# The Politics and Public Culture of American Jews

The Modern Jewish Experience
Paula Hyman and Deborah Dash Moore, editors

ARTHUR A. GOREN

# The Politics and Public Culture of American Jews

INDIANA UNIVERSITY PRESS

*Bloomington and Indianapolis*

This book is a publication of
Indiana University Press
601 North Morton Street
Bloomington, Indiana 47404-3797 USA

www.indiana.edu/~iupress

*Telephone orders*   800-842-6796
*Fax orders*   812-855-7931
*Orders by e-mail*   iuporder@indiana.edu

The paper used in this publication meets the minimum requirements of American National Standard for Information Sciences—Permanence of Paper for Printed Library Materials, ANSI Z39.48-1984.

Manufactured in the United States of America

**Library of Congress Cataloging-in-Publication Data**

Goren, Arthur A., date
    The politics and public culture of American Jews / Arthur A.
    Goren.
        p.     cm. — (The Modern Jewish experience)
    Includes bibliographical references and index.
        ISBN 0-253-33535-3 (cl : alk. paper).  — ISBN 0-253-21318-5 (pa :
alk. paper)
        1. Jews—United States—History—20th century.  2. Jews—United
States—Politics and government.  3. Immigrants—United States—
History—20th century.  4. United States—Ethnic relations.
I. Title.  II. Series: Modern Jewish experience (Bloomington, Ind.)
E184.35.G67  1999
306.2'089'924073—dc21                                            98-52677

1  2  3  4  5    04  03  02  01  00  99

To My Sons

Avner and Amos

# Contents

# Acknowledgments

Two friends and colleagues, Ezra Mendelsohn and Deborah Dash Moore, persuaded me to bring together these articles in a book. Published separately over a long period of time and often in places beyond the reach of all but specialists, the articles, they believed, focused in an original way on a central theme of American Jewish life: the ways Jews sought to maintain a sense of community, and their uses of politics and public culture to do so. I am grateful to them for the thought they gave to helping me shape the book. Despite their sound advice, I absolve them of responsibility for the outcome, which is mine alone.

It was my good fortune that Janet Rabinowitch, senior editor at Indiana University Press, agreed that I had a book. Her wise advice and words of approbation have fallen on open ears. Dee Mortensen, her associate, has tied together the loose ends editorially with professionalism and forbearance. I also want to thank Michael Baker for his careful copy-editing. A grant from the Lucius N. Littauer Foundation made it possible to complete the book on an illustrated note.

For more than a generation, I have been fortunate to have been associated with two renowned universities as both student and teacher: the Hebrew University in Jerusalem and Columbia University in New York. For twenty years I was a member of Hebrew University's Department of American Studies, and for the past eleven years I have been a member of Columbia's History Department and its Center for Israel and Jewish Studies. I owe an enormous debt of gratitude to my teachers, colleagues, and students at these two distinguished and very different universities. Over the years, I discussed chapters of this book with Jerusalem colleagues Yehoshua Arieli, Emily Budick, and Shlomo Slonim. At Columbia, department chairs—from Jack Garraty, upon my coming to Columbia, to Martha Howell, the current chair—have been supportive in every way. So have Yosef Yerushalmi and Michael Stanislawski. They have also presided over an intellectual feast—the University Seminar in Israel and Jewish Studies—which has provided an incomparable forum for presenting work-in-progress. Two Columbia doctoral students, Arthur Kiron and Annie Polland, helped me with the research. Nearby, David Nasaw and Dinitia

Smith offered not only hospitality but a discerning ear to my ideas. My heartfelt thanks to this good company of people.

It is a pleasure to acknowledge the help of the staffs of the following libraries and archives: in New York, the YIVO Institute, the Jewish Division of the New York Public Library, the Jewish Theological Seminary, the Columbia University Libraries, and the Jacob Blaustein Library of the American Jewish Committee; in Jerusalem, the Central Archives for the History of the Jewish People, the Central Zionist Archives, the Jewish National and University Library, and the Steven Spielberg Jewish Film Archives of the Abraham Harman Institute of Contemporary Jewry at the Hebrew University.

Conferences provided opportunities to present early versions of several chapters in this collection. I note with appreciation the following: the Bicentennial Conference on the American Historical Experience, Hebrew University, 1976 (chap. 1); American Jews and the Establishment of the State of Israel, Ben-Gurion University of the Negev, 1985 (chap. 7); YIVO Conference on Kinship, Mobility and Community among American Jews, 1989 (chap. 10); New Perspectives in American Jewish History, Center for Israel and Jewish Studies, Columbia University, 1990 (chap. 9); Envisioning Israel: The Changing Ideals and Images of North American Jewry, Ben-Gurion University, 1993 (chap. 8).

I have shuttled between Jerusalem and New York since 1951. The reader may find traces of the "living-in-two-cultures" syndrome in this book. If so, it reflects not only cultural geography but family. Ayalah Goren-Kadman filled our home with the sounds and movements of Israel's ethnic culture and dance, and then summoned us to her festivals and workshops. Yet in time of need she put her work aside to foray into the archives and libraries with *my* research list. For all this and more, I am grateful. During the course of writing the articles that make up this book, our two sons, Avner and Amos, to whom this book is dedicated, grew to manhood, took part in Israel's defense, married (one Brooklyn-born, the other a *sabra*), and presented us with five grandchildren, third-generation American Israelis. Most of all, they surrounded us with jollity and camaraderie. At discouraging moments, their good spirits were like balm from Gilead.

Earlier versions of essays in this volume have been previously published. The author wishes to thank the following for permission to reproduce them here.

Chapter 1, "Strategies of Survival: American Jews and the Uses of Pluralism," in *The American Experience in Historical Perspective*, ed. Shlomo Slonim (Jerusalem: Hebrew University, 1979), 99–121.

Chapter 2, "Pageants of Sorrow, Celebration and Protest: The Public Culture of American Jews," from *Studies in Contemporary Jewry, Volume XII, Literary Strategies: Jewish Texts and Contexts*, ed. Ezra Mendelsohn. Copyright (c) 1997 by Oxford University Press, Inc. Used by permission of Oxford University Press, Inc.

Chapter 3, "Sacred and Secular: The Place of Public Funerals in the Immigrant Life of American Jews," *Jewish History* 8, nos. 1–2 (1994): 269–305.

Chapter 4, "A Portrait of Ethnic Politics: The Socialists and the 1908 and 1910 Congressional Elections on the East Side," *Publications of the American Jewish Historical Society* 50 (March 1961): 202–238.

Chapter 5, "Orthodox Politics, Republican and Jews: Jacob Saphirstein and the *Morgen zhurnal*," *Proceedings of the Eighth World Congress of Jewish Studies: Jewish History* (Jerusalem, 1983), 63–71.

Chapter 6, *National Leadership in American Jewish Life: The Formative Years*, Ninth Annual Rabbi Louis Feinberg Memorial Lecture, April 1986 (Judaic Studies Program, University of Cincinnati, 1989), 1–26.

Chapter 7, "Spiritual Zionists and Jewish Sovereignty," in *The Americanization of the Jews*, ed. Robert M. Selzer and Norman J. Cohn (New York: New York University Press, 1995), 165–192.

Chapter 8, " 'Anu banu artza' in America: The Americanization of the *Halutz* Ideal," in *Envisioning Israel: Changing Ideals and Images of North American Jews*, ed. Allon Gal (Jerusalem: Magnes Press, Hebrew University; Detroit: Wayne State University Press, 1996), 81–113.

Chapter 9, "A 'Golden Decade' for American Jews: 1945–1955," *Studies in Contemporary Jewry*, Volume VIII, *A New Jewry? America since the Second World War*, ed. Peter Y. Medding. Copyright (c) 1992 by Oxford University Press, Inc. Used by permission of Oxford University Press, Inc.

Chapter 10, "The New Pluralism and the Politics of Community Relations," *YIVO Annual* 19 (1990): 169–198.

The Politics and Public Culture of American Jews

# Introduction

In blending Judaism with Americanism . . . compromises will be unavoid-
able. . . . But these compromises will never be such as to obliterate or muti-
late the character of either party. . . . In the great palace of American civilization we [Jews] shall occupy our own corner, which we will decorate and
beautify to the best of our taste and ability, and make it not only a center of
attraction for the members of our family, but also an object of admiration
for all the dwellers of the palace. . . . We see a community . . . blending the
best it possesses with the best it encounters, . . . adding a new note to the
richness of American life.

—Israel Friedlaender[1]

On December 15, 1907, Israel Friedlaender, thirty-one-year-old professor
of Bible at the Jewish Theological Seminary, addressed the Mikve Israel
Association of Philadelphia on "The Problem of Judaism in America." In
one way or another, the issue Friedlaender chose to discuss is at the core
of most studies of American Jews. How could the ancient faith, or "culture" as Friedlaender defined it, survive the extraordinarily benign conditions of American freedom? Experience had shown that overcoming the
vicissitudes of Exile was no assurance of group survival. On the contrary,
in West European states, Jews finally attained political and civil rights but
at the cost of minimizing or forgoing their cultural and communal distinctiveness.

"The Problem of Judaism in America" was, in a sense, a manifesto—a
pessimistic analysis of the spiritual state of modern Jewry followed by a
call to American Jews to fill the vacuum and accept the mantle of diaspora
leadership. It was also an American-centered declaration, an ode "to the
great American Civilization" in which American Jews would find their
place and to which they would make their contribution. Friedlaender's
analysis was accepted by communal activists who held a centrist position
in Jewish life; like Friedlaender they gave primacy to the precept of "the
unity of Israel" and consequently championed a Jewish community that
was inclusive and pluralistic. This view of American Jewry and its place in
American life informs the chapters that follow. The timing of Friedlaen-

der's talk is also significant. It was delivered in the midst of the peak years of the great Jewish exodus from Eastern Europe. Between 1904 and 1908 over 100,000 Jews arrived in the United States annually; in 1906 the number skyrocketed to just over 150,000. Economic destitution, Czarist oppression and a new wave of pogroms accelerated the mass migration which had been underway since the 1880s. Part 1 of *Politics and Public Culture* considers the public life of the immigrants who were simultaneously recreating the Jewish cultural world they brought from Europe and adjusting it to the American milieu. Thus a consideration of Friedlaender and his Philadelphia lecture aptly serves as a prelude to this book of essays.

In his opening, Friedlaender felt it necessary to justify his speaking on the subject at all. He had come to the United States, he explained, a mere four years earlier, and yet he now had the temerity to address an assembly of men and women who were "deeply rooted in American soil and intimately associated with American life." (The Association was sponsored by Congregation Mikve Israel which was founded in 1771, and the meeting took place on its premises.)[2] The fact of the matter was that soon after Friedlaender's arrival in America, he became active in a range of communal undertakings. No less interesting than his rapid entry into Jewish life in the dual role of scholar and public intellectual was his personal odyssey. After a traditional upbringing, he followed a path taken by scores of young Russian Jews who were drawn to academic studies in Germany. For Friedlaender it was first Berlin and then Strassburg, where he received a Ph.D. in Semitics. Soon after, Solomon Schechter, the new president of the Jewish Theological Seminary, invited him to join the distinguished faculty he was in the process of recruiting. Friedlaender's biography, tragically cut short when he was murdered in 1920 while on a relief mission in the Ukraine, suggests some of the themes that are amplified in the chapters that follow: the mass migration from Eastern Europe, in Friedlaender's case motivated by the craving for intellectual freedom and growth, and his vision that American Jewry was destined to replace a ravaged Russian Jewry as the great center of the diaspora. His move from Germany to America stemmed from this perception. American Jewry's population increase, wealth and security provided an auspicious setting, Friedlaender argued, for spiritual and cultural growth. (Of Germany, once the mecca of Jewish scholarship, Friedlaender wrote, "[W]e stumble on all sides against indifference and apostasy, and her [Germany's] intellectual productivity shows an appalling decline.") Crucial for our discussion was his vision of a creative diversified community living in concord at a time when most observers stressed the fragmentation and intellectual poverty of American Jewry.[3]

For Friedlaender, the overarching challenge facing American Jewry was to maintain its cultural integrity while encouraging the participation of the individual in society in general. Everywhere else in the West, the effort had failed; would it fail in America? Friedlaender quoted "an experienced Jewish minister from New York" who for a quarter of a century had witnessed the stunning growth of the Jewish population of the city. "What will our second and third generation be a quarter of a century hence?" the rabbi asked. "American? Yes. Jewish? Perhaps." For the more skeptical, Friedlaender commented, the "perhaps" turns into a plain "no." The Judaism which withstood the "billows of hatred and storms of persecution," he declared, was "melting away like wax under the mild rays of freedom." "Is there no hope," he asked, "for the Jews to participate in the life and the culture around them and yet remain Jewish?"[4]

Friedlaender responded by describing an era in Jewish history when toleration had allowed for full participation in the life and culture of the host country. During the Judeo-Arabic period, the so-called "Golden Age of Spain," Jews spoke and wrote Arabic, studied Arabic literature, and held an "honorable" place in the economic, political and cultural life of the nation. Yet "never before or after in the lands of the exile" had there been such an outpouring of Jewish spiritual and cultural creativity. Here was a precedent and paradigm, and America provided the auspicious setting for once again "living harmoniously in two cultures." In a statement that is a precursor of what would soon become well known as "cultural pluralism," Friedlaender declared: "The true American spirit understands and respects the traditions and associations of other nationalities, and on its vast area numerous races live peaceably together, equally devoted to the interests of the land." What was required of American Jews was the abandonment of "the narrow frame of a creed"—the price paid for gaining civic equality in Europe and presumably required for full social acceptance in America—and the resumption of Judaism's "original function as a culture, as the expression of the Jewish spirit and the whole life of the Jews." In numbers, wealth, power and cultural and spiritual resources, the conditions existed for American Jewry to become "the center of Judaism, of the spiritual life of the Jewish people in the Dispersion." It was the Jewish people's best hope.[5]

"The Problem of Judaism" as Friedlaender understood it, including the problem of defining it, was no mere intellectual exercise of theological, historical or sociological analysis. It was preeminently a matter of politics, the politics of winning a following for a set of principles, sentiments or doctrines and providing the wherewithal to transform sympathizers into

a movement. One need but mention the fluctuating course of two established movements—Reform Judaism and Zionism—as they accommo-
dated themselves ideologically and institutionally to a changing America
and a changing American Jewry to appreciate the adaptability of Jewish
communal politics. "Strategies" in the title of the essay "Strategies of Survival" (chapter 1) implies this sort of politics.

"Strategies," as opposed to "tactics," also suggests a long-range view and
ideological coherence. The social critics and religious thinkers included in
the chapter addressed Jewish issues in this spirit. They searched for a collective self-definition that would sustain a variegated communal life in an
open society, and they undertook to interpret America's democratic doctrine in a way that endorsed particularistic group loyalties. In "Paths of
Leadership" (chapter 6), the relationship between ideology and communal
politics becomes explicit. The chapter considers the rise of a national Jewish leadership, that is, the appearance of public figures who headed country-wide constituencies and were accepted as representatives of American
Jewry. The 1930s and 1940s produced such "giants" as Stephen S. Wise and
Abba Hillel Silver; then, popular opinion has it, the giants disappeared and
were replaced by communal functionaries. Chapter 6 argues that the emergence of a national leadership was linked to the rise of popular movements
during the second decade of the century and particularly during World
War I. Probably no other period in the communal life of American Jews
was as contentious. Internal class and cultural divisions fomented dissension and discord that on occasion became venomous. At the same time, all
parties recognized the need to provide relief and political support for millions of Jews suffering from the chaos of war particularly in Eastern
Europe. Collaboration was essential. The tangibility of the issue—who
represents American Jewry and therefore who makes policy—illuminated
the inner dynamics of Jewish communal politics and the limits of communal collaboration.

Politics of another order is discussed in "Spiritual Zionists and Jewish
Sovereignty" (chapter 7)—the politics of dissent. On two critical occasions
in the history of American Zionism, influential Zionists challenged the
movement's basic premises. In 1917 when the Balfour Declaration promising British government support for a homeland in Palestine for the Jews
raised Zionist expectations that a Jewish commonwealth was attainable,
Israel Friedlaender and Judah L. Magnes questioned the feasibility, probity
and necessity of a sovereign state. The political goal of sovereignty, they
believed, would divert Zionism from its primary purpose, the cultural ren-
aissance of the Jewish people. (The influence of cultural—or spiritual Zi-

onism—on the Jewish community has received far less attention than the impact of political Zionism.) Twenty-five years later the controversy was renewed when American Zionists declared a Jewish Commonwealth the operational goal of the movement (the Biltmore Program of 1942). Once again, two eminent Jewish leaders who were also influential religious thinkers and respected Zionists, Mordecai M. Kaplan and Louis Finkelstein, questioned the primacy of the demand for statehood. Internationalists and moral teachers, they feared the chauvinism bred by ethnic minorities and small nationalities demanding political independence. Both World Wars, they believed, had shown that national ambitions were destabilizing, played into the hands of aggressive imperialist states and were obstacles to attaining an effective world order. For the Jews, other arrangements beside a sovereign Jewish state—a United Nations trusteeship, or regional federation—would assure the necessary degree of autonomy to enable the National Home to fulfill its double role as haven for the homeless and the cultural-spiritual center of the Jewish people, functions vital for the well-being of American Jewry.

Parallel to these expressions of internal Jewish politics, Jews as citizens participated in the public realm of municipal, state and national politics. A considerable literature describes the radicalism of the Jewish immigrants, the New Deal liberalism of the second generation, and the gradual move to the center of the third generation. Three chapters in *Politics and Public Culture* examine the Jewish involvement in domestic American politics. "Socialist Politics on the Lower East Side" (chapter 4), focuses on the congressional elections of 1908 and 1910. The "case study" approach made it possible to follow the campaign trail in the immigrant quarter. It opened a window into the world of contending class, ethnic and party interests and to the political culture of the Jewish quarter with its fusion of European ideological movements, special interest politics, American socialism, and urban machine politics. "The Conservative Politics of the Orthodox Press" (chapter 5) continues the story of the political culture of the immigrant quarter by singling out the conservative strand among the Jewish immigrants which has received less notice from historians. The *Morgen Zhurnal*, the centerpiece of the essay, was a religiously Orthodox daily and supported the Republican Party. Publishers of the Yiddish press like the *Morgen Zhurnal*'s Jacob Saphirstein wielded considerable power in the community and they intervened aggressively in day-to-day party politics.

Three decades later, American Jewry showed its adeptness for mobilizing political support for causes it deemed important. Emerging from the war a self-assured affluent community, American Jews expanded their communal institutions and at the same time provided the main financial and political support for the Jewish state-in-the-making and for Jews in need elsewhere in the world. The Zionists spearheaded these efforts, and in the process built an extraordinarily effective coalition which embraced nearly the entire spectrum of Jewish organizations. American Jewry also adopted a liberal stand in domestic American affairs especially in opposing racial, religious and ethnic discrimination. Based on these two public commitments—assuring Israel's security and striving for a liberal America—American Jews appeared to have achieved a durable consensus for the first time in their history. "The 'Golden Decade': 1945–1955" (chapter 9) surveys these developments. Chapter 9 also considers the lingering sense of vulnerability the community felt because of the conspicuous presence of Jews among the radical Left and the criticism Jewish intellectuals leveled at the shallowness of Jewish life. "Inventing the 'New Pluralism' " (chapter 10) takes up American Jewry's preoccupation with eliminating discrimination in American life. During the 1940s and 1950s, Jewish intergroup agencies—once known as "defence agencies"—broadened their historic purpose of combating antisemitism to include fighting bigotry in all its forms. They launched innovative educational programs and took a leading part in the legal and political struggle for civil rights and civil liberties. Their vigorous stand was a source of pride and even self-congratulation. In the latter half of the stormy 1960s when black nationalism and the white backlash polarized American society, Jewish organizations began turning inward.

In no small measure, the dramatic events of May and June 1967, when the Arabs' threats to Israel's survival were followed by their stunning victory in the six-day war, contributed to this "closing of ranks." (A number of African American leaders and liberal Christian ministers, former comrades-in-arms in the civil rights struggle, were critical of or indifferent to American Jewry's support of Israel.) No less pivotal in understanding the changed Jewish temper was worry over the growing estrangement of the young from Jewish life, the dissatisfaction of others with the quality of Jewish life, and the rising rate of intermarriage. Nevertheless, alongside the first steps in a search for answers, several Jewish organizations addressed what some observers called "the national identity crisis," i.e., the ongoing debate over the nature and limits of ethnic pluralism in the civic life of the nation.

Especially notable were the initiatives of the American Jewish Committee, the oldest and most prestigious of the Jewish intergroup relations agencies, which promoted the concept of the "new pluralism." Revising the liberal model of cultural pluralism—the ethnic group was a voluntary association; one belonged by choice—the committee's policy makers presented ethnicity as a permanent feature of American society. White ethnic groups alongside Latino and other ethnic minorities needed public recognition and redress for their legitimate grievances. Only then could racial tensions be "depolarized" and a creative and balanced pluralism emerge.

Alongside Jewish politics in its internal (Jewish) or external (American) expression, another arena of Jewish communal life existed—the domain of Jewish public culture. (The two realms frequently overlapped.) At least since the beginning of the century, Jews expressed their Jewishness by participating in great public events that marked some auspicious occasion in the life of the people. Mass meetings and rallies, parades, pageants and other public displays enabled the participants to affirm a collective identity. Held in the public sphere and open to all, these gatherings transcended cultural and class divides as well as organizational affiliation or its absence, and served as communal rituals of affirmation and self-definition.

"Pageants of Sorrow, Celebration and Protest" (chapter 2) examines three memorable events that took place in late 1905: the funeral of the Yiddish writer Nahum Meyer Shaikevich, the 250th anniversary of Jewish settlement in America, and the demonstration march in protest against the October 1905 pogroms in Russia. Taken together they serve as a paradigm of the public culture of American Jews. Thousands participated, and the extensive press coverage communicated the aura and message of the formalities to many times that number. In accordance with their intent, these solemn affairs drew upon hallowed ritual, emulated the American penchant for commemorating historical beginnings, or borrowed from American and European practices of populist protest. One form of communal bonding discussed in chapter 2, the public funeral in homage of a revered sage, literary figure or political hero, is the subject of "The Rites of Community" (chapter 3). The essay traces the rise and fall of the funeral pageant over a period of half a century. For much of this time, the collective mourning of a distinguished Jewish notable became the occasion for calls for solidarity and for rededication to the values of the departed leader and guide. But the celebrated dead represented divergent ideological and political camps; rituals and symbols once shared by all splintered into secular and sacred rites. Nevertheless, a countertrend developed. Religious customs were adjusted by the traditionalists to enhance their image before the public at large, and the secular rituals that the radicals invented to foster class solidarity were modulated to appeal to wider Jewish circles.

Zionism contributed notably to the making of a Jewish public culture. A mass movement in its structure and ambitions, Zionism—particularly the Zionist Organization of America, the largest and most American of the Zionist parties—used the medium of the public event to popularize its message. Political, educational, revivalist—the boundaries were usually blurred—Zionist appeals reached well beyond the organization's membership. Two prototypical instances are edifying. On May 11, 1920, a parade held in New York in conjunction with the convening of an "extraordinary Zionist convention" celebrated the awarding of the Palestine mandate to Great Britain (the San Remo Declaration of April 24, 1920). Fifty to one hundred thousand (estimates differed) marched from the Lower East Side to Central Park. Behind the slogan "*Geulah*—Redemption," flag-bearers carried the American, Zionist and British flags. First in the line of march were Jewish war veterans, survivors of the "Lost Battalion," followed in turn by 1,800 members of the Jewish legion who fought in Palestine, 2,000 American Legionnaires, and Hadassah women dressed in white and wearing blue sashes. Thirty marching bands were dispersed among twenty-seven divisions who made up the parade "representing all Jewish organizations."[6] More grandiose than the parade was the pageant that took place on July 3, 1933, at Soldier Field, Chicago, marking "Jewish Day" at the Chicago World's Fair. One hundred and thirty thousand spectators filled the stadium to watch the Zionist-inspired pageant *Romance of a People*, with a cast of 5,000, depict the 4,000-year history of the Jews. The final episode, "The New Liberation," consisted of two sequences: America—the mass unfurling of the Stars and Stripes; and Palestine—throngs of young people dressed as Zionist pioneers (*halutzim*) carrying hoes and sickles running on stage singing the *halutz* folk song, "We have come to the land to build it and to be rebuilt."[7]

With such episodes in mind, "Americanizing Zionist Pioneers" (chapter 8) focuses on the ways the pioneering ideal—*halutziut*—was presented to American Jewry as the central myth of Zionism. Producers, publicists and educators used folk song and dance, documentary films, exhibitions, and religious school curricula to popularize the "heroic" *halutzim* who were "conquering" the ancestral land with their labor. With the achievement of political sovereignty in 1948 the ideal turned into practical-minded demands. Israel's leaders called on American Jews to do more than provide political and economic aid. Their skills, professional experience, and the democratic values they had absorbed while growing up in America were needed in Israel. The ensuing controversy between the two world centers of Jewish life over mutual obligations and expectations—the meaning of Jewish "peoplehood" and the interdependence between diaspora and homeland—stirred much self-searching and creative thought over the basics of self-definition and illuminated the singularity of American Jewry and the depth of its American roots.

The studies that make up *Politics and Public Culture* appeared in various journals over the course of a number of years, one as early as 1961, although the majority appeared during the 1980s and 1990s. The collection reflects my abiding interest in the unfolding communal life of American Jews— the way Jews transplanted, changed and invented their social institutions and ideologies and created over time an impressive organizational culture. I hope the chapters' diverse perspectives and variety of historical materials, stemming from their origin in individually conceived studies, will prove provocative. The collection reflects the density of Jewish public affairs; it also records the disposition of some in every generation to view Jewish life as a time of decline. In this sense, the essays register the communal fragmentation of the first decades of the century, and the foreboding of the final decades of the century that meaningful group survival for Jews was in jeopardy.

*Politics and Public Culture* also presents voices in counterpoint: the inventiveness that the four generations who pass through this book have shown in maintaining a remarkably resilient community. During the early 1900s, the established Jewish community, the cohesive circle of Americanized Jews of German origin, acted in concert with the new immigrants at moments of crisis, especially when calls came to aid Europe's Jews and the tiny Zionist settlement in Palestine. The establishment of the American Jewish Joint Distribution Committee during World War I is a case in point. This collaboration, sometimes half-hearted, nevertheless continued and, in the face of more terrible disasters, increased in power. At home, as the two million Russian immigrants moved upward socially and economically, they recast the traditional institutions and folkways that they brought from Europe to meet their changing middle-class American tastes and needs. The rise of the Conservative wing of Judaism and the community-center movement are examples of this process. The two faces of Jewish communal life—the political and philanthropic connection to world Jewry, and the domestic religious, cultural and defense needs of American Jewry—reinforced one another.

How successful was the effort? In his 1907 lecture, Friedlaender paired his pessimistic review of the state of American Judaism with an idyllic vision of what might come to be. Writing thirty-five years later, Salo Baron, the eminent Jewish historian, struck his own balance. In the opening chapter of his monumental study of the Jewish community from post-biblical times to the end of the eighteenth century, Baron devoted a few remarks to American Jewry by way of underscoring America's "exceptionalism." He referred to the enormous role voluntarism played in the civic and social life of the nation and the importance of the separation of church and state. Baron praised "the amazing record of the American Jewish community." That "amazing record," he wrote, was achieved by "communal organisms [that were] entirely optional." Baron admitted that about half the Jews failed to identify with any form of organized Jewish life. However, those who did identify with a Jewish institution, Baron continued, brought a "superior vitality" to their "optional organizations" which was incomparably greater than in the case of European Jewish communities with their quasi-legal status.[8]

In the 1990s, half a century after Baron's ambiguous judgment—on the credit side, the Jewish community's "amazing record," and on the debit side, the unaffiliated half of America's Jews—academics, policy-makers, and communal leaders debate with unprecedented intensity and anxiety ways of reversing the accelerating erosion, as they see it, of Jewish life. Now, instead of Baron's "unaffiliated half," they point to the half who are intermarrying. On the Jewish communal agenda, ensuring "Jewish continuity" has an equal place with Israel's security and community relations (issues such as antisemitism and black-Jewish relations), and demands abound that investing in continuity must be prioritized. Historians are wary of crossing the line into the domain of the policy-makers. The manner in which Jews handled issues of collective identity and group commitment in the past will hardly provide solutions for today. However, knowing the story may give the fourth and fifth generation of the descendants of those who came in the great migration—they make up most of America's Jews—a sense of the continuity of the community and its problems.

# Part One

## Immigrant Encounters with America, 1900–1940

# 1 Strategies of Survival and the Uses of Pluralism

The quandary Jews in America have faced in their striving to survive as a communal entity while aspiring for integration into the society at large is marked by a special poignancy. Whether Jewish particularism should be maintained—to what degree, in what way and for what reason—or should be abandoned for a higher cosmopolitan fellowship has, of course, been one of the central themes in modern Jewish history. Though other groups have been torn between a desire to maintain their ethnic identity and an eagerness for full merger into the American mainstream, the strain within the American Jewish group has been especially intense. For generations before coming to America Jews were preoccupied with their predicament as an alien minority in a generally hostile society. Be it as members of self-segregated communities guided by their sacred code, or as "co-religionists" associated in a *Kultusgemeinde* while participating in the newly opening secular society, or as devotees of social movements having despaired of achieving the political emancipation prevailing elsewhere, Jews for the most part affirmed their group identity in one form or another. Arriving in America at different historical times and from widely different circumstances, Jewish immigrants brought vast and varied experiences of accommodation to the majority culture and regime. The very diversity of approaches coexisting and competing for hegemony agitated the community. It also generated much creative thought and experimentation which informed not only the immigrant generation but those that followed as well.[1]

In America, profoundly dissimilar conditions—conditions of freedom and tolerance—cast the question of group survival in a completely new light. In contrast with their countries of origin, in relation to other minorities in America, and in comparison with conditions in other democratic societies, Jews had an unmatched opportunity, so it seemed, of being absorbed into American society—and for those who wished—to the point of loss of their ethnic identity altogether. Over the years not a few followed this path. The material and cultural achievements of American Jews, and the dramatic success of some, gave credence to the American promise of reward, recognition and acceptance for the deserving individual. One suspects that the conventional wisdom that prevailed among the first and second generation was that individual Jews could, if they so chose, disengage themselves from the group and unobtrusively blend into the cultural mainstream of the nation. Those who did, it appears, encountered less deprecation from their people and experienced fewer pangs of conscience than would have been the case elsewhere. For, except where conversion was involved, the departing or lapsed son or daughter retained the American component of their dual identity—loyalty to the "American Way of Life"—an identity shared and praised by all. Faith in the openness of the society—the ethos of a nation still in the making—made the process of disassociation from the ancestral group less acute. Not infrequently the Jewish public claimed an illustrious personage as one of its own, alienated and indifferent as the person might be to his or her ethnic origins, to reflect glory upon itself.[2]

The twin desires for ethnic survival and personal acceptance into American society were rarely posed as an either-or choice. Much of Jewish communal thought was directed toward formulating strategies and programs to mitigate tensions through compromise and accommodation, or by redefining the group's Jewish identity and the character of American nationality. The debate over Jewish education in the 1910s, the height of the mass migration, offers an insight into this process.

Confronting the chaotic state of religious education, a circle of American-trained Jewish educators faulted both the old world's Orthodox ways and Reform Judaism's methods for their ineffectualness in imparting an understanding of and loyalty to Judaism or Jewish culture to the young. These young educators, recruited by Samson Benderly who headed the newly established Bureau of Jewish Education (the first agency of its kind), called for a new educational system that would employ modern methods, textbooks, and trained pedagogues to transmit the sacred texts and religious teachings of Judaism to the next generation. They also believed that fostering Hebrew culture would enrich American Jewish life by linking it to the national revival in Palestine. Yet these educators opposed the establishment of Jewish parochial schools—several existed at the time—which would have privileged Jewish studies. Writing in 1910, Benderly summed up their position:

> As the great public school system is the rock bottom upon which this country is rearing its institutions so we Jews must evolve here a system of Jewish education that shall be complementary to and harmonious with the public school system.[3]

Benderly admitted that the Catholic parochial school offered a remarkable example of a community's commitment to its spiritual values and culture, but he rejected the Catholic model as un-American. Isaac B. Berkson, a Benderly protégé and a student of John Dewey and William H. Kilpatrick at Teachers College, articulated what by 1920 became the dominant view among Jewish communal leaders:

> The Jewish parochial school, like the Catholic system, segregates the children along lines of creed. The essential point of having the various elements of the population, during the formative period of childhood, associate with their neighbors with whom they are destined to live together as American citizens remains unfulfilled.

Though Berkson justified "the perpetuation of significant elements of the culture of ethnic groups" as consonant with American democracy, "segregation along any lines of ethnic creed or race was thoroughly undemocratic." There was a limit beyond which the ethnic or religious group ought not go in educating its young. Berkson suggested the afternoon supplementary school, which left intact the public school and was a compromise between the inadequacy of the Protestant Sunday school and the "dangerous" segregation of the Catholic parochial school.[4]

A famous case of a redefinition of the Jewish collectivity and its relation to the larger polity was Reform Judaism's Pittsburgh Platform of 1885. The rabbis who gathered in Pittsburgh drew upon their European background and American civic and religious perceptions and declared the Jews of the modern world no longer a nation. They were bound together by a "progressive religion ever striving to be in accord with the postulates of reason." The rabbis rejected all ceremonies and religious laws "not adapted to the views and habits of modern civilization" and called on all people of good will to join in the common endeavor to establish "the reign of truth and righteousness among men." The broad, humanistic pronouncement reflected the astonishingly rapid acculturation of the mid-nineteenth-century Central European immigrants, as well as the prompt acceptance by their ministers of the "advanced" social theories of the times. On the eve of the first wave of the mass migration from Eastern Europe, these spokesmen for Reform Judaism, by then the dominant ideological current in American Judaism, had reformulated Jewish identity in accordance with the congenial model of nineteenth-century liberal American Protestantism.[5]

Forty years later, Mordecai M. Kaplan, son of an Orthodox rabbi from Eastern Europe, but himself ordained at the Jewish Theological Seminary and a distinguished member of its faculty, rejected the Reform and Ortho-dox understanding of Judaism. He interpreted Judaism as "the civilization of the Jewish people." More a program than a theology, what came to be called Reconstructionism spoke to the children of the East European im-migrants who had come of age in America. Acculturated, religiously skep-tical or apathetic, but nevertheless bound to one degree or another to an ethnic culture permeated with religious nuances, these Americanized Jews sought a mode of group identity compatible with their liberal-secular out-look. Kaplan's "civilization" was ethnic and communalistic in tone and program: "the living, dynamic process of intellectual, social and spiritual give-and-take of Jews in the course of their relationship to one another as individuals and as members of various groups." His definition embraced all manner of Jewish expression and identification. It included all of the elements in what was termed the cultural life of a people, "such as lan-guage, folkways, patterns of social organization, social habits and stan-dards, spiritual ideals, which give individuality to a people and differenti-ate it from other peoples." Kaplan also accorded a central place to the upbuilding of the national home in Palestine in his schema and called for an all-encompassing Jewish communal polity, "the organic community." At the same time, he acknowledged the prior lien of America and its civi-lization on the individual's loyalty and interest. He, too, dismissed the Jew-ish parochial school as "a futile gesture of protest against the necessity of giving to Jewish civilization a position ancillary to the civilization of the majority."[6]

Horace Kallen's interpretation of America as a "democracy of nation-alities" was shaped to no small extent by his Jewish concerns. However, unlike the Reform rabbis thirty years before, his argument did not begin with internal communal considerations, reformulating the meaning of Jewish group existence. His celebrated essay, "Democracy Versus the Melt-ing Pot" written in 1915, analyzed the nature of American society as cul-turally pluralistic thus legitimizing ethnic group life.[7] What is noteworthy from the Jewish perspective was not only his insisting on the tenacity of ethnicity ("Americanization has not repressed nationality, Americaniza-tion has liberated nationality"). Of equal significance was the greater weight Kallen gave to the secular rather than to the religious sphere in his analysis of ethnicity.[8]

Kallen, of course, noted the role of religion as a stimulus to the self-pres-ervation of the "nationality" group. Religion is "often the sole repository of the national spirit, almost always the conservator of the national lan-guage and of the tradition that is passed on with the language to succeeding generations." But in playing out this role, religion did more. It contributed to the uncovering of a "higher type of personality" among the immigrants, their "*natio.*" The latter "assumes spiritual forms other than religious." Thus, for example, the parochial school, "to hold its own with the public school, gets secularized while remaining national."[9] The Poles, Kallen wrote,

> Exploited by both their own upper classes and the Russian conqueror . . . have clung to their religion because it was a mark of difference between them and their conquerors. Because they loved liberty they made their language of literary importance in Europe. Their aspiration, impersonal, disinterested, as it must be in America, to free Poland, to conserve the Polish spirit, is the most hopeful and American thing about them.[10]

Similarly, in describing the rich texture of life in the Jewish quarter of New York, Kallen treated religion as ancillary to the main course of ethnic group development.

> Once . . . the Jewish immigrant takes his place in our society as a free man and an American, he tends to become all the more a Jew. The cultural unity of his race, history, and background is only continued by the new life under the new conditions. . . . [The Jewish quarter] has its sectaries, its radicals, its artists, its literati; its press, its literature, its theater, its Yiddish and its Hebrew, its Talmudical colleges and its Hebrew schools, its charities and its vanities, and its coordinating organization, the Kehillah. . . . Here not religion alone, but the whole world of radical thinking carries the mother-tongue and the father-tongue, with all that they imply. Unlike the parochial schools, their separate schools, being *national* [italics added], do not displace the public schools; they supplement the public schools. . . . As was the case with the Scandinavians, the Germans, the Irish, democracy applied to education has given the Jews their will that Hebrew shall be coordinate with French and German in the regent's examination.[11]

The prescription Kallen proposed—in form a federal republic, in substance "a democracy of nationalities, cooperating voluntarily and autonomously in the enterprise of self-realization through the perfection of men according to their kind"—suited his own ethnic predilections. For the irreligious Kallen, who had rebelled against his father's Orthodox Judaism as a youth, had then returned to what he called "the Hebraic, the secular, the non-Judaistic component of the entire heritage." Hebraism, Kallen wrote in 1910, was what "Israel has stood for in history, the life of the Jews, their unique achievement—not as isolated individuals, but as a well defined ethnic group." What it stood for, moreover, had powerfully influenced the genesis of the "American Idea." Common to both were the precepts of the Old Testament prophets and their social and spiritual ideals. (This he had learned as a Harvard undergraduate.) Thus Kallen's Americanism countenanced his commitment to Jewish group survival on two accounts: Hebraism and democracy (ethnic "self-realization"). For Kallen this led logically to Zionism.[12]

In 1955, forty years after the appearance of Kallen's seminal essay, Will Herberg published his *Protestant, Catholic, Jew*. He subtitled his book, "An Essay in American Religious Sociology." Herberg's schema of "the three great religious communities" constituting "the three basic subdivisions of the American people" led him into a sweeping analysis of the social, cultural and spiritual condition of the nation. His main theses proved to be short-lived. Few viewing American society during the late 1950s and early 1960s foresaw the turbulence just beyond the horizon: the new-found militancy of African Americans demanding civic and social equality, the crisis in the churches and decline of religious influence, and the contentiousness and confrontation exacerbated by the escalating war in Vietnam permeated public life. In retrospect, Herberg's book, so widely acclaimed when it appeared, proved to be a tract for its time. His depiction of the "American Way of Life" as America's religion, his exposition of the three great "religions of democracy" as serving as three "pools" within which the old ethnic boundaries of religiously related groups were being eroded, accorded with the climate of national consensus and self-confidence. Jewish circles found Herberg's analysis especially appealing.

The Jews, Herberg stated, exemplified "the fundamental restructuring of American society which transformed 'the land of the immigrants' into 'the triple melting pot.' " He found the key for understanding this development in a little-noticed address that the historian Marcus L. Hansen published in 1938, "The Problem of the Third Generation Immigrant." Hansen claimed that "what the son wishes to forget, the grandson wishes to remember." However, the third generation, fully Americanized, could not embrace the Jewish ethnic world of the immigrants, which had all but vanished with the second generation. Instead it identified with its own congenial rendering of the religious tradition. "Hansen's law," Herberg suggested, explained the religious revival then current in the country. Religion was a surrogate for ethnicity, a more acceptable basis for group distinctiveness.[13]

Just as Kallen's view and use of Hebraism stemmed in no small part from a personal search for self-identity, so, too, did Herberg's explanation. Herberg described an "American religion" which was an integral part of the "American Way of Life" and rooted in a "Jewish-Christian faith." That faith acknowledged the particularity of its constituent "three great religious communions" while recognizing the "common 'spiritual' foundation of basic 'ideals and values.' " Judaism, centerpiece of the Judeo-Christian tradition (no less than Kallen's Hebraism was to the "American Idea"), placed Herberg and his "communion" in the mainstream of America's cultural and spiritual tradition.

Herberg's journey of self-discovery and "return" was stormier and more protracted than Kallen's. Herberg's intellectual odyssey led from the atheism and radicalism imbibed from Russian immigrant parents, to communism at a young age, to Marxist dissent, to disillusion, to a search for a "true faith" to replace the one he had lost—finally culminating in his conversion to Judaism. It was, then, a profoundly religious identification in which the intellectual-theological considerations were paramount if not exclusive. This was evident in Herberg's essay, published in 1947, describing his way from Marxism to Judaism which concluded with a call for a "great theological reconstruction" of Judaism. (The article carried hardly an allusion to the tragic and heroic events which had been taking place in the Jewish world.) In like manner, Herberg ended *Protestant, Catholic, Jew* by pointing to the need for true religious discourse. Indeed, he concluded his critique of the quality of American religion on a note of hope by invoking God's "redemptive purpose."[14]

The melting-pot triad thus held out for Herberg a dual promise: the acceptance of Jews as a major partner in the cultural and spiritual world of America; and the expectation that with the dissolution of ethnicity, Jews like their fellow Americans of other faiths, would focus on their religious heritage. According to both Kallen's and Herberg's doctrines, the secular and the sacred, the Jewish entity had cause to survive.

At both extremities of the survivalist-assimilationist spectrum were the maximalists. At one end, the advocates of self-segregation saw such a course as the one guarantee of survival. The rabbi of Slutzk, Jacob David Willowski, on a visit to the United States in 1900, chastized his audience of Orthodox Jews for having emigrated to this "trefa land where even the stones are impure." In his introduction to a volume of commentaries and to one of responsa, he described the demoralization and disintegration which had beset Orthodox life in America. Among the causes he enumerated was the use of English in religious instruction and in sermons delivered by "so-called rabbis." (At a time when few Orthodox teachers and rabbis had a command of English, knowledge of the vernacular implied exposure to heretical beliefs.) Attempts were made to enforce European norms. The Rabbi Isaac Elchanan Talmudical Academy, for example, prohibited its students from attending secular higher educational institutions on the pain of losing their stipends, and it refused to introduce secular studies, including English, into its curriculum—a situation which led to student strikes and ultimately to the establishment of a liberal arts college.[15]

At the other extreme, Felix Adler, a maximalist of another sort, led his followers out of the radical wing of Reform Judaism in his pursuit of universalism and humanism. Rabbi Charles Fleischer of Boston's reformed Temple Israel proclaimed at the turn of the century that "We of America are . . . the 'peculiar people' consecrated to that 'mission' of realizing Democracy [which] is potentially a universal spiritual principle, aye, a religion." A decade later Fleischer severed his ties with his temple and announced that "America needs and deserves its own particular type of religion."[16]

Nor was the cosmopolitanism of the Jewish socialists essentially different from Adler's Ethical Culture or Fleischer's religion of democracy from the perspective of Jewish group survival, though the outward thrust of the former was blocked by language and immigrant status. Arguing in 1907 against the establishment of a Yiddish-speaking section of the Socialist Party, Michael Zametkin wrote (in Yiddish, of course): "Self-isolation in any form is a sickness which can and must be cured. Only the carriers of an epidemic should be quarantined. Lepers are put in isolation." On a less emotional note his coworker on the *Forverts*, Samuel Peskin, pointed out that the psychology of all nationality groups led to amalgamation in the cosmopolitan American nation.[17]

Theorists of survivalism undoubtedly influenced communal policy. However, it was the Jewish community's pragmatism which produced a functional pluralism. Faced with a host of problems in the wake of the mass migration and calls to aid suffering kinsmen in Europe, the community invented techniques and reached understandings that were crucial to the struggle for self-preservation. The early decades of the century witnessed some of the most important of these developments.

At no time in the history of American Jewry was it as fragmented, was it riven by so many passionately held doctrines, and did it face social problems of such staggering proportions as during these years. The great waves of East European Jewish immigrants who crowded into downtown ghettos established scores or hundreds of synagogues (depending on which city one has in mind), religious schools, mutual aid societies and social and benevolent orders. Less numerous, but more vociferous and provocative, were the ideological movements and trade unions founded by the newcomers. Profound rifts ran through the Jewish populace. Crucial for the course of Jewish communal development was the presence of the old-stock, German-Jewish group. Americanized and prosperous, separated from the Jewish quarter by a cultural and social chasm, these well-established Jews did not, fortunately, remain aloof. Prompted by noblesse oblige—the compulsions of conscience and ancestral loyalty—and self-interest, the "uptown" Jews undertook to Americanize, uplift and control an alien element with which they were identified. Thus they became involved and embroiled with the immigrant Jews in working out patterns of communal organization which would bring some order and offer some signposts for this conglomerate public to follow.[18]

Notable, in viewing the period as a whole, is the measure of tolerance which did exist and, although grudgingly given, opened lines of discourse among the heterogeneous groups. Communal pluralism was a functional necessity. Banker-philanthropist Jacob Schiff, uncrowned prince of the community, might denounce adherence to Zionism as disloyalty to the United States, yet at the same time he did collaborate with Zionists. In a private letter to Israel Friedlaender which dealt with his great concern for creating an effective Jewish educational system, Schiff expressed his ambivalence toward a key figure in the educational effort, Judah L. Magnes, a former rabbi of Temple Emanu-El, head of the New York Kehillah, and the most popular Zionist speaker of the time. Magnes, Schiff wrote, "whose manly qualities and devotion to Jewish affairs I highly respect, but whose intense Jewish nationalism . . . makes him blind to everything outside of this, constitutes a grave danger to many things we need hold dear, a danger greater because of the magnetism of the man which, perhaps even unbeknown to him, hypnotizes many who come in closer touch with him." Yet were Magnes to withdraw, Schiff concluded, "his loss to the cause of Jewish primary education and other problems would be so great as to become almost fatal.[19] For the sake of Jewish education, which was to save the youth of the ghetto from delinquency and assimilation, the philanthropist was prepared to cooperate with a fanatic, hypnotic Jewish nationalist.

There is an additional dimension to Schiff's behavior which becomes explicit in his dispute with Solomon Schechter, again over Zionism. In response to Schechter's widely publicized statement explaining his joining the Zionist organization, Schiff countered with a letter to him, which was also quoted in the *New York Times*, declaring the incompatibility of being loyal to Zionism and to America. In the same letter, Schiff also defended Schechter's right to hold whatever religious or political views he wished, and not to have to suffer criticism for it. (Schechter had complained bitterly of the wild attacks he had endured following his statement.) "I freely concede," Schiff wrote, "the right of whosoever may choose to do so to join the Zionist movement, and cannot see any good reason why anyone who becomes a Zionist, so long as he does this from honest motives, should draw upon himself the attacks of others who may think differently."[20]

Schiff was not being very consistent, but he was being very American. As an American Jew he was profoundly disturbed by the "mischief" Zionism might do. The charges of dual loyalty were uppermost in his mind. Moreover, Zionism challenged his entire conception of Judaism, which was classical Reform. Zionism was wrong and dangerous. However, freedom of speech and association required him to let the matter stand. No less important, democratic principles enabled him to declare his disapproval and yet legitimately maintain contact with people and organizations whom he could not readily dominate, but whose behavior he hoped to moderate.[21]

Another American principle—separation of church and state (for American Jews the capstone of American democracy)—was intuitively applied to internal Jewish affairs, smoothing the way for a functioning communal pluralism. The American Jewish Committee, which conceived of itself as the council of elders of American Jewry and defender of its interests, rejected at its inception congregational representation as a basis of organization. No less significant was the elimination from the proposed formulation of the Committee's purposes the phrase, "to promote the cause of Judaism." The amended version—one might call it a secular or "nonpartisan" formulation—read, "to prevent infringement of the civil and religious rights of Jews and to alleviate the consequences of persecution."[22]

The key figures in these discussions in fact defined American Jewry as a religious community, and most subscribed to classical Reform's deethnicized definition of Judaism. However, realists that they were, they understood that erecting a communal body based on a religious definition, or raising the banner of the faith, would cause endless contention. "To promote the cause of Judaism," Seligman J. Strauss remarked, "would lead to strife, instead of creating unity it would arouse sectarian feelings." A group of prominent rabbis and lay leaders refused to attend a preliminary meeting because, like Strauss, they objected "to the term used, 'The cause of Judaism.'" It was "exceedingly vague and opened the door to all sorts of attempts on the religious liberty of the Jews and the autonomy of the existing congregations and fraternities."

The argument was overstated and was, in part, a pretext for opposing the creation of a new coordinating body at all. Nevertheless, it carried weight. Even the support of such influential figures as Louis Marshall and Cyrus Adler for the phrase, "the cause of Judaism," failed to convince the majority, which included Oscar Straus. Straus opposed forming a national body for religious purposes because "it would be divisive." To Straus's mind the only ground for united action was the need to counter discrimination or to raise funds for suffering brethren.[23]

What was discussed with restraint at the founding of the American Jewish Committee was debated with much agitation at the preliminary conferences which led to the establishment of the New York Kehillah. Starting in the fall of 1908, the steering committee of that conference, a far more diverse group than the American Jewish Committee, deliberately skirted the issue. It formulated the purposes of the proposed organization in the most innocuous language:

> The purpose of this organization shall be the formation of a representative community of the Jews of New York City. It shall act for them as necessity requires; and it may promote and foster such organizations, institutions as will fulfill its purposes.[24]

The American-born Orthodox rabbi, Bernard Drachman, challenged the formula. A declaration of principles which did not affirm "the protection and care of the interests of the Jewish faith" as its central purpose degraded Judaism. Henry Moskowitz, leader of the Madison House settlement, and Nachman Syrkin of the Socialist-Zionists, responded with a secularist counterproposal; the Kehillah was to devote itself to the interests of "the Jewish people that are national, cultural, social and economical, etc." The innocuous, neutral formula was accepted.[25]

Federations of Jewish philanthropies, which by 1917 existed in all major centers of Jewish population, held to the view that the Jewish communal polity must distinguish between the religious, which was private and sectarian, and the nonreligious which was communal. The New York federation at its inception excluded "philanthropic religious activities" from its scope as had its predecessors. Religious instruction, the federation's founders ruled, was a congregational function not a communal service. Only after intensive lobbying did the federation allow a crack in the "wall of separation" to the extent of agreeing to extend aid to six religious schools. The justification offered was that the schools were not affiliated with synagogues; they were community schools serving, among others, children of the poor who were unable to pay tuition fees. Boris Bogen put the matter succinctly in his textbook, *Jewish Philanthropy*, which appeared in 1917. While indicating his reservations about the separation of functions he wrote, "For some time this arrangement was considered rather favorable, as it was thought that the analogy of separating the state from religion, or the school from the church, holds good in this case [the federation]."[26]

Such ground rules were suprisingly effective in assuring the minimal operation of a communal polity. The very challenges to the validity of a pluralistic community of such latitude—and the challenges were continuous and pressed with vigor—became part of the ongoing, many-sided internal struggle to achieve power and influence. Thus schismatic, centrifugal tendencies were by and large contained. They were contained by stretching communal pluralism to the breaking point, through compromise and stalemate, and by countenancing incongruities and inconsistencies. The issue of forming an American Jewish congress illustrates this process.

For three years beginning in the fall of 1914 a public debate raged over the question of creating a democratically elected central organization to represent American Jewry. Its advocates claimed that only such a body, a "congress," would have the moral authority to mobilize support for Europe's Jews in their impending struggle for political and cultural rights. The men of the American Jewish Committee correctly understood the proposal as a challenge to their hegemony. They viewed the congress movement, moreover, as exploiting the "terrible distress of our brethren abroad" in order to "consolidate the Jews of America into a separate nationalistic group." When an agreement was finally reached, promoters of the congress like Louis D. Brandeis and Stephen S. Wise viewed the decision as a victory for democracy over the "plutocracy." But the victory was actually attained only when the pro-congress leaders made major concessions to the American Jewish Committee and its confederates. The congress was to be constituted on condition that it disband after completing a specific, single assignment: sending a delegation in the name of American Jewry to the future peace conference to lobby for recognition of a "Jewish home" in Palestine and for granting "group rights" to Jews in those European states recognizing national minority rights. Thus, in order to limit the scope of the congress, the opposition joined it. The socialist camp, long-alienated from the Jewish community, followed suit. Reluctantly, it joined forces with the American Jewish Committee to check the "nationalists."[27]

The congress controversy also indicated the growing role of the secular agency as an integrating force in the community. This development is most apparent in the rise to preeminence of the American Jewish Joint Distribution Comittee (JDC) and the Zionist Organization during the war years. In both cases, groups holding disparate, indeed at times antagonistic views established tenuous yet operable alliances. The JDC, dominated by the German Jewish philanthropists' American Jewish Relief Committee, co-opted relief organizations sponsored by Orthodox circles (the Central Relief Committee) and by the Jewish radical movements (the People's Relief Committee). The unprecedented sums required to aid the war sufferers and the political and administrative problems entailed in transferring and distributing funds required collaboration. The Zionists possessed their radical and orthodox wings as well as a center group which was by no means homogeneous. Nevertheless, both bodies succeeded in building impressive structures which linked a central administration with a nation-wide constituency.

Both groups, furthermore, attracted lay leaders of a younger generation, who directed campaigns which enrolled thousands of members and raised tens of millions of dollars. The central administrations recruited professional cadres, formulated development plans, and carried on diplomatic negotiations with the government and with international bodies. Between 1914 and 1918, the JDC raised slightly over $16.5 million, and in the two postwar years it raised $27.4 million. Its top leadership included Felix Warburg, Paul Baerwald, Herbert Lehman, James H. Becker, Joseph C. Hyman and James N. Rosenberg—all drawn from the second generation of the American Jewish elite. By 1920, the JDC had established a vast relief network in Europe staffed by scores of field workers and specialists who had risen to prominence in American Jewish communal service—men like Boris Bogen, David Bressler and Julius Goldman. The Zionist Organization, under Louis Brandeis's leadership, attracted to its upper echelons Felix Frankfurter, Julian Mack, Horace Kallen, Eugene Meyer Jr., Benjamin V. Cohen, Elisha Friedman, Louis Kirstein, Bernard Flexner and Robert Szold. American-born or nearly so, highly successful professionals or businessmen, most were unattached to synagogue or temple, and in a number of cases removed from Jewish institutional affiliation prior to joining the Zionist Organization. In the years 1917–1920 almost all held prominent places in government service—a time of 100 percent Americanism and anti-hyphenism. The Zionist Organization grew from 12,000 members in 1914 to 144,000 in 1918. It successfully challenged the established Jewish leadership and, through the congress movement, attained coequal status with the American Jewish Committee-JDC; it also became a powerful force in world Zionist politics.[28]

The creation of these broad alliances with their utilitarian programs (alongside explicit or implicit ideological stands) did not diminish a continuing attention to the question of ethnic self-definition. Ideologues, from the Reform theologian Kaufmann Kohler, to the Yiddishist diaspora nationalist Chayim Zhitlovski, offered philosophies which addressed the question of group survival in America. However, less systematic thinkers, the communal functionaries and the lay leaders—the broad, middle range of pragmatic people—lived by a pliant biform identity. Could not one emphasize, when conditions called for it, the religious component of the ancient heritage: God, the prophets, the divine law—in short, Jews as a religious community? Or pay passing deference to the religious heritage, and then define one's Jewishness as a nationality, a people, or, to use the term of those years, a race—all appellations with strong secular colorings?[29]

Here is Julian Mack, presiding judge of Chicago's Juvenile Court, addressing the National Conference of Jewish Charities in 1906:

> The question arises, why should we confer on Jewish charity? Aye, why have we Jewish charities? *The Jew seeks no separation. He is at one with the followers of all other religions in a common American citizenship* [emphasis added].

The answer Mack gave was embarrassingly apologetic: the promise made to Governor Peter Stuyvesant of New Amsterdam that the Jews would provide for their poor. Mack continued:

> The Jew conceives it to be his duty—no longer to his fellow Americans, but to himself, to his religion, to his fellow Jews—faithfully to carry out this pledge given by his ancestors. This explains the need of our own separate charities, to better and to strengthen their work, for creating this National Conference.[30]

Nine years later Mack again stated his position, which was now akin to the Zionists. In an address before the American Jewish Committee, of which he was a vice president, he stated:

> The only conception of nationality that I can see is that of the Jews as a people. There is no difference in my mind between the nationality of the Jews of this country and the nationality of the Germans and the Irish of this country—and that makes them none the less Americans.[31]

Both elements—the national-secular and the religious—could coexist and contend with one another within the same statement, within the same mind, reflecting a bifurcated self-perception of the group. In 1910, Brandeis, responding to a question regarding his interest in Zionism, answered:

> I have a great deal of sympathy for the movement and am deeply interested in the outcome of the propaganda. These so-called dreamers are entitled to the respect and appreciation of the entire Jewish people. Nobody takes greater pride than I do in the success of individual members of my race. . . . I believe that the Jews can be just as much of a priest people today as they were in the prophetic days.

But then Brandeis goes on to say that American democracy has no place for hyphenated Americans:

> This country demands that its sons and daughters whatever their race—however intense or diverse their religious connections—be politically merely American citizens. Habits of living, of thought which tend to keep alive difference of origin or to classify men according to their religious beliefs are inconsistent with the American idea of brotherhood and are disloyal.[32]

Brandeis soon moved to a position of outright ethnic pluralism. Five years later, in a July 4th oration in Boston's Faneuil Hall, he declared that: "the new nationalism adopted by America proclaims that each race or people, like each individual, has the right and the duty to develop, and that only through such differentiated development will high civilization be attained." He could then say, in other speeches, that because Jews by reason of their tradition and their character were peculiarly fitted for the attainment of American ideals, to be good Americans meant being good Jews which meant becoming Zionists.[33]

The seesaw play of different images of identity comes through with great clarity in a sharp, acrimonious exchange between Magnes and the Reverend Frederick Lynch, a prominent Protestant minister. The occasion was the launching of the New York Kehillah in 1909. Magnes, the moving spirit behind the Kehillah and its chairman, delivered a sermon entitled, "A Republic of Nationalities." Lynch's sermon in rebuttal, reported in the New York Times, warned:

> Our Hebrew friends are continually complaining of being treated as a race apart and yet they often seem to be doing their best to separate themselves from the rest of the community.

Magnes responded:

> The Jews have the right and duty to organize themselves into as strong a
> body as possible. They must be organized both for the sake of their Ju-
> daism and for the sake of the country in which they live. [Magnes is re-
> ferring to the need to meet social problems of the immigrant commu-
> nity.] Their Judaism requires of them that they be a race apart. . . . The
> destruction of historic races is . . . not the highest conception of the fu-
> ture of America. The Reverend Lynch might consider the possibility of
> a variety of races dwelling peacefully together, and each of them con-
> tributing its share to the sum total of American culture.

So what were the Jews, a race with a culture? Magnes continued, shifting,
to a clearly religious definition of Judaism:

> Judaism, as the religion of a minority of the people, must, as must any
> other minority religion, have minority interests. . . . We Jews shall con-
> tinue to insist upon the rights of Judaism just as we trust that Chris-
> tians may insist upon the rights of Christianity.

The Reverend Lynch, still puzzled, replied:

> If Rabbi Magnes thinks, as he seems to, that as a race Italians, Irish,
> Jews, or any other foreign race can be at the same time foreigners and
> Americans, he will find it cannot be in America. . . . One cannot be a
> Jew (except in religion) and a real American at the same time.[34]

The presence of "biformities," as historian Michael Kammen has suggested, is central to understanding the American national character. "The
push-pull of both wanting to belong and seeking to be free has been an
ambivalent condition of life in America, the nurture of a contrapuntal
civilization."[35] The insight is a useful one in understanding not only America's pluralistic society, but in comprehending the internal pluralism of the
American Jewish collectivity. This biform construct of identity aided
them in locating and relocating themselves in the "unstable pluralism"
which was, and continues to be, characteristic of the nation as well as of
their own ethnic community. During the first quarter of this century, the
coupling of mass immigration with the need to become protector of war-
torn Europe's Jews, and the nascent Zionist settlement in Palestine, resulted
in a particularly creative period in American Jewish group life.

The consequences are still evident in the community's institutions and
in its pattern of communal pluralism, notwithstanding the continued pace
of integration of American Jews, most of whom are now three and four

generations removed from their immigrant origins. American Jews now define themselves as a religious community at the expense of their once robust secular-ethnic components. Yet they are no less engaged in secular politics than in sacred rituals. In world affairs, the pivotal role they played in the establishment of Israel, their continued support of the state, and their political intervention on behalf of Soviet Jews stand out. At home, Jewish communal agencies, leaders in the civil rights movement of the 1960s, are immersed in the public policy debates over government recognition and empowerment of minority groups (affirmative action) and in redefining American pluralism (multiculturalism). At the same time, American Judaism's religious establishments have carried the burden of transmitting the historical heritage however it be understood. Organizational diversity, ideological ambiguity, and even contentiousness appear to be endemic to the communal experience of American Jews. This communal temper goes far to explain American Jewry's inventiveness in its endeavors to maintain its American and Jewish collective identities.

## 2 Pageants of Sorrow, Celebration and Protest

Over a span of eight days during late November and early December 1905, three mass events took place in which hundreds of thousands of Jews participated and about which millions more read in the general and Jewish press. Two of these events were commemorated throughout the United States; the third occurred in New York City alone. The first in time was the funeral of the popular Yiddish novelist and dramatist, Nahum Meyer Shaikevich (better known by his pseudonym, Shomer), which was held on November 26. Nearly 100,000 turned out to honor the writer, lining the funeral route and following the hearse through the streets of New York's Lower East Side and across the Williamsburgh Bridge to Union Hills Cemetery in Brooklyn. Four days later, on Thanksgiving Day, in scores of public meetings and synagogues across the land, American Jews celebrated the 250th anniversary of Jewish settlement in America. Governors, mayors and a former U.S. president Grover Cleveland participated in the festivities. The celebrations were followed on December 4 with protest demonstrations mourning the victims of the October pogroms in Czarist Russia. Two hundred thousand participated in the New York protest march, with more modest demonstrations occurring in other cities and special memorial services conducted in Jewish communities throughout the United States.

Taken together, these three episodes offer a paradigm of the public culture of American Jews. They were communal observances that were in part civic rituals of affirmation and self-definition and in part ideological and political statements in the guise of ethnic pageantry. These pageants of commemoration, celebration and protest provided opportunities for transcending cultural and class disparities and enmities. For the medium and the message of these public events—crafted with due deliberation—endeavored to embrace great numbers, new immigrants no less than old settlers, the religious and the secular. They were appeals to "the community" in its totality even though their sponsors were often party people with partisan designs. They took place, furthermore, in the city's main streets, public squares, concert halls and sports arenas so that the general public and the press would also take notice.[1]

The Jews who gathered to mourn their luminaries, demand redress for brethren in peril, and invent an American Jewish past were creating a public culture that exists to this day, although the form and idiom have changed. American Jews continue to resort to similar devices and tactics as a means of providing some sense of collective identity. For an ethnoreligious community whose sense of self is increasingly marked by ambiguity if not vacuity, the incentive to nurture a Jewish public culture is compelling. The grandly staged pageants of the 1930s and 1940s— *The Romance of a People* (1933), *The Eternal Road* (1937), *We Will Never Die* (1943) and *A Flag Is Born* (1946)—which sought to raise Jewish morale, mobilize public opinion and unify American Jews in efforts to save the Jews of Europe, is a latter-day expression of this public phenomenon. The year-long tercentenary celebration beginning in the fall of 1954 of the first Jewish settlement in America, the Israel Independence Day Festivities with the parade up New York's Fifth Avenue as its centerpiece, the great 1987 "March on Washington" on behalf of Soviet Jewry, and the opening of the United States Holocaust Memorial Museum in 1993 are more recent instances of this process. This study examines the three 1905 episodes that exemplify the early makings of this public culture, the separate strands that shaped it, and the collective memories that legitimized it.

Of the three events, the funeral of Shaikevich (Shomer) represented the most venerable expression of communal celebration. One can indeed argue that in traditional European Jewish society the public funeral of an illustrious scholar or communal leader was the most significant event in the life of the community. It was a time not only of mourning but of rededication, uplift and communal solidarity. Each detail of the ritual was charged with meaning: those chosen to maintain the final vigil, carry the coffin, and deliver the eulogies; the public places where the procession paused for prayers; and at the cemetery, the location of the grave itself. The orchestration of the funeral ranked and classified the deceased among the community's worthies who had gone to their reward. In the popular mind, the number of mourners who accompanied the deceased to the grave served as the measure of esteem. Though secularization breached the walls of the traditional, organic Jewish community of Eastern Europe, and the passage to America reduced them further, the need to rally forth on the death of a distinguished person in a communal act of solidarity and contrition remained intact. Time-honored religious custom still resonated in freethinking America.[2]

Shomer, who came to the United States in 1889 with a considerable reputation, had made his name as the most prolific writer of his time. The author of more than two hundred novels and scores of plays (many of both genres adapted and popularized from the works of others), Shomer was the master of what we would call today low-brow literature. (His critics, among them Sholom Aleichem, called him the "father of *shund*," literary trash.) His was a popular, accessible literature, and the masses soaked up its social messages and stirring historical tales of Jewish heroism. Typical of the former was *Der yidisher poritz* (*The Jewish Mogul*), a novel Shomer later adapted for the stage, which was a devastating portrayal of the fanaticism, imperiousness and arid piety of the shtetl autocracy. An example of the latter was *Der letzer yidisher kenig* (*The Last Jewish King*), a drama of the Bar Kochba–led revolt against the Romans. His collaboration with the pioneers of the Yiddish theater began in Europe and continued in New York, where his plays on immigrant life and current affairs became staples of the Yiddish stage. His novels were serialized in the *Morgen Zhurnal* and *Tageblat*. David Blaustein, the director of the Educational Alliance, recalled reading Shomer's novels as a young boy: "I was one of many who was started on the road to culture (*bildung*) by Shomer's writings." When Shomer died, the Jewish immigrant quarter responded in the traditional way to the call to honor an important figure—a writer and teacher of the people, or a great *maggid*, a beloved preacher.[3]

Yet who in fact determined the degree of honors Shomer should receive? Who planned the funeral, chose the honorees, the eulogists, the order of march, the procession's route? In a word, who defined the community's character and its self-image? In those towns the immigrants came from where the traditional community (the *kehillah*) was still in place; the *kehillah* leadership, including its rabbis and learned men, made these determinations. Where the traditional leadership was challenged, an unresolved struggle for hegemony ensued. In New York, the Yiddish press decided, a press that spoke for distinct ideological camps. The day of Shomer's death (a Friday, which allowed more time for preparations, since the funeral could not be held until after the Sabbath), the publishers of the Yiddish dailies met at the Educational Alliance, the uptown-supported social and cultural center of the immigrant quarter. All Yiddish journalists, artists and intellectuals (*maskilim*), the publishers resolved, should join in making the funeral a "general one," that is, nonpartisan, and urge all Jews of New York to take part. Jacob Saphirstein, the publisher of the politically conservative and religiously Orthodox *Morgen Zhurnal*, and David Blaustein of the Educational Alliance were charged with making the arrangements. To advise them, an executive committee of two representatives of each paper was appointed. The Educational Alliance was chosen for the memorial meeting. The proprietors of the Yiddish theaters, the various actors' unions and their chorus, and the typesetters union announced that they would come in organized contingents, and the choristers volunteered to sing at the services.[4]

For three days, the conservative *Tageblat* and *Morgen Zhurnal*, and the socialist *Varheyt* and *Forverts* sang Shomer's praises. The *Forverts*, a harsh critic of Shomer in the past, remarked: "Whatever one might say of the literary worth of his works, they were of great value for a large part of the Jewish people. Through Shomer's novels many thousands learned to read." Furthermore, he had imbued them with a thirst for culture and self-improvement. The *Forverts*, like the other papers, urged all classes to attend and outlined the funeral route.[5]

In reporting the funeral, the Yiddish press struck an inspirational and ecumenical note. The *Tageblat* began its account: "Where else can one find a city like New York and where else can one find such Jews as in New York. In no country, and in no city, and at no time in history has one witnessed such an exalted expression of *Judenthum* [Jewishness] as at Shomer's funeral." The *Forverts* proclaimed: "Young and old, religious and freethinkers, Jews of all hues and types came to honor and accompany the deceased to the grave." The *Tageblat* estimated that at least a hundred thousand crowded into the side streets near the Educational Alliance and along the route of the cortege.[6] As the hearse traversed the East Side, the *New York Times* reported, "Jacob P. Adler, the tragedian," walked to the left of the hearse and by his side Saphirstein of the *Morgen Zhurnal*. At each synagogue along the way "the procession stopped and the rabbi and congregants came out and sang a hymn for the dead."[7]

Traditional in form, the funeral was arranged with great care. The planners stressed inclusiveness and aesthetics, taking into account both the sensibilities of the acculturating, "modern" Jews and the curiosity of non-Jewish observers. The arrangements commmittee announced through the Yiddish press that notables and family friends wishing to pay their respects prior to the funeral should appear at the Educational Alliance for an identity button allowing them into the Shomer home. At the appointed time, writers, actors and representatives of the theater and typsetters unions carried the coffin to the hearse, and a combined choir of the Yiddish theaters, chanting psalms, marched before the hearse over the short distance to the

Educational Alliance. Admission to the memorial service was by invitation only. The list of eulogists represented the range of Jewish political and cultural life: Adolf Radin, rabbi of the Alliance's People's Synagogue (who spoke in German); David Blaustein, the Alliance's director; socialist Abe Cahan of the *Forverts*; John Paley of the *Tageblat*; Joseph Barondess, Zionist leader and radical; Boris Thomashafsky, the actor and stage director; and the Orthodox preacher, Zvi Hirsch Masliansky. Between speeches the theater choristers alternated with the downtown cantors' choir in chanting psalms from the funeral service. Downtown's renowned cantor, Pinkhas Minkovsy, concluded the service with the memorial prayer, *El male rahamim*. All of the accounts stressed the sense of exhaltation that permeated the meeting and the perfect order that marked the procession.[8]

In its editorial the day of the funeral, the *Tageblat* offered some interesting reflections on the event's wider significance. The column was subtitled: "The Future City of Historical Jewish Funerals." Shomer's funeral, the paper predicted, would be the third funeral of historic proportions that New York Jews had participated in, if size and feelings were the criteria. First had come the unforgettable mass funeral in 1902 of Jacob Joseph, the eminent Vilna preacher who was invited to serve as "chief rabbi" in the abortive experiment to strengthen the communal life of New York's Orthodox Jews. At least 100,000 took part. And in January 1905, Kasriel Sarasohn, publisher of the *Tageblat* and patron of downtown charities was similarly honored. In both cases, not only the Yiddish but the general press gave detailed coverage in laudatory, even reverential, terms. And now, all within a mere three years, the third historic funeral was about to begin. "In no other city in the world," the *Tageblat* declared,

> have there been such grand funerals. Our generation and the next to come will have the task of rendering final tributes to the illustrious figures of the Jewish world when their time will come to take leave. New York is at present the greatest Jewish center in the world. Within the next five years all the distinguished Jews in Russia will have settled among us.[9]

During the lifetime of the immigrant generation, religious, cultural and political associations organized funeral pageants for their luminaries, providing the Jewish public for a moment with a sense of uplift and communal solidarity. (This aspect of the Jewish public culture is discussed in chapter 3.)

A commemorative event of a different order was the celebration of the 250th anniversary of the first Jewish settlement on the North American continent. In 1654, twenty-three Jews arrived in New Amsterdam aboard the *Sainte Catherine*, expelled from the Dutch colony of Recife in Brazil after its conquest by the Portuguese. The proposal to commemorate the establishment of the first settlement originated among the elitist circles of the established Jewish community. Their intention was to enshrine the event—heretofore hardly noticed, let alone celebrated—in the nation's pantheon of founding myths. Turning the anniversary into a nationwide commemoration offered a superb opportunity to achieve several goals: prove the venerable lineage of America's Jews; reiterate once more the presumed affinity of Americanism and Judaism; and have others—mainly the non-Jewish notables and newspaper editorialists—praise both the rectitude and civic virtues of the Jews and their material and cultural contributions to the nation.[10]

Historians have explained the mind-set of the planners as stemming from the conflicted soul of the ambitious and insecure. Eminently successful in business and the professions, immigrants or children of immigrants from German-speaking Europe (their success achieved in a single generation), fervently American and craving acceptance, they faced the social impediments of a pervasive antisemitism. They were barred from the proper clubs, boards of trustees, and philanthropies; their children were blocked from attending the desired private schools; their sons and daughters were excluded from some colleges and from the better fraternities; and they suffered from the intellectual antisemitism common in literary and academic circles. To add to their disquiet, like a plague from Egypt came the Jews from Russia. Their coreligionists' startling distinctiveness (Jewish but so alien) and their utter poverty made the responsibilities that kinship imposed especially burdensome—an obstacle in the pursuit of social inclusion. Understandably, the Jewish elite became preoccupied with a dignified refutation of those antisemitic canards of parasitism, duplicity and disloyalty that were cast at them.[11]

There was also a more sanguine face to the importance assigned by Americanized Jews to the 250th anniversary. An authentic interest in historical roots and processes was astir in America. Kindled by an energetic secularizing nationalism sometime in the 1870s, Americans began celebrating their past with unprecedented zeal. History became the medium for defining their national identity and glorifying what they perceived to be the moral superiority of the Republic. On a local level, commemoration of the anniversaries of Revolutionary War battles, Civil War heroes and pioneer settlements became widespread. Cities observed the bicentennial or centennial of their founding in festivities that sometimes lasted as long as a week. Nationwide, the Centennial Exposition of American Independence held at Philadelphia in 1876 and the 1893 Columbian Exposition in Chicago stand out. A patrician expression of this phenomenon, initiated by the first professionally trained historians (the new guardians of the past), was the formation of the American Historical Association in 1884. Dedicated to a "scientific" reconstruction of the past, the association drew to its ranks Brahman amateur practitioners as well as the new breed of academic historian.[12]

Six years later the American Jewish Historical Society was established for some of the same reasons by a similar mix of professionals and interested patricians. At the first "scientific meeting" of the society, founding president Oscar Straus, scion of the well-known mercantile family and author of a book on Old Testament influences on the origins of republican government in America, declared: "The objects of our Society . . . are not *sectarian*, but *American*—to throw an additional ray of light upon the discovery, colonization, and history of our country." For Straus, that "additional ray of light"—the exploration of the part Jews played in the early settlement of the colonies—was a way not only of contributing "to the general history of our country" but of uncovering for Americans and Jews the authentic identity of American Jewry. Straus and others of the founders would play a central role in the 250th anniversary celebration.[13]

Among America's ethnic groups, Jews were not alone in displaying a self-consciousness and assertivenesss that developed in tandem with the nation's intensified reverence for its past. Ethnic associations participated in the local celebrations, marching in the parades dressed in their ethnic costumes and often mounting historical floats. At the Philadelphia Centennial Exposition, six ethnic and religious groups had their "days"—a parade culminating in the unveiling of a monument on the fairground. The Jewish monument, commissioned by the B'nai B'rith and executed by the American Jewish sculptor Moses Ezekiel, represented "religious freedom": "The statue of a woman, symbolizing religious liberty, dominates the monument, her right arm sheltering a boy holding a flaming lamp representing faith in a higher power, her left arm pointing to the scroll of the constitution." Interestingly, the Germans, Irish, Italians and African-American monuments depicted ethnic heroes: Wilhelm Humboldt, Father Matthew (an Irish temperance advocate), Christopher Columbus and Richard Allen (an ex-slave who founded the African Methodist Episcopal Church).[14]

Perhaps the most impressive event of the sort anticipating the 250th American Jewish celebration was the German-American celebrations of

1883. Marking the bicentennial of the founding of Germantown, Pennsylvania, by thirteen families from the Rhenish town of Krefeld, German cultural and social associations staged impressive pageants in the major centers of German-American population. The central feature of the day was the parade, which included floats depicting the history of German Americans—the founding of Germantown, German participation in America's wars, and German-American economic contributions—in addition to marching rifle companies and bands. (In a number of cities, the 1883 bicentennial inaugurated an annual "German Day.") Five years later Swedes, concentrated in the Midwest, celebrated the 250th anniversary of the founding of the first Swedish settlement at Fort Christina on the Delaware River. In both cases, tentative steps were taken to establish historical societies. Thus ethnic Americans promoted their own founding myths, insisting on equality of place.[15]

In February 1905, the proposal to observe the 250th anniversary of Jewish settlement on a nationwide scale was broached by two separate bodies: New York's Congregation Shearith Israel (the oldest Jewish congregation in the United States) and the American Jewish Historical Society at its annual conference. By spring, a joint ad hoc committee had appointed an executive committee to direct "the Committees in Charge of the General Celebration"—which gives one a notion of the scope of the planning. The executive committee, a mix of wealth and intellect, was headed by the bankers Jacob Schiff (chairman), and Isaac N. Seligman (treasurer) and included other leading establishment personages such as Cyrus Adler, Daniel Guggenheim, Adolph Lewisohn, Louis Marshall, Oscar Straus and Judge Mayer Sulzberger. All of the states as well as Alaska, Puerto Rico and the Indian Territory were represented on the two-hundred-member general committee which was apparently a purely honorary body. No Russian Jews served on the executive committee, though eight Russian Jews, including the editors of the Yiddish dailies and several prominent rabbis, were appointed to the general committee.[16]

The executive committee chose Thanksgiving Day as the appropriate occasion for the celebration, and launched an educational campaign to make Jews conscious of their American origins. Lecturers spoke on the topic and lengthy articles appeared with regularity in the Anglo-Jewish press. In early May the Anglo-Jewish press published long excerpts from papers delivered at a meeting of the "Judaeans," a social-literary society of the New York Jewish elite. In June, the Boston [Jewish] *Advocate* reported on the first of a series of celebrations that would continue until the "general celebration" on Thanksgiving Day. In the issue of the *Advocate* that appeared following the 4th of July, the lead banner read: "On Thanks-giving-Day next, the Hebrew Communities of the United States will com-memorate fittingly the 250th anniversary of the arrival of their Pilgrim Fathers," and readers were informed that the Boston committee had cho-sen Faneuil Hall, "the cradle of liberty," as the site of the Thanksgiving Day convocation.[17]

In a widely reprinted lecture, Louis Marshall captured the mixture of apologetics and self-assertiveness that became the leitmotif of the anni-versary:

> It has been a popular fallacy, that the Jew has been a latecomer on
> American soil; that he has been unwilling to undergo the hardships of
> the pioneer, or to create new paths for industry and commerce; that his
> admittance within our gates has been a matter of grace and bounty, and
> that his rights are inferior in antiquity to those of our population who
> have other racial and religious affinities. But when we remember that
> the settlement at Jamestown, Virginia, was in 1607, that of the Dutch at
> New Amsterdam in 1614, that of Pilgrims at Plymouth Rock in 1620 and
> that the first settlement of the Jews in New York occurred in 1655, the
> latter are to be regarded as of equal rank with the most ancient Ameri-
> can settlers.[18]

In October, the committee distributed a pamphlet, "Notes Relating to the Celebration," which included guidelines for observing the approach-ing jubilee. Congregations were instructed to hold special services on the Saturday or Sunday preceding Thanksgiving Day, and an "Order of Serv-ice" for that Sabbath was attached. The service was prepared by a commit-tee of eminent rabbis representing the various denominations that in-cluded the Orthodox Dr. H. Pereira Mendes, the Conservative Professor Solomon Schechter, head of the Jewish Theological Seminary, and Re-form's Dr. Kaufman Kohler, head of the Hebrew Union College. A reprint of Cyrus Adler's history of the Jews in America from the recently pub-lished *Jewish Encyclopedia* and an annotated bibliography were included. In addition, long accounts of the history of American Jews were featured in major newspapers and periodicals.[19]

November was not a good month for festivities. Details of the death and devastation of the October pogroms (400 Jews were killed in Odessa alone) and further outbreaks in the first week of November galvanized the estab-lished community as well as the immigrant community to an unprece-dented outburst of activity. Relief committees were formed, protest meet-ings held, and memorial services called. Under these circumstances, some communities—Chicago, Milwaukee, Cincinnati, Philadelphia—abandoned plans for mass celebrations and held their anniversary meetings in the larger synagogues. The national anniversary committee announced that the subscriptions it had solicited for a memorial statue to mark the 250th anniversary would be directed "to the immediate relief of the distress of our unfortunate brethren there." However, despite the pall of the pogroms, the national committee went ahead with the central event of the country-wide celebration, which took place in New York's Carnegie Hall.[20]

The "great celebration" in Carnegie Hall, the *Times* reported, "resolved itself into a demonstration likely to become historic in the annals of that famous meeting place." The setting was indeed an august one. The exercises began with the honored guests and members of the executive committee led by Jacob Schiff marching into the hall single file to the strains of Mendelssohn's "March of the Priests" from *Athalie* played by the New York Symphony Orchestra. To the thunderous applause of a packed house of 5,000, the dignitaries took their places on a stage already crowded with the People's Choral Union and the Downtown Cantors' Association. The lavish decor of the hall added to the majesty of the occasion. The lower boxes were draped in bright red decorated with the coats of arms of the different states; green hangings "embossed with golden bucklers emblematic of Jerusalem," according to the *Times*, adorned the second tier; and "festoons of American flags" bedecked the galleries and stage. Befitting the aura of an affair of state, the speakers included ex-president Grover Cleveland, Governor Frank Higgins of New York, and New York City's mayor, George B. McClellan; and a letter from President Theodore Roosevelt was read. The committee had chosen the other speakers with a shrewd diplomatic eye. Temple Emanu-el's rabbi opened the meeting and Shearith Israel's rabbi closed it; the Episcopal Bishop of New York spoke; and the "oration" was delivered by Judge Mayer Sulzberger of Philadelphia, a rising figure in Jewish communal life and a Jewish scholar of some breadth. The capstone of the musical program—the program itself included choruses from Mendelssohn's *Elijah* and Bruch's *Kol Nidre*—was the singing of "Adon Olam" by the Downtown Cantors. "The solemn hymn," the *Times* remarked, "was beautifully sung. . . . Their voices would have done credit to the Metropolitan Opera House." For the planners, the cantors symbolized the Jewish immigrant presence in the ecumenical homage to the Jews of America.[21]

Two of the recurring themes in the anniversary addresses deserve special attention. The first linked the twenty-three Jews who had landed in New Amsterdam in 1654 on the *Sainte Catherine* with the band of Pilgrims who had arrived at Plymouth Rock on the *Mayflower* thirty-four years earlier. In impressive historical detail, speaker after speaker spun out the remarkable interlocking fate of Pilgrim and Jew. Persecuted and hunted because of their religious faith, both had found haven in tolerant Holland. Soon after the Pilgrims left for the New World, the Jews left Holland for the Dutch colonies in Brazil and, when expelled by the Portuguese, found refuge in New Amsterdam. Philadelphia's Rabbi Joseph Krauskopf declared (in words echoed by other orators): "Within the cabins of the *Mayflower* and the *Sainte Catherine* were those principles conceived that gave birth to the battle cry of 1776." Oscar Straus embellished the Pilgrim/Puritan-Jewish-Dutch connection by pointing out that at the very time that the Dutch West Indies Company deliberated over the petition to grant Jews leave to remain in New Amsterdam, Rabbi Menasseh Ben Israel of Amsterdam met with Oliver Cromwell to negotiate the resettlement of the Jews in England. Among the supporters of readmission was Roger Williams, founder of the colony of Rhode Island and defender of religious liberty ("Soul-freedom"), who was completing a stay in London on the eve of the negotiations. Thus, Straus and his fellow speakers stressed, from America's earliest history, the Jews were linked with the champions of religious liberty.[22]

"Columbus," the other motif, provided two inspiring images. Speakers cited historians and quoted sources that coupled the launching of Columbus's expedition with the expulsion of the Jews from Spain. As Columbus sailed out of the harbor of Palos with his little fleet to discover the New World, the audiences were told, he passed ships laden with Jews being expelled from Spain: as one great center of Jewish life lay in ruins, another was being prepared to replace it. Providentially, the passing of the ships occurred on the Ninth Day of Av, the day of fasting and lamentations over the destruction of the Temple and the day, according to Jewish legend, that the Messiah would be born.[23]

There was also a more direct tie between the end of Spanish Jewry and the discovery of America. To escape from the Inquisition, some Jews had joined Columbus's expedition. The physician, the overseer of the crew and the translator, it was claimed, were of Jewish origin. Moreover, Isabella's financial advisors, who made the expedition possible, were of Jewish lineage. These conclusions were based on the latest research on Columbus by the Budapest Jewish historian, Meyer Kayserling. Commissioned by Oscar Straus in 1891, Kayserling's *Christopher Columbus and the Participation of the Jews in the Spanish and Portuguese Discoveries* appeared in 1894. By 1905, its findings were accepted in Jewish circles as historical truth. When, for example, Rabbi Krauskopf of Philadelphia addressed the New York 92nd Street YMHA on the occasion of the 250th anniversary, the *Times* carried this bannerline: "A Jew First to Land of Columbus's Party."[24] The *Tageblat* presented the same "historical facts" to the Yiddish-reading public: "In the archives of Seville are listed, black on white, the sums of money that the Jew, Luis de Santangel, gave for Columbus' expedition." Probably "half a *minyan* of Jews" were in the discoverer's crew—including the first white man, Luis de Torres, to step on the shores of the New World. "Consequently," the *Tageblat* concluded, "we Jews have a full claim to America and we should not be ashamed to call America our home. . . . We have an [American] ancestry older than all other nationalities, even antedating the English and Dutch."[25] Partaking in the very discovery of America, the Jews were indeed "present at the creation."

The Yiddish press split along class lines in reporting the Carnegie Hall meeting. For the *Tageblat*, "the jubilee celebration was the most magnificent and radiant gathering ever held by Jews in America." All sections and strata of Jewry were present in the packed hall—bankers, merchants, workers, craftsmen, rabbis, statesmen—"and all united in giving thanks for this place of refuge for our homeless and plundered nation." The *Tageblat* in fact printed the texts of the main addresses in the "English Department" of the paper.[26] In contrast, the *Forverts* concluded its account with this observation: "The festivities did not impress one as a people's celebration; besides the wealthy Jewish classes no other class was present. It was a festival for wealthy Jews who gathered to praise God for his benevolence to them." In a long essay, Benjamin Feigenbaum, the socialist firebrand, elaborated on the class theme, turning on end, the compliments that Grover Cleveland and others had showered upon the Jews. "The Jewish contributions so praised by the speakers [their enriching the American economy, their individual success, and their respect for the law] had served to strengthen an unjust order that benefited the millionaires." He continued, "A time will come in America when in speaking of what Jews have accomplished, people will no longer have in mind the great Jewish merchants and bankers but the Jewish masses, the tailors and operators who played a critical role in freeing America from the capitalist yoke." The *Varheyt*'s editorial, "Jubilee of the Jewish Bankers," was written in the same vein. It attacked "the people from Wall Street, Lexington Avenue, Fifth Avenue, West End Avenue and Riverside Drive" for declaring their celebration "a holiday of the Jewish people" while ignoring the "Jews of Hester Street, Norfolk Street, Houston Street and East Broadway." More grievous was the festive character of the exercises: "The Jewish masses are not actors. They cannot go out one day with trumpets, cymbals and dance, give thanks to God, and then the next day march in the streets bemoaning the victims of the pogroms." In fact, the *Tageblat* and the Anglo-Jewish press did report anniversary celebrations held in the more established, immigrant synagogues. The *Times* described an anniversary meeting at the Rumanian congregation Shaarei Shamayim on Eldridge Street, which featured festive speeches and 800 Talmud Torah children carrying American flags marching in a procession led by the band of the Hebrew Sheltering Orphan Asylum.[27]

For days the Yiddish press prepared the public for "der groyser troyer marsh" (the great mourning march) to be held on December 4. Shomer's funeral was a street pageant in the tradition of an East European Jewish community honoring a great personage; the 250th anniversary was held in elegant halls and imposing temples, an American creation; and the "troyer marsh," a mass demonstration of unity drawing on modern politics and Jewish religious ritual, returned the act of communal bonding to the city's streets. In fact, in early November, the *Forverts* set the tone for what would become repeated calls for popular activism. In a front-page banner headline the paper called, "To Washington! Thousands to Washington! March to the White House! Let the Blood of Our Dead Be Heard." "The greatest catastrophe in Jewish history" had taken place, the *Forverts* editorialized. "If [President] Roosevelt so wished, America could help. How can we make the Jewish voice heard? Demonstrate in Washington." Little came of Cahan's call, though later in November several mass marches did take place. In one case, it was the theater unions that organized the demonstration, which concluded with a benefit performance of the play, *Khurbn Kishinev* (*The Destruction of Kishinev*). In the other instance, the Odessa *landsmanshaft* associations sponsored the march, and in Philadelphia there were organized street demonstrations.[28]

The principal demonstration took place in New York, planned and directed by the newly established Jewish Defense Association. Founded in the beginning of November with the purpose of raising funds to buy arms for clandestine Jewish self-defense groups being formed in Russia, the Association succeeded in gaining the participation of broad segments of the downtown Jewish political spectrum. It also had the support of some establishment leaders. From the start of the preparations, the Association spoke in the name of Jewish pride, "manhood" and unity. In addition to protest and fund-raising, the Association provided the means for fulfilling the mitzvah of remembering and honoring the dead—sisters, brothers, parents—and to shed tears over graves they could not visit.[29]

Critical to the success of the undertaking was the collaboration of the Yiddish press. For six continuous days preceding the march, the Yiddish dailies published what were in effect "orders of the day," long columns of notices from societies to their members and from the arrangements committee to the societies. All organizations—lodges, labor unions, political parties, *landsmanshaft* associations and synagogues—intending to participate were instructed to designate an assembly point for their members and to inform the arrangements committee. Musicians and choral groups wishing to offer their services were to contact the committee. Owners of halls and meeting rooms were asked by the arrangements committee to provide them gratis; businesses were ordered to close on the day of the march, and workers were urged to leave their shops and take part. On the morning of the "troyer marsh," the papers published final instructions informing the participating groups where each would gather before joining the march.[30]

The several hundred participating organizations were divided into eight divisions to assure order and efficiency, each headed by a "marshal" who was subordinate to the parade's "grand marshal." The march began at Rutgers Square, facing newspaper row in the heart of the Lower East Side, followed a familiar route through the Jewish quarter and then turned north on Broadway to Union Square. Residents were urged to hang black bunting from windows and fire-escapes along the line of march. The Yiddish press also announced that meetings would be held at eight designated theaters at the conclusion of the march. The published list of speakers, as one would expect, reflected the span of downtown ideologies.[31]

The *Times* called the march "one of the largest parades this city has ever seen." Thirteen hundred police were required to keep order, although all observers emphasized the decorum of the crowd. According to the *Times*, 125,000 were in the line of march, and a similar number crowded the sidewalks. What stands out in the press descriptions and photographs is the mix of bereavement and protest—of a "phantom funeral" and a military formation—that was symbolized by the flags carried at the head of the parade. The *Forverts* described the red and black banners waving in the wind, the workers' flag and the flag of mourning. (The *Times'* account differed on the last point: "A corps of men carried black banners, American flags and what has become known as the Jewish flag—the banner of Zion—with the blue, six-pointed star of David in the centre." Where the

*Forverts* saw red, the *Times* reported blue and white.) Behind the flag-bearers came a fifty-person band. Other marching bands were placed at intervals in the line of march. Those who marched in the procession wore black or a crepe around their sleeve or hat, except for the detachments of the Zion Guards from New York and New Haven and the Manhattan Rifles. Banners identified organizations, and large placards in Yiddish—"Mourn Our Dead," or slogans denouncing the Czar—were held aloft.[32]

The general press coverage expressed empathy for the demonstration, as the following quote from a *Times* report indicates:

> The bands between the sections rang out in funeral strains the note of grief [which were] accentuated by similar strains further down the line. Men and women burst into tears, some moved by their losses, others by the dramatic intensity of sound and scene. Occasionally, at a concerted signal, the bands would stop playing. Above the murmur of the moving throng would arise softly at first then swelling to full tone, the voices of the synagogue boy choirs in a hymn for the peace of the dead.[33]

And when the main column approached the synagogues on Norfolk and Rivington Streets, "the procession halted. Bearded rabbis appeared in the little alcoves under the lights and the strangely carved doorways, clasped their hands, prayed for a moment, and then chanted a solemn dirge." When the first division reached Union Square, it filled the park, and it became necessary to proceed with reading the resolutions before all the demonstrators had arrived. One of the resolutions (which carries an uncanny contemporaneity) reads:

> We call upon the Government of the United States and upon all the Governments of enlightened lands to enter their protest against the criminal slaughter of innocent persons, against the brutal massacres which violate all laws of humanity. . . . It is the duty of a power like that of the United States to put a halt to the fiendish atrocities.[34]

None of the establishment leaders took part in the "troyer marsh." A letter to the editor of the *American Hebrew*, the weekly they all subscribed to, deplored the absence of uptown Jews in the line of march. Their presence "would have gone far to break down the barriers of caste and class." It was regrettable, the writer stated, that her fellow Jews were unable to overcome those constraints of their middle-class mores that found street demonstrations repugnant and dangerous.[35]

However, the "uptowners" sought other ways of identifying with the protest. Across the land they gathered in their temples on December 4 for memorial services, addresses and condemnations, and calls for extending ever more aid to the afflicted. Furthermore, the Schiffs, Marshalls and Strauses were working diligently to alleviate the suffering of Russian Jews—lobbying in Washington for diplomatic intervention or sanctions, raising large funds for relief, and coordinating their efforts with world Jewish leaders. Tacitly, the establishment leaders approved of the "troyer marsh" as the justifiable "manly" expression of anger of Russian immigrants for kin fallen victim to Czarist hooligans or in imminent danger of new excesses. Moreover, the demonstration was a "success"—massive and orderly—winning the approbation of the general press. In fact, the "troyer marsh" complemented the establishment's political and financial efforts.[36]

One should take note that the "troyer marsh" borrowed much from its American setting. True, the parade had a distinctive Russian-Jewish texture. In one respect, it recalled the European funeral procession of a famous personage with eulogies and pauses at synagogues along the route of the procession. In another respect, the flags, slogans and speeches reminded some spectators of the radical rallies (such as the May Day demonstrations) that, by the late 1890s, were taking place—clandestinely to be sure—in the centers of Jewish socialist activity in the Pale of Settlement. However, the arrangements, structure and pace of the 1905 "troyer marsh" derived from American practice. The "divisions" and "marshals," the marching bands and flags, the holiday dress of the participants, and the culminating speeches and resolutions in the public square were borrowed from the recently invented May First demonstration, which leaned on the German-American flair for pageantry. In the first May Day labor demonstration in 1890 (part of the eight-hour-day movement), 9,000 Jewish workers participated in the New York parade in what became an annual event. At preliminary meetings in Lower East Side halls, the Jewish cloakmakers, dressed in their finest, listened to speeches and to bands playing revolutionary songs before joining the German and American contingents in the march to Union Square. At the square, separate speaker's stands for the German-, English- and Yiddish-speaking orators were set up in different areas to enable the demonstrators to hear the addresses in their own language. By 1903, the United Hebrew Trades had organized its own supplementary march on the day following the general demonstration with marshals heading divisions and the parade ending at Hamilton Fish Park to hear a battery of Yiddish speeches. Two and a half years later, the experience gained by Jewish radicals in celebrating the international workers'

May Day would be added to the experience of the religiously traditional immigrants who mounted the great public funerals in 1902 and 1905 of "Chief Rabbi" Jacob Joseph and the *Tageblat*'s Kasriel Sarasohn.[37]

How shall we understand these communal rites that encompassed hundreds of thousands of Jews? In the first place, a handful of notables and communal functionaries and, concurrently, the editors of the Yiddish dailies orchestrated the commemorative events to meet the needs and sentiments of the Jewish multitudes. At a time when a diffuse and divided American Jewry had no organizational core and informal committees of the wealthy and well-connected filled the vacuum in times of crisis, the dimension and scope of the 1905 celebrations of solidarity advanced the belief in a holistic community. Moreover, it promoted the movement for communal collaboration and the related demand for a publicly recognized leadership.[38] A second, crucial revelation of the 1905 events deserves notice. However dissimilar the public commemorations and demonstrations were—reflecting cultural, ideological, regional and class differences and disparate goals—they demonstrated a degree of collective self-assurance that was remarkable. The organizers staged their pageants in the public place in order to activate, uplift and educate maximum numbers of Jews; and they paraded Jewish culture, Jewish accomplishments and Jewish remonstrations before the American people to win its sympathy and respect. This was true even in the most parochial of the three events described above, Shomer's funeral. The immigrant community united in order to display for all the cultural values it honored. The *Times* remarked that the immigrant Jews lamented the passing of one of its literary heroes with the same passion and in the same numbers that it had the victims of the pogroms in a protest march only days earlier.[39] Taken together, these pageants of celebration, protest and sorrow formed overlapping social and cultural orbits. Made up of Jews with varied pasts who had come at different times to so singular a nation, these overlapping orbits constituted the building blocks of the public culture of American Jews.

Public culture is no substitute for the communal web of religious observance, institutional loyalty, ideological commitment and ethnic fellowship. At best, it supplements a sense of community through participation in the occasional rites of community. But where the community's institutional life often produced more divisiveness than solidarity, the triad of communal observances that took place in late November and early December 1905 disclosed the unifying quality of a public culture in the making. The communal rites and civic pageants considered here, arranged and directed by communal powers, brought American Jewry together, bound it with its past and defined its collective identity at least for the moment. Fragile and fluid as it has been, the public culture of American Jews has provided an important arena for self-definition. Since 1905, there have been highs and lows in this process that have paralleled the complex interweaving of social and cultural change. Uncovering this history, which requires looking beyond the conventional boundaries of institutional life, should contribute to our perspective on the dynamics of the communal life of American Jews.

# 3   The Rites of Community

Beginning in the early 1900s and continuing for some forty years, massive funerals were held, particularly in New York City, to honor distinguished Jewish figures. The funerals of "Chief Rabbi" Jacob Joseph (1902), the Orthodox *Yiddishe Tageblat*'s publisher Kasriel Sarasohn (1905), popular Yiddish playwright Jacob Gordin (1909), the beloved Yiddish writer Sholom Aleichem (1916), and the Jewish socialist leaders Meyer London (1926), Morris Hillquit (1933), and Baruch Charney Vladeck (1938) brought out crowds of mourners which numbered in the tens of thousands and sometimes in the hundreds of thousands. Then, in the 1940s, the character of the public funeral changed. When Bernard Revel, the president of the Rabbi Isaac Elhanan Theological Seminary and Yeshiva College, died in December 1940, several thousand—mostly faculty, students, and prominent rabbis—attended the funeral services which were held in the college auditorium. Louis Brandeis's funeral service (October 1941) was private. About fifty assembled at the Brandeis home in Washington, D.C., where a quartet of violins played Beethoven and Dean Acheson, Assistant Secretary of State and former law clerk to the justice, and Felix Frankfurter eulogized him. The family requested that no flowers be sent, and the body was cremated. No longer was the Jewish public exhorted to leave their shops or close their stores and take their place along the designated route of the funeral procession to pay homage to the revered leader, writer or rabbi.[1]

On first sight, the rise and demise of the public funeral as mass event can be understood as the inevitable course of acculturation. At Jacob Joseph's and Kasriel Sarasohn's funerals, police were required to control the nearly hysterical crowds eager to touch the coffin ("a plain unpainted pine box") as the funeral cortege moved through the streets of the Lower East Side and paused for prayers at various synagogues. Forty years later, only invited guests were allowed into Carnegie Hall for the funeral service for Stephen S. Wise ("a severely plain walnut coffin with bronze handles in the center of the stage"). The overflow audience stood in the nearby streets and listened in restrained grief to the proceedings over loudspeakers.[2] Understandably, time had wrought changes in dress, social convention, formal practice, and urban geography (most obviously, the demise of the old immigrant neighborhoods). However, acculturation and the different urban setting as explanatory devices gloss over cultural subtleties and adjustments which in fact served as bench marks for the immigrant generation. Public funerals, viewed as communal observances, were rituals of collective affirmation. They extended the boundaries of private grief and adoration—and often guilt—to embrace the kinship of community and nationality by celebrating the virtues of the fallen leader or mentor. Such celebrations were also ideological and political declarations. In paying tribute to the dead and to the past, the celebrants addressed the present by calling for rededication to the departed hero's way of life and goals. But no less important than the rhetoric was the symbolism which was linked to every phase of the rites. Sacred custom was manipulated by the traditionalists, without violating religious law, to enhance their image among their own people and before the gentiles. Secular radicals invented their own tradition in order to forge a group solidarity and willy-nilly define their identity. This chapter examines a little-studied aspect of the public culture of American Jews. It seeks to sort out some of the elements of the public funeral as civic pageant played out in the streets of New York and in the press, for all to see.[3]

Jews memorialized their great men and women with public funerals and annual visits to their graves beginning in Talmudic times. This practice struck deep roots in the religious culture of East European Jewry. A funeral of an illustrious rabbi would be postponed to enable notables from afar to be present. The funeral procession of a saintly scholar, philanthropist, or important communal functionary would pause at the synagogue and other institutions with which the deceased was associated. At each station, and at the cemetery, distinguished members of the community eulogized the deceased and then interred him among the esteemed who had gone to their reward. All who possibly could paid homage to a person of such standing by accompanying the coffin to the cemetery. Many left their workplaces, and children were excused from school in order to attend the funeral and gain religious merit. On the anniversary of the death of a famous and revered figure, disciples and admirers would visit the grave and call on the departed for divine intervention on behalf of the community or support for a personal petition. The pilgrimages of the Bratslaver Hasidim to Umsk to visit the grave of Nahman of Bratslav is a famous instance of this practice.[4]

These extraordinary occasions rested on a highly disciplined communal order which dealt with death whenever and for whomever it occurred. Religious law and custom dictated the precise details of the rituals: the vigil maintained as death came, the preparation of the body for burial, the prayer services and eulogies, the order of the funeral procession, the choice of burial plot, the interment service, and the mourning arrangements. Responsibility for the preparations and their execution belonged to the *hevra kadisha* ("the holy burial society"), which also had exclusive control of the communal cemetery. Since attending the dying and burying the dead without personal gain, as Jewish law required, was considered the most exalted of mitzvahs, only devout and established members of the community were eligible for membership in the society. By virtue of its members' social standing and its monopoly over burial, the *hevra kadisha* acted for the community in passing public judgment on the deceased through the details of the final rites of passage. The society also applied sanctions against those who had violated communal norms. It charged the heirs of a wealthy person who had been uncharitable in life exhorbitant burial fees, and buried drifters, criminals or apostates "near the cemetery fence." In this manner, where traditional institutions still possessed some influence and control (in the nineteenth century there were breaches in the communal order and a spreading erosion of its authority), the community reaffirmed its common values.[5]

Although secularization increasingly challenged religious tradition, in matters of death the traditional establishment in Eastern Europe gave ground grudgingly. In what was no isolated instance, the *Forverts* reported on its front page on February 28, 1903, the clash that took place in the Polish town of Suwalki between the religious functionaries of the local burial society and the socialist revolutionaries who brought their dead comrade to the cemetery for burial. When the socialists began delivering speeches in praise of his revolutionary activities and interspersed them with revolutionary songs, the burial society officials threatened to leave the corpse unburied. "But the revolutionaries shouted them down," the *Forverts* informant wrote, "and, singing the Marseillaise and other such songs, the comrades laid their friend to rest."[6] But such victories were only occasional ones. However, in the case of Hirsch Lekert, the young Bundist who was hanged for attempting to assassinate the governor of Vilna in June 1902, Jewish socialists speedily established a memorial day for their new folk hero beyond the reach of the traditionalists. Since the Czarist police buried Lekert in an unmarked grave, a funeral was impossible and with it the demonstrative effect of a revolutionary hero's burial and a confrontation with the *hevra kadisha*. Instead, each year the Bund commemorated Lekert's martyrdom with mass meetings where popular songs, poems, and literary readings composed for the occasion were presented. Bund leaders reminded the assembled of Lekert's courage. On the gallows, when the noose became entangled, Lekert calmly slid it into place, and then adamantly refused the attending rabbi's entreaties to recite the traditional prayer of repentence.[7]

In America, affiliation by choice and the privatization of religious rituals further eroded the Orthodox institutions the immigrants brought with them. The communal management of death as it was practiced in Eastern Europe quickly crumbled, and with it one of the sources of authority the Orthodox establishment might have retained. The 1912 murder of a notorious Jewish gang leader, Jack Zelig, illuminates the process. Zelig's underlings hired a well-known funeral director who arranged one of the most dignified and celebrated funerals the Jewish East Side had known. Talmud Torah children marched in the funeral procession, a prominent rabbi delivered the eulogy, and the gang leader was laid to rest between the grave of playwright Jacob Gordin, one of the Jewish quarter's most illustrious figures, and an "eminent rabbi." In Europe, all three features of the Zelig funeral—religious school children leading the cortege, a rabbinical eulogy, and burial among the elect—were reserved for the most distinguished departed alone. In the "old home," the entire Yiddish press fulminated, a common criminal like Zelig would have been ignominiously buried "beyond the cemetery fence." Indeed, in an immigrant quarter fragmented by the parochialism of old-town loyalties and engulfed by conflicting ideologies, who awarded the "high honors," and to whom, and why?[8]

The advent of the mass funeral in the early 1900s addressed some of these issues. Ad hoc "arrangements committees" filled the absence—and impossibility—of judgment by conventional communal authority. Drawn from circles associated with the personage to be memorialized, committees summoned the public to take part in a demonstration of mourning and unity. How high the honors bestowed was measured by the numbers who attended the funeral and their fervor.

The first mass funeral on the Jewish East Side—estimates ran from 50,000 to 100,000—was in honor of Rabbi Jacob Joseph, the most eminent East European rabbi in America at the time of his death. In 1888, a number of East Side congregations had banded together and invited Jacob Joseph, the community preacher of Vilna, to serve as their "chief rabbi." The association's lay leaders hoped that Rabbi Joseph's renown as one of Vilna's leading rabbis—his Talmudic erudition, piety, celebrated preaching and communal experience—would enable him to rebuild the Orthodox communal life of New York's immigrants. The experiment was a dismal failure. Before long the congregations faulted on their financial commitment to the rabbi, he took ill, and on July 28, 1902, he died in poverty. Historians who have taken note of the funeral have presented it as the denouement of the one attempt to create in America an Orthodox authority as it existed in Eastern Europe; or, they have focused on the riot that erupted when Irish factory workers pelted the cortege as it passed their place of work. However, neither the denouement nor riot perceptions of the funeral should distract us from the event itself as public drama in which thousands took part. The summons to pay one's last respects to the saintly rabbi by accompanying him to his grave, made more poignant and compelling by the years of indifference to his plight, was a call for spiritual awakening and communal solidarity.[9]

In many respects, as one would presume, the funeral resembled that of the burial of a great rabbi in Eastern Europe. The funeral of Rabbi Isaac Elhanan Spektor of Kovno, the most illustrious of the East European rabbis of his time, offers a basis for comparison.

News of the Kovno sage's death in the early hours of Friday, March 6, 1896, spread by word of mouth throughout the city and neighboring villages. In Vilna, mourning notices were posted in the courtyards of the synagogues early enough for a delegation of prominent rabbis and laymen to arrive in time for the interment. In Kovno, stores, workshops and schools closed as "men, women and children" streamed to the rabbi's home waiting for the funeral to begin. (Meanwhile, the ritual washing of the body, *tahara*, took place in the home.) Students of the rabbi's academy, the *perushim*, carried the coffin on their shoulders from the home to the synagogue he frequented, and then, at the request of the head of the municipal council, along the main avenue to a more spacious synagogue for the eulogies. Following the eulogies, the thousands of mourners—newcomers adding to the congestion—followed the coffin by foot to the cemetery where more eulogies were delivered before the interment. Because of the onset of sabbath, the funeral was held the same day, and the leading rabbis and public figures of Russian Jewry who were informed by telegram were unable to attend. During the procession, police and "high officials" enforced order, mounted police opening a wedge for the procession while others protected those carrying the coffin from the crush of the crowd. The governor of the province, chief of police, and the mayor of the city joined the procession.[10]

In describing the demeanor of the thousands of mourners, the accounts in the Hebrew press stressed the unrepressed expressions of grief. The "tens of thousands following the coffin walked and wept, walked and mourned, and there was no end to the hot tears that were shed." And, not only the Talmud Torah youngsters and the scholars from all the schools chanted aloud the [verse] "Righteousness shall go before him and shall set his steps on the way," but everyone joined in repeating the psalms and prayers as they accompanied the sage to his final resting place. And the voices of the mourners rose and were heard from afar and touched the hearts and innermost being of all.[11]

The score of eulogies dwelt on Isaac Elhanan's merits: his wisdom and compassion, the profundity and originality of his writings, his humanity in interpreting personal law, his public service as conciliator and diplomat, and his humility. Nearly all of the eulogies were delivered by eminent rabbis who interspersed their orations with learned expositions of Biblical and Talmudic texts. The didactic purposes were evident in the calls for religious rededication and piety.[12]

In some respects the public funeral of Jacob Joseph could have taken place in Vilna or Kovno, but mingled with the traditional notes were also American ones. Surely, the role of the press was the most innovative, both in its immediate and exhaustive coverage of the events and in its hortatory role. On July 29, 1902, the Yiddish dailies informed New York's Jews of Jacob Joseph's death. The *Tageblat*'s headline proclaimed: "The spiritual giant of our generation died yesterday at midnight; from a poor family grew a living encyclopedia who made a great name for himself in two worlds." The paper called on all New York Jews to close their stores and pay the great scholar the high honor in death which they had not rendered him in life by attending the funeral. Newspaper accounts described the rabbi's final hours, named the lay leaders and rabbis who came to the family home on Henry Street to bid farewell to the dying rabbi, and noted the arrival of the *hevra kadisha* to perform the ritual washing. The *New York Times* reported:

> By daybreak, Henry Street, for several blocks in both directions, had become crowded to suffocation with the mourners. Men and women of all ages, long-bearded patriarchs, mothers with babies in their arms, young girls and boys jostled and pushed each other, all trying to get as near the house as possible. The wailing and chanting echoed from all sides.

Finally, the remains, in an "unpainted white pine box," were taken to the waiting carriage, a task that required police reinforcements to complete.[13]

As the funeral procession proceeded along the predetermined route "thousands of Jews," the *Tageblat* wrote, "pressed forward, endangering their lives, hoping to touch the hearse, at least with a finger." The police officers marching in front and alongside the hearse were swept aside, the

*Times* reported, by "enthusiastic" spectators. Ahead of the hearse, Talmud Torah children walked reciting psalms followed by Orthodox rabbis from New York and other cities. Behind the hearse came several thousand on foot; then came more than 200 carriages carrying representatives of synagogues and institutions, each carriage with the organization's name displayed on the window, and others occupied by the prominent mourners. Tens of thousands packed the sidewalks, tenement-house roofs, stoops and fire-escapes. Frequently, the line of march was disrupted temporarily as the teeming crowds spilled onto the street. The procession paused in front of a number of synagogues where prayers and brief tributes were offered. At the Beth Hamidrash Hagadol on Norfolk Street the original plan of bringing the coffin into the synagogue and delivering the main eulogies had to be abandoned. When the riot broke out at the Hoe and Company factory on Grand Street—the fracas lasted about an hour—the hearse and many of the mourners had reached the East River ferry house on the way to the Union Fields Cemetery in Brooklyn.[14]

At the cemetery, the mood of reverence, remorse, fervor and commotion continued. Horse cars brought nearly 15,000 persons to the cemetery well before the hearse and the carriages arrived. Five hours had elapsed since the funeral had begun, and the assembled were clearly impatient and under enormous emotional stress. When the hearse approached "the pushing and shoving was terrible," the *Tageblat* wrote. "The crowd knocked over tombstones and climbed over fences in order to be close to the hearse." An hour went by until a place was found where the eulogies could be delivered. The eulogists extolled the virtues of the late chief rabbi, "the star in the heavens which has been extinguished," and chastised New York's Jews who had "torn the leaves and branches from their greatest and most wonderful tree." With tears of grief and contrition the assembled acknowledged their sins in failing to honor the saintly sage in his lifetime and to live up to his teachings. The waning day did not allow for all of the important rabbis present to deliver their eulogies. The time for the interment had arrived and with it a dispute as to where the grave should be dug. It was decided that the grave should be in the middle of an open area which would allow for burial plots to be sold to those who would pay for the privilege of being buried near the saintly rabbi.[15]

Arduous negotiating over the choice of the cemetery had preceded the wrangle over the location of the grave. The day of Jacob Joseph's death, a committee representing some of the synagogues that the chief rabbi had nominally served met to make the funeral arrangements. (At the same time the formation of a committee to raise funds for the support of the widow was announced.) The main issue the arrangements committee faced was which congregation would win the privilege of having the deceased interred in its cemetery land. Having the saintly rabbi buried in a congregation's cemetery added to its sanctity and raised the value of the burial plots. Unseemly as the bidding between the congregations may appear (the Beth Hamidrash Hagadol on Norfolk Street won out), it was a means of raising funds for a pension for the rabbi's widow whose consent was necessary for the choice of a burial site; and one must assume that the future cemetery profits were intended to support the synagogue. In the end, the episode with its competitive and commercial overtones, an impossibility in Europe, cast but a small shadow on the first massive display of old-country Orthodoxy in the great metropolis.[16]

Indeed the public display of Orthodox Judaism received laudatory and even reverential treatment in the mass-circulation press, an impossibility in Europe. In announcing Jacob Joseph's death the *New York Times* embellished its account by titling him "the highest official in the orthodox Jewish religion in the United States." Reporting on the funeral the following day, the paper explained that "never had a man so well beloved by the Orthodox Jews died in this country, nor had there been another opportunity since those Jews came to number hundreds of thousands in this city for them to unite in a public observance that appealed so strongly to every one of them." For the general public the description of the funeral and the interpretation of the ritual were both edifying and touching. Detailing the arrival at the rabbi's home of the *hevra kadisha* bearing "an unpainted white pine box," the report explained that "like others of his belief, he was to be buried in this unadorned box, an outward indication that death leveled all equally." The entire Jewish quarter "from the wealthy storekeeper to the pushcart man," the *Times* account noted, were in mourning for the dead leader "who, although he had a chance to accumulate a fortune, spent all his money for charity." The facts were embellished with the best of intentions.[17]

The didactic opportunity Jacob Joseph's funeral presented is especially evident in the English page of the *Tageblat*. For Kasriel Sarasohn, the Orthodox publisher of the *Tageblat*, the "English Department" of his daily was the medium for interpreting Orthodox Judaism to the non-Yiddish reader. The report of the funeral began with the words, "Never before has one been given so thrilling a conception of the austerity, the inspiring simplicity of Judaism." Scores of thousands accompanied "the righteous traveler on his last journey," the account continued, "huddled close to the plain black hearse, in which the plain pine box reposed, holding the remains of

*The Rites of Community* 55

the plain man, garbed in plain white, shrouded in his *talith* and *kittel*, who wended his way to his simple grave in the same simple manner he lived." There were no "crashing bands," no "panoply of purple," and no flowers (possibly an illusion to Italian funerals and to the majestic funeral of the recently deceased Catholic Archbishop of New York). A simple informality marked the occasion.

> New York's Jewry left the work bench, put down its tools, closed its shops and stores, and went out to accompany this simple man for at least part of the way on his final journey, went out in their workday costumes—without ornament, not even the formal black, to bid him farewell, with all the thrilling, awe-inspiring simplicity that is the sweetest charm of Judaism. . . . The solemn procession passed through the ghetto without order and yet without confusion.[18]

Two years later the death of Sarasohn himself was the occasion for another public expression of bereavement for a leading figure of New York's Orthodox Jewish community and an opportunity to reaffirm the values of Orthodox Judaism and demonstrate its sentimental hold upon the Jewish masses. Scion of a line of rabbis and scholars, Sarasohn was best known as the founder and publisher of the first Yiddish daily newspaper. He was famed for his philanthropy and support of Orthodox institutions, most notably the Hebrew Sheltering Home (*Hachnoses Orchim*) and the Machzikei Talmud Torah. His contribution to the Beth Hamidrash Hagadol had enabled the congregation to gain the honor of burying Jacob Joseph in its cemetery. On Sarasohn's death, the congregation rewarded him with the plot closest to the chief rabbi.[19]

In its broad contours, the Sarasohn funeral was identical to the funeral of Jacob Joseph. Yet there were some significant differences. Most obvious was the turnabout in the relations between the police and the Jewish public. The entire press commented that the police had learned much from the earlier funeral when they had failed to respond to the disorders in time and in adequate strength, and then had acted brutally, prompted in no small measure by anti-Jewish feelings.[20] At the start of Sarasohn's funeral, when it became apparent that double the estimated 50,000 mourners would turn out, 200 additional policemen under the personal command of the inspector of police were rushed to the scene. Although force was used at several points to prevent the hearse from being mobbed and later on to block frenzied mourners from storming the Beth Hamidrash Hagadol where the main eulogies were held, the *Tageblat* praised "Inspector Titus and Captain Shaw and everyone of the three hundred men under their command for excellent work." Both the Inspector and the Captain, the *Tageblat* emphasized, had taken particular pains "to instruct the policemen under their command that the crowds were to be handled with the utmost gentleness." The *New York Sun* explained that the police had been informed of "the orthodox Hebrew superstition which makes it an honor to touch the coffin of a rabbi or holy man. They were prepared for a rush, therefore, when the coffin was carried to the hearse and met it with drawn clubs and managed to hold the line."[21]

The arrangements committee's most sensitive task was choosing the eulogists. In this connection the committee orchestrated a precedent-making mix of Old World Orthodoxy, incipient New World Orthodoxy, and uptown establishment Jewry. At the Beth Hamidrash Hagadol, where the coffin had been placed in the center of the sanctuary, the rabbinical orators, in the Old World tradition, used the awesome presence of the body of a revered leader, to call for repentence and rededication. As the *Evening Post* expressed it, "Except for Dr. [H. Pereira] Mendes"—the one non–East European rabbi to speak—"the object of every rabbi was to excite the audience by his speech to tears and loud lamentations." Sarasohn was extolled for his piety, modesty, learning and generosity. Well before he became renowned for his philanthropy, the assembled were told, while still struggling to support his family, he shared the "food on his table" with the less fortunate. There were so many speakers, the *Evening Post* noted, that each was limited to five minutes. The eulogy by the English-speaking Rabbi Mendes, the honored places in the synagogue assigned to Rabbi Bernard Drachman, Harry Fischel and Joseph H. Cohen—all representing modern Orthodox institutions—and the five-minute limit on eulogies were all signs of a modernizing Orthodox Judaism.[22] More notable and more noticeable was the prominence given to representatives of the established Americanized Jewish community, and above all, to the banker and philanthropist Jacob H. Schiff. Schiff eulogized the publisher at the Hebrew Sheltering and Old Age Home, the first stop the cortege made. His remarks were the most widely quoted of all the eulogies. Schiff spoke of his long acquaintance with Sarasohn and of his magnanimity. "Although rigidly Orthodox, he was not narrow. He was the friend of all movements for the benefit of his brethren, and his sympathies were broad. He was the link connecting the two elements [uptown and downtown]."[23]

To properly honor and highlight the participation of representatives of uptown Jewry, the arrangements committee named them "honorary pallbearers," a titular designation unknown in the Jewish burial rite. The list of honorary pallbearers was published in the English daily press when the arrangements for the funeral were announced but did not appear in the *Tageblat*. The list included, in addition to Schiff, such other uptown notables as Louis Marshall, Nathan Bijur, and Henry Rice; communal functionaries Lee K. Frankel, Philip Cowan, and David Blaustein; and Orthodox lay leaders Joseph H. Cohen and Harry Fischel. The *Tageblat* did single them out by name as those who accompanied the body from Sarasohn's residence on East Broadway to the Hebrew Sheltering Home several buildings away, and from there to the Beth Hamidrash Hagadol. Their participation symbolized an extension of the commemoration beyond the downtown Orthodox. That act and the satisfactory handling of the funeral were, one may assume, the result of the experience and skills gained in the wake of the Jacob Joseph episode no less than the ambitions of the deceased publisher and his followers.[24]

The funeral of Jacob Gordin, the celebrated Yiddish dramatist and political radical, which took place on Sunday, June 13, 1909, introduced a new cultural, indeed, political content to the solemn observance. The funeral was secular; thus it allowed paying homage—civic homage—to a playwright, whose vocation as artist and social critic and whose flamboyant public behavior hardly met the criteria for a traditional tribute. But the idiom of remembrance combined the worldly with the godly. "Hold this day sacred," the *Forverts* wrote. "Gather together at his grave. Gather together in your meeting halls. Bring wreaths of flowers with you. Jacob Gordin is dead."[25] Every Jew and every child of the Jewish people, the *Varheyt* urged, "should accompany one of the great poets of all peoples . . . to his eternal rest, he who years on end ploughed the soil of his people and planted there the seeds of culture, civilization and progress."[26] The summons to escort a revered figure to his grave was, of course, in keeping with age-old practice. Bringing wreaths of flowers was not. It violated Orthodox custom which insisted on the austere and the avoidance of the pleasurable; flowers were associated with funerals of Gentiles.

The *Forverts* and the *Varheyt*, which previously had been at loggerheads in judging Gordin's artistic worth, now united in praise of him. The "people's tribune," both agreed, had dedicated his life and work to the moral and cultural elevation of his fellow Jews. His plays, panned by important critics when they appeared, were now lauded for the depth and truth of their message. His strident polemics, particularly his long-standing feud with Abe Cahan, editor of the *Forverts*, were buried beneath the paper's adulations. And if the socialist camp quite properly claimed him for theirs, both papers emphasized Gordin's universal message and called on all Jews of all political and religious views to attend the funeral and honor the mentor and bard of the Jewish people. The day before the funeral the *Varheyt* expressed its wish this way:

> We hope the funeral will pass into American history as the funeral of General Grant had, and we hope that the funeral of Jacob Gordin will be even greater and nobler than Grant's, because Gordin's greatness was achieved not on the field of battle, war, ruin, and blood, but on the field of labor, culture, civilization and progress.[27]

The intended nonpartisan cast of the funeral was personified by Joseph Barondess who agreed to head the arrangements committee of seventy-five. Barondess's fame as the popular leader of the Jewish labor movement in the 1890s still resonated a decade later. By then he had become the proverbial *klal tu'er*—the ubiquitous communal doer—and beloved master-of-ceremonies, parade marshal and eulogizer. Barondess also commanded incomparably greater organizational resources than had the sponsors of the Jacob Joseph and Sarasohn funerals. By Friday evening—Gordin died shortly after midnight on Friday—trade union locals, political party branches, and literary societies were meeting to issue memorial resolutions and announce their participation in the funeral procession and memorial meeting. The Friday and Saturday editions of the *Varheyt* and *Forverts* carried reports of these meetings, lists of participating societies, and updated details of the funeral arrangements including the names of the memorial meeting speakers (in some cases with their political affiliation). The *Varheyt* pointedly noted the consultations that were held between Barondess and the police and between the police and the *Varheyt*. In fact, the paper informed organizations intending to march with flags and music that the police prohibited such demonstrations because of the Sunday blue laws.[28]

The funeral procession left Gordin's home in Brooklyn along a designated route across the Williamsburgh Bridge to the Thalia Theater on the Bowery near Canal Street, the site of the memorial meeting. None of the religious rites were observed. Soon after Gordin's death, Sigmund Schwartz, the funeral director, arrived at the deceased's home with "embalmers" who in the presence of Gordin's friends carried out the procedure which was against Jewish practice. Nor was any part of the interment service recited at the cemetery, although he was buried in a Jewish cemetery in a plot close to the grave of a rabbi.[29]

The crowds lining the streets on the way to the Thalia and from the theater along a circuitous route through the Lower East Side and back again to the bridge were as large as on the earlier occasions. (The *Varheyt* claimed that 20,000 marched in the procession and 200,000 watched.) The poet Morris Rosenfeld, who reported on the funeral for the *Forverts*, described "the earnest stillness" of the standing crowds. "People felt as though a friend had died, the herald of free thought, and fighter for a better society." The *Varheyt* evoked "the wonderful sense of orderliness . . . and the aura of solemnity and sanctity" that prevailed. Rosenfeld's pathos and the hyperbole of the *Varheyt*'s reporting and editorials prior to the funeral contributed to the mood of collective bereavement. In a Rosenfeld vignette, which he appended to his account of the funeral, the poet-journalist cast some light on the commercial side of bereavement. "Thousands of vendors," he remarked, "sold black mourning bands, buttons bearing Gordin's picture, wreaths and a choice of photographs of the deceased—the healthy Gordin, the robust, the fiery-eyed, the dying Gordon on his deathbed with a compress on his head, and the dead Gordon." Selling souvenirs at the funerals of the famous went back at least to the funeral of Archbishop Michael Corrigan of New York in 1902. The *Times* reported that "vendors of photographs and memorial buttons of the dead Archbishop . . . had to keep constantly adding to their supply to meet the demand."[30]

Descriptions of Gordin's memorial meeting stressed the perfect decorum that prevailed, in the eyes of the participant-observers proof positive of the solemnity of the occasion and the reverence harbored for the deceased. Ushers assured that ticket-holders only were admitted and were seated in good order. At 9:45 A.M., representatives of several hundred organizations and institutions, bearing wreaths and garlands of flowers, filed through the theater and placed their tributes on the black-and-purple-draped stage in front of a giant picture of Gordin. Promptly at 10:00 A.M.—as announced—eight of the leading figures of Yiddish cultural and radical life carried in the coffin. The audience rose, the theater choir sang the prologue from Gordin's famous drama, *God, Man and Devil*, and a wave of sobbing swept the theater. Barondess, who was presiding, quieted the audience with the admonition that consideration for the presence of the bereaved family required self-restraint. When in the midst of his eulogy the actor Jacob Adler broke down "wailing like a child," the audience wailed with him until Barondess signaled for silence. There were other outbursts of weeping which he swiftly quieted. At the conclusion of the speeches, Barondess with a sure hand orchestrated and supervised the recessional. All waited in their places until the coffin, borne by a second group of eight prominent artists and literary figures, and the family, left the theater; then Barondess dismissed the assembled row by row as though it were a school assembly.[31]

The program itself began with the Halevi Choral Society singing the Pilgrim's Chorus from Wagner's *Tannhauser*. ("People sobbed quietly," Rosenfeld wrote, moved by the musical image of "the great pilgrim's *oleh regel* pilgrimage to the temple of the immortals.") Sixteen speakers—one account had the number as thirty—drawn from the East Side's lecture platforms and theater world followed. From among the former, the majority—Morris Winchevsky, Louis Miller, Chaim Zhitlovsky, Hillel Zolotarov, Saul Yanovsky, and Abraham Goldberg—belonged to the national-radical intelligentsia. (Cahan's absence from the list of eulogists should be noted; however, two of his *Forverts* co-workers, Rosenfeld and Avraham Liessen, delivered eulogies at the grave.) Boris Thomashevsky, David Kessler, and Adler spoke on behalf of the Yiddish actors. All spoke in Yiddish. During the more than two hours of eulogizing, the coffin's lid was removed. The *Varheyt* noted that "Gordin's body was in full view not only of those on the stage, but of the entire theater. Anyone who stood-up could see his beautiful countenance." The open coffin violated religious law.[32]

Rosenfeld summed up the memorial meeting well:

> When all the eulogies and lamentations were over, people didn't want to leave the theater. An inner feeling drew them to the stage. One wanted to cheer and shout the familiar—"Gordin, bravo Gordin." Instinctively, one's hands wanted to applaud for the author, calling him to the stage, at least for one brief moment . . . but the funeral director [Barondess] ordered the coffin removed. . . . The curtain remained open, but the author failed to appear.[33]

Indeed, public funerals made good theater, good parades and good press copy. For four days the festival went on. Scores of organizations met to discuss their part in the funeral, and the Yiddish dailies turned these meetings and the planning of the funeral into banner news for a million Yiddish readers. When the climactic day came probably a quarter of downtown's Jews took part in the procession and provided the stuff for the following day's papers. The funeral pageant was one sort of endeavor to sanctify the radical and secular view of Jewish life. The arrangements committee, the eulogists and the bearers of the coffin represented a spectrum of the secular left. They were able to rally around the death of a literary figure because, on the one hand, he was identified with Jewish radicalism, and, on the other hand, as a dramatist he was above political factionalism and sectarianism.[34] It was a rare moment of unity made possible by the massive, predictable response of the Jewish public to a hallowed rite. However, the secular celebration also made a provocative statement. Embalming (rather than the *tahara*), *Tannhauser* (rather than the *El male rakhamim* prayer), hundreds of wreaths, and—most distressing because it ran counter not only to Jewish practice but to Jewish sensibility—exposure of the corpse (the centerpiece of the memorial meeting) were for many not only sacrilegious, but a vulgar aping of the gentiles.

Interestingly, in reporting the funeral, the *Morgen Zhurnal*, the conservative Orthodox daily, showed remarkable restraint. Its page 1 account, although barely a column in length, was straightforward and respectful. However, the paper simply ignored those acts that ran against the Orthodox grain, sanitizing the funeral for its readers. It showed no similar restraint in attacking "Gordinism." The day of the funeral the *Morgen Zhurnal* began its editorial by declaring that it had nothing against Gordin personally. He was the product of time and place. Growing up in Russia under the influence of "the intellectual and moral nihilism" of the 1870s and 1880s, he had become completely Russified, and by the time he came to America, he was too old to change his ways. He brought with him the Russian school of "fanaticism" and "class enmity" that was "corrupting" and "destructive," and this "fallacious radicalism" had to be opposed. "It was a matter of principle," the editors concluded.[35]

"Matters of principle" were at the core of the dispute over honoring the dead of the calamitous Triangle Waist Company fire (March 25, 1911), in which 146 garment workers perished. The disaster, caused by flagrant violations of safety regulations including illegally locked exit doors, unleashed a wave of protest as intense as the mourning that enveloped the Jewish quarter.[36]

A *Morgen Zhurnal* headline, "Grieving and Wailing in All the Streets," captured the depth of the calamity. Day after day the press provided the public with graphic accounts of the disaster and its aftermath. Photographs showed bodies of those who had leapt in desperation from the windows of the ninth- and tenth-floor premises of the factory strewn on the sidewalk, and of the lines of corpses "set up head to head in two rows" in the temporary morgue waiting to be identified. The English as well as the Yiddish papers were filled with stories of the individual tragedies. The *New York Times* told of a young woman whose charred body was finally identified by a relative who recognized the signet ring and a gold cuff button he had given her.

She had taken an active part in the shirtwaist workers' strike last year in which the Triangle Company was the storm center . . . and was several times arrested and taken before the Magistrate . . . along with other girl victims of the fire. She was Yetta Goldstein.

Yetta was about to be married, the *Forverts* reported. The paper called on all Bialystock *landsleyt* to attend the funeral. Fifteen-year-old Esther Rosen was summoned by the police to identify her mother, a widow. She did so by the hair she had braided for her. Four days later she returned to the morgue and identified her seventeen-year-old brother by a ring. About their funeral the *Forverts* wrote, "three orphans followed the coffins crying and screaming, the streets packed until the bridge."[37]

Jewish organizations began functioning at once. Families belonging to fraternal orders, *landsmanshaft* societies, or synagogues could expect the necessary services. In fact, funerals were announced in the Yiddish press by the name of the order or organization arranging the funeral. For the considerable number of families or single people without such affiliations and without the means of paying the costs of a funeral and cemetery plot, communal agencies intervened. Several free burial societies and the Work-men's Circle fraternal order, which also handled referrals from the shirt-waist makers union, arranged funerals and provided burial plots without cost. The undertaker Sigmund Schwartz announced his readiness to bury the Triangle fire victims free. A bare eighteen hours after the fire, the ex-ecutive committee of the New York Kehillah ("The Jewish Community of New York City") met with representatives of the agencies concerned, and with representatives of the Yiddish newspapers, to coordinate emergency aid and raise funds "in view of the loss to many families of their wage earners." The Kehillah, established in 1909 by prominent figures from the established and immigrant communities and led by Rabbi Judah L. Magnes, claimed to speak for the majority of the Jewish organizations of the city. In that capacity, it issued a public statement expressing "its horror and sorrow at the calamity that has befallen so many of its children and the children of other people in the terrible fire," and its readiness "to be of service to the city government in taking proper steps to remove condi-tions that could have permitted such a harrowing catastrophe."[38]

Almost immediately, the question of prerogative was raised. Who were to be the chief mourners? To which community did the victims belong? The great majority of the shirtwaist makers who perished—mostly young women—were Jewish. However, a considerable number were of Italian ori-gin. The Triangle workers were also closely identified with a trade union that considered itself guardian and chief plaintiff of its membership; and it claimed the privilege to bury, commemorate, and avenge its dead. In the fall of 1909, members of Local 25 of the International Ladies Garment Workers Union (ILGWU), the "martyred" Yetta Goldstein among them, had led the walkout which triggered the general strike of the shirtwaist industry. During the four-month strike, the women of Local 25 had won fame and sympathy for maintaining the picket lines in the face of police brutality and attacks by hoodlums. More than any other strike, the "Uprising of the 20,000" dramatized the economic discrimination and sexual harassment working women faced. Now the union intended to mobilize the entire labor movement and turn the funerals and memorial meetings into giant demonstrations against the manufacturers, the capitalist system and lax municipal regulations and regulators. Feminists, particularly the Women's Trade Union League (WTUL), who had collaborated so fully with the shirtwaist makers' union in 1909, protested the powerlessness of women, but they offered no woman's way of commemorating the mass death of women workers. They gave skills, money and leadership to help organize the demonstrations, and also the protest movement's most effective voice, Rose Schneiderman, the WTUL and union organizer.[39]

The unions and their ally were challenged by a third authority asserting its prerogative: the mayor, William J. Gaynor, representing the diversity of New York's citizenry. His commissioners of police, fire, and charities, declared the municipality responsible for honoring the victims, investigating criminal acts that may have occurred and encouraging the charitable initiatives of civic bodies.[40]

Protest meetings, memorial meetings, and meetings to raise funds took place beginning the day after the fire and continued for more than a week. The first, on March 26th, met under the auspices of the WTUL at its headquarters and called for a citizens' committee of inquiry. On the 28th, Local 25 of the ILGWU held its protest meeting at Grand Central Palace where the audience interrupted Abe Cahan's address to hiss the mayor's name, then sobbed—scores fainting—when Jacob Panken, the chairman, asked for a moment of silent tribute, and resumed listening attentively to the conventional political speeches that followed. At a Cooper Union memorial on the 31st, sponsored by the suffrage league, socialist leaders Meyer London and Morris Hillquit joined Dr. Anna Shaw, the noted suffragist, in addressing the meeting. Once again the political message dominated. Two meetings took place on April 2nd, one held by the cloakmakers at the Grand Central Palace, and a second one at the Metropolitan Opera which was opened by Jacob Schiff and addressed by the city's leading civic and religious leaders. The climax of the second meeting, where a number of resolutions were passed and appeals for contributions made, was Rose Schneiderman's slashing assault on the assembled. "We have tried you, citizens," she said.

> We are trying you now, and you have a couple of dollars for the sorrowing mothers and daughters and sisters by way of a charity gift. . . . I can't talk fellowship to you who are gathered here. Too much blood has been spilled. I know from experience it is up to the working people to save themselves. And the only way is through a strong working-class movement.[41]

But by far the most impressive and moving commemoration of the tragedy was the funeral of the seven unidentified victims. Bringing the unidentified dead to an honorable burial quickly claimed the public's attention. The press accounts of the scores of funerals with their focus on families grieving over their loved ones, contrasted sharply with the other dead, unknown by name and unmourned by kin. Civil sensibility and religious precept demanded that the community, the surrogate family, conduct these final rites with reverence and remorse. However, in many circles the victims in their namelessness represented all who had perished, "murdered," in the *Forverts'* words, "by the profit fiend named 'capitalism.' "[42]

On March 28th, the third day following the fire, Local 25 of the Shirtwaist Makers Union, the WTUL, and the Workmen's Circle, announced plans for "a great silent procession" that would follow the bodies of the unidentified from the morgue to Mount Zion Cemetery. Representatives of the main garment industry unions, building-trade unions, and Socialist Party branches pledged themselves to call upon their members to stop work and participate in the march. The date of the funeral demonstration depended upon the coroner's release of the bodies.[43]

Negotiations with the mayor and coroner to finalize the date became entangled in a jurisdictional issue. The Hebrew Free Burial Society, which had buried twenty victims of the fire, was prepared to bury the unidentified dead (there were twenty-nine at the time), on the condition that the proposed procession be cancelled. The society's director, H. E. Adelman, told the *Times* that "such a procession smacks of vainglory or advertisement (even if the advertising is of labor itself) . . . at a time of calamity and bereavement." Furthermore, during the Hebrew month of Nissan, which was about to begin, funeral orations and demonstrations were prohibited by Orthodox practice. In the *Morgen Zhurnal,* Adelman claimed that most of the victims were children of Orthodox parents "who should be buried in a strictly Orthodox cemetery without parades and marches." The officers of the shirtwaist makers union argued that since most of the dead were union members "they had a right to bury them which ever way they thought best."[44]

Two more days of negotiations were necessary before the problem was resolved. At one point, Charities Commissioner Michael Drummond, the city official most directly involved, consulted Archbishop John Murphy Farley on the proposal to bury the unidentified bodies in a Jewish cemetery. At another point, the union's manager, Abraham Baroff, told Mayor Gaynor that "it was a point of union pride that decent burials had always been furnished every worker, whether in the union or not." Adelman of the Burial Society pressed his point that a political demonstration, even a "silent march," was an affront to observant Jews and a dishonor to the dead. Finally, the mayor accepted Commissioner Drummond's recommendation that the Charities Department bear the expenses of the funeral and bury the dead in city-owned plots as a way of resolving the dispute. The burial ground was to be nonsectarian, to which the union agreed. The commissioner also recommended that the funeral be "private" preventing the "hysteria" that a "labor parade" would foment. The union objected, and, as we shall see, a compromise was arranged. Friday, March 31st, the coroner announced that the unclaimed bodies would be released for burial on Wednesday, April 5th.[45]

The two events took place simultaneously but separately—the burial of the unidentified seven, and the *troyermarsh*, the funeral march, sponsored by the garment unions and the Women's Trade Union League. The march was organized in two sections. The first consisted of the "Jewish unions"— as the *Forverts* put it—who assembled at Rutgers Square at the foot of the Forward Building. At 1:30 P.M. the procession began, an empty hearse drawn by six horses at its head, followed by the survivors of the fire, the shirtwaist makers union and contingents from sixty other garment workers unions. Most wore black and many wore badges with the legend, "We mourn our loss." The uptown section—the "non-Jewish unions," leaders of the suffrage movement and socialists—which had assembled at Fourth Avenue and Twenty-Second Street, met the downtown marchers at Washington Square. At the last minute the police diverted the downtown section from passing by the Asch Building where the Triangle Company was located. But the building was seen from a distance, and that was the one occasion when the silence of the marchers was broken by uncontrolled weeping. The two segments, now joined, proceeded up Fifth Avenue dispersing at Madison Park. At its head, marching arm in arm, were Rose Schneiderman, suffragist and labor organizer, Mary Dreier, the wealthy and socially prominent president of the WTUL, and Helen Marot, the league's secretary. Despite pouring rain, 120,000 people took part, according to the police estimate, and twice that number watched. Shops and factories closed. By agreement with the police, there were no banners or placards. The "silent march" lasted six hours. The day of the funeral the *Morgen Zhurnal* called on the organizers to avoid turning the occasion into a political demonstration, pitting class against class. "Ideologies and politics should be set aside, opponents and enemies forgotten, and all should bow their heads and grieve silently over the victims of the horrendous misfortune." For the *Forverts*, the *troyermarsh* was a demonstration of nobility and sense of duty, and of the unity and strength of the unions.[46]

Only an official party of six was present when the seven coffins, six women and one man, were taken from the morgue to the Twenty-third Street ferry where several hundred mourners joined the party. A few thousand more waited at the entrance of the Evergreen Cemetery, part of the Cypress Hill Cemetery, in Brooklyn. The burial rites were ecumenical. At the graveside, Commissioner Drummond spoke briefly of the city's sorrow. A Catholic clergyman read the service over one body, an Episcopalian minister over a second, and Rabbi Magnes recited the *kaddish*. A quartet from an Elks Lodge sang "Abide with Me" and "Nearer, My God, to Thee." The demonstration was another matter. It blended class and gender, personified by the shirtwaist makers union with its largely female membership and by the loyal support of the WTUL and the garment unions. Class and gender were also multiethnic. The thousands of handbills distributed during the days before the funeral urging all workers to leave their shops and factories and participate in the march appeared in English, Yiddish and Italian. In sheer numbers and influence—victims and survivors, union leaders and members, organizational support and public protest— the Jewish immigrant populace contributed most to the Triangle affair. Notwithstanding, in the realm of *public commemoration* hardly a distinctly Jewish voice was heard or a Jewish symbol seen.[47]

Sholom Aleichem's public funeral in May 1916 differed from all of its American predecessors. For a moment, it promised a restoration and American adaptation of the venerated tradition of an entire community paying homage to a revered figure and by that act reaffirming its basic unity and sense of common fate. Sholom Aleichem, one of the giants and founding fathers of modern Yiddish literature, may well have been the most illustrious Russian Jew to settle in the United States, although he arrived in New York only in December 1914, just a year and a half before his death. His fame as the self-effacing but wise observer of the tribulations of shtetl life had won him international notice. More importantly, his work was acclaimed by all sectors of the Yiddish public. In America, the Orthodox *Tageblat*, the socialist *Forverts*, the radical *Varheyt* and the nationalist-centrist *Tog*, in turn, praised his empathy for tradition, his social criticism and proletarian sensibility, and his nationalist pride. All four papers had published his stories at one time or another. In short, more than Jacob Joseph, Jacob Gordin or the Triangle fire tragedy, Sholom Aleichem's death provided the opportunity to bring together the most disparate elements of the Jewish immigrant community in a demonstration of affection and reverence.

In her fine study of the funeral, Ellen Kellman examined the manner in which the planners seized the opportunity. Soon after his death in his Bronx apartment, the family, together with close friends of the author, chose an arrangements committee which requested Judah Magnes to organize the funeral. As chairman of the New York Kehillah, Magnes was nominally the most representative figure of the Jewish community and much-esteemed by immigrant and establishment leaders alike. Using the Kehillah organization, he was in a position to move quickly in planning and coordinating the event. The Yiddish press enabled him to provide the public with details of the preparations for the funeral and cues for understanding its communal character: the names of the arrangements committee and the cooperating bodies, the route of the march, the places the procession would pause for memorial prayers and eulogies, and the roster of speakers. Jews were implored to stop work and attend the funeral. "Jewish workers, it is your Sholom Aleichem," the *Forverts* declared.[48]

Kellman argues that by directing the funeral, Magnes hoped to bolster the Kehillah's standing at a time when the organization was "facing a deep crisis of confidence." Caught in the bitter controversy between radical, Zionist and "establishment" circles over the proposal to create a democratically elected American Jewish Congress—in which the Kehillah was playing a mediating role—and opposed by the more conservative Orthodox rabbinate, Sholom Aleichem's death "provided the Kehillah with an opportunity to assert the unity of New York's Jews through the symbolism of the funeral pageant."[49]

Unlike Gordin's funeral, Sholom Aleichem's funeral rigorously followed traditional ritual, although the writer himself was not observant. However, unlike Jacob Joseph's funeral, but foreshadowed by Sarasohn's funeral, the content and symbolism of Sholom Aleichem's funeral were designed to appeal to the different factions in Jewish life. Kellman has examined the intertwining of the two components of the funeral: the "pageant" itself, and those who played a public role in the proceedings. The arrangements committee had a distinctly Zionist complexion, more cultural than political. All except Magnes were Yiddish-speaking secularists and several—the playwright Dovid Pinski and the prominent Russian revolutionist, Pinhas Rutenberg—possessed respectable radical credentials.[50] The first decision of the committee was to invite over a hundred Yiddish writers, probably none of whom were observant, to take turns keeping vigil over the body. The Orthodox precept not to leave the body unattended—Sholom Aleichem died Saturday morning and the funeral was held on Monday— was thus given a dramatic and ecumenical twist. Ten prominent Yiddish writers were chosen to carry the coffin from the house to the horse-drawn hearse. A contingent of Yiddish writers was first in line in the procession. Finally, five of the eleven eulogists were Yiddish writers. As Kellman notes: "The extensive involvement of Yiddish writers in the public ceremonial aspects of the funeral added much to its solemnity and pageantry, and brought the image of Sholom Aleichem as an icon of the Jewish nation into relief." One might add that the choice of writers, drawn from every literary and political strand of the Yiddish cultural world, also appeased those radicals who may have been discomfited by the prominence of the Kehillah and its "bourgeois-Zionist promoters."[51]

The funeral details were orchestrated with great care. Just prior to the funeral the *Tog* described the "three old Jews with long beards" from the Pereyaslaver *landsmanshaft* society arriving to perform the *tahara* and clothe the body in shrouds and prayer shawl. (The widow was from Pereyaslav.) As the coffin was taken from the house, Kellman points out, the *El male rakhamim* memorial prayer was chanted by the cantor of a Bronx Reform temple, and at the head of the funeral procession, children from an Orthodox Talmud Torah and from the National Radical [Yiddish] School marched reciting psalms. The first stop the cortege made was the Ohab Zedek congregation, a modern Orthodox synagogue located in Harlem. On the steps of the synagogue, the congregation's famous cantor, Yossele Rosenblatt, chanted the *El male rakhamim*. The cortege continued south along Fifth Avenue and then Madison Avenue until it reached the United Hebrew Charities Building, on Twenty-First Street and Second Avenue, which housed the Kehillah offices. Crowds as large as those in the Bronx and Harlem awaited the cortege. The Yiddish Writers and Newspaper Guild, which had assembled in the Forward Building, marched four abreast up Second Avenue to join other delegations for the memorial service in front of the Charities Building which were led, once more, by Rosen-blatt. As the procession continued on toward the Lower East Side, the num-bers of marchers and onlookers grew. Six mounted policemen now led the cortege, and a line of police flanked the hearse on each side. The cortege passed by the Yiddish theaters. Opposite the headquarters of the Hebrew Actors Union, a company of actors led by Jacob Adler fell into line behind the hearse. At the Educational Alliance the procession halted, and the cof-fin was brought into the auditorium for the main memorial service. Mag-nes spoke in English and read the ethical will Sholom Aleichem had asked to be opened on the day of his death. Pinski, the poet Yehoash (Solomon Bloomgarden), and the popular preacher Zvi Masliansky spoke in Yiddish; Israel Friedlaender of the Jewish Theological Seminary followed in He-brew. The dignitaries on the podium included Jacob Schiff, Rabbi Joseph Silverman of Reform Temple Emanu-El, Rabbi H. Pereira Mendes of the Spanish and Portuguese Synagogue, Leon Sanders, the president of He-brew Immigrant Aid Society (HIAS) and a former municipal judge, several orthodox rabbis associated with the Kehillah, and Jacob Adler, Chayim Zhitlovski, and Leon Motzkin, the European Zionist leader. As the *Ameri-can Hebrew* expressed it, "On the platform and in the audience were the leaders of Jewish life." The procession stopped once more, at the HIAS headquarters, where Rosenblatt repeated the memorial prayer.[52]

The funeral procession had traversed the entire length of the city, from the Bronx, through Manhattan to the Lower East Side, and then through Brooklyn to the Mount Nebo cemetery in Cypress Hills. People joined it at various junctures, others waited along the way for the cortege to pass, and many gathered at the designated stations for the memorial services. Altogether, between 150,000 to 250,000 participated in the funeral pag-eant. A considerable number traveled to the cemetery to be present at the interment where additional eulogies were offered. The Yiddish writers Sholem Asch and Abraham Raisen spoke, as well as the Yiddish socialist poet Morris Winchevsky, the socialist-Zionist publicist Nahman Syrkin, and the visiting European Zionist leader Shmaryahu Levin.[53]

Sholom Aleichem's funeral was a remarkable event. The organizers adapted the religious commandment to "accompany" a famous personage from home to cemetery to the geography of the metropolis and its dis-persed centers of Jewish population. (*Der Tog* commented that there were in fact three separate funerals: the Bronx, Harlem and the Lower East Side.)[54] They also orchestrated, with much circumspection, the mode of communal homage paid to the beloved writer. The European custom of routing the funeral procession of an eminent figure past the institutions he was associated with was applied in Sholom Aleichem's funeral to stress the existence of a united community. The combination of institutions selected for the sites of the memorial prayers evoked, in Kellman's words, "the domains central to conventional Jewish life: religious practice, self-government, education, and charity."[55]

Sholom Aleichem himself sounded two dissenting notes apropos his own funeral. In his will he asked that his burial be temporary until circumstances allowed permanent reburial in Kiev, Russia. He was, after all, a sojourner in America, linked even in death to the "old home." (In 1921, when it became clear that his wish to be buried permanently in Russia could not be met, he was reburied in the Workmen's Circle Mount Carmel Cemetery.) Sholom Aleichem also requested that he "be buried not among aristocrats, but among ordinary Jewish working folk," in defiance of European convention but surely in accord with the ideals of his radical admirers. For immigrants, agitated and alarmed over the fate of family and friends in war-torn Eastern Europe, mourning and honoring him became a collective act of grief for the world he portrayed, which was also the world they had so recently abandoned. For the planners, the pageant was intended to be a paean to Jewish unity at a time of national crisis.[56]

It was the closest to a state funeral one could come to, a final rite of passage for the humble hero who had served his people faithfully and whose memory and writings would be a source of national inspiration. Only the funeral of the Yiddish writer Isaac Leib Peretz, a year earlier in Warsaw, rivaled the funeral of Sholom Aleichem. In the midst of war and devastation, in a city overrun with refugees, the death of Peretz—the teacher and comforter of his people like Sholom Aleichem—united the "folk-masses" in grief. Delegations representing the entire spectrum of organized Jewish life—from Hasidim to Polonized Jews—marched in the massive funeral procession that brought Peretz to his grave; and youth, "some with red insignia and others with blue and white insignia, kept order along the march." Thus a particular concurrence of events produced the statelike funeral of Sholom Aleichem: acute anxiety pervaded New York's immigrant public; a renowned, noncontroversial figure who personified the shared concerns and culture of the Jewish populace had died; and an ostensibly all-embracing communal agency sponsored the pageant.[57]

Such a confluence of circumstances would not occur again. The death of Jacob Schiff, American Jewry's greatest philanthropist and one of its most eminent figures, brought no mass funeral pageant, nor would the consummate patrician or his family have allowed it. (Schiff left instruc-

tions that there be no eulogies and that no flowers be sent.)[58] The funeral
(September 1920) was a restrained affair. The service was conducted in
Temple Emanu-El by the congregation's rabbi in the presence of Governor
Al Smith, John D. Rockefeller Jr., Oscar and Nathan Straus and other distinguished guests. Outside the temple, crowds gathered, including many
who had walked from the Lower East Side. Following the services, as the
Times reported, "Governor Smith and the members of his military staff
followed the pallbearers from the church, preceding the surviving members of the family." When the procession turned into Park Avenue, delegations from Jewish societies fell in line and marched the twenty blocks to
the Queensboro Bridge. The courtly tribute paid to Schiff stands out in
dramatic contrast to the Sholom Aleichem pageant.[59]

Nor did the funeral of Rabbi Moses S. Margolies (Ramaz), the dean of
the American Orthodox rabbinate who died in 1936, evoke the mass participation and emotion that Jacob Joseph's funeral had, Ramaz's spiritual
predecessor. Rabbi for thirty-one years of the affluent Kehillath Jeshurun
Congregation on the upper East Side, he had played a leading role in the
major educational and philanthropic enterprises of the Orthodox community. The memorial services took place in the synagogue in the presence of
four hundred rabbis, according to the Times.[60] Three rabbis, representing
the institutions Ramaz had been most closely identified with, delivered the
eulogies: Joseph H. Lookstein, the associate rabbi of Kehillath Jeshurun
Congregation and grandson of Ramaz; Bernard Dov Revel, dean of Yeshiva College; and Joseph Kanowitz, president of the Agudat Ha-rabanim
(the Union of Orthodox Rabbis). (At Ramaz's home, prior to the memorial
service, eight rabbinic scholars delivered eulogies following the tahara.)
The Morgen Zhurnal described the anguish that overcame the eulogists
forcing them to interrupt their remarks and the sobbing that swept the
packed synagogue in response. The paper estimated that five thousand
mourners waited in the street in front of the synagogue. The Times noted
that sixteen policemen were sufficient to keep order. (One should recall
that two to three hundred policemen were necessary to handle the crowds
at the Lower East Side funerals.) At the conclusion of the services, when
the coffin was taken out of the synagogue, the waiting crowd wept. A mo-
torcycle police escort led the funeral procession of thirty cars to the Mount
Carmel Cemetery in Cypress Hills.[61]

In the 1920s and 1930s, the Jewish labor movement alone maintained the
tradition of the funeral pageant. Alongside continuities, there were also
new emphases that reflected changing self-perceptions and an altered political and cultural context. The public funerals of London, Hillquit, and

Vladeck were, predictably, more in keeping with Gordin's funeral than Sholom Aleichem's. In burying their leaders, Jewish radicals refused to compromise their agnostic, freethinking faith. However, in paying homage to political leaders, rather than to cultural heroes, a nonsectarian civic tone tinged the ceremonials, which was reminiscent of the Triangle fire commemorations. The pageants' organizers turned outward. Nevertheless, in the late 1930s there were those in the leadership of the Jewish labor movement who also wished to assign to it the responsibility of keeper of American Jewry's historical consciousness, indeed, creator and guardian of an American Jewish "valhalla."[62]

London, who died as a result of an automobile accident (June 6, 1926), held a unique position in the Jewish labor movement. The first socialist to serve in Congress, and reelected twice more, he carried the fame of having been one of the two national legislators representing his party in Washington. A pragmatic reformer and civil libertarian while in Congress, London had acquitted himself with honor. In 1922, he refused to run for reelection when his Lower East Side district was gerrymandered. In the Jewish labor movement, London's standing was legendary. For over two decades, he served as the legal counsel for many of New York's garment unions and was one of the founding fathers of the important institutions created by the movement—the *Forverts*, the Workmen's Circle fraternal order, the arbitration mechanism in the needle trades (the "protocol of peace"), and the People's Relief during World War I. The five organizations under whose auspices the funeral was held accurately reflected London's constituency: the *Forward* Association, the Workmen's Circle, the Socialist Party, the Jewish Socialist Farband, and the United Hebrew Trades.[63]

In important ways, London's funeral was innovative. The traditional visit by friends to the home of the deceased prior to the funeral—following Sholom Aleichem's death thousands came—was transferred in London's case to the Forward Building's hall where the body was brought for public viewing. Around the building, the *Forverts* reported, an honor guard of New York socialists was drawn up. Wearing "black and red armbands, dressed in simple workers' clothes, and standing in perfect order, the 'red guard' gave the street, where thousands waited [to enter the building], an atmosphere of festivity and solemnity like Kol Nidre night in an Orthodox synagogue." Twenty-five thousand "women, children and workmen" passed by the open coffin which was banked by wreaths of red and white roses and flanked by members of the honor guard. They came "with bowed heads to see the beloved face of their beloved leader, to see the lips

*The Rites of Community* 73

that had spoken so magnificently, moving people to tears and eliciting the most beautiful and noblest of feelings." Among the mourners were old Jews who needed help climbing the stairs, mothers who raised their children to view the corpse, and high school youth sent by their teachers. There were also non-Jews, and in particular, the *Forverts* noted, negroes who "with full hearts and wide-eyes passed by the bier. For them London was more than a socialist and labor leader. In Congress he had fought for their interests and for their honor with the same bitterness as one of their own representatives."[64]

The memorial service began at 10:45 when Baruch Vladeck, the veteran Jewish socialist, poet and business manager of the *Forverts*, instructed the undertaker to close the lid of the black coffin. Vladeck's words—"the most exquisite vase in our house is broken to pieces, the most beautiful flower in our garden has been crushed"—evoked a wave of sobbing. Cahan of the *Forverts*, who followed, pointed out the diversity of people who had come to mourn London including elderly Orthodox Jews. (In a boxed, front-page brief, "Stirring Moments at London's Funeral," the *Forverts* described how when the funeral procession passed the Anshe Kaminetz Congregation on Pike Street, the rabbi chanted the *El male rakhamim* prayer from the synagogue steps and the congregants recited psalms.) Among the speakers who followed were Victor Berger, the socialist congressman from Milwaukee, the socialist leaders Norman Thomas and Morris Hillquit, Lillian Wald of the Henry Street Settlement House, the socialist municipal court Judge Jacob Panken, and representatives of the Jewish trade unions, the Workmen's Circle, and the Bund. The recurring motifs were London, the fighter for humanity and socialism, and his devotion to the working class. In Rutgers Square and Seward Park, opposite the Forward Building, 50,000 listened to the speakers over loudspeakers. It is noteworthy that a photograph of the coffin being carried out of the *Forverts* building quite clearly shows a sumptuous oak wood casket with brass handles.[65]

Mounted policemen led the cortege followed by six carriages filled with flowers. The *Times* estimated that 50,000 walked behind the hearse along the main streets of the Lower East Side and then north on Second Avenue to London's home on Eighteenth Street where the funeral procession ended. Many paraded in groups carrying the signs of their organizations. "It seemed as if every organized labor body in the city was represented in the line," the *Times* remarked. Both the *Times* and the *Forverts* found it newsworthy to mention that a large delegation of striking furriers—according to the *Forverts*, 1,500 in number—marched in the procession despite the union's communist leadership which London had fought bitterly.

The furriers carried a placard: "We mourn the death of Meyer London, the founder of our union." Five hundred thousand lined the streets. In many store windows memorial candles were lit, black banners hung from tenement houses, and mourners carried pictures of London taken from the front page of the *Forverts*. From London's home, several thousand continued to the Workmen's Circle Mount Carmel Cemetery in a motorcade of over a hundred cars and buses. At the cemetery, on a platform decorated with an American flag and red and black banners, a number of Jewish labor leaders spoke briefly. Among them were Alexander Kahn and Abraham Shiplacoff of the *Forverts*, Abraham Beckerman of the Amalgamated Clothing Workers Union (ACWU), and Saul Yanovsky, the *Freie Arbeiter Shtimme*'s editor. Algernon Lee of the Rand School and James O'Neil of *The New Leader* spoke for the Socialist Party. When the time came for the interment, someone distributed white flowers to the mourners who flung them into the open grave. London was buried in the row of graves of the labor movement's luminaries to the left of Sholom Aleichem.[66] The funeral pageant was indeed a Jewish labor movement affair. But the Jewish radical camp also addressed non-Jewish socialists and progressives, and it responded with warmth to the notion that religious Jews also mourned the loss of their leader.

Homage on a different scale and in a different tone was paid to Morris Hillquit, who died on October 7, 1933. Both he and London had done their socialist apprenticeship as young immigrants immersed in the struggle to make a living and the equally demanding struggle to unionize their fellow Yiddish-speaking workers and win them over for socialism. Both also served the garment workers unions as legal advisors. But Hillquit rose quickly to the national leadership of the Socialist Party, represented it at international socialist conferences, and before his death served as the party's national chairman. Proudly, the *Forverts* portrayed him as the incomparable teacher, thinker, and leader. For Vladeck, Hillquit was one of the two greatest leaders American socialism had known. The other was Eugene V. Debs. "Debs was the soul of the movement, Hillquit the brains." Cahan's front-page eulogy recalled the forty-three years Hillquit and he had worked together, from the pioneer days when Hillquit had played a key role in establishing the Yiddish unions, Yiddish socialism, and the Yiddish socialist press, to the time when he became the pragmatic centrist leader of the party who was under continuous attack from its right and left wings. The *Forverts* coverage was massive. Norman Thomas and Algernon Lee wrote major articles. The verbatim texts of the condolence messages were printed. Those published on the front page alone included condolences sent by President Roosevelt (a brief perfunctory message), Governor Lehman, Phillip Green, the president of the American Federation of Labor, David Dubinsky in the name of the ILGWU, and European socialist leaders Leon Blum, Arthur Henderson and Karl Kautsky.[67]

The *Morgen Zhurnal-Tageblat* offered another perspective of Hillquit's public life. Hillquit, the paper wrote, had "quickly distanced himself from Jewish concerns. He believed in the older, cosmopolitan militant ideology and didn't change his views to the end. . . . He remained far from Jewish national interests and Jewish culture."[68]

The locations and tone of the commemorative ceremonies reflected the *Morgen Zhurnal*'s understanding. The Rand School, the educational center of the Socialist Party, was chosen for the public viewing of the body (by then an established feature of the funeral rites of Jewish radical leaders). In the school's auditorium (the walls draped in black), Hillquit's body was placed upon a pediment. Masses of floral wreaths were placed behind the body in a semicircle. The largest of all was sent in the name of the Socialist Party. Others were sent by the Socialist International, the Polish Socialist Party, the Polish Bund, the *Forverts*, and scores came in the name of ILGWU and ACWU locals and Socialist Party branches. An honor guard of young socialists stood next to the body; two others, holding red flags, remained at the door of the auditorium. For an entire day and night, the body was on view. Twenty thousand persons came to pay homage to Hillquit. The following day, on the way to Cooper Union, where the memorial meeting took place, the cortege—the hearse followed by a car carrying the family and open cars with flowers—paused before the headquarters of the ACWU and the ILGWU. The streets around Cooper Union were cordoned off and loudspeakers installed to carry the proceedings to the overflow crowd of several thousand. Seventy-five patrolmen were assigned to maintain order. The meeting opened with a string quartet playing Chopin's funeral march and the assembled rising in tribute to Hillquit. August Claessans, the secretary of the Socialist Party of New York, presided and introduced Abe Cahan. Among the speakers representing the Jewish trade unions were Dubinsky, Abraham Miller of the ACWU, Morris Feinstone of the United Hebrew Trades. Nathan Chanin spoke for the Jewish Socialist Federation and Joseph Weinberg for the Workmen's Circle. The socialist mayor of Milwaukee, Daniel Hoan, and other socialist leaders—James O'Neal, Charles Solomon, Louis Waldman, and Harry Laidler—spoke. Algernon Lee concluded the program. The eulogists paid tribute to Hillquit as "the architect of the Socialist Party," "builder of the world of the future," "defender of labor," and the "great intellectual and humanitarian." Then the cortege made a final stop at the Forward Building where many had gathered. As the procession halted, the *Forverts* wrote, "[the throng] broke out with the *International* and other revolutionary songs which resounded with sorrow for the dead hero. . . . Young socialists raised their arms, fists clenched in the workers salute and unfurled the red flag." Since Hillquit requested that he be cremated, only the family and close friends proceeded to the crematorium.[69]

More than any other contemporary figure, Baruch Vladeck personified the ideals of the Jewish labor movement and its new-found influence. When he was fatally struck by a heart attack at his desk at the *Forverts* offices, on Friday, October 28, 1938, at the age of fifty-two, he had been serving on Mayor Fiorello H. La Guardia's New York City Housing Authority and had recently been elected to the City Council on the American Labor Party ticket. Together with Dubinsky, whose ILGWU had grown phenomenally since 1933, and other Jewish trade union leaders, Vladeck had formed the American Labor Party in 1936 as a way of moving Jewish trade union socialists from the radical periphery into mainline New Deal politics.[70] No less important was Vladeck's involvement in Jewish communal affairs. Beginning in World War I, he had played an important role in organizing the overseas relief efforts of the Jewish immigrant community through the establishment of the People's Relief Committee in 1915 and the American ORT federation in 1923. Relief work brought him into the counsels of the Joint Distribution Committee, the most important agency in the field which was led and financed by American Jewry's philanthropic elite. In 1934, Vladeck was instrumental in forming the Jewish Labor Committee—"to fight Fascism and Nazism . . . and to represent organized Jewish labor in all Jewish problems"—and became its first chairman. In effect, he represented the non-communist Jewish left in the informal leadership group of the American Jewish community. Vladeck also possessed attributes that enhanced his stature as a leader of the Jewish left: his legendary revolutionary past in Russia (illegal work for the Bund, arrest, imprisonment, escape), for one; and his Yiddish literary bent (poet and literary critic), for another.[71]

The memorial meeting opened with the Workmen's Circle choir singing *Di sh'vu-e* ("the oath") in Yiddish, the revolutionary hymn of the Bund. "Brothers and sisters of toil and hardship . . . the banner is ready. / She flutters with wrath, and is red with blood! / . . . / Heaven and earth will hear us, . . . an oath of blood and tears! / We swear it! / We swear it!" The list of speakers who followed demonstrated the extraordinary honor being accorded the *Forverts*' business manager and was a tribute, no less, to the influence and power Vladeck's supporters wielded. Governor Herbert Lehman spoke followed by Mayor La Guardia, who had ordered flags on all municipal buildings lowered to half-staff. Then Senator Robert Wagner and City Council president, Newbold Morris, spoke. For the 900 "important guests" crowded into the hall of the Forward Building, the 50,000 gathered in Seward Park listening over a public address system, and the millions who would see the photographs and read the news accounts the following day, the magisterial aspect of the event must have been stirring. It was reinforced when the governor, senator, mayor, and city councilmen walked behind the hearse in the front rank of an estimated 30,000 marching mourners. At Grand Street, the *Forverts* informed its readers, the procession halted momentarily to enable Governor Lehman, fatigued by election campaigning, to enter his car. Although he invited La Guardia and Wagner to join him, they and Newbold Morris at the head of the city councilmen continued on foot until the conclusion of the procession at Fourteenth and A Streets.[72]

Thirteen other speakers eulogized Vladeck during the memorial meeting. They represented the Jewish trade unions (Dubinsky, Hillman, Zaretsky), the American Federation of Labor (Matthew Woll), the Workmen's Circle (Josef Weinberg), the American Labor Party (Alex Rose), the Socialist Party and its rival the Social Democratic Federation (Norman Thomas and Algernon Lee), and the *Forverts* staff (Adolf Held and Hillel Rogoff). The novelist Sholom Asch, and Abraham Liesin, the poet and editor of the *Zukunft*, spoke for the Yiddish literary world. Liesin's ode on the death of Vladeck brought the audience to tears. Because the Jewish speakers were drawn from the Jewish labor movement, the presence of Rabbi Jonah B. Wise, national chairman of the Joint Distribution Committee, was especially noteworthy, although not unexpected. The *Forverts* quoted from his "moving eulogy": " 'They' elected Vladeck councilman, but we Jews elected him in our special way to be our leader." Vladeck's involvement in the plight of world Jewry was a recurring theme of the eulogies, along with his humanity and his "fight for the underprivileged of all peoples." Dubinsky called Vladeck "the ambassador in America of the oppressed Jews of Europe." Asch began his tribute, "A great captain has fallen in Israel, prince of the Jewish working people and of Jewish poverty." However, Vladeck, Asch continued, also "spoke to the world not only of Jewish need, but he represented the [interests] of our entire Jewish people, indeed, of our entire [human] race." Crying into the open coffin, Asch called out, "You died a hero in our people's struggle."[73]

The *Forverts* camp's eagerness to stress Vladeck's and its own standing *within* the Jewish community expressed itself in various ways. The day of the funeral the paper announced that not only would garment factories release their workers to attend the funeral, but most offices of Jewish organizations and institutions would close in honor of Vladeck. Among the hundreds of condolence cables that arrived in the *Forverts* office, the paper highlighted the fact that one of the first received was from Tel Aviv from the executive of the Histadrut, the Jewish Labor Federation, and a second message came from David Ben-Gurion, Berl Katznelson, Moshe Shertok and Berl Locker, Histadrut leaders then on a political mission in London. It is significant that the list of honorary pallbearers—the *Forverts* explained its symbolic importance to its readers—included a number of uptown Jewish notables who would not have been approached to accept the honorific designation by the organizers of the London or Hillquit funerals, nor would the designees have agreed if asked. On Vladeck's list were: Paul Baerwald, George Becker, Jacob Billikopf, Benjamin Buttenweiser, Ira A. Hirschmann, James Marshall, Arthur Hays Sulzberger, Edward Warburg, and Rabbi Stephen S. Wise. Albert Einstein also appeared on the list in a paragraph by himself. Following the established Jewish labor tradition, the exposed body lay in state in an open coffin in the hall of the Forward Building the entire day prior to the funeral with an honor guard of Vladeck's close associates in attendance. Thousands of all classes, ages, and ethnic backgrounds, the *Forverts* stressed, passed by the bier, and out-of-town delegations and representatives of hundreds of trade union locals and Workmen's Circle branches joined the long lines.[74]

The memorial service itself concluded with the Workmen's Circle choir singing David Edelstadt's workers' hymn, "Mein Tsvo'o"—My Will. ("Good friend! When I die, / carry to my grave our flag— / freedom's flag with its red color, / soaked with the blood of the workingman.") According to the *Times*, 500,000 lined the procession's route through lower Manhattan and Brooklyn. The *Forverts* estimated the number at a million. Vladeck was buried in the section of the Workmen's Circle Mount Carmel Cemetery reserved for the movement's heroes. Five thousand were present at the interment. The scene was an intimate one. "Old socialists, labor leaders, communal activists and writers—the most important personages in the socialist movement and in the world of Yiddish literature were there." Joseph Weinberg, president of the Workmen's Circle, opened the proceedings by saying that until now the eulogies had dealt with Vladeck's broad interests. The time had come to address his Jewish socialist work. An old comrade of his Bundist years in Russia recalled what Vladeck had meant to the movement then and what he meant to the Polish

Bund today. "They have been orphaned," he cried. Louis Boudin, the socialist lawyer, praised Vladeck's work for ORT. But Jacob Panken spoke mostly of the thinning ranks of the founding generation of the socialist movement: London, Hillquit, Debs, Berger, and now Vladeck had gone. Not all on Weinberg's speakers list had spoken, but the time had come. The body was interred as the assembled sang once more the Bundist anthem, "Di shvu-e."[75]

For the Jewish labor movement, the Vladeck pageant was a reaching outward. It neared, but did not merge with, the mainstream of public life, still proudly retaining its identity. The movement had demonstrated its wherewithal, experience and passion in mounting an enormous celebration in homage to its dead leader and proven its worth to its own followers as well as to the wider public. No other Jewish organization could or wished to do the same. The Jewish labor movement also approached, but did not merge with, the main currents in Jewish communal life, guarding its secularism and maintaining its socialist rhetoric. One need only compare Vladeck's public funeral with those of London and Hillquit to realize the distance the movement had come, and to recall the Sholom Aleichem pageant to measure the disparity that remained. Undoubtedly, beneath the ceremonials and eulogies a liberal-ethnic consensus was taking form driven by domestic conditions and the gathering storm in Europe.

Although Vladeck's funeral symbolized the movement at its summit, the more reflective leaders were troubled over its future. Panken had expressed his fears over Vladeck's grave: the ranks are thinning; a generation is passing; who will follow if no one remembers? Aside from the public funeral—a passing event no matter how momentous—how could one maintain and strengthen the sense of common history?

In an introduction to the 1939 annual report of the Workmen's Circle Cemetery Department, Mikhl Ivanski, a member of the National Board of Directors of the order, grappled with the problem of nurturing the historical consciousness of American Jews. "In ancient times, in Rome and Athens," he wrote, "temples were built called Pantheons, Temples for the Gods. In modern times Pantheons are also built, not for mythical figures but for the nation's civil and spiritual heroes." Ivanski described the role of London's Westminster Abbey, the "Pantheon of the English people," where Britain's kings, great military commanders and statesmen were buried and where her best-known poets and scientists found their resting place. "Here, English history is hallowed." Indeed, "all civilized people honor their great men with monuments and temples that are designed to glorify those who shaped their history." The French had their Pantheon, the Germans Victory Boulevard in Berlin's Tiergarten, and America its Arlington Cemetery. But the Jewish people were different. "We are an ancient people possessing a long historical memory, but our history has taken us to all the corners of the earth." Although the Jewish settlement in America was young, it had made history nevertheless. "Occupying an honored place in the history of the Jews of America is the Jewish labor movement which is dedicated to the ideals of justice and brotherhood." American Jews could not survive without ideals, and the ideals required the guidance of "our spiritual leaders." But their ranks were thinning, their successors few. It was incumbent upon the "organized Jewish workers of America to fill the vacuum and repay the national debt of the Jewish people to its great men and women." The cemeteries of the Workmen's Circle were fulfilling that function. "There is a corner in the Mount Carmel Cemetery of the Workmen's Circle," Ivanski continued, "which may be truly called the Valhalla or Pantheon of our literary giants and leaders of the labor movement. Sholom Aleichem, Meyer London, Philip Krantz, Vladimir Medem, Morris Rosenfeld, Abraham Raisen, Morris Winchevsky, the victims of the Triangle fire"—and the list goes on—"all found their last resting place in the heroes section."[76]

The fact is that the Jewish labor movement held no other funeral pageants on the scale of Vladeck's commemoration. In its form, Abe Cahan's public funeral in 1951 followed the earlier ones. The body lay in state in the Forward Building for the entire day before the funeral. A number of the garment unions called on their workers to stop work for one hour at the time of the memorial service. As befitting the patriarch of the Jewish labor movement, distinguished figures eulogized him. Among them were Maurice Tobin, Secretary of Labor, Abba Eban, Israel's Ambassador to the United States, and David Dubinsky. Ten thousand people, according to the *Times,* listened to the speeches standing in Rutgers Square or else waited along the route for the cortege to pass. The *Forverts* estimate was 25,000. The cortege took the usual route through the Lower East Side to the Williamsburgh Bridge and on to the cemetery. Cahan was interred in the "heroes' section" of the Mount Carmel cemetery where more eulogies were given. In comparison to London's, Hillquit's and Vladeck's funerals, the atmosphere was muted and venerative, appropriate to the ninety-one-year-old editor and his aging followers.[77]

The life of the funeral pageant lasted a generation, shorter for the Orthodox, longer for the labor movement, and briefest for the Zionists. It was a characteristically immigrant phenomenon. (The giant funeral of

Menachem Mendel Schneerson, the Lubavitcher Rebbe in 1994, bears this out.) The factors that linked it to immigrant life explain its dynamics: population density, the ability of a denomination or organization to command the loyalty of its followers, the cultural-religious tradition of participating personally in the collective mourning of a great figure, and the power and interest of the Yiddish daily press in transforming the public funeral into a public and political spectacle. Surely, the mundane and the traumatic contributed to its eclipse. On the one hand, suburbanization and embourgeoisement presented geographic and cultural impediments to participation in such mass events as public funerals. The decline of the labor movement and the Americanization of Orthodoxy explain much about the demise of the public funeral. On the other hand, World War II and the destruction of European Jewry called for a reassessment of the dimension and object of public grieving. The most dramatic instance of this was the 1943 "We Will Never Die" pageant produced in Madison Square Garden by Billy Rose and directed by Moss Hart with a script by Ben Hecht and music composed by Kurt Weill. In the early postwar years, memorializing the victims of the Holocaust was gradually included in the calendar of Jewish religious and civil life. State funerals and days of national remembrance in Israel were also, to an extent, surrogates for those occasions of collective mourning that were once typical of Jewish life and were transferred to America to be transmuted into the religious and secular funeral pageants we have considered. Collective mourning also presumed consensus, at least for the moment: a coming together of the scattered flock to remember the fallen leader. This, as we have seen, was hard enough to achieve during the immigrant generation, although the need remained and strenuous attempts were made. Mount Carmel Cemetery never became Valhalla. For half a century, now, the heroes, martyrs and saints honored are those who died in the Holocaust and in Israel's wars. Pilgrimages to the sites, monuments and museums tied to those events, and annual religious services and civic ceremonies to commemorate them are the ways collective remembrance and the reaffirmation of kinship are fostered. But they belong to a venerable tradition of which the public funerals we have discussed have a place.

# 4 Socialist Politics on the Lower East Side

In the course of the first two decades of the twentieth century the Socialist Party gained relatively important footholds in two metropolitan areas, German-populated Milwaukee and the Jewish Lower East Side of New York. Both districts sent socialists to Congress in the latter half of this period and in Milwaukee notable victories were registered in municipal elections.

By 1900, the Ninth Congressional District of New York, carved out of the heart of the Lower East Side, had become the most densely populated area of Russian-Jewish immigration. It had also acquired its reputation as the habitat of a vigorous, young radical movement. The year 1904 saw the District's socialist candidate poll 21 percent of the vote. Two years later Morris Hillquit raised the socialist share of the vote to 26 percent. Eventually, Hillquit's successor as candidate, Meyer London, was elected to Congress from the "Ninth."[1]

The East Side political campaigns attracted considerable attention. Progressives saw the socialist "David" pitted against the Tammany "Goliath." Others, disquieted by the frenzied agitation of the East European radicals, found support for their immigrant restriction stand. Americanized coreligionists of the Jewish immigrant populace feared antisemitic repercussions that would ultimately endanger their hard-won position.

Of all the parties in the immigrant quarter, the Socialist Party was least responsive to the ethnic interests of the residents. Cosmopolitan in outlook and faithful to its class allegiance, the party was hostile to what it considered to be the conflicting loyalties invoked by "nationality." Furthermore, despite the ethnic locale, in its political ambition to embrace the American working class it sought to avoid the suspicion of domination by "foreigners."

The central theme of this investigation of the 1908 and 1910 political campaigns on the Jewish East Side is the impact on an ethnic-centered, new immigrant community of a political ideology posing imperatives transcending the ghetto parochialism. The unexpected dimensions of Morris Hillquit's defeat in 1908 and his replacement in 1910 by Meyer London indicate the conflict and the compromise the socialist politician was compelled to make in his encounter with the immigrant community. The two campaigns also form part of a transition period in the history of the Socialist Party. By 1910, the East Side radicals were elevated to the status of a "serious threat." This new show of strength was possible only when due recognition was given to the local interests of the immigrant quarter.

On October 31, 1908, the socialist *New York Evening Call* carried on its front page in large type and framed in a black border Eugene Debs's "A final word to you on the eve of battle." Debs did not address his order of the day to all the socialist forces. He singled out the voters of the Ninth Congressional District of New York for these special words of encouragement.

> The East Side [he wrote] is destined to be a historic battleground. It is here that capitalism has wrought its desolation, here that it has spread its blighting curse, like a pestilence, to destroy manhood, debauch womanhood and grind the blood and flesh and bones of childhood into food for mammon. It is here on the East Side where the victims of capitalism struggle and suffer, that the hosts of freedom must spring from the soil, fertilized by the misery of their class. Hillquit, the working class candidate for Congressman, can and should be elected so that the working class may have its first representative in the national Congress.[2]

There were other indications besides Debs's appeal to the voters of a particular district that the Socialist Party had mounted a major offensive on the Lower East Side. In the two assembly districts, the sixth and eighth, which made up much of the Lower East Side, Hillquit's running mates were Robert Hunter and James Graham Phelps Stokes who were also drawn from the first echelon of the national leadership. "The Ninth" offered the best chances for a breakthrough. In the logic of the socialist analysis it possessed the basic elements needed for victory: the "desolation capitalism has wrought" was nowhere more evident; its socialists were alert, militant and numerically significant; and they were appealing to a public consisting by and large of impoverished wage earners.

To this socialist dialectic, Hillquit, in an interview granted to a *New York Times* reporter, appended an analysis of the political balance of power in the district which he predicted would spell out his election. The Democratic vote for Congressman would be reduced by these factors: the stringent new election law decreasing the number of enrolled voters in the District would eliminate Tammany floaters and repeaters; the presidential campaign would preclude the Republican machine "voting openly" for the

Democratic candidate for Congress as in 1906; and finally, Hearst's Independent League candidate would remain in the field at Tammany's expense. Thus, four candidates were vying for 11,000 votes. The one receiving 4,000 votes, Hillquit reasoned, was assured of election. In the light of this campaign arithmetic, Hillquit needed to improve his 1906 showing by three hundred votes to win. The reporter compared the "luke-warmness" of the other campaigns to the "enthusiasm, buoyant and bubbling over, among the socialists of the Lower East Side." Republican and Democratic leaders, he concluded, saw much truth in Morris Hillquit's prediction.[3]

The stir created by the Debs presidential campaign and the support of a strong local ticket were additional sources of Hillquit's optimism. However, aside from such political variables he undoubtedly postulated the uncompromising support of the growing socialist movement in the Jewish quarter. The Jewish trade unions, the backbone of the movement, provided functionaries and rank-and-filers who were gaining political experience in each succeeding campaign. The *Forverts*, the socialist daily, possessed organizational and financial resources of consequence. Particularly striking was the growth of Workmen's Circle (*Arbeiter Ring*), a fraternal order of Jewish workingmen allied to the Socialist Party. Its New York City membership increased from 5,103 in 1906 to 10,233 in 1908. Meanwhile, the booming Russian immigration brought reinforcements of highly literate, "ready-made" socialists.[4]

The socialists conducted their most vocal and best-organized campaign to date. Outside help augmented the party's district organization. Hillquit, in his autobiography, tells of the "hordes of young intellectuals [who] came down daily to speak at street corners." William Dean Howells endorsed the socialist ticket. Lincoln Steffens remembered his days on the East Side as a police reporter and backed Hillquit and his comrades as the only way of breaking the evil machine. Charles Edward Russell chose the week before election to join publicly the Socialist Party and endorse Hillquit.[5] In the final weeks of the campaign the Socialist Party was averaging twenty-five meetings a night with audiences aggregating 25,000, the *New York Times* estimated. The *New York Evening Call* found confirmation of the effectiveness of the East Side campaign in the dissension and panic reportedly rampant in Timothy ("Big Tim") Sullivan's downtown Tammany domain. "Tammany Hall on East Side Panicky," one story ran ten days before election. A week later a page 1 headline read, "Tammany Heelers Are Desperate." A sense of confidence unusual for socialist leaders led them to expect the votes of sympathizers reluctant in the past to waste their ballots on a socialist candidate with no chance of winning. A week before election Hillquit felt certain enough of victory to declare that were the opposition to combine behind a single candidate he would still be able to win. The *New York Times* in a survey of the congressional election campaign saw no likelihood of change in New York with the exception of the "Ninth."[6]

Yet, when the returns were counted, Hillquit ran a distant second behind Tammany's Henry Goldfogle. His total vote was nearly a third less than his 1906 showing and one had to look back to the lean election years of the first part of the decade to find a comparably bad showing. The post-mortems offered by the socialist commentators were quick to explain the defeat: a deal between the Democrats and the Republicans to defeat the socialist at all costs; Tammany terror; the continual movement of socialists out of the Lower East Side to Brownsville and the Bronx leaving a mounting residue of Tammany-dependent shopkeepers and peddlers. One *Forverts* commentator appended a psychological explanation: the Old World antipathy of the Russian Jew for all bureaucratic activity explained his indifference to becoming naturalized, registering and finally voting.[7] However, in their analysis of the defeat, most socialist commentators ignored the issues which revolved around the ethnic interests of the population of "the Ninth."[8]

"The Ninth" was not merely the district of tenement house slums, sweatshops and immigrant radicals. The heart of the Jewish ghetto and the point of concentration of Yiddish-speaking Russian Jews served as the unofficial reception center of the newly arrived immigrants during the decade of their highest influx into the country. An uninhibited, self-contained social and, in certain respects, economic life, eased the ordeals of its inhabitants. Four Yiddish daily newspapers and a score of periodicals published on the East Side offered the comfort of the familiar word and the full range of political and literary tastes. "Here a man was . . . safe among his own kind." This sentiment found expression in the preeminence of the *landsmanshaft* societies in the ferment of East Side communal life. Formed by immigrants from the same town or region in the old country, the ascendancy of the *landsmanshaft* in Jewish life represented the binding ties of the "old home" and the constant concern for the kinsmen left behind. Consequently, not only the synagogue and the mutual aid society were established on the *landsmanshaft* principle but the majority of the socialist-oriented Workmen's Circle branches were as well, despite the socialist injunction calling for class unity above all. Just as the Yiddish press coverage revealed the apprehension of the newly arrived immigrants for the well-being of their family and townspeople on the "other side," so much of the activity of the *landsmanshaft* was attuned to the reception and initial settlement of the newcomers.[9] In fact, during the four years prior to the 1908 campaign anxieties intensified in the aftermath of a new wave of pogroms in Russia and the extinction of all radical and progressive hopes for a more liberal Russian policy. The tempo of relief work rose sharply. Prominent individuals, including radical intellectuals heretofore passive in Jewish communal life, now accepted a more active role. Immigration figures continued to climb. The prevalent feeling was stronger than ever that the Jews of Russia had no alternative but flight.[10]

This atmosphere of crisis coincided with the public discussion on immigration: the renewed attempt to enact a literacy test, the establishment of the Dillingham Commission, the negotiations on Japanese immigration, Russia and the American passport debate. Jewish organizations, ambitious to play a role in Jewish communal life, joined in the fight against the "restrictionists." Thus, on the individual and institutional plane the note of anxiety and fear lest the doors of asylum close dominated the immigrant ghetto. This anxiety expressed itself in a high-pitched sensitivity to the immigration restriction issue. One can appreciate, then, the shrillness of the debate when this very issue was injected into the campaign in the Ninth Congressional District and the accusation of supporting the restrictionist stand was hurled at the downtown socialists.[11]

Not unrelated to the immigration issue was a second theme which ruffled the pride of the Jewish quarter. For the social reformer, immigration restrictionist, socialist and uptown co-religionist, the ghetto of the Lower East Side epitomized a host of evils—crime, prostitution, disease, machine politics at its worst, and cultural backwardness. Though much of this picture of the degrading conditions of the ghetto was drawn by those wishing its inhabitants well, the Jewish quarter rebelled against this image. Characteristic of this sensitivity was the reaction to an article by the Commissioner of Police, General Theodore Bingham, which appeared in the September 1908 issue of the *North American Review*. By implication the Commissioner attributed 50 percent of all crimes committed in New York City to Jews. While Louis Marshall and other respected Jewish citizens from "uptown" cautioned restraint and sought to deal with the incident away from the public's eye, protest meetings were held on the East Side. The *Tageblat* called for mass demonstrations demanding Bingham's resignation for besmirching the name of the Jews of the East Side. The good intentions of Lincoln Steffens's muckraking letter or Debs's rhetoric on behalf of Hillquit emphasizing the need to "clean up" the abominations of the East Side were equated by many with Bingham's accusation.[12]

At the first Hillquit rally in the 1908 campaign, which Abraham Cahan, editor of the *Forverts*, chaired, the candidate for Congress said:

> The issues thus defined by the Socialist Party in its national platform are also the issues in this Congressional District of New York. . . . It is true that our district is inhabited largely by a foreign-born population. . . . [That] the naturalized citizen of Russian-Jewish origin is as much a citizen as the native American of Dutch or Puritan origin is fact as well as theory. The interests of the workingmen of the Ninth Congressional District are therefore entirely identical with those of the workingmen of the rest of the country, and if elected to Congress, I will not consider myself the special representative of the alleged special interests of this district, but the representative of the Socialist Party and the interests of the working class of the country so understood and interpreted by my party.[13]

The irony of two Russian Jews, Morris Hillquit and Abe Cahan, solemnly declaring they recognized "no special interests" in the Lower East Side may have been lost to the socialist audience of Russian Jews. The rhetoric delivered by known citizens of the ghetto in the language of the ghetto obscured the anomaly. Nevertheless, in the maze of ghetto organizations dedicated in one fashion or another to ethnic continuity, socialism was unique in preaching an involvement in American life and concern for issues transcending the ethnic group.

On the day before election Louis Miller, Abe Cahan's old comrade and now archrival of downtown's mainline socialists, wrote in his *Varheyt*:

> The American people has one position of high honor, the office of the President. For this highest office it seeks out its finest, most famous, most devoted and loyal son. We Jews in the quarter possess only the office of congressman. It is not much, perhaps, but it is all we have. To whom shall we give this office, to a person who has always been with us, or to a person who never cared to know us and has no desire to know us now, who when he comes among strangers denies that he is a Jew, who was, is and will always remain a renegade. Morris Hillquit's coming to us Jews when he wants our vote should by itself be sufficient reason for not voting for him.[14]

With the refrain, "Where was Morris Hillquit when . . . ," the *Varheyt* itemized its charges of indifference to the interests of the Jewish quarter:

the strike of tenants over the raising of rents in January 1908; the organized boycott of the kosher meat wholesalers who raised prices in 1907; Julia Richman's campaign urging deportation of immigrants guilty of violating the pushcart ordinance; the bankruptcy of fraternal and benevolent funds during the 1907–1908 crisis; Bingham's accusation of criminality among the Jews.[15]

The catalogue of indifference concluded with this accusation:

> Where was Morris Hillquit in the days of the pogroms when old, infirm people marched and women threw their jewels into the collection plates to help, when the entire Jewish people, radicals and conservatives, young and old, united in brotherhood in the great day of tragedy?[16]

The reference was to the burst of mass meetings and appeals for funds triggered by the Kishinev pogrom in 1903. Months of agitated activity had reached a climax on December 4, 1905, when 125,000 Jews dressed in mourning garb marched to Union Square from the Lower East Side. A young, American-born Reform rabbi, Judah L. Magnes, headed the sponsoring organization, "The Jewish Defense Association." Serving on the executive committee was the Reverend Zvi Hirsch Masliansky, renowned Orthodox Jewish preacher, and representatives of the Bund. A former trade union leader and socialist candidate for Congress from the Ninth Congressional District, Joseph Barondess, acted as Grand Marshal of the procession. Jacob H. Schiff, philanthropist banker, personification of propriety and Americanism, made his contribution to a fund avowedly buying arms for clandestine Jewish defense units in Russian towns. For the moment it appeared that fraternal factionalism and strife had been forgotten in the name of "brotherhood in the great day of tragedy." Three years later the *Varheyt* reminded the voters of Morris Hillquit's abstention.[17]

The crime of indifference became one of outright treason in the conservative *Tageblat*'s arraignment.

> Morris Hillquit belongs to those who hide their Jewish nationality . . . who crawl after the Gentiles on all fours. It was not enough for him to change his name [from Hilkowitz]. Not only did he run away from his people, he . . . backed closing the door of the land of freedom to those who like himself wished to find a home in America.[18]

"The assimilationist, alienated from his people, ashamed of his nationality," Morris Hillquit could not represent the million Jews of New York!

Every right-thinking Jew will recognize that the Jews of New York should have as their representative in Congress a Jew who bears in mind Jewish interests. If Morris Hillquit were to be elected it would mean that New York Jewry would have no representative in the Congress of the United States.[19]

In the general elections the Jew had the same interest as any other citizen. The campaign within "the Ninth," however, was unabashedly a Jewish campaign. It became so the moment Hillquit declared it was not.

As the campaign entered its final week, the *Tageblat*, the most conservative and nationalist of the Yiddish dailies, intensified its attacks on Hillquit and his fellow socialists. The paper berated them for claiming that ignorance and moral depravity were endemic to the Jewish East Side, proof of capitalism's decadence. Hillquit and "his friends" were slandering the good name of the immigrant Jews and American Jewry as a whole and providing fodder for antisemites. "We are greenhorns. We must guard our honor and the fate of those who must yet come." Such propaganda, the *Tageblat* declared, was ammunition in the hands of the enemies of the Jews:

> They [the socialists] must show how low society has fallen under the present system. They tell the whole world that they come to rehabilitate the filthy, backward Jews. . . . No wonder the anti-Semite hurls his lies at the East Side. No wonder the public considers the East Side a center of crime. It is enough for a gentile to hear Morris Hillquit's speech to label the East Side the hell of America and the Jews who live there the worst of all nationalities in America.[20]

In this manner, "the socialist Bingham," as the *Tageblat* dubbed Hillquit, would speak to Congress endangering the Jews of America.

> It is the lowest lie that the East Side is immoral or is as poor as the "comrades" say. . . . We are citizens, as upright and as honest as others. . . . He who says the East Side is filled with corruption, neglect and filth must not represent the East Side.[21]

Hillquit was certainly the commanding figure of the Socialist Party in the East. A person of consequence at party conventions, delegate to international congresses, and leading theorist, his interests and ambitions lay on a national plane. As Debs himself had put it, his election would give Congress a representative of the working class. He had long outgrown the confining parochialism of local politics. The opposition, however, campaigned on no other level.

Sensational appeals to ethnic sentiments could in part be met by Hillquit's national reputation and his fame as a lawyer, a socialist version of the American success story: Russian immigrant, formative years amidst the poverty of the East Side, early struggles to improve conditions there, on to law school to become a fighter for the oppressed of the world. Running mates Max Pine in the Fourth Assembly District, veteran organizer of the United Hebrew Trades, and popular orator Jacob Panken in the Eleventh Senatorial District, together with Abe Cahan and his *Forverts*, spoke the language of the ghetto and muted Hillquit's cosmopolitan stance. The socialists did take up the cudgel of race pride sufficiently to be rebuked by the *Tageblat* for their brazenness in appealing for Hillquit as a Russian Jew.[22]

But interlaced through the diatribes appeared the dominant strand of the immigration issue. A leader of American socialism, Hillquit was held accountable for all actions of his party. A moderate, he was roundly rebuked for his own ambivalence on immigration and tagged a restrictionist and enemy of the immigrant workingman.

David Shannon has aptly summarized the Socialist Party's official policy on immigration as a straddling of two opposing principles. On the one hand, the socialist scripture called for the international solidarity of the working class. On the other hand, cooperating with the trade unions and wooing the American laborer required a stand favoring immigration restriction.[23]

In 1904, Hillquit, representing the American socialists at the International Socialist Congress in Amsterdam, supported the minority resolution of restriction of immigration from "backward races." Three years later, Hillquit went to the Socialist Congress in Stuttgart instructed by the national executive of the party to "combat importation of cheap labor calculated to destroy labor organization, lower the standard of living of the working class and retard the ultimate realization of socialism." When Hillquit wrote that he opposed the immigration of workers from industrially backward countries "who are incapable of assimilation with the workingmen of the country of their adoption," he was referring to Asiatic immigration. Its applicability to Russian immigration was not overlooked on the East Side. Just five months before the 1908 campaign, the Socialist Party convention meeting in Chicago had avoided acting on a resolutions committee draft of an anti-immigration plank by appointing an investigating committee to report to the next convention. The delaying action did not conceal the vigorous restrictionist sentiment at the convention.[24]

At the opening rally of the campaign, Hillquit deftly sought to identify the socialist restrictionist sentiment with the problem of Asiatic immigration. "As for the question of Asiatic exclusion," he remarked, "it may be an issue for the workingmen of the Pacific slope, but the workingmen of this congressional district have but a remote abstract interest." By referring to a basic tenet of international socialism, the demand "that the doors of all civilized countries be left open to the unfortunate working men . . . especially the victims of political oppression," he sought to deflect the attack.[25]

In Daniel De Leon, the Socialist Labor Party's candidate, Hillquit faced a shrewd opponent who waged his campaign with single-minded purpose: to embarrass and abuse his old adversary, Morris Hillquit. Fully aware of Hillquit's vulnerability on the question of the Socialist Party's position on immigration, De Leon adopted a double line of attack. The Socialist Party had violated socialist canon and Hillquit had inspired that policy. Louis Miller's widely read *Varheyt* trumpeted the De Leon exposés throughout the ghetto. Proposals offered by Hillquit to convention committees were exhumed from protocols. Bund (Jewish Social Democratic Party in Russia) representatives were quoted as saying that Hillquit's resolution at Stuttgart "was like a knife plunged into live flesh."[26]

In the closing weeks of the campaign immigration had become the pivotal issue. The rebuttal Hillquit offered to the accusations of being an immigration restrictionist revealed a master debater arguing the more difficult side of the proposition. Referring to the 1907–1908 depression with the resulting decrease in immigration and sharp increase in departing immigrants Hillquit declared immigration a nonissue. "The problem [was] how to stop emigration." Hillquit offered the following syllogism: "The capitalist system forces the worker to emigrate from land to land in search of bread; this cannot be stopped as long as capitalism exists"; hence the socialists by destroying capitalism will solve the immigration issue. As in his earlier speech, he invoked socialist humanitarianism. The party stood for an open door, he declared, "especially for the sufferers of economic exploitation, race and political attacks, and refugees like the Russian Jews." However, the Socialist Party, opposed "the abuse of immigration." Capitalist shipping companies artificially stimulated emigration of European workers. Socialists and union men had been called upon at Stuttgart to prevent the importation of strike-breakers and contract labor thus recognizing that immigration was not always desirable.[27]

Establishment of a category of "undesirable immigration" was not likely to allay the fears of the Jewish quarter. A single desperate logic ruled the immigrant community: an open door for immigration; restriction in any form would eventually affect Russian immigration. In such a situation, however brilliantly Hillquit couched his reservations, the Jewish quarter insisted on an unqualified stand for unrestricted immigration. As a spokesman of American socialism, Hillquit could not meet this sectional demand. He spoke with the circumspection of a presidential nominee and not with the regional partiality expected of a congressional candidate.

In the course of the acrimonious campaign, Goldfogle, the incumbent congressman, received slight attention in the pages of the Republican-prone *Tageblat*, the Hillquit-flaying *Varheyt*, and the Socialist *Forverts*. The radical journalist Hillel Rogoff, a keen observer of the East Side, has provided us with a partial explanation. "Campaigning," he noted, "was done almost exclusively by the socialists, Tammany relying upon the effective work of their henchmen on Election Day."[28]

Goldfogle found little need to conduct an active campaign. For the opposition, Tammany was the villain and Goldfogle a mere tool. The disregard for the latter, however, may have reflected other considerations than disdain or lack of newsworthiness. Goldfogle, as representative of the Lower East Side, was not particularly vulnerable. In the tradition of American political life, Congressman Goldfogle championed the special interests of his district. As a freshman in Congress, he introduced the "Goldfogle Resolution" which called on the president to use his good offices for equal treatment of all American passport holders. He thereafter became the defender of naturalized Jewish citizens of Russian birth who were discriminated against while traveling in Russia. He became chief protagonist of the honor of the American passport, placing principle above material gain (insisting that the commercial treaty with Russia not be extended), America's egalitarianism above Czarist prejudice. On the other hand, socialist ire was not likely to be aroused by a fight to abrogate an 1832 Treaty of Commerce and Navigation with Russia. Nevertheless, in the eyes of the Jewish public the issue touched their sense of dignity and belonging. Similarly, the day in December 1905 when the Jews mourned the victims of the Russian pogroms, Goldfogle offered a resolution calling on the House of Representatives to express its profound sorrow and horror at the massacres and calling on the president to use his good offices to prevent such outrages from reoccuring. When Police Commissioner Bingham's article incensed New York Jewry in September 1908, Goldfogle addressed the emergency conference of communal leaders. Goldfogle's vulnerability lay not in his record but in his connection with the machine. Tammany, therefore, became the more likely villain.[29]

Observers miscalculated socialist strength by employing the faulty index of campaign ardor. "Whenever we had a Socialist procession march through the streets the enthusiasm was tremendous and spontaneous," Charles Edward Russell wrote in retrospect. "When election day came around . . . we had the cheering and the old parties had the votes." In the aftermath of the 1908 election when the campaign processions no longer marched, M. Baranov, a socialist journalist, explained the phenomenon of loud cheers and few votes. He wrote:

> It would be a good thing if the comrades of downtown would establish a committee whose task would be helping Jewish workers become citizens. It now seems that we Jews make the most noise before the elections and make fools of ourselves when we can't vote on election day.[30]

The Census of 1910 bore out what East Siders knew so well. Only 18.6 percent of the foreign-born males of voting age in the Second, Fourth and Eighth Assembly Districts were naturalized. The new wave of Russian Jewish immigrants, containing many influenced by the Jewish socialist movement in Russia and seared by the Russian Revolution of 1905, was bringing ready-made socialists to America. These socialists were attending campaign meetings but they did not yet qualify for citizenship and many would not be going to the polls in significant numbers until after 1910.[31]

Yet despite the debacle, Hillquit ran well ahead of his party's standard-bearer, Eugene Debs. The East Side voter was splitting his ballot. Hillquit claimed that the Republican machine, seeing no hope for its candidate and fearing a Socialist upset, connived with Tammany, instructing its followers to "split for Goldfogle." An examination of the election returns for offices in the Ninth Congressional District other than that of Congressman discloses a significant pattern of party irregularity. The Republican presidential nominee, William Howard Taft, ran 5 percent ahead of his running mate for governor, Charles Evans Hughes. Undoubtedly, Taft's favorable statement on the passport issue, made from an East Side platform late in the campaign, together with the goodwill harbored for Theodore Roosevelt, contributed to Taft's stronger showing in the Jewish quarters. More difficult to explain was the 7 percent difference in the Socialist vote and the 11.5 percent difference in the Republican vote for assemblymen in neighboring districts. Obviously, personalities weighed heavily with the East Side voter. As the Jewish immigrant boy who made good and as the advocate of the laboring man, Hillquit carried an appeal beyond the Socialist ranks. Thus, we can understand his 21 percent of the vote compared to Debs' 13.5 percent in the Ninth Congressional District. On the other hand, Hillquit appeared in too controversial and equivocal a light to command the broad support of the population of the Jewish quarter. The hard political facts pointed to his 1,133 loss in votes compared with his 1906 total rather than to his lead over running mate Debs.[32]

That the Socialist Party was in the process of learning the lessons of the campaign was borne out by the new candidate it offered to the electorate of the Jewish quarter in 1910. With Meyer London, the socialists strove to avoid a conflict of interests. The party began to recognize grudgingly what an increasing number of Jewish socialists were agitating for: that socialism operating in the ghetto must acknowledge the legitimacy of the ethnic loyalties of its inhabitants. The Jewish socialists coming in the new wave of immigration were making their presence felt within the Jewish labor movement and in the periodical press. The lines of ideological conflict were evident. Newer immigrants, radical but committed to a Jewish ethnicity, opposed the older, cosmopolitan leadership anxious to merge with their American radical comrades.

At the socialist congress held in May 1910, London was one of two delegates representing the Jewish Agitation Bureau which was organized in 1907 for the purpose of recruiting Jewish workers for the Socialist Party and trade unions. It was suspected of Jewish "nationalist" tendencies by the "old guard." (In New York City, the party leadership was especially antagonistic to the bureau, and when the national executive hired an organizer for the Yiddish-speaking membership, Hillquit moved to have him recalled.) Early in the congress proceedings, London raised the question of the voting rights of the bureau's delegates. Hillquit, the chairman, ruled that representatives of foreign language organizations were not delegates. They had only advisory status, and were unable to vote or serve on committees.

Weeks later, London received the socialist nomination in the Ninth Congressional District. Hillquit, high in the inner councils of the Party, was replaced by London who never rose above leader of the East Side. Hillquit was enmeshed in the compromises of national politics while London, single-mindedly, served the interests of his constituency. His biographer, possibly with Hillquit in mind, said this of London:

> The older labor and socialist leaders on the East Side considered his presence among them as temporary. It was expected that he would gradually attach himself to the general American movement and go into the non-Jewish sections to live. But he did not. London was drawn more and more into East Side socialist and trade union activities. He remained on the East Side because his services were needed there, because his heart was there.[33]

It was London who served as legal counsel of the Workmen's Circle in these critical years of growth. And it was London who participated in the key conferences of the Joint Board of Cloakmakers Unions in August 1908 to consider the calling of a general strike. In the throes of union disorganization and financial distress, the union leaders convened in an air of utter despondency. London's role in encouraging them became legendary.

In the summer of 1910, as counsel for the cloakmakers he stood at the helm of the "revolt of the 70,000." London emerged in the fall of 1910 as a popular hero of the Jewish labor movement and his party's leading candidate for public office. The *Forverts* boasted that the Socialist Party has proven "it is a 'workers party' with brilliant possibilities of winning the campaign . . . because this year [the Party] established close ties of cooperation with the broad laboring masses."[34]

At the socialist convention in Chicago, the immigration issue sent to committee two years before for further study was again discussed. The majority report submitted called for "unconditional exclusion" of all Mongolian races. Refusal to exclude certain races and nationalities, the committee declared, "would place the Socialist Party in opposition to the most militant and intelligent portion of the organized workers of the United States."[35] From the floor of the convention, Hillquit offered a substitute resolution which placed the party on record favoring legislative measures to "prevent the immigration of strike-breakers . . . and the mass importation of workers . . . for the purpose of weakening the organization of American labor." The resolution, at the same time, opposed the "exclusion of any immigrants on account of their race or nationality" and demanded that the United States be "maintained as a free asylum" for the persecuted. The resolution was accepted 55 to 50. David Shannon in his history of the Socialist Party wrote pointedly that "the first paragraph . . . was one that might have been written by an American Federation of Labor convention; the second paragraph might have been written by an International Congress of Marxists." London who opposed any form of immigration restriction reluctantly supported the Hillquit compromise because it rejected race as a basis for exclusion. In the Jewish quarter, London was still perceived as a powerful voice for open immigration within socialist circles. No longer was the local candidate being identified with the entire party.[36]

A colleague of Cahan and Hillquit in the early days of socialist activity, the pragmatic London had allied himself with the vital movements on the East Side. He could make his bid for the support of "ordinary people" as well as literate socialists. This is born out by the following interview with a storekeeper which the *Forverts* published during the campaign:

As a businessman I will work and vote for Meyer London. Our interests demand this. . . . The politicians sap the blood of us businessmen. . . . The honest businessman must have someone who will take his part, [someone] the politicians will fear. . . . When Meyer London will be elected he will be under no obligation to anyone. As a citizen of the East Side he will be in a position to accomplish a great deal. He will liberate us from graft. . . . The East Side has no father or mother, no spokesman. When Meyer London is elected to Congress he will be the spokesman of the Jewish quarter both in Washington and in New York.[37]

The authenticity of the "interview" is impossible to determine. It may have been composed in the editorial room of the *Forverts*. This would not alter the fact that in 1908 the *Forverts* had not appealed to "storekeepers and businessmen." It had portrayed Hillquit as representing the "working class" in Congress and not the Jewish immigrant quarter. The putative 1910 interview was indicative of a change in campaign tactics as different from 1908 as the candidates were different.

Following the 1910 election, a series of letters to the editor of the *New York Evening Call* in response to Louis Boudin's article, "Milwaukee and New York," corroborated the change in tactics. In Milwaukee, there had been less than a 10 percent difference between the highest and lowest vote polled on the Socialist ticket. In the Ninth Congressional District, London had run more than two to one ahead of the party's candidate for governor. According to Boudin, "in the London campaign, racial and subracial prejudices of voters were appealed to. The Russian-Jews were appealed to because Comrade London was also a Russian Jew." A member of London's campaign committee replied that London had been selected to run because of his "tremendous popularity with the workers of the East Side." As for the accusation of appealing to "racial prejudices," the campaign worker wrote, "we have not made any stronger use of it not withstanding the temptations which came from the enemy."[38]

Other letters indicated that an effort had been made to appeal to non-socialists. A Professional League had been organized. The Workmen's Circle and the Cloakmakers Union campaign committees had soft-peddled socialism. They had highlighted London's character, and Tammany's infamy. As one writer put it, "the keynote of the campaign was 'split for London' and with this race prejudice was appealed to, nationality was appealed to, and, in fact, everything except the class consciousness of these workers." It was freely admitted that the vote of the small businessman and professional had been energetically pursued.[39]

London's 33.09 percent of the vote was 11.86 percent better than Hillquit's 1908 showing. In 1908, except for congressman, the socialist vote in the Ninth Congressional District for other city and state offices ranged from a high of 17.87 percent to a low of 12.88 percent. In 1910, again excluding the vote for congressman, the socialist vote carried from 15.78 percent to 15.12 percent. A consolidation and a moderate gain in the straight-ticket party vote had taken place. (Hillquit, the socialist candidate for Associate Justice of the Court of Appeals in 1910, received 15.8 percent of the votes cast for that office.) The growth in socialist strength did not preclude London receiving two votes for every one the remainder of his ticket received. The London campaign and London's appeal had reached well beyond the regular Socialist following.[40]

What the Boudins and Hillquits regarded as a "pestilential atmosphere generated by the appeal to national or race feelings . . . [and] unsocialistic practice" denoted, rather, recognition by the local party that "special interests" indeed existed. The impassioned debate two years before had revealed the depths of these national and race feelings. Anguish for the fate of brethren left behind and dedication to the task of their removal to America transcended other loyalties. These emotions together with the continued efforts at restricting immigration heightened group allegiances. Rather than expose conditions on the East Side, the representative of the Ninth Congressional District was expected to defend the good name of his district and its citizens. The socialist, London, rooted in the East Side, responded to these demands.

Two more campaigns were necessary before London won the East Side congressional seat. In 1912, he garnered 31 percent of the vote to Goldfogle's 39 percent, Tammany Hall's perennial victor. In all likelihood, the Progressive Party's candidate, Henry Moskowitz, who won 22 percent of the vote, cost London the election. Finally, in 1914, London won with an impressive 10 percent margin over Goldfogle. Observers agreed that the growing numbers and organizational strength of the garment workers trade unions sent him to Congress. London told his victory rally:

> When I take my seat in Congress I do not expect to accomplish wonders. What I expect to do is take to Washington the message of the people. . . . I want to show them what the East Side of New York is and what the East Side Jew is.[41]

Reelected in 1916 and elected for a third term in 1920, London played out his political career within the confines of the Jewish East Side. The period of his rise and victories coincided with the crystallization of the

"Jewish Socialist Federation," the last of the Socialist Party's language federations to be organized. The federation, never a large organization, represented the ascendancy of the new wave of immigrant intellectuals who prized Jewish ethnic identity. Beginning in 1909, the Jewish labor movement entered its period of gigantic growth. London had been associated with both. The "old guard" socialists—ironically London had been one of them—became inactive in the Jewish quarter or underwent a change of heart and accepted the ethnic factor as a legitimate one. The 1908 and 1910 campaigns on the Lower East Side illustrate the turning point in this process.

# 5 The Conservative Politics of the Orthodox Press

The study of the political culture of American Jews has centered almost exclusively on its radical-liberal character. Scholars have been fascinated by what they have seen as the anomalous political profile of America's Jews, particularly those of East European origin. The starting point of their analysis is the fact that over the generations, as Jews rose in the economic and social scale, they remained left-of-center in their political behavior, unlike other groups which had attained an equivalently high educational, professional, and class standing. True, the passing of the immigrant generation brought a diminution in socialist zeal. Nevertheless the grandchildren of the immigrants remained committed to economic, political, and social justice, and the obligations of government to aid the downtrodden. In fact, to some Jewish intellectuals of the second and third generation the continued allegiance of America's Jews to an activist liberalism was the only meaningful remnant of their Jewishness.[1]

What intrigued political scientists and historians were the origins and persistence of this Jewish exceptionalism. Scholars agreed that the East European Jewish immigrants possessed a protean radicalism, and they offered a number of explanations: the religious heritage of the Jews fostered a social ethic which in the secular context of American life was transformed into social reform; or, centuries of suffering as a persecuted minority produced a set of responses and group norms which fit the ideology of liberalism; or, the emancipation of West European Jewry wedded Jews to the secular, democratic camp, while in Eastern Europe revolutionary socialism became the one way to challenge a ruthless Czar and gain emancipation.[2]

Admittedly, inconsistencies existed in this ideal radical-liberal portrait of the American Jew, particularly as it represented the experience of the immigrant generation. The same religious tradition which taught a universal-humanistic ethic also contained an overriding commitment to group survival, parochial in its thrust, which surely was not a liberating social ideology. Thus one could interpret the low percentage of voter participation among the more traditionally minded Jewish immigrants as reflecting insularity and political indifference. However, the political arithmetic of the Jewish immigrant neighborhoods shows that voting Jews rarely deviated from the national trend, and on the local level they generally voted for the candidates of the party machine. Nevertheless, the radical-liberal image has remained intact with most scholars celebrating the socialist-radical pedigree of the descendants of the East European Jewish immigrants.

The centerpiece of these accounts is the Jewish labor movement with its trade union base, Yiddish literary life, and abundance of ideologies and parties. However, this portrait has ignored another element in the political culture of the immigrant years. Ordinary folk, a multitude of tractable townspeople, related to a nonideological, functional and interest-driven politics when it purported to answer their needs. They were responding to the authentically American practice of politics.

Linked to the notion of a latent radicalism Jewish immigrants possessed is the view of their lack of political experience on arriving in America. This was as true for immigrants who had been sheltered from secularist influences in Europe as for those who had been exposed to political movements. Irving Howe succinctly summarized this judgment in his influential book, *The World of Our Fathers.* "To the Orthodox," Howe stated, "the idea of a secular politics was inherently suspect, to the radicals an untried if tempting possibility. In the political life of czarist Russia, Jews had been allowed at most a token representation, more humiliating than enabling. Many were still in the grip of the traditional Jewish persuasion that it was best to keep as far away from politics as possible." Consequently, Howe continued, the immigrants "tended to look upon the politics of American cities as still another antic of the gentiles."[3] Thus for some influential interpreters of the immigrant experience, the newcomers in addition to their inbred tendency toward radicalism were political innocents.

A starting point for reconsidering these widely held conceptions is the political career of the Bialystock-born Orthodox Jew, Jacob Saphirstein, who immigrated to the United States in 1887 and began publishing the *Jewish Morning Journal*, the *Morgen Zhurnal*, in 1901. Conservative on social and religious issues, Saphirstein turned his paper into the aggressive defender of Orthodox Judaism and the Yiddish voice of Republicanism.

A remarkable event indicative of Saphirstein's loyalty to the Republican Party and his influence among the Jewish immigrants occurred in January 1912. Saphirstein organized a ball to raise funds for his favorite charity, the Daughters of Jacob Old Age Home located on East Broadway. Ten thousand attended the affair, the *Morgen Zhurnal* claimed. It was held in the

71st Regiment Armory on Park Avenue, and Judge Otto Rosalsky, an Orthodox Jew and a Republican, presided. The guest of honor was William Howard Taft, President of the United States.[4]

Only a month before, on December 15, 1911, Taft announced his instructions to the American ambassador in Moscow to officially notify the Russian government of the American government's decision to abrogate the commercial treaty between the two countries. The controversy over abrogating or renegotiating the treaty focused on the Russian government's refusal to allow Jews holding American citizenship entry to Russia. Supporters of abrogation portrayed the Russian government's policy as an affront to the United States and America's acquiescence as implicitly discriminating between its Jewish and non-Jewish citizens. Some American Jewish leaders believed that abrogation would also serve as a major diplomatic rebuke of the Czar's anti-Jewish policies. Taft had acted reluctantly. For nearly two years, Louis Marshall of the American Jewish Committee and an important Republican had orchestrated a remarkable campaign which included meetings with the President, mobilizing congressional support, and holding protest meetings. Finally, following a nearly unanimous vote for abrogation in the House of Representatives and a vote pending in the Senate, Taft issued his order. One might have expected that Taft's first public appearance before a Jewish group following the most important pro-Jewish act a president had ever taken, as it was understood by many, would be at an event sponsored by the Jewish notables most of whom like Marshall, Jacob Schiff and Oscar Straus were loyal Republicans. Instead, on a visit to New York City, that honor went to the Daughters of Jacob Old Age Home, obviously in appreciation of Saphirstein's loyalty and the *Morgen Zhurnal*'s friendship. At the start of a presidential election year, Taft, seeking a second term, probably calculated that there were more Jewish immigrants than Jewish notables.[5]

Another indication of Saphirstein's influence found expression in the initiative taken by Judah Magnes, head of the New York Kehillah and close to the German-Jewish elite, to establish a rival Yiddish daily which would be "responsible and upstanding." (In 1902, Marshall and his circle had founded a Yiddish daily with the same purpose in mind, only to have the paper fail two years later.) Clearly, the prestige that went with the appearance of wielding influence in the Republican Party had enhanced Saphirstein's position in internal Jewish communal affairs. In these matters, the established Jews—the uptown notables—considered him a disrupting and benighted force. In a memorandum addressed to Jacob Schiff, Felix Warburg, and Marshall soon after the 1912 elections, Magnes related how

Saphirstein had "received at least three signed letters from the President of the United States, who saw fit to lick the boots of a corrupt Jewish editor for the sake of the political gain he thought he could secure." The president had also "issued a luncheon invitation in honor of the nephew of this editor," Magnes reported, and "Secretary of Commerce and Labor Charles Nagel made a special trip from Washington to take dinner with this man who would not be welcome at the table of any poor, self-respecting Jew."[6]

In fact, at least as early as January 1911, Saphirstein began corresponding with the president, sending him translations of *Morgen Zhurnal* editorials on topics of interest to the administration, such as the proposed changes in the immigration laws, anti-trust legislation, and the abrogation of the commercial treaty with Russia. Saphirstein also drafted a statement on immigration policy for the president's consideration for inclusion in his letter of acceptance of renomination. When the international executive of B'nai B'rith at its meeting in Berlin awarded Taft its annual medal "for accomplishing more for the Jews of the world than anybody else," Saphirstein forwarded his paper's effusive editorial of how well Taft deserved the award. Nor did Saphirstein allow the Tafts' celebration of their twenty-fifth wedding anniversary to pass without a note of congratulations. The president cordially acknowledged the letters, editorials and advice.[7]

For a new immigrant group, the politics of symbolism carried a compelling importance. A public gesture brought recognition and self-esteem. How sensitive the immigrants were to the symbolic act is apparent in the *Morgen Zhurnal*'s account of the president's visit to the Daughters of Jacob ball. Taft came "in evening dress to a social affair and accompanied by a lady of the family, not as a political official or candidate, but as a participant in our joy, as an intimate friend of our big family." Such an event, the *Morgen Zhurnal* rhapsodized, could not have taken place in "constitutional" England or even in "Republican" France. "When once the Jewish immigrant realizes that he is the full equal of the American people and perceives the friendship the government harbors for the Jews he becomes an enthusiastic patriot." It should be noted that prior to the president's appearance at the ball, he had attended a dinner of the Ohio Society, the West Virginia Society, and the Aero Club. Taft's party-hopping that evening obviously did not detract from the sense of pride the assembled felt when he finally appeared at their affair, at least not according to Saphirstein's account.[8]

No other Yiddish daily outdid the *Morgen Zhurnal*, defender of Orthodox Judaism, in singing the praises of America. And during the years of

Republican ascendancy, when Saphirstein was publisher and managing editor of the *Morgen Zhurnal*, to be an American patriot was to be a Republican. When Jewish interests were at stake the *Morgen Zhurnal* took a vigorous stand. Issues such as immigration restriction legislation, toughening the enforcement of the immigration laws, the passport issue, and the celebration of Christmas in the public schools filled the pages of the paper. These issues, the *Morgen Zhurnal* emphasized, were not peculiarly Jewish. They were questions which concerned all Americans, for they called into question the nation's fundamental principles.[9]

The *Morgen Zhurnal* was not unique in its agenda of concerns. However, among the Yiddish newspapers, it displayed a political subtlety and nuanced response which is worth noting. When Taft proved sluggish during the first two years of his term in dealing with the passport issue, the *Morgen Zhurnal* refrained from criticizing him. Saphirstein's patience was rewarded by the president's friendship. The paper's stand on the strict enforcement of the immigration regulations was also surprisingly mild. Jewish establishment spokesmen no less than the other Yiddish dailies bitterly criticized the Department of Commerce and Labor's policies. However, following a meeting of editors of the foreign-language press with the president and Secretary of Commerce and Labor Charles Nagel in January 1911, the *Morgen Zhurnal* remarked that "accidental incidents [of deportation] must not be transformed into . . . the false impression . . . that the stream of immigration is to be checked or stopped." In their "friendly conference" with the editors, Taft and Nagel had shown understanding and goodwill.[10] On a local matter, Christmas celebrations in the New York public schools, the *Morgen Zhurnal* joined the militants—the Union of Orthodox Jewish Congregations and the *Tageblat*, the other conservative Yiddish daily—in calling for a strike of Jewish children. On December 24, 1906, nearly 30,000 children on the Lower East Side and in Brownsville remained home from school. The paper's stand on the strike and its aftermath deserves attention.[11]

The *Morgen Zhurnal* justified the strike as an "American way of expressing our disapproval of the un-American attitude of the Board of Education." In one celebrated *cause célèbre*, a Brownsville elementary school principal admonished the largely Jewish school body at a Christmas assembly "to be more like Christ." Parents petitioned the local school committee to dismiss the principal. The hearings and the appeals lasted for over a year and provoked a rash of accusations of Jewish children being proselytized at Christmas exercises. When the Board of Education postponed action on the demand of "prominent members of the Jewish faith" that "the singing of denominational hymns . . . the holding of festivities in which clergymen make speeches, and the use of the Christmas tree" be abolished, the strike followed. The *Morgen Zhurnal* editorialized the following day:

> We are more than satisfied with the splendid showing our Jewish children made. . . . It was not a religious controversy, but a manly American stand, and we hope our Christian brethren will understand the spirit that prompted the protest.[12]

A year later the *Morgen Zhurnal* counseled restraint. Despite dissatisfaction with the Board of Education's compromise formula for "sanitizing" Christmas observances, it opposed another strike. The presence of Jewish children in school during "the pre-winter vacation exercises," the paper argued, would pressure the principals and teacher to comply with the new regulations and pressure the authorities to remove the remaining offensive practices. In dealing with the affair, the *Morgen Zhurnal* had initiated the public into the possibilities and the limits of confrontation politics: much had been achieved, but to continue with aggressive tactics would alienate the authorities and public opinion. During the months of the controversy over Christmas in the public schools, the paper also attended to the political education of its readers. Editorials and articles explained the constitutional issues involved, analyzed the New York State Constitution and then described the historical complexities of church-state relations.[13]

The Republican paper's discreet support of Henry Goldfogle, the Lower East Side's Democratic congressman, provides another example of the *Morgen Zhurnal*'s political prudence. Saphirstein was well aware that there was little chance of electing a Republican in the face of the strong Tammany machine. At best, a strong Republican showing would benefit the Socialist Party's candidate. Moreover, Goldfogle represented Jewish interests in Washington commendably. These circumstances required reaching an understanding with the rival party. And indeed, Goldfogle could count on a friendly *Morgen Zhurnal*. Saphirstein was following normal American practice: political reality and group interest led him across party lines.

One interesting episode which involved President Theodore Roosevelt illustrates the collaboration between Saphirstein and Goldfogle and the weight given to the politics of the personal gesture. It also underscores Saphirstein's grasp of the praxis of American politics. In 1906, Shmaryahu Levin, the eminent Russian Zionist leader and recently elected to the Russian Duma, arrived in the United States on a lecture tour on behalf of Russian Jewry. Early in Levin's visit, Saphirstein, cognizant of the publicity that would accrue from a meeting between the Russian Jewish statesman and congressional leaders, arranged for a visit to the capital. Saphirstein, Peter Wiernik, his managing editor, and several other New York Jews including Israel Friedkin, Saphirstein's nephew and the future publisher of the *Morgen Zhurnal,* accompanied Levin on the visit to Washington which coincided with the opening of the winter session of Congress in December 1906. Goldfogle took the delegation in hand and arranged for meetings with Joseph Cannon, speaker of the house, and Vice President Charles W. Fairbanks. Saphirstein hoped for an interview with the president. Goldfogle led the group to the White House. There, the *Morgen Zhurnal* reported with pride, all doors opened to the Jewish congressman. Without a prior appointment, the president received the entire party. Under the *Morgen Zhurnal*'s banner headline, "Dr. Levin Sees Roosevelt," came the subheadline, "Goldfogle's Influence in Washington." For twelve years he served in Congress before going down to defeat in 1914. Saphirstein's death in June 1914, Wiernik suggests in his memoirs, removed one of the Democratic congressman's main supports.[14]

Where was this political adroitness acquired? Much about Jewish life in Eastern Europe prepared the immigrants to be public persons and provided them with skills applicable to the American political scene. In Europe, the Jewish communal system of voluntary institutions and organizations bound together society and polity and enabled a broad stratum of the populace to find its place in the public life of the community. The immigrants who came to America were, in a sense, organization men and women from the outset. They were conversant with associational life— constitutions and elections, factions and politicking, collecting and distributing funds. They were also wise in and wary of the ways of their *shtadlanim,* those who spoke for them before the authorities. Observant Jews like Saphirstein, who lived in Bialystock until 1879 and then moved to Warsaw to become a Hebrew book publisher, and Peter Wiernik, who grew up in Vilna and lived in Riga and Bialystock before emigrating to the United States in 1885, had witnessed an ongoing power struggle within the religious camp and between that camp and the various shades of acculturated Jews for control of the Jewish community and its institutions. A pluralist Jewish communal politics, though constricted, nevertheless existed. The Jewish secular movements which gained momentum by the beginning of the twentieth century widened the cleavages in the community. They also broadened the range of communal politics and created new modes of political activity. These developments were not lost upon Orthodox Jewry.[15]

Saphirstein's opposition to the New York Kehillah in the first years of its existence, from 1909 to 1914, offers some insight into the political world of Orthodox Jews as they applied their European experience to Jewish affairs in America and by extension to American politics.

Initially, the *Morgen Zhurnal* welcomed the formation of the Kehillah. It was, after all, the most ambitious and promising attempt yet made in America to create an integrated community, to bring some order into the existing communal chaos, and to strengthen their own religious institutions thereby. The paper even approved of the Kehillah's ties with the American Jewish Committee—the most controversial question attending the formation of the organization. Such ties, the *Morgen Zhurnal* pointed out, assured the cooperation of the wealthy Americanized Jews. Nor did the committee's condition for joining the Kehillah—that the Kehillah defer to the committee on all external matters—disturb Saphirstein so long as democratic elections assured the immigrant population control of internal Kehillah policy like Jewish education and supervision of kashrut. Indeed, the *Morgen Zhurnal* proclaimed that Orthodoxy could learn much from collaborating with Reform Jews. With its numbers and institutions, Orthodoxy could become the dominant influence in the internal life of the Jews. When these expectations were not realized—and in Saphirstein's eyes the assimilated Jews' domination of the Kehillah threatened Orthodoxy's control of its religious institutions—the *Morgen Zhurnal* called on the leaders of Orthodoxy to secede from the Kehillah and establish a separate community.[16]

The tactics Saphirstein resorted to are revealing. The *Morgen Zhurnal* launched a massive crusade to discredit the Kehillah through innuendo and distortions, techniques borrowed from the American yellow press. It described a conspiracy directed by the uptown moguls to capture or subvert Orthodoxy's holiest institutions. It highlighted a story that the head of the Kehillah's bureau of Jewish education was an apostate. At the same time Saphirstein created a rival center of authority by bringing Rabbi Gabriel Ze'ev Margolies (Reb Velvele) to New York and proclaiming him *rav ha'kolel*, chief rabbi. Margolies had held important rabbinical posts in Europe before settling in Boston, and the *Morgen Zhurnal* presented him as the one authoritative figure who could save Orthodox Judaism. Then the paper enthusiastically supported the formation of a federation of Orthodox congregations led by Reb Velvele to compete with the Kehillah.

When the attempt failed, the *Morgen Zhurnal* threw its support behind the Adas Israel Society, a large downtown burial society eager to enlarge its activities and become the leading force in New York's Orthodox Jewish community. Saphirstein was endeavoring to manipulate public opinion and to combine traditional sources of authority with American forms of organization in order to create an Orthodox power base.[17]

He resorted to a third tactic. In 1912 and again in 1913 when the Kehillah sought incorporation through an act of the New York State legislature, the *Morgen Zhurnal* launched a letter-writing campaign against the incorporation bill. In January 1913, a delegation from Adas Israel met with Al Smith, the speaker of the State Assembly, to explain their opposition to a state charter. (Formally, opponents objected to the descriptive title of the organization in the proposed charter—"The Jewish Community of New York"—which created the danger that the corporate body could legally claim to represent all of New York's Jews.) Smith assured the delegation that "my point of view on this bill as in all other bills depends completely on the wishes of my constituents. I always felt that the Yiddish press represented its readers' views faithfully." A year later, only after significant changes were made—most importantly, "Jewish Community of New York" was replaced by "New York Kehillah"—did the bill of incorporation become law.[18]

During the anti-incorporation campaign the *Morgen Zhurnal* explained its viewpoint of Jewish communal politics in an editorial which disclosed the gist of the political credo of Orthodox Jews. The editorial compared communal politics in New York and Warsaw. Despite basic differences in the legal status and character of the two communities, there were striking similarities in the assumptions which guided New York's and Warsaw's Jewish leaders. In Warsaw the majority of the electorate, Hasidim, invariably elected "deitschen," assimilated Jews, to head the *gemeinde*, on the assumption that these Jews could best represent the entire community before the authorities. An unwritten understanding existed that the "deitschen" would not interfere in the internal affairs of the observant Jews. In fact, the *Morgen Zhurnal* emphasized, the Orthodox Jews preferred a coalition with the assimilated Jews rather than with the Zionists. Zionism, with its expansive ambitions to embrace all of Jewry, posed a greater danger than the assimilationists. The Zionist slogan, *kibbush ha-kehilot* ("the conquest of the communities"), implied meddling in the *gemeinde*'s institutions. In America, the same sort of understanding existed between the observant and the nonobservant. The *Morgen Zhurnal* explained that Orthodox immigrants applauded the Americanized Reform Jews who spoke out in defense of Jews. "One requires from today's Jewish statesman no more piety than from the old *shtadlan*." However, the paper warned, "let him not mix into our internal religious affairs. He should be a spokesman on matters over which we do not quarrel among ourselves and nothing more."[19] Group interest was the driving force in Orthodox Jewish politics as in orthodox American politics.

This case study of Jacob Saphirstein and the *Morgen Zhurnal* suggests that contrary to the prevailing historical view, the immigrant leaders and opinion-makers of Orthodox Jewry were political sophisticates. They understood the American style of politics—the uses of power and influence, political horse-trading, and the importance of the political gesture. They demonstrated an affinity for orthodox American politics which was non-ideological, interest-group oriented, and sugarcoated by the conventional rhetoric that it wasn't. Jewish political culture in America had its roots in the Jewish communal life of Europe—quickened, enriched, and elaborated by the experience of late-nineteenth- and early-twentieth-century changes in Eastern Europe. The guiding principle, both in outward and inward expression, was the pragmatic use of politics to defend the integrity of Orthodox Judaism. In this sense, Orthodox Jewish immigrants in America were not that different from the Irish, the most famous practitioners of nonideological orthodox American politics. This tradition deserves more attention than it has received.

# 6 Paths of Leadership

At all times in Jewish life there have risen men who have endeavored to lead the masses for their own purposes. It began at the dawn of history, it began when our forefathers were about to enter the land of promise, when Korach arose and said to Moses and Aaron—"we are all leaders, we are all prophets"—and what was the consequence? Our forefathers were on the border line of the promised land, and just as they were to enter it, God in his wisdom ordained "you shall stay forty years, a full generation, in the desert until the present generation shall have gone out of existence and a united Israel alone shall enter the promised land." And so it is now again here with us. Do we really want, just as we are on the borderland and have actually gone across the border line . . . [to] the United States of America, . . . do we want again to have this firebrand thrown into our midst, this firebrand which says we do not trust our old leaders, we want new leaders chosen upon a democratic basis? If you really want to do this, I say to you, leaders cannot be elected. True leaders must develop, true leaders must have proved their value. Office holders can be elected, but we Jews, to gain what we must obtain, not for ourselves but for our unhappy and miserable brethren in Europe, must have proved leaders, and not office holders. . . . [1]

—Jacob Schiff, 1915

It is the essence of the democratic spirit wisely to choose and reasoningly to follow high leadership. . . . Through the centuries Israel ceaselessly renewed its quest for leadership in the words of our fathers, "na-aseh-rosh,"—let us choose for ourselves a leader. The leadership which Israel has always rejected has either been imposed by outward authority or unendowed with inward authority. . . . The time is come for a leadership by us to be chosen,—a leadership that shall democratically and wisely lead rather than autocratically and unwisely command.[2]

—Stephen S. Wise, 1916

During the first half of this century American Jews produced a succession of commanding figures whom the community acknowledged as national leaders although they held no formal mandate. These leaders created national organizations and movements, defended Jewish interests at home and abroad, and shaped Jewish communal policy. It was a time, as the historian Melvin Urofsky expressed it, when "there were giants on the earth." Louis Marshall, Jacob Schiff, Louis Brandeis, Henrietta Szold, Stephen Wise and Abba Hillel Silver have had no counterparts in the nearly four decades since the last of them, Wise and Silver, departed from the public stage. In Urofsky's words, "A generation of titans has given way to a generation of managers."[3]

Like most aphorisms the statement is an oversimplification. Among the "titans" of the earlier generation were zealous managers. Brandeis's exhortation to "organize, organize, organize, until every Jew in America must stand up and be counted," his call for "members, money, discipline," and his attention to the minutest administrative detail during the years he actively headed the Zionist movement carries the contemporary ring of a federation of Jewish philanthropies chief. On the other hand, the role Philip Klutznick of B'nai B'rith played in our time was no mere managerial one. For his part in expanding the scope and influence of the mass organization he served and in recasting the structure of national Jewish leadership, Klutznick ranks high among twentieth-century leaders.[4] Nevertheless, Urofsky's observation is a highly suggestive one, for it coincides with a watershed in American Jewish life—the years from the end of the Second World War to the establishment of the Jewish state—which had a profound effect upon the community and undoubtedly upon its leadership.

These years witnessed an unprecedented level of unified communal activism. Propelled largely by the urgency to resettle and rehabilitate the one-third of European Jewry who had survived the Holocaust—a task which merged with the struggle for Jewish sovereignty in Palestine—American Jewry mobilized its organizational, financial and political resources in a massive display of support. It emerged from the trial fortified and optimistic, standing on the threshold of a new era. Of course, more was involved than the invigorating effect of the collective effort to save the "surviving remnant" and support the struggle for a Jewish state. Generational succession, acculturation, affluence and social acceptance combined with the searing historical events to produce a consensual outlook, communal stability and group self-consciousness and self-confidence that had not existed before.

With these developments in mind, this chapter focuses on an earlier period, the years prior to the outbreak of war in 1914 and the war years themselves, which formed the pivotal stage in the creation of a tradition of national leadership. The chapter concerns itself with modes of leadership, the paths to attaining communal power and the exercise of that power implied by the "titans to managers" thesis.[5] Remarkably, the figures who cast their shadow on two generations of Jewish public life achieved their reputation as national leaders during an era when American Jewry was divided socially, culturally and ideologically. Polarized at the start of the era by class, language, communal tradition, and political outlook (in the American as well as in the Jewish realm), the segmented Jewish public produced different types of leaders with contrasting bases of authority and accountability, and conflicting methods of exercising their influence. The test of national leadership became the ability to navigate this stormy cultural and political sea to reach a wider constituency or to form a coalition of constituencies. Consequently, one must first consider the social, cultural and ideological influences which shaped the various patterns of leadership.

By 1900, the established community—prosperous, Americanized or native-born, and sharing common German origins for the most part—considered itself part of mainstream America. Reform Judaism best expressed the group's self-definition. In well-appointed temples, an increasingly American-trained rabbinate articulated the Reform credo of a historical religious fellowship united by the belief in the prophetic ideals of universal brotherhood and good works. The Reform minister, despite his standing as spokesman of the faith, rarely engaged in public leadership roles. Congregation members and trustees expected him to serve them as preacher, pastor and educator. Those outstanding rabbis who did become national leaders—Stephen Wise, Judah Magnes, and Abba Hillel Silver, to name the most eminent—achieved that station not as representatives of denominational constituencies but as heads of secular movements.[6]

In addition to its temples, the established community maintained "nonsectarian" philanthropic agencies, social clubs and fraternal orders. Taken together a network of secular and religious institutions provided proper middle-class ways of social endeavor that were much influenced by American norms and liberal Protestantism's notions of spiritual uplift, stewardship, and noblesse oblige.[7]

In keeping with this tradition, the community's leaders were its men of means and social standing—mostly businessmen but sometimes lawyers and other professionals—who supported and controlled their chosen institution or association. Increasingly, as the need for communal services grew, paid specialists in addition to the religious functionaries were employed to administer the agencies and supply the necessary skills. A corporate business model came to dominate Jewish organizational life although it soon had to contend with alternative, radically different models introduced by the immigrants. Directors or trustees (the concerned elite), approved by the contributors (stockholders), then hired professionals to carry out the directors' policies. The appearance of federations of Jewish charities in the large Jewish population centers exemplified this development. (Between 1895, when the first federation was established, and 1920, 32 local federations were founded.) The federations, with their coordinated fund-raising campaigns and allocations of income, promised a more efficient, rational use of philanthropic resources. Nevertheless, the institutions developed by the established community remained staunchly autonomous.[8]

Two national organizations should be mentioned, the Union of American Hebrew Congregations, a loose alliance of Reform synagogues, and the B'nai B'rith fraternal order, democratic in structure and secular in its program of social service and defense of Jewish rights. Both organizations appealed to the broad, middle-class stratum of acculturated Jews, and their leaders sought recognition as spokesmen for American Jewry. Leo N. Levi who headed the order from 1899 to 1904, Adolph Kraus who was elected president in 1905, and Simon Wolf who represented the order and the Union of American Hebrew Congregations in Washington interceded regularly on the highest governmental levels in matters of Jewish concern.[9]

However, by and large, central leadership was increasingly concentrated in the hands of a group of New York notables who exercised it in an informal way as the need arose. The most prominent among them were the banker Jacob Schiff, the diplomat-politician Oscar Straus, and, soon to join them, the lawyer Louis Marshall. Each of them, it should be noted, was active in American public affairs as well as in Jewish matters. The issues that most often moved them to take action as communal advocates was the anti-Jewish policies of the Czarist government, the periodic waves of pogroms, and the resultant rise in migration to the United States, beginning in 1882, of impoverished, Yiddish-speaking Jews. The plight of persecuted Jews abroad merged with the problems of the social and cultural integration of those who settled in America.[10]

The newcomers, while preoccupied with eking out a living and making their initial accommodation with the startlingly different society they encountered, also transplanted much of the intensive, diversified and self-enclosed Yiddish-speaking communal life they had known in Eastern Europe. Indeed, the immigrants used the freedom they found in America to broaden and elaborate it. They established trade unions to meet their economic and social needs, created and transplanted organizations and parties to propagate their cultural and religious views, and supported a highly politicized Yiddish daily and periodical press which interpreted American and Jewish life through a variety of ideological lenses.

Within the immigrant community, leadership was as varied in style, function, and source of authority as the heterogeneous public it served. At one end of the spectrum, the received religious leadership attempted to reestablish its hegemony over the Orthodox community but with little success. In America, where religious organization carried no governmental sanction and survived only through the voluntary efforts of its supporters, the Orthodox rabbi's role as expounder of religious law, arbitrator, and overseer of communal institutions atrophied. The balance and collaboration between received leadership and lay leadership which existed in Eastern Europe collapsed leaving almost unlimited power in the hands of the latter. The well-off, like their uptown counterparts, exerted their authority through the charities and religious institutions which they sponsored. However, their influence rarely extended beyond the local organization they supported and headed.[11]

One illuminating exception is the case of Harry Fischel, a harbinger of future developments. The New York builder was a director of nearly all of the Orthodox educational and social welfare institutions which were community-wide in scope—the Etz Chaim Yeshiva, the Hebrew Loan Society, Beth Israel Hospital, and the Daughters of Jacob Old Age Home. As national Jewish organizations evolved (a development discussed below), Fischel's role broadened. In 1909, he was instrumental in uniting two smaller charities into the Hebrew Immigrant Aid Society (HIAS) which became the central agency dealing with new immigrants, and he served as its treasurer for the next thirty-seven years. In October 1914—a time of intensified communal activity kindled by the outbreak of war—Fischel received unusual recognition. He was invited to serve on an ad hoc committee of five that led to the establishment of the American Jewish Joint Distribution Committee (JDC) which would soon become the major overseas relief agency. The other members of the ad hoc committee were Oscar Straus, Louis Brandeis, recently elected to head the emergency Zionist body (the Provisional Executive Committee for General Zionist Affairs), Judge Julian W. Mack, the personal advisor to Julius Rosenwald, the Chicago philanthropist, and Meyer London, the socialist labor lawyer.[12]

The Yiddish press offered another avenue to power and influence. For the Orthodox, splintered into scores of autonomous congregations and welfare societies, the religiously conservative dailies provided an authoritative voice. The publisher of the first Yiddish daily, the *Tageblat*, founded in 1885, was the Orthodox Jew Kasriel Sarasohn, who served for a year as a rabbi in Syracuse, New York, before returning to New York City in 1874 to launch a Yiddish weekly. In 1901, Jacob Saphirstein founded a second Orthodox daily, the *Morgen Zhurnal*. Both publishers vigorously defended Orthodox Judaism, diligently reported on its institutional life, denounced Reform Judaism and socialism as blasphemous, and rallied support for the partisan causes they favored. The *Morgen Zhurnal* was also aggressively Republican, and Saphirstein carried weight in New York Republican circles. In addition to the influence they wielded among their readers, Sarasohn and Saphirstein personally shouldered communal responsibilities by raising funds and heading some of the Orthodox community's major institutions. Sarasohn died in 1905 and Saphirstein in 1914. Their heirs, Sarasohn's son-in-law, Leon Kamaiky, who was also a part owner of the *Tageblat* and later of the *Morgen Zhurnal*, and Gedaliah Bublick, editor of the *Tageblat*, continued the tradition of combining journalism with communal leadership. When the Central Committee for the Relief of War Sufferers was established in October 1914 to coordinate the raising and distribution of funds by the Orthodox community, Kamaiky was elected chairman. (Fischel served as treasurer.) Meanwhile Bublick lined up the *Tageblat* behind the movement to establish a democratically elected congress to speak for American Jewry and joined the organizing committee when it was formed in March 1915. Two years later the movement culminated in the calling of the American Jewish Congress, and Bublick was elected one of the vice presidents.[13]

The Jewish labor movement stood at the other end of the spectrum of immigrant life. There, the leadership track to power led most often through the garment industry trade unions whose membership was largely Jewish. For a few, the radical Yiddish press also provided entry into the higher echelons of labor movement leadership. The daily *Forverts*, in particular, played a decisive role in shaping the Jewish labor movement's identity and direction. The *Forverts*, under the guidance of its formidable editor, Abe Cahan, not only provided a rich fare of popular education, belles lettres and socialist pep talk. The paper raised funds for strikers, provided the communication net between workers, their locals and the union leadership. Individual staff members held posts in the trade unions and radical parties, and the Forward Building served as a socialist "house of assembly."

Beginning in 1909, a series of successful strikes brought tens of thousands of Jewish workers into the garment unions. By 1918, 250,000 belonged. Organized by shop and in trade locals which then federated into city-wide joint boards and finally into national associations, the union members elected hundreds of representatives and functionaries who manned the different levels of the trade union organizational structure. During the great strikes of the period, which sometimes lasted months, union management raised hundreds of thousands of dollars in strike funds, maintained picket lines in the face of violence and intimidation, set up committees which supplied food, legal aid and medical services for the striking workers, and sustained workers' morale through mass meetings, benefit affairs and union newspapers. In these protracted confrontations, the unions could count on the support of their allies, in reality organizations with overlapping memberships. The Workmen's Circle fraternal order, the Jewish Socialist Federation, the United Hebrew Trades, and the *Forverts* Association—all of whom possessed aggressive leaders—packed the protest meetings, contributed from their treasuries to the strike funds, and exhorted the strikers to carry on. Together, they formed a highly self-conscious working-class community which also included a number of small but highly articulate ideological parties either brought over from Europe or else reflections of the American socialist movement.[14]

However, the main arena for exercising power remained the trade unions. Young, innovative and forceful leaders succeeded in rising quickly in the union hierarchy despite factional and, at times, ruthless infighting. The founders of the Jewish labor movement—men like Cahan, Joseph Barondess, Max Pine, Meyer London, Joseph Schlossberg and Morris Hillquit—were mostly in their twenties in the 1890s when they organized the early unions. The first president of the newly organized International Ladies Garment Workers Union (1903) was twenty-seven-year-old Benjamin Schlesinger. In 1910, Sidney Hillman, aged twenty-three, led 38,000 of Chicago's clothing workers to a path-breaking victory. Five years later, the founding convention of the Amalgamated Clothing Workers of America elected him president. During these years, the best of the Jewish trade union leaders proved to be gifted negotiators and executives. They pioneered a program of social unionism which included medical care, cooperative housing, recreational programs, unemployment insurance, and worker education. In terms of popular democratic leadership, the activation of sheer numbers, and the creation of effective mass organizations, the Jewish union leaders created a unique leadership tradition in Jewish life. It was also a highly politicized tradition. Leaders connected with the Jewish trade unions regularly ran for public office under the Socialist Party banner. The Jewish labor movement's greatest triumph was Meyer London's election to Congress in 1914 and his reelection in 1916 and 1920 from a preponderantly Jewish-populated district on New York's Lower East Side. There is a link between the mass protest demonstrations of the 1930s against Nazi atrocities that were led by Wise, those of the 1940s for a Jewish state that were led by Silver, and the strikes and protest marches of the Jewish labor movement in the 1910s and 1920s.

Ambivalence if not outright estrangement characterized the relationship between the leaders of the labor movement (less so the rank and file) and the organized Jewish community. The regnant socialist ideology was assimilationist and indifferent to the notion of ethnic loyalty. Preoccupation with ethnic group maintenance was inimical to class interest, to the amalgamation of all nationalities into a progressive, cosmopolitan nation, and to the vision of a humane international order. There were influential voices who combined socialism with some form of Jewish nationalism, but they were in the minority. The majority railed against the benighted Orthodox and the misguided Zionists in their midst and dismissed the welfare and Americanization programs sponsored by the German Jewish patricians as unwanted tutelage and devices for silencing social protest.

Ironically, these socialist leaders addressed a Yiddish-speaking public which was rooted in its ethnic culture. To advance their program of class interests and class solidarity, the radical leaders had no choice but to participate in the Jewish communal life of the immigrants; they either muted their disdain for Jewish survivalist ideologies, or by engaging them in debate acknowledged their influence and legitimacy in the life of the Jewish quarter. Occasionally, the radical leadership was reluctantly drawn into the vortex of Jewish communal politics. An interesting example (discussed below) was the controversy over the establishment of a democratically elected body to speak for American Jews, an American Jewish Congress.[15]

The leaders who represented the central bloc of immigrant organizations, whose constituencies were middle-class in social standing or aspiration, were eclectic in their style and tactics. They drew upon the experience of their radical and Orthodox counterparts. Most of all, they emulated American models of leadership which reached them by way of the established German Jewish community.

The best example is the Zionist movement which was democratic in structure and populist in intent. It hoped to win a mass following from among all segments of the Jewish population. A federation of autonomous branches allowed for diversity. At annual conventions delegates contested policy, elected the movement's officers and proclaimed its unity with the world organization. An outreach program of mass meetings, popular fund-raising events, public lectures, and publications was flexible enough to appeal to the immigrant quarter (the use of Yiddish) and to the English-speaking public. The Zionists issued periodicals in Yiddish and English. Yet the Zionists chose leaders in the patrician mold—Richard Gottheil, Professor of Semitics at Columbia University, Herbert Friedenwald, a distinguished Baltimore opthalmologist, Louis Brandeis, the "people's attorney," and Julian Mack, a founder of the American Jewish Committee and judge on the U.S. Circuit Court of Appeals. All were American-born of central European origin. Only occasionally did the plebeian leaders of East European origin, men like Louis Lipsky and Abraham Goldberg who were journalists by profession or paid Zionist officials, assert themselves.[16]

The fraternal orders provide an additional perspective of the community's centrist leadership tradition. The orders attracted the ideologically uncommitted by federating hundreds of *landsmanshaft* societies. The Order B'rith Abraham and the break-away Independent Order of B'rith Abraham, the largest of these fraternal associations, followed the B'nai B'rith model. They were secular organizations which offered their members fellowship, social and welfare benefits, and a pledge "to take an active interest in Jewish affairs." They produced middle-of-the-road leaders who were amenable to communal collaboration and tended to accept the direction of the notables. B'rith Abraham's long-incumbent Grandmaster, Samuel Dorf, was invited to join the executive of the American Jewish Committee when it was founded in 1906. He was also a director of New York's United Hebrew Charities and served on the executive committee of the New York Kehillah. Leon Sanders, who headed the rival order, served as president of HIAS from 1909 to 1917, and was a member of the executive of the New York Kehillah and a vice president of the American Jewish Congress. During the drawn-out controversy over holding a congress, Sanders, who belonged to the Congress Organization Committee, the Provisional Zionist Committee and the rival American Jewish Committee, sought to play a mediating role. He also moved easily from Jewish communal leadership to Democratic Party politics and back. Elected twice to the State Assembly on a Tammany ticket and to a municipal judgeship in 1904, Sanders failed to win the party's nomination for judge of the state Supreme Court in 1914. Two years later he won the party's nomination for Congress but lost to the socialist incumbent, Meyer London, in a campaign in which he highlighted his many Jewish organizational connections. Eager to build a broad base of goodwill, an attitude in accord with his Tammany training, Sanders was the ubiquitous communal officeholder. He was one of the most popular chairmen and toastmasters at the numerous testimonial and fund-raising dinners that characterized the organizational world of the immigrant middle class.[17]

From the Kishinev pogrom in 1903 to the outbreak of the First World War, a succession of upheavals shook East European Jewry and left its mark on American Jews. The rash of pogroms in 1905 and 1906, followed by heightened Czarist oppression, resulted in a mass flight that doubled the Jewish population of America in the decade preceding the outbreak of war. These events led to a flurry of activity to meet the new burdens. It became necessary for the Jewish notables to formalize their de facto standing as national leaders. The result was the establishment of the American Jewish Committee (AJC) in 1906 which was dominated by the New York patrician group of Schiff, Marshall, Oscar Straus and Cyrus Sulzberger, and by two of Philadelphia's leading figures, Mayer Sulzberger and Cyrus Adler.

This oligarchy of the German Jewish elite maintained its primacy in Jewish affairs by the sheer weight of its prestige, wealth, political connections, and dedication. Yet from the start the AJC was sufficiently uneasy about maintaining its hegemony to occasionally co-opt other "leading Jews" to its ranks. The AJC's support of the New York Kehillah can be seen as an attempt to bolster and extend its authority by forging an alliance with the moderate leaders of the immigrant community. In the AJC's table of organization, the Kehillah became district twelve (New York City), and the twenty-five members of its elected executive committee assumed their places on the AJC's general council. Hopefully, other cities would establish "kehillot" under the aegis of the committee and become districts in its domain. Interestingly, the founders limited the organization to the "non-controversial" areas of "fighting discrimination and aiding suffering brethren." It excluded from its purview cultural or religious questions, avoiding as the founders explained, "arousing sectarian issues." In its agreement with the Kehillah, the latter was to have complete autonomy over "internal" matters including education and religion, but was to yield on "external" (national and international affairs) to the committee.[18]

The AJC's initial successes were impressive. Especially notable was its three-year campaign of quiet but firm diplomacy—from 1908 to 1911—to abrogate the Russo-American treaty of commerce. The Czarist government's refusal to allow American citizens who were Jewish entry to Russia was presented as an affront to the United States. The campaign was a paradigm of committee strategy. Direct negotiations with President William Howard Taft and Secretary of State Philander C. Knox went hand in hand with cultivating the support of key members of Congress that led eventually to an overwhelming congressional vote in favor of abrogation. The committee prepared thoroughly researched background papers, ensured that the question was discussed in the nation's leading papers and periodicals, and at a crucial point arranged public meetings where prominent non-Jews joined in attacking Russia's anti-Jewish policies. At stake, they argued, was "the sanctity and integrity of American citizenship" and impression of acquiescing to Russian tyranny.[19]

The appearance in 1909 of the greatly expanded HIAS represented a new level of immigrant assertiveness. By 1914, the organization had reached beyond providing the newly arrived immigrants with social and legal services. HIAS developed a national network of agents and committees for locating kin and assisting the newcomers in reaching the interior cities. It began publishing information bulletins and educational material, and it opened employment bureaus and Americanization classes. The organization also maintained a Washington office that not only handled deportation appeals but lobbied against immigration restriction legislation. On one occasion—an indication of its self-assurance—a committee of HIAS leaders that included Kamaiky and Fischel met with President Taft and then lunched with the Secretary of Commerce and Labor to win government approval for opening a kosher kitchen on Ellis Island.[20]

By the eve of the First World War, HIAS had built a nationwide membership of individuals and organizations that reflected the spectrum of Jewish immigrant life from the Orthodox to the socialists. In addition to men like Sanders, Fischel, and Kamaiky, HIAS's governing board included other centrist leaders like Bernard Semel, the president of the Federation of Galician and Bucovinean Jews and, significantly, Adolph Held and Alexander Kahn, representative figures of the Jewish labor movement, who were connected with the *Forverts.*[21]

The war years witnessed a further acceleration of organizational activity that completed the formation of a national leadership structure that would remain in place until after World War II. The need to help the victims of famine, mass expulsions and pogroms became a matter of overwhelming urgency. With it went the awareness that the American Jewish community was the one center of affluence and influence unscathed by war. In addition to massive relief, Russia's Jews required political intervention and the final securing in the postwar Europe of equal rights and, where appropriate, "group" or minority rights.

An extraordinary eruption of communal energy that encompassed all sectors of the Jewish public followed fast upon the outbreak of the war. Within three months, beginning at the end of August 1914, the following major events occurred: the Zionist movement established the Provisional

Executive Committee for General Zionist Affairs to mobilize political and financial support to save the hard-pressed Jewish colonies in Palestine from Ottoman repression; Orthodox circles formed the Central Relief Committee; and through the initiative of the AJC, forty national Jewish organizations met to create the American Jewish Relief Committee for general relief purposes. Soon after, the two relief committees organized the American Jewish Joint Distribution Committee (JDC) to coordinate the transfer and distribution of relief funds overseas. In November 1915, the People's Relief Committee, established the previous summer by radical circles, joined the JDC. By that time, the Jewish Congress Organizing Committee and the National Workmen's Committee on Jewish Rights were operating in the political field mobilizing support, as we shall see, for or against a congress.

The tumultuous times induced persons of stature to join the first rank of national leadership. Felix Warburg, Jacob Schiff's son-in-law and a partner in Kuhn, Loeb and Company, accepted the chairmanship of the JDC. Joseph Barondess, Bublick and Sanders, all of whom were identified with the immigrant community, won national attention lobbying for the congress idea; from the radical camp, Max Goldfarb, J. B. Salutsky, Max Pine and Nachman Syrkin—unknown beyond the Jewish labor movement—now became players in the Jewish political arena. But surely Brandeis's sudden entrance into the thicket of Jewish communal affairs as chairman of the Provisional Zionist Council was the most notable instance of the appearance of a new national leader.[22]

With so eminent and energetic a figure heading the movement, Zionists who had been inactive for a variety of reasons returned to leadership roles and others gained prominence for the first time. Stephen Wise, Julian Mack, Horace Kallen, and Felix Frankfurter are representative of this development. One of Brandeis's first steps was to launch an emergency campaign to raise $100,000 to save the Zionist colonies. It became necessary to coordinate the campaign with the initiatives taken by the AJC which included transferring food to Palestine on an American naval vessel. The new leaders with no past ties to the establishment leadership now demanded a share in directing the course of Jewish affairs. The call for a congress—an elected body to represent a united American Jewry—became the vehicle for challenging the German Jewish notables.[23]

By the spring of 1915, the public debate over establishing a congress was in full pace continuing for three more years until the congress convened on December 15, 1918. During this time, alliances were formed and broken, ad hoc committees appointed, and pro-congress and anti-congress conferences called that brought together hundreds of delegates. Unaffiliated organizations like the B'nai B'rith attempted to mediate but to no avail. Negotiators, chief among them Marshall and Brandeis, reached or nearly reached agreements over such matters as representation, scope, a predetermined agenda, and the date for convening the new body, only to have them rejected or postponed by their respective organizations.

Entwined with the questions of pride, procedure, governance and institutional power were the polarizing issues of how American Jews defined themselves. Never before had the entire ideological and organizational spectrum of Jewish life become engaged in direct debate in public forums over the meaning of being Jewish in America. The controversy and its irresolution would affect the practice of leadership in directing Jewish communal life for a generation.

The Yiddish press fueled the debate. Graphic reports from the Russian front agitated a public largely cut off from family and townsfolk so recently left behind. Alongside the war news, each of the fiercely competitive dailies aligned itself with one of the increasingly polarized camps contending for the political leadership of the struggle on behalf of Europe's Jews. The *Tageblat* spearheaded the attack on "the self-crowned aristocrats of the American Jewish Committee" for attempting "to kill the whole [congress] movement." In an acrimonious editorial in February 1915 (one of many to follow), the paper appealed "directly to the people, to the millions of Jews in America . . . who have a good heart and sound Jewish patriotism" to oppose the AJC's tactics. "Fearful of its authority," the AJC was scheming to "smother" the congress movement by announcing its own conference of national organizations. The *Tageblat* called for a "people's conference," not one that would be "a footstool to the throne from which a handful of German Jews may rule over the Jews of America." Bublick, the *Tageblat*'s editor, did more than write pro-congress editorials. He assumed a leadership role in the steering committee of the congress movement.[24] The *Forverts*, on the other hand, first leveled its criticism at its bête noire, the pro-congress radical nationalists within its own camp, and in particular the small but vociferous socialist-Zionists. Describing a labor conference which ended in pandemonium (where the radical nationalist demand for a broad-based congress was defeated), the *Forverts* reported: "One felt at once that these [the radical nationalists] were people used to collecting shekels [Zionist dues] for the Jewish past and voting resolutions for the future. . . . They defended their resolutions with wild fanaticism, like people from a *kloyz* [small synagogue], not like people from the labor movement." The paper supported the establishment of the National Workmen's Committee as a means of stemming the tide for the congress. In the realignment of forces, the traditional radical leadership now shared a common animus with the AJC: the congress movement as a Zionist stratagem to create a Jewish nationalist entity in America.[25]

To appreciate the legacy of the congress controversy one needs to consider the depth of the rancor harbored by the leading protagonists, Schiff and Marshall for the AJC, Brandeis and Wise for the Zionists. In May 1915, in a private letter to Judah Magnes, Schiff expressed the establishment's near panic: "This proposition for an American Jewish Congress is nothing less than an attempt to weld together the Jewish population of this country into a racial or nationalistic organization. . . . Let this attempt succeed and it will not be long before we shall witness in this country an anti-Semitism which does not now exist." In a slashing public address, Marshall carried the attack further. The pro-congress "agitators" were endangering the statesmanlike efforts of discreet and experienced leaders who were dealing with complex and sensitive issues. They were doing so for reasons of self-aggrandizement. A congress, Marshall continued, would create a platform for impolitic, ethnocentric leaders playing to the masses with their "inflammatory rhetoric" and preposterous demands. Public criticism of Russia (whose goodwill was necessary for relief work), praise of Germany (with whom the United States was on the brink of war), and Zionist demands for a Jewish homeland (angering the Turks and thus endangering the local Jewish population) would prove disastrous. Writing to Adolf Kraus, the head of B'nai B'rith, several months later, Marshall described his opponents as "blatant demagogues, principally nationalists [Zionists] and radical socialists" who lived on notoriety. "If they can make a speech in which they can denounce everybody and everything they will be perfectly happy, even though the destruction of our European brethren might immediately follow."[26]

With negotiations proceeding at a snail's pace and public agitation escalating, Brandeis concluded that the time had come to deliver a major address on the congress issue. At Carnegie Hall in late January 1916, at the height of his popularity, revered chief of the growing Zionist organization, an authoritative figure no less than Schiff, Marshall or Straus, Brandeis presented a sweeping analysis of the "Jewish problem." His point of departure was his liberal democratic credo, the core value of his American and Jewish patriotism, and the key to understanding and resolving the Jewish problem. The war, he told the packed hall, was not the fundamental cause of Jewish misery. It had magnified and intensified Jewish suffering tenfold.

Only radically changed conditions after the war could end the oppression and discrimination suffered by more than one-half of the Jewish people. Fundamental changes meant full political rights guaranteed by democratic governments who accepted the "new nationalism," a doctrine that proclaimed that "each race or people, like each individual, has a right and duty to develop." Then alone would "minorities be secured in their rights . . . and with it, the solution of the Jewish Problem." The war, Brandeis continued, had shown that the rights of the Jewish people can be gained only by

> traveling the same road as other peoples travel—the road of democracy—through the people's asserting their own authority in their own interest. The demand for democracy in the consideration of the Jewish problem is not a matter of form. It is of the essence. It is a fundamental Jewish conception, as it is the basic American method. It rests upon the essential trust in the moral instincts of the people.[27]

Having taken the "high road" to the issue at hand, Brandeis then underscored the need for an open and permanent democratic congress. It was no end in itself but rather "an incident of the organization of the Jewish people—an instrument through which their will may be ascertained, and when ascertained, may be carried out." Only in this way could Jewish public opinion find expression, wise decisions be reached, elected spokesmen speak with authority, and a permanent "machinery" created to assure that whatever gains were made at a peace conference would be "maintained by the united effort of the Jews."[28]

Grueling negotiations continued with the AJC making concessions no doubt influenced by the groundswell of pro-congress sentiment and addresses like that of Brandeis. Stephen Wise, the popular Reformed preacher, veteran Zionist and social progressive, now replaced Brandeis on the public platform. Nominated by Wilson four days after his Carnegie Hall address, Brandeis was finally confirmed by the senate on June 1, 1916. He felt constrained to play too visible a role in Jewish communal politics. More fiery and less cerebral than Brandeis, Wise threw down the gauntlet in a keynote address in March 1916, before a conference in Philadelphia charged with arranging the calling of the congress. His address turned into a clarion call for a democracy in Jewish life:

> The people are resolved to be free of their masters whether these be malevolent tyrants without or benevolent despots within the life of Israel.

... Are we forever to suffer men to think and act for us, not because we have chosen and named them, but because they have decreed that we are not fit to be trusted with the power of shaping our own destiny? ... Shall we be the last to welcome the renewal of the spirit of democracy? Shall we in this democratic land renounce our democratic ideals, and by so much forswear the passionately democratic faith of our fathers?

The *American Hebrew* captioned its report of the address, "Leadership in American Jewry."[29]

Judged by Brandeis's and Wise's rhetoric, the ultimate resolution of the congress issue was disappointing. True, nominating conventions and then direct elections of delegates were held as the pro-congress committee had insisted. In May and June of 1917, 335,000 ballots were cast for organizational lists. Finally, after repeated delays, on December 15, 1918, the American Jewish Congress assembled in Philadelphia following three years of public debate, involuted and often devious negotiations, power plays, and dizzying realignments and schisms among the contending parties. Three hundred and sixty-seven delegates from eighty-three cities attended, and 5,000 filled the opera house at the festive opening with thousands more outside. In stormy debates in the plenum and in committees, the congress hammered out the provisions for political and minority rights to be presented to the peace conference for inclusion in the treaties to be negotiated and elected the delegation to represent it.[30]

These were signal accomplishments. Nevertheless, at every step the limitations of imposing majoritarian rule upon a voluntaristic communal order was evident, how much more so, when such an order embraced so heterogeneous a public. The bloc of anti-nationalist radicals—spokesmen for the Jewish trade union movement, the Workmen's Circle, and the Jewish Socialist Federation—boycotted the congress elections (although some individual branches and trade union locals ignored the decision). After much vacillation, the radical bloc sent a token delegation. Not a single major trade union leader attended, although a small delegation representing the Jewish labor movement attended. Thus the largest, best-organized sector in American Jewish life remained standoffish. The AJC, battling for its preeminence, won important concessions. The most crucial one was the unconditional proviso that the congress disband after hearing the report of its peace delegation. The AJC insisted that the congress be a temporary body to meet an emergency situation, limited to the single undertaking of obtaining political rights at the peace conference. Thus Brandeis's vision of reordering American Jewish communal life along democratic lines and Wise's goal of replacing self-appointed notables with the people's choice came to naught.

Yet for the chief protagonists, the two titans of the drama, Marshall and Brandeis, visions and ultimate goals were negotiable. Both were brilliant litigators and agile mediators. The conservative, elitist Marshall, no less than the liberal, democratic Brandeis plotted their strategy pragmatically, fully cognizant of the other side's strengths and weaknesses, and determined to make the best possible bargain they could. The negotiating sessions between them and the representatives of the various factions had all the earmarks of labor arbitration meetings in the Jewish garment industry which both knew so well. In the case of the congress controversy the anti-establishment side (the Zionists and their bourgeois immigrant allies) made some significant gains, the most important one being its legitimization as a party to the dispute. Moreover, the precept of the "democratization of Jewish life" continued to provide an avenue for challenging the established leaders. However, the old establishment maintained much of its power because it dominated the other major concern of American Jewry, overseas relief work and the politics that went with it.

In important respects, the politics of relief had a more lasting influence on the structure and dynamics of Jewish leadership than the struggle for a congress. The two movements were also interrelated. Both had an almost identical cast of characters. The American Jewish Relief Committee, the Central Relief Committee, the People's Relief Committee, and the JDC, headed respectively by Marshall, Kamaiky, London, and Felix W. Warburg—Brandeis was a member of the American Jewish Relief Committee's executive and headed its New England region—brought together establishment Jews, Orthodox, radicals and Zionists. The collaborative effort raised, transferred and distributed $38 million of overseas aid during the years 1914 to 1920.[31]

This tenuous collaboration was marked with bickering and discord. For example, at first Marshall opposed separate funds assuming that the current emergency could be met as previous ones had, by soliciting the circle of wealthy and generous patricians. However, he and his coworkers quickly recognized the enormity of the catastrophe and the anxiety and anguish that gripped the immigrants who spontaneously launched their own relief campaigns. Moreover, there were legitimate interests and particular needs that drove these separate efforts. For the Orthodox, aid to religious scholars and institutions carried a high priority, and their fund-raising took place largely within the precincts of the synagogue. The radical camp opposed the very notion of philanthropy, stressing the need for reconstructing the social and economic fabric of Eastern European Jewish life. These goals could best be achieved, it insisted, by bolstering the fraternal parties and institutions. Moreover, for the radicals mass participation in fundraising was as important as the amounts raised. For the Zionists, an international movement with major branches in the belligerent countries, the distribution of funds in Europe was as important as assuring that the needs of the Jewish population in Palestine be met.[32]

The case of the Zionists offers an illuminating example of the political ramifications of overseas relief. The Provisional Zionist Committee had little choice but to work through the American Jewish Relief Committee—the AJC's satellite and the dominant partner when the JDC was established. This was true even when dealing with Palestine relief operations. The Zionists' ability to raise large sums of money was limited. To meet the initial emergency call for Palestine aid, each agency pledged to meet half the goal set. From that moment friction between the relief committee and the Zionists escalated. The Zionists complained that they were not receiving due credit for the amounts they raised; Palestine was not getting its agreed share of funds; nor had they gained recognition for their part in the stunning diplomatic feat of gaining U.S. government help in transmitting money and food to Palestine and evacuating Jews forced to leave the country. The Zionist leadership charged that the relief committee's moguls intended to eliminate Zionist influence.[33]

However, more was involved. In a letter to Otto Warburg, the German Zionist leader, written in April 1916, Brandeis described the subordinate position the Zionists held within the JDC. Although Zionists were to be found in all of its constituent agencies, they were "very much in the minority" whenever the joint executive committee dealt with "a clear Zionist question." Despite his repeated objections, Brandeis continued, JDC relief monies were channeled to Poland through the Juedisches Hilfskomite (the coordinating committee in Germany for aiding Jews in German-occupied Poland). The Hilfskomite was dominated by the anti-Zionist Hilfsverein. Thus in the event Polish territory should be reoccupied, Polish Jews would be accused of receiving aid from the enemy. No less distressing for Brandeis, the distributing agency, the Hilfskomite, was under the control of "assimilationists."

Brandeis described some of the minor concessions he had won from the JDC. Some payments would be sent directly to the American consulate in Warsaw for direct distribution to the local committee (where the Zionists were represented). He had also succeeded in having Otto Warburg, himself, and Max Bodenheimer, another leading German Zionist, added to the Hilfskomite. Surely, the inferior position of the Zionists in the JDC apparatus contributed to Brandeis's decision to place himself at the head of the congress movement after his initial hesitations. In all likelihood, this wartime experience influenced Brandeis's bitter fight to prevent his Zionist rival, Chaim Weizmann, the leading figure in the World Zionist Organization, from establishing the Keren Hayesod (Foundation Fund) campaign in the United States in the 1920s. Controlling the American operation of the main fund-raising instrument of the world organization constituted power. It meant directing (usually through proxy) the fund-raising apparatus with its functionaries, body of loyal contributors, many-sided public relations operations, and sometimes, the power of the purse. In the years to come, the path to national leadership included directing the campaigns.[34]

Nevertheless, controlling, or next best, holding the purse was not all. In the name of a functional consensus—a modicum of harmony—concessions were necessary. Despite the overwhelming power of the philanthropic purse which the Marshall-Warburg group possessed (71 percent of the JDC funds raised for overseas relief up to 1918 came from the American Jewish Relief Committee), the "big givers" bent their principles and practices to maintain JDC unity. Each organization preserved its autonomy even at the cost of duplication. Nor were all of the monies raised by a given organization channeled through the central coordinating body as they should have been. Marshall's mollifying reply to an angry letter by Warburg threatening to break off all ties with the Peoples Relief Committee captures the ruling sentiment of forbearance. "I sympathize very much with your criticism upon the Peoples Relief Committee," Marshall wrote.

> Their attitude is, to my mind, reprehensible. . . . There is, however, a point of view which you must not overlook, and which I believe to be of controlling importance. That is, "That it is better to bear the ills we have than to fly to others that we know not of." . . . It is always better to keep men of this kind within an organization than to deal with them when they are on the outside. They are less apt to do harm and mischief in the one case than in the other. Under existing conditions we can outvote them anyway in the Joint Distribution Committee.[35]

As in the case of the congress episode, wartime overseas relief tended to neutralize the contentiousness of American Jewry. As the congress movement provided an arena for new leadership talent, raising millions of dollars for relief work demanded innovative methods and cadres of administrators and specialists to deliver the services. Even the leaders of the American Jewish Relief Committee had no choice but to adapt the populist tactics of the Zionists and the radicals, fund-raising through mass meetings. In the prestigious halls of the main cities across the land the best orators of the affluent Jewish community exhorted middle- and upper-class gatherings of two and three thousand people to give. The prominent philanthropists announced their pledged sums prior to the general canvassing for contributions; women dropped their jewelry into baskets that were passed around.

President Wilson designated January 27, 1916, American Jewish Relief Day. In 1917, when the relief committee announced a goal of ten million dollars, Julius Rosenwald pledged $100,000 for every million dollars raised. When the goal was reached, Rosenwald received a letter of congratulations from President Wilson. Professionals and lay leaders carefully planned and orchestrated the events. The relief committee also reached out to the smaller communities. For the year 1918 it received contributions from 1,652 different localities. Horace Kallen noted that the success of the local relief campaigns was the result of the "democratization of American Jewish life," democratization, one should add, not in the sense of governance but rather as broad-based participation in fund-raising.[36]

The transfer and distribution of relief entailed negotiations with government authorities, with Jewish relief agencies abroad and with foreign powers. It required an administrative apparatus and a highly professional staff. To supervise these activities the governing body of the JDC attracted a younger generation of leaders especially those in finance. Its top leadership, in addition to Warburg and Marshall, included Paul Baerwald, Arthur and Herbert Lehman, Joseph C. Hyman and James N. Rosenberg— all drawn from the second generation of the American Jewish elite. The professional staff constituted an impressive Jewish civil service. Men like Jacob Billikopf, Boris Bogen, David Bressler, Julius Goldman, and Joseph A. Rosen managed the campaigns in the United States and vast relief network in Europe. Solomon Lowenstein, Lee K. Frankel, and Bernard Flexner, experts in child care, social work organization, and health, respectively, were sent on special missions to Europe. A member of the administrative committee described the division of responsibilities on the topmost level in this fashion: Marshall was in charge of political and legal matters, Arthur Lehman supervised business affairs, Cyrus Adler dealt with Jewish questions, Boris D. Bogen handled administration, and Warburg coordinated the entire operation.[37]

Later Jewish communal developments bear out the notion that the exercise of national leadership was limited to spheres of Jewish life which allowed the possibility for coalition building. Relief work—from the 1920s on, "constructive relief" such as support for Zionist settlement in Palestine—continued to offer the main area for the exercise of national leadership. One hears little about the democratization of Jewish life after 1920. The reconstituted American Jewish Congress was a pale replica of the original. But one does hear much about the politics of fund-raising. A weakened Zionist movement, prodded by Chaim Weizmann, invested most of its energies in organizing an American Keren Hayesod campaign, as we noted, which later developed into the United Palestine Appeal. The Zionists used it as a lever to bargain with the old establishment whose power base continued to be the JDC. Eventually, in 1929, after five years of maneuvering and negotiating—no less intricate than the earlier congress negotiations—Zionists and non-Zionists created the Jewish Agency on a common platform of the economic upbuilding of Palestine (which was in part an answer to the end of free immigration to America). Ironically, and understandably, the American Zionists were ambivalent about the entire undertaking. The chief architects were Marshall and Chaim Weizmann who represented the World Zionist Organization not the American Zionists. Brandeis's position during these years is also indicative of the submergence of the democratic issue. Limited to a behind-the-scenes role by his position as a Supreme Court justice, he nevertheless waged a bitter struggle to depoliticize the control of Zionist fund-raising. In 1920, Brandeis broke with Weizmann over the issue of introducing the Keren Hayesod campaign in the United States. Brandeis favored planned private investment in building up Palestine. In essence, he opted for business efficiency over democratic "inefficiency."[38]

In this context, Stephen Wise's standing and influence as a national leader is highly suggestive. Upon Brandeis's appointment to the Supreme Court in 1916, Wise assumed the direction of the congress movement and thus became the leading advocate of democracy in Jewish life, the masses against the classes, as the phrase went. But the masses weren't enough. Only in the mid-1930s would Wise return to center stage after a decade and a half in the Jewish political wilderness. President of the Zionist Organization of America and of the American Jewish Congress, and chairman of the executive committee of the World Jewish Congress and of the United Palestine Appeal, he once again invoked the principle of democracy in Jewish life. However, it was more a matter of recruiting numbers than electing leaders, and more a strategy for raising and controlling funds than creating a democratic polity. Membership lists and fund-raising campaigns were crucial in confronting the conservative opposition. Wise and, soon to follow him, Abba Hillel Silver now had the power base of the organizational infrastructure of the United Palestine Appeal in addition to a populist platform.

Beginning in 1939, the decisive struggle for power within the American Jewish community took place within the precincts of the United Jewish Appeal, established that year to coordinate the fund-raising campaigns of the Joint Distribution Committee and the United Palestine Appeal. In the 1940s, the younger Silver, who succeeded Wise as chairman of the United Palestine Appeal in 1938, challenged Wise's leadership of the growing Zionist camp. He used the basic organizational campaign methods to build the nationwide Zionist lobby that would prove so effective in winning American support for the establishment of the Jewish state in May 1948. Then, in early 1949, Silver himself was defeated in his bid to retain the commanding position he had won as the aggressive and imperious leader of American Jewry. Silver attempted to consolidate his position by insisting on the autonomy of the American Zionist movement in its relationship with the Jewish state. He argued that American Jewry, led by the Zionists, was an independent and coequal partner with Israel in Jewish affairs. The downfall of this last of the titans came not over the question of principle—what should be the relationship between Diaspora Jewry and the sovereign State of Israel?—but over control of the United Jewish Appeal. Who indeed should control the funds raised by American Jews? When he lost that battle he was effectively removed from office.[39]

In the years that followed such confrontations were avoided. The consensus among American Jews in support of Israel, welded during the struggle for the state and by the threats to its existence that followed, has held firmly. Ideological and social boundaries that once divided Zionists from non-Zionists and anti-Zionists have all but disappeared. For these reasons the national leadership of the consensus years have had less need for titans.

דער גרעסטער אידישער מארטש אויף דער װעלט.

"The Greatest Jewish March in the World," according to *Forverts*, December 5, 1905.

Vol. VIII. No. 24.　　　New York, June 9, 1916.

דער ענטפער · דער ארגומענט

"The Argument/The Answer." Could Jews be loyal Americans and also Jewish nation-alists? In the right panel of this sketch, the Jewish weekly *Der Groyser Kundes* (*The Big Stick*) of June 9, 1916, portrays banker Jacob Schiff who declares that "a Jew cannot be a Jewish nationalist and a good American at the same time." In the answer, on the left, Uncle Sam invites Louis D. Brandeis, "an enthusiastic Zionist and president of the American Zionists," to take his place on the Supreme Court.

Picnic of the Vilna Revolutionary Women's Branch of the Workmen's Circle, founded by immigrant members of the Russian Jewish labor Bund. Socialist women provided the backbone for such militant unions as the shirtwaist makers. Courtesy of YIVO Institute.

"She recognizes the 'unidentified.'" The Triangle Waist Company fire on March 25, 1911, took the lives of 146 garment workers, mostly young Jewish women, eight of whom were unidentified. The woman on the left represents the working class. The kneeling woman on the right holds a wreath labeled "From the Rescued." The artist's caption reads, "The working class—no matter where they came from and who they might be, they are my sacrifices—I know them, I know them." *Der Groyser Kundes*, April 7, 1911.

Sholom Aleichem's funeral, New York, May 14, 1916. The Jewish community united in paying homage to the Yiddish writer in a massive funeral. In the photograph, the cortege is moving along Yiddish newspaper row on East Broadway. Courtesy of YIVO Institute.

Collage of mastheads of Jewish newspapers and periodicals published in New York in 1917. Five Yiddish dailies, 16 weeklies, 4 monthlies, 17 trade union and professional journals, and 4 juvenile periodicals appeared regularly.

אין דער וועלט פון כל טוב

דרײ אין איינס — ראבי סטיפען ווייז

A satirical view of Jewish leaders. Each week *Der Groyser Kundes* lampooned a Jewish leader under the banner "In the ideal world." From right to left: "Rabbi Stephen S. Wise, his friends say, is the Herzl of the Jewish people [wordplay on *herz*, "heart," and Theodore Herzl, founding president of the World Zionist Organization]. His enemies say he is a pushy Jew. The truth is, his great eminence lies in his tongue." April 7, 1916.

אין דער וועלט פון כל טוב

דרײ אין איינס — לואיס מארשאל.

This cartoon depicts Louis Marshall. From right to left: "His friends say he illuminates Judaism. His enemies say he is Jacob Schiff's busybody. The truth is, he is a self-crowned monarch of a people without a land." July 21, 1916.

136

This cartoon satirizes Judah L. Magnes. From right to left: "His friends say he is a Jewish field marshal. His enemies say he is in the palm of Louis Marshall's hand. The truth is, he is the chief waiter of the Yahudim [German Jews]." December 8, 1916.

The Hadassah contingent, wearing the colors of the Allies, marching in a parade that opened the convention of the Zionist Organization of America, in Pittsburgh, June 1918.

A Zionist pioneer holding a rifle is juxtaposed against a minuteman of the American Revolution to identify the Zionist "freedom fighter" with the American struggle for independence. *New Palestine*, October 4, 1946. Courtesy of the Zionist Organization of America.

Jewish war veterans demonstrate against British policy in Palestine near the British Consulate in New York. Some of the signs read, "We Reject Partitioning. A Decimated Palestine Spells Death to Our People." "Palestine Is the Lidice of 1946." "We Support the Haganah." Courtesy of the Central Zionist Archives, Jerusalem.

Protest demonstration in front of the British Consulate in Philadelphia on July 17, 1946, sponsored by the American Zionist Emergency Council. Courtesy of Urban Archives, Temple University.

The Pioneer Women of the Labor Zionist Organization greet Golda Meir at their 1949 convention. Meir's American background, her commitment to Palestine, and her leading role in the labor movement made her a favorite of American Jewish circles.

President Dwight D. Eisenhower with Ralph E. Samuel, vice president of the American Jewish Committee and the chair of the Tercentenary Steering Committee, at the National Tercentenary Dinner launching the year-long celebration of the first Jewish settlement in the United States. Eisenhower delivered the keynote address. The tercentenary logo in the background shows a menorah capped by five-pointed "American" stars. Courtesy of YIVO Institute. October 20, 1954.

Marilyn Monroe joins leaders of the Junior Division of the United Jewish Appeal of Greater New York at a fund-raising dinner circa 1955. Courtesy of the Central Zionist Archives, Jerusalem.

Rabbi Abraham Heschel presenting Dr. Martin Luther King, Jr., with the Judaism and World Peace Award of the Synagogue Council of America on December 6, 1965. In his acceptance speech, King called for a negotiated end to the Vietnam War and warned that "an ugly, repressive sentiment to silence peacemakers is assuming shape." Courtesy of the American Jewish Historical Society, Waltham, Massachusetts.

# Part Two   Communal Politics and
## Public Culture, 1940–1990

# 7 Spiritual Zionists and Jewish Sovereignty

In a seminal essay, "The Americanization of Zionism, 1880–1930," Ben Halpern compared two strands of Zionism. One, secular and political, associated with Louis Brandeis, came to dominate the American Zionist scene. But in fact, the other, cultural and spiritual, Halpern claimed, was the more "thoroughly American variant of Zionism." It "succeeded most fully in impressing its stamp upon American Jewry at large." It was led by a group of "rabbinical Zionists around the Jewish Theological Seminary, beginning with their ally Judah Magnes and culminating in the fully developed theories of Mordecai Kaplan. Their religious revision of the ideas of Ahad Ha'am and Dubnow fitted well into the place allotted to the Jews as a religious community in the American scheme of things."[1] The discussion that follows examines one facet of this cultural-spiritual strand of American Zionism. It probes the response of four influential figures who defined themselves as cultural or spiritual Zionists to the two penultimate political events in Zionist history: the Balfour Declaration's expression of support for a Jewish national home in Palestine and the final struggle for the establishment of the Jewish State. Following the British cabinet's issuance of the Balfour Declaration in November 1917 and for several years thereafter, Israel Friedlaender, professor of Bible at the Jewish Theological Seminary, and Judah Magnes, an ordained Reform rabbi close to Seminary circles and chairman of the New York Kehillah, were the most important spiritual Zionists to contribute to the public debate that ensued. Nearly two and a half decades later, in May 1942, an extraordinary conference of American Zionists adopted the Biltmore Program calling for the establishment of a Jewish commonwealth in Palestine. From that moment until the Jewish state was proclaimed six years later, the question preoccupied the organized Jewish community. Once again, two spiritual Zionists, this time Mordecai Kaplan, long associated with the Seminary, and Louis Finkelstein, the Seminary's president, grappled with the meaning of Jewish sovereignty. For these Zionists, Jewish political sovereignty was problematic. The reason for this brings into focus some of the dilemmas inherent in spiritual Zionism and explains in part the political reticence of its ideologists, except for a brief period during the early years of the American Zionist movement.

During that short but revealing period, spiritual Zionists, in fact, directed the affairs of the movement. From 1905 to 1911, Magnes and Friedlaender held high office in the Federation of American Zionists and were its most prominent spokesmen. In 1905, Solomon Schechter, the esteemed president of the Seminary, officially joined the Federation and soon after issued his influential statement on Zionism which stressed its religious-national character. "The rebirth of Israel's national consciousness and the revival of Israel's religion," he declared, "are inseparable."[2] Although Magnes, Friedlaender and their coworkers among the leaders of the movement subscribed to Schechter's pronouncement, their conception of what Zionism should be in America was more inclusive than his. Their beliefs are best understood through a brief consideration of the Zionist program they formulated.

The hallmark of their program was their calculated attempt to integrate the needs of American Jews with Zionism's goals. These pragmatic spiritual Zionists emphasized those phases of the world Zionist platform that they believed best enabled the American movement to appeal to the masses of American Jews, and they sidestepped ideological positions that appeared inappropriate in the American context. One example, their shunning of the preeminence that the world movement assigned to political action, will suffice. In June 1906, in a plaintive letter to David Wolffsohn, the president of the World Zionist Organization, Magnes, the newly elected secretary of the Federation, requested a presidential message of encouragement for the Federation's annual convention. While not questioning the "thorough political character" of the world movement, Magnes asked Wolffsohn, "if not officially, at least morally," to sanction the support of "active work in Palestine." The world organization's preoccupation with political work, Magnes complained, important as it was "from the point of view of the development of politics in Europe," was of no interest to American Jews.[3]

In fashioning an indigenous American Zionism that would speak to American Jewry as a whole, the spiritual Zionists confronted, as their predecessors had, the dilemma posed by the fundamental premise of classical Zionism: Jewish homelessness, a problem that was to be solved only through geographic concentration in Eretz Israel, did not apply to American Jews. Indeed, on first sight, the mass migration to America disproved the central thesis of Zionism's solution of the Jewish problem. In coping with the paradox, the spiritual Zionists expanded upon the formulations they inherited from such early leaders of the movement as Richard Gottheill. In the first place, the basic tenant of Zionism was declared valid for the *other* Jewish diasporas—not for the American diaspora, which was exceptional. *To keep it exceptional,* immigration was best deflected to Palestine, which would advance the cause and avert the creation of a "Jewish problem" in America. In the second place, the spiritual Zionists explicitly accepted the permanency and desirability of Jewish life in America. Although never stated so baldly, self-interest demanded a strong Zionist movement in America, both to channel immigration elsewhere and to enrich culturally and direct spiritually a community made up of growing numbers of new immigrants adrift in a sea of social and personal turmoil. The programmatic side of the dual strategy the spiritual Zionists adopted consisted, on the one hand, of organizational innovations such as establishing a Zionist fraternal order to appeal to the immigrants' predilection for mutual aid societies, and the publication of a Yiddish weekly to address the same public. But the leadership failed dismally in these undertakings. On the other hand, the leaders located American Zionism firmly within the Jewish community. The demand for the democratization of Jewish communal life, a cardinal precept of Zionism in Europe, was adapted to American circumstances. The examples par excellence of this strategy were the early attempts to create a nationally representative body to speak for American Jewry (a "congress"), and on a local level to elect councils, *kehillahs*, to support and coordinate the philanthropic, educational and religious undertakings of the community.[4]

The other component of the program the spiritual Zionists espoused—its cultural and spiritual dimension—was its most important legacy. Israel Friedlaender, Judah Magnes, and Mordecai Kaplan—and, hovering in the background, Solomon Schechter—placed great stress on the benefits Zionism would bring to American Jews. Simply put, they presented Zionism as a cultural and spiritual movement that would become, in the words of Schechter, "the mighty bulwark against the incessantly assailing forces of assimilation." At the core of their Zionism was Judaism, as Schechter had formulated it, which Friedlaender defined as "a national religion, its bearer a national community." The national religion had preserved the memory of a national life in the land of Israel and the hope for the return to Zion. The rebirth Zionism promised would bring about a rapprochement between the contending definitions of the Jewish people which had marked its entry into modern life: a religious faith or a national entity. Fulfilling Zionism would go hand in hand with a religious revival anchored in historic Judaism.[5] However, in contrast with Schechter who rejected any compromise with Jewish secularism, the Magnes-Friedlaender group posited a different priority.[6] Magnes aphorized, "Zionism means battle on behalf of Jews and Judaism. There can be no Judaism without the Jews. Zionism is the battle to save Judaism by saving the Jews." For the Jews of Eastern Europe it meant fighting "for their equal political rights, for their economic betterment, for an eventual place of refuge for thousands in our ancient home, the land of Israel." Borrowing from Ahad Ha'am, he continued, "If in the lands of oppression, the Jews be held in bodily bondage, in the lands of freedom all too many are spiritual slaves." Zionism's task was "to make Jews free . . . in body and spirit."[7]

The spiritual Zionism of Friedlaender and Magnes was, consequently, all-inclusive. As nationalists, they considered the preservation of the Jewish people wherever it might be, as transcending all particularistic conceptions of Judaism and Zionism. Each saw himself primarily as an educator of American Jewry. On the lecture circuit, in articles and books, and not infrequently from the pulpit or university podium, they addressed the contemporary problems of American Jews: Jewish group survival, cultural and spiritual continuity and revival, and the place of Zionism and Judaism in the life of American Jews. They rejected with vehemence the negation-of-*galut* concept. If they despaired at times about the cultural and spiritual state of the new Jewish center in America, the Zionist revival in Eretz Israel promised to radiate spiritual and cultural sustenance. Here was the importance of Zionism for American Jews. In a word, for these Zionists, education, rather than politics, was the decisive Zionist act.[8]

This spiritual conception of an Americanized Zionism coexisted with a secular version that rather quickly became the prevailing one with the advent of Brandeis to leadership in 1914. The reasons are known: the increasing secularization of Jewish life, the political cast of the new Zionism, and the "nonsectarian" emphasis of a movement seeking the broadest common denominator. But surely the most powerful and immediate factor was the cataclysm of war. With all of European Jewry caught up in the conflagaration and the tiny Zionist settlement in Palestine facing annihilation, forceful leaders were required more than devoted educators. It was this sense of extreme peril that explains Brandeis's astonishing acceptence of the leadership of American Zionism. "Organize," "mobilize," "numbers," "fundraising," "efficiency" became the watchwords.

In accounting for the enormous growth of the movement under Brandeis's leadership, more was involved than his eminence, political acumen and organizational ability. At a time when a militant nativism increasingly demanded unconditional assimilation, and the compact masses of Yiddish-speaking immigrants loomed so large and threatening in their alienism in the eyes of the acculturated Jewish establishment, Zionism's ultimate goal of national sovereignty for the Jewish people raised the specter of dual loyalties. Spokesmen for Reform Judaism aggravated these fears by intensifying their ideological war against Zionism, which they considered not only historically and theologically false but politically perilous. Brandeis addressed these issues. Melvin Urofsky in his studies of American Zionism has ascribed the movement's success to Brandeis's seminal role in formulating an American Zionist ideology which legitimized it in American terms. By defining Zionism as the highest ideal of the Jewish people— the quest for social justice—and equating that ideal as America's highest as well, Brandeis identified Zionism with Americanism. A typical Brandeis remark pointed to the "self-governing" Zionist colonies being built by "our Jewish Pilgrim Fathers." These models of progressive democracy were proof of the compatibility of American and Zionist values. "The descendents of the Pilgrim Fathers," he commented on another occasion, "should not find it hard to understand and sympathize with it [Zionism]."[9]

However, the Brandeisian formula failed to lay to rest an inner disquiet. Whenever Jewish sovereignty in Palestine became an international issue, it distressed American Jews, including some Zionists. In fact, when the Balfour Declaration was issued, Brandeis wrote privately that he neither advised nor desired an independent state. He considered statehood "a most serious menace."[10] At such times, the spiritual Zionists could be eloquent defenders of the Zionist cause. Religious figures occupied a respected place in American public life. When the spiritual Zionists invoked scripture and theology, they effectively refuted the attacks of classical Reform Judaism and Christian anti-Zionism. By placing Zionism in the prophetic tradition one stole the thunder of the Reformers and spoke to Christian America in terms it understood. Friedlaender chided a gentile American journalist who had asked why Jews required a distinct nationhood. "The Jewish prophets," Friedlaender explained, "were both universalists and nationalists, believing in the realization of the universal ideal through the channel of national existence." But "nationhood" (or, later, "peoplehood") was not sovereignty. Once the sovereignty issue arose, the spiritual Zionists had to grapple with politics.[11]

When the British issued the Balfour Declaration, neither Magnes nor Friedlaender held Zionist office. Magnes had resigned his office in 1915; Friedlaender followed a year later. Both men were casualties of the Zionist challenge of the hegemony the elitist American Jewish Committee had maintained in national Jewish affairs. They had belonged to both groups. Magnes remained with the Committee while Friedlaender withdrew from both bodies. Where Magnes moved into the broader sphere of American politics, becoming a leading spokesman of the anti-war movement and an advocate of civil liberties and other radical causes, Friedlaender continued to maintain close ties with the Zionist leadership. In fact, until his departure for Europe in January 1920 on a relief mission that ended tragically with his murder in the Ukraine, he served as one of the movement's best public advocates.[12]

Friedlaender's first published response to the Balfour Declaration came only weeks after it was issued. The article, entitled "Zionism and Religious Judaism," appeared in the the *New York Evening Post*, at that time New York's most liberal newspaper, in December 1917. It was reprinted shortly thereafter in pamphlet form by the Zionist Organization of America. The article, addressed to a wide public, expounded the significance of the Balfour Declaration on the high ground of religious ideals.[13]

It was an effective apologia. Clearly, Friedlaender wrote, the importance of Palestine as the connecting link between three continents and three religions was incalculable, whether considered from the political, economic, or religious point of view. Friedlaender chose to deal with Jewish resettlement from the religious perspective. For those Jews who believe that Judaism "has a religious message to the world and to those Christians who share or appreciate these sentiments," the religious aspect was of "paramount consideration."

The "religion of Judaism," Friedlaender explained, was indissolubly bound up with the homeland of the Jewish people. Only in the middle of the nineteenth century had some modern rabbis, catering to the desire for civil and political emancipation, begun preaching the dispersion of the Jews as divine providence. In a phrase that surely challenged the Reformers and his Christian readers, Friedlaender asserted that the "restoration of Israel to its ancient soil was an indispensable condition for the realization of the religious mission of Judaism." Judaism was embodied in "concrete human institutions, in a nation, a commonwealth, a state. . . . The ideal of Jewish prophecy, Justice and Righteousness, presupposed a definite social order, such as can only be realized in a body politic." No conflict existed between renewed nationhood and universalism. "Zion is conceived as the place where in an ideal future the 'Word of the Lord' will proceed to the rest of the world."[14]

Six months later, in June 1918, in an address delivered at Carnegie Hall at the opening of the annual convention of the New York Kehillah, Friedlaender dwelt on the historic significance of the Balfour Declaration. He acclaimed Britain's role. "A great Government has recognized the right of the Jewish people to be a people, and the claim of Palestine to be Eretz Yisrael, the Land of Israel." It was not political expediency that had prompted Britain to act, but the manifestation of "that large-hearted policy which modern England has always pursued toward our people." The declaration had also vindicated Wilson leading the American people into war. Victory would assure the rights of the smaller nationalities. "Palestine represents [to us] the same ideals for which our country, for which the United States, is fighting, . . . ideals of justice and righteousness, the ideals that right stands above might, that spirituality stands above materialism."[15]

In his peroration, Friedlaender mentioned "commonwealth" with its implied notion of Jewish political sovereignty. The passage reads:

> Upon the gates of the Third Jewish Commonwealth will be inscribed the same prophetic words which greeted the establishment of the Second Jewish commonwealth:
> "Not by might, nor by power,
> But by My spirit, saith the Lord of Hosts."[16]

The optimistic and congratulatory tone of the address is understandable given the time and place. A wartime America was in the grips of a patriotic fever that few (Magnes being one of them) dared resist. Britain was about to complete the conquest of Palestine, and Wilson's pronouncements on the postwar peace were clothed in prophetic visions. Friedlaender's assignment was to call for Jewish unity, inspire and encourage, and stimulate material support for Zionist work. He used "commonwealth" not as a political term—it aroused no controversy—but as an inspirational text, a rallying cry of the spirit.

Much as the Zionists played down the question of Jewish political sovereignty, indeed, evaded it when they could, opponents of Zionism focused on it. One line of attack faulted a policy that led to a Jewish state when Arabs outnumbered Jews six to one. How could one ignore "the Arab problem"? In an internal memorandum addressed to the Zionist Organization of America, "A Few Suggestions Concerning the Relations between the Jews and the Arabs," Friedlaender defined the importance of the issue. (Undated, the memorandum was most likely written in early 1919 at the time that the Middle East was a center of intense diplomatic maneuvering at the Peace Conference.) Among the American Zionists none but Magnes had given the matter any serious thought until then. Friedlaender brought to bear the authority of the expert, an Arabist and scholar of medieval Arab-Jewish history.

The realization of the Zionist claims, Friedlaender explained, would undoubtedly stimulate Arab national aspirations. The "Arab problem" would surely affect *"the future Jewish Commonwealth in Palestine* [emphasis mine]. Whatever may prove to be its geographic extension, it is bound to appear as a tiny Hebrew island in the midst of an Arabic ocean." Not only will the Jews in Palestine be surrounded by a "politically rejuvenated Arabic speaking population" from the Atlantic in the West to Persia in the East, but within "the future Jewish Commonwealth itself, the Arabic element will, for a considerable time at least, form the majority, and for a much longer time, a substantial minority of the Palestinian population." Rather than ask how a Jewish commonwealth would govern under such circumstances (which Magnes did), Friedlaender proposed a program of education and public relations. Jews would learn about Arabic life and culture. The Arab world would be informed about the vast Jewish literature in the Arabic language created during the "Golden Age."[17]

In April 1919, Friedlaender published his most notable defense of Zionism, a rejoinder to a sweeping indictment of Zionism by Herbert Adams Gibbons, author of *The New Map of Europe* and Paris correspondent of *The Century*. Friedlaender dismissed the objections Gibbons had based on geopolitics, religion, and moral law. He was especially irked by Gibbons's argument that "a Zionist state in Palestine" flouted the Wilsonian vision of a just peace because of the enormous Arab majority. It was "the only objection that is apt to command the serious attention of the Zionists," Friedlaender wrote, "because in their desire to establish a commonwealth on the foundations of the ancient Jewish ideals of justice and righteousness, they are anxious to avert anything that might in the slightest degree conflict with these ideals." Friedlaender cited the Emir Feisal's public assurance of his readiness to cooperate with the Zionists, and he rejected the claim that the Palestinian Arabs were in fact opposed to Zionism. Arab opposition came almost entirely from Syrian Arabs and Egyptians, Friedlaender claimed. The country had room for large population growth, and the rights of the "non-Jewish communities" were safeguarded. However, the thrust of his argument was that Palestine was "neither historically nor emotionally" an Arabic country. "When the Arabs dream of their ancient glory . . . they think of Nejd and Hedjaz, the cradle of their race and religion; they think of the splendor of the Ommiads at Damascus, of the magnificence of the Abbassides at Bagdad, of the power of the Fatimites at Cairo; but they do not think of Jerusalem." During the twelve hundred years the Arabs had lived in Palestine they "had never developed an Arabic culture worth speaking of." The handful of Zionists who had come to Palestine and been willing "to brave the dangers and hardships, which can be paralleled only by the similar experiences of the early colonists of New England, have succeeded in setting up . . . the beginnings of a civilization which . . . is the greatest cultural factor in Palestine today."[18]

It was a brilliant exposition for the general public, weaving the religious and political imperatives into a tight design, and then embellishing them with biblical and American motifs. Friedlaender was at his most eloquent pleading the religious and moral case. The Zionist Organization promptly reprinted the article for mass circulation.[19]

Of the four spiritual Zionists we are considering, Magnes was the most political and the most fearless. Under enormous pressure to cease speaking on behalf of pacifism and radicalism lest it stir up antisemitism ("you are giving aid and comfort to the enemy," Louis Marshall, his brother-in-law, told him), Magnes rejected the demand. For Magnes, higher principles, Jewish and American principles, compelled him to follow his conscience. "This is not the first time that the Jews have been threatened with, or have had to suffer from antisemitism because of their convictions," he explained in a letter to a friend. Zionism and Jewish sovereignty were no exceptions to the moral compulsion to speak the truth.[20]

In December 1917, soon after the Balfour Declaration was issued, Magnes addressed a fund-raising meeting sponsored by the People's Relief Committee. The talk masked a philosophic rejection of Jewish political sovereignty. Under the title "The Jewish People—A Spiritual Force," Magnes offered the familiar notions of a "Jewish national spirituality" with its "international" commitment to the universality of humankind. Jewish nationalism was not arrogant, he declared. It "stood for the eternal right of every minority to be true to its innermost convictions." It did not "desire the territories of other men, it is not a material, an economic, a political imperialism." It sought "an empire of the spirit, that is, the recognition by all men of the Fatherhood of God and the Brotherhood of Man."[21]

Lest his universalism be equated with what he considered to be the vapid, passive rhetoric of Reform Judaism, he lashed out at the war patriotism of "the Reformed Jewish Church." It had made a sham of its doctrine of Israel's mission to bring the prophetic message of brotherhood to the world. Not a single Reform leader had spoken out on "behalf of the revolutionary Jewish idea of the Fatherhood of God and the Brotherhood of Man" and the Jewish people's "inherent repugnance to the spilling of blood."[22] (Privately, Magnes put the matter even more explicitly: he praised "the anti-militarist outburst on the part of the Jewish masses and their elemental passion for peace." That "the Jewish masses have expressed themselves as they have," was one of the glories of Jewish life. It distinguished "*Jewish prophetic nationalism* [emphasis mine] from the heathen nationalism of the Christian nations.")[23] In concluding his address, Magnes gave Palestine its due. The land was offering "this ancient people a renewal of youth." Perhaps, he mused, "new thoughts, new ideas, radical and revolutionary action will come from the Jewish Center."[24] But neither at this time nor in speeches that followed did Magnes criticize the Balfour Declaration directly. Clearly, he was curbing his impulse to lash out at the declaration, as he later did, as the misbegotten offspring of British imperialism.

Finally, in August 1921, Magnes published a letter on the political significance of the declaration in the London *Jewish Chronicle*. Years later he explained the circumstances that led him to break his silence on the subject. His manifesto—for it was more a manifesto than a letter to the editor—was composed immediately after the Jaffa riots of May 1921 when forty-seven Jews were killed. The letter was also "an answer to a question of some of my friends in America as to why I could not reenter Zionist life." Obviously the timing of the letter was Magnes's way of reentering Zionist life. It appeared a week before the first World Zionist Congress convened following the war.[25]

"Wartime Zionism," Magnes began his piece, "aroused swollen expectations among the Jews, just as the war did among other peoples. Palestine was to be presented to the Jews as a political gift, and the Jewish people was to be delivered bag and baggage, to a single Imperialistic Government in return for a political declaration." The Jews should have learned long ago that "Jewish politics must be independent politics and skeptical of all political favors."[26] Palestine could be won, not through war or political privilege or the oppression of one's neighbors, but on equal political terms with others. All the Zionists required were the "rights of free people anywhere in the world," certainly the rights of Jews in Palestine, "of free immigration, free land purchase, and free cultural development." This was not political favoritism. It did not "compel good men to interpret 'self-determination' as meaning one thing throughout the world and another thing for Palestine." Referring to the rejoicing that followed the San Remo conference, which had incorporated the Balfour Declaration in the League of Nations mandate and conferred it upon the British, Magnes wrote:

Almost every principle of democracy, of self-determination is denied. The fact is that Palestine has five or six times as many Arabs as Jews. You speak of "historic rights" of the Jews to offset the claims of the present-day Arab majority. I am aware of the way in which historic rights and strategic rights and economic rights have been manipulated whenever it suited the needs of the conquerors. Yet, I, too, believe in the "historic right" of the Jewish people to the Land of Israel . . . the free and unhindered opportunity to come into the land . . . and to become, in the course of time, if they can, the preponderant element of the population.[27]

A remarkable dualism marks Magnes's political philosophy. Realism led him to admit that the mandate offered the Jews opportunities for developing the country. Yet it was folly not to recognize the harsh truth that "economic imperialism" was not to be relied upon. This was all the more reason to remember the old adage, "Put not your trust in princes." What remained? "The one kind of *realpolitik* with any chance," Magnes concluded, "must be based upon simple justice, because this is the Jewish tradition." It was just, for example, for the Zionists "to be inexorable and unyielding" in the struggle for free Jewish immigration.[28]

Soon after the publication of the manifesto-letter, Magnes settled in Jerusalem. In 1930, when he had become chancellor of the Hebrew University, he published a small booklet, *Like All the Nations?* It was prompted by the Arab riots of August 1929 in which more than four hundred Jews were killed or wounded. Magnes included the 1921 letter in the booklet "in order to show that my present attitude is not new, and that it is the result of a view of life and a conception of the ethical function of Judaism, and does not just spring from tactical or strategic motives."[29]

Neither Louis Finkelstein nor Mordecai Kaplan is associated with the great debate that rose over the question of Jewish sovereignty in the early 1940s and which culminated in the declaration of the State of Israel in 1948. However, like Friedlaender and Magnes, Finkelstein and Kaplan were authentic voices in the tradition of spiritual Zionism. Peripheral as their positions were to the political struggle for statehood, their thoughts on sovereignty are important for understanding that strand of thought among the spiritual Zionists that I have discussed thus far.

Kaplan, in his sixties during the period we are considering, was at the height of his influence in his dual capacity as a member of the faculty of the Jewish Theological Seminary and leader of the Reconstructionist movement. Finkelstein had recently become president of the Seminary. A prolific scholar, he became an innovative administrator. He not only broadened the Seminary's influence in the Jewish community at large, but he also created a center where scholars and clergy of all faiths examined the moral and social issues that appeared so acute in the dark years of the war.

Kaplan and Finkelstein shared a similar Zionist outlook. They supported a Jewish national home in Palestine, saw it as an asylum for persecuted Jews, acclaimed the accomplishments of Zionist pioneering, were inspired by the revival of Hebrew culture, and assigned the national home a major place in building a creative Jewish life in America. They insisted that Jewish nationalism and religion were inextricably linked. In these sentiments, they faithfully reflected the views of a large segment of American Zionists, and in time, of most of American Jewry.

However, in the critical years leading to the establishment of the state, they entertained serious reservations about statehood as the immediately attainable or desirable goal. In maintaining their position they were moved by several political considerations: belief in liberal internationalism as expressed in America's war aims and dread that the struggle for statehood would bring war and destruction to the Yishuv. Finkelstein also feared that a secularized state would compromise Judaism's moral and spiritual values. Kaplan weighed the effect of a sovereign Jewish state on the unity of the Jewish people.

Today, more than fifty years after the Second World War ended, it is difficult to comprehend the depth of faith many Americans had in the new international order that they hoped would assure peace and guarantee human rights. Harry Truman captured this sentiment when he told the founding conference of the United Nations in June 1945, "Before us is the supreme chance to establish a world-rule of reason—to create an enduring peace under the guidance of God."[30]

However, during the interwar years, only a small band of internationalists—keepers of the faith—lobbied and preached for that "supreme chance." It included pacifists, champions of disarmament, and supporters of a stronger League of Nations and world court. Liberal church organizations and leading Protestant ministers and theologians were prominent advocates of one or another of the programs. For Christian liberals, internationalism was an integral part of a religious commitment to social justice.[31] So it was with the Central Conference of American Rabbis. From the early 1920s to the mid-1930s, the conferences adopted strong antiwar positions and resolutions calling on America to join the League and the

World Court. In 1932, the Rabbinical Assembly followed suit. It formed a Committee on Social Justice that established ties with the National Council for the Prevention of War and the Committee of International Justice of the Federal Council of Churches, among other groups. The committee's first public statement, addressed to the Geneva Disarmament Conference, was a resolution favoring universal disarmament and expressing the need for "instruments and agencies" to resolve international disputes.[32]

The cumulative effect of the failures to contain aggression in the 1930s, the outbreak of world war, and finally America's entry into the war fomented a national debate on organizing the postwar world. Civic agencies appointed planning commissions and recruited experts to prepare proposals. The Federal Council of Churches, for example, established the Commission to Study the Bases of a Just and Durable Peace in December 1940. Almost simultaneously the American Jewish Committee created the Research Institute on Peace and Post-War Problems, and the American Jewish Congress and World Jewish Congress established the Institute for Jewish Affairs. After Pearl Harbor, pressure mounted on the State Department to begin designing an international organization to keep the peace.[33]

Of particular significance for the debate over the wisdom of pressing for a Jewish commonwealth, which was about to begin, was an early notion of the direction the organization of peace should go. John Foster Dulles articulated the sentiment well in an address before a Methodist conference in May 1941. The moving spirit behind the formation of the Federal Council's Commission on a Just Peace and its chairman, he undoubtedly reflected in his remarks several months of commission deliberation. "The sovereignty system," Dulles stated, "is no longer consonant either with peace or justice. It is imperative that there be a transition to a new order."[34] That such thoughts were current in liberal internationalist circles is corroborated by a letter Judah Magnes sent to Felix Frankfurter from Jerusalem in November 1941. Magnes, whose views on international affairs were deeply influenced by these circles, wrote: "I come more and more to the conclusion that there should be the smallest possible number of small states with independent armies and independent foreign policies. Armies and foreign relations should be in the hands of unions or federations. Of course to work out 'the national genius,' a state ought to be absolutely and completely sovereign and independent. But the ills resulting from this are so massive that it is better that the 'national' genius suffer than that these states and peoples plunge the world into misery through their exaggerated national egos."[35]

Finkelstein, as we shall see, shared these views in common with the group of Protestant theologians at the Union Theological Seminary who were among the most influential activists in the cause of internationalism. He also shared with them a broader concern: mobilizing the spiritual and moral resources of the nation, no less than its material resources, in a total war against the forces of darkness. The ecumenical notion of a Judeo-Christian tradition answered the nation's need for unity and amity. It also enjoined Christians to repudiate the central thesis of Nazi ideology—the demonic, depraved nature of Jews and Judaism—and to link the war against Nazism and antisemitism with the defense of democratic values. At the annual Conference on Science, Philosophy and Religion and Their Relation to the Democratic Way, which Finkelstein was instrumental in organizing, Christian theologians portrayed the Judeo-Christian tradition as the "spiritual underpinning of democracy" and the antithesis of fascism. The Hebrew prophets served as the hyphen that made the tradition one. On a more profound level, Reinhold Niebuhr reflected in 1944 on how as a Christian theologian, he had "sought to strengthen the Hebraic-prophetic content of the Christian tradition." Thus much of the rhetoric explaining America's war aims carried the universal message of the prophetic ethic.[36]

Finkelstein brought this world view of a Judeo-Christian universalism to bear on specific Jewish questions. Two of Finkelstein's essays on Zionism illustrate this milieu. Both were published in the *New Palestine*, the journal of the Zionist Organization of America, the first in May 1943 and the second in September 1944. Their titles are illuminating: "Judaism, Zionism, and an Enduring Peace," and "Zionism and World Culture." The core idea of these essays is the universal significance of the Jewish experience.

As one would expect from Finkelstein, his argument was historical and theological. His 1943 essay began by expounding the place of Palestine in Judaism. "For the Jewish religion," Finkelstein explained, "Palestine is the land of the Lord, set aside from the beginning as a unique sanctuary for distinctive forms of communion with God." Although "especial merit attaches to those who dwell in the Holy Land . . . the Jew regards his native land, wherever that may be, as his hearth and home." Palestine was the spiritual home for all Israel. How then was Palestine linked to world peace? The prophetic vision of redemption, of the brotherhood of man, and of a world of enduring peace included the reestablishment of a Jewish homeland in Palestine. In the world struggle between pagan chauvinism and the prophetic doctrine, "the prophetic and rabbinic form for world peace" mandated the "restoration of Judaism to Palestine." As Palestine, the "home of the prophetic tradition," distilled the "moral basis for medieval and modern civilization, so the Holy Land potentially could unify all mankind."[37]

In discussing Judaism and world peace, Finkelstein echoed Reform Judaism's classic formulation. Providentially, history had prepared Israel for its unique role. Scattered across the earth, the Jews had become conversant with different civilizations. "Parent to Christianity and Islam, Judaism bears certain similarities with the Oriental faiths." The reestablishment of a Jewish homeland in Palestine would be the means of developing better mutual appreciation between East and West. Finkelstein failed to mention "exile," so central to the Judaic tradition. The Jews had been prepared by their bondage in Egypt to proclaim freedom to the world and by medieval persecution to defend their right to be different; their dispersion among the nations was fortuitous. With its nucleus in the Holy Land, Judaism was prepared to serve mankind.[38]

Finally, Finkelstein considered the political history of the Jewish national home, which he infused with transcendent significance. Echoing his generation's dashed hopes in the aftermath of the last war, he wrote: "At the end of the First World War mankind was on the threshold of prophetic fulfillment. A world association of nations all but emerged; and with it a recreated Jewish homeland in Palestine. But mankind faltered. The League of Nations became an instrument of power-politics, and the resettlement of Palestine was caught in calculations of empire." Only if mankind proved capable of rising to "Prophetic spiritual levels would a world association of nations emerge and under its aegis a Jewish homeland in Palestine."

Finkelstein acknowledged the encouraging signs of a spiritual rebirth in Jewish Palestine. Without parallel in modern times, the Yishuv was attempting to implement the prophetic and Talmudic ideals of justice, and alone among the peoples of the world it opened its arms to the stricken. But, he warned, Jewish national secularism would subvert the promise. Indeed, in his 1944 article, Finkelstein complained that the basic concept of Judaism as a ministry and a service, and of the Jewish people as a Kingdom of Priests had all but disappeared. "We have failed to make the world understand that we Zionists consider the establishment of a Jewish Palestine indispensable to a reformation of world culture as well as one of the major expressions of that reformation itself."[39]

Dominant though the religious motif was in his interpretation of Zionism, with its implicit rejection of a secular state, Finkelstein objected to a Jewish state on other grounds. "The creation of an enduring peace," he wrote in his 1943 essay, "presupposes an active cooperative relationship among nations and peoples, which make the question of statehood less and less relevant; while emphasis on national sovereignty anywhere must be fatal to civilization."[40]

The influence of internationalist thought is apparent in Finkelstein's remarks before an executive committee meeting of the American Jewish Committee in October 1943. The meeting was called to decide whether to withdraw from the American Jewish Conference after it had gone on record in favor of a Jewish commonwealth in Palestine. Finkelstein opposed a commonwealth and favored withdrawal. Morris Waldman, the executive secretary of the committee, describing the meeting in his memoirs, noted how influential Finkelstein's remarks were. Among other reasons, Finkelstein opposed a Jewish commonwealth because "by saying we want the Jewish commonwealth in Palestine . . . we are helping to defeat that which is the salvation of the Jews, as of all other people, namely, the creation of states on political and economic and geographical bases and without regard to ethnic religious and other divisions." In the mind of many liberal thinkers the national state had fostered the chauvinism, intolerance and extremism that had culminated in the satanic power now threatening to subjugate the free world. Surely other political arrangements were possible which would further the Zionist undertaking in Palestine. In fact, abandoning the unrealistic demand for a Jewish commonwealth would place the Zionists and their confederates in a far stronger position to gain concessions from Britain, above all the abrogation of the White Paper.[41]

If liberal internationalism rooted as it was in religious and humanistic visions of a better world shaped Finkelstein's understanding of Zionism, Kaplan, the pragmatist, approached Zionism as a resource for maintaining Jewish life in the diaspora. Living in two civilizations the American Jew, in Kaplan's celebrated analysis, subordinated the Jewish to the American. "Judaism is unlikely to survive, either as an ancillary or as a coordinate civilization, unless it thrive as a primary civilization in Palestine."[42] Only in the environmental conditions of a Jewish national home could Judaism become a modern, creative civilization. Writing these words in 1934, Kaplan contended that the Yishuv was, in fact, fulfilling this mission. "Palestine has become to the Jews everywhere 'a symbol of corporate existence.' All Jewish activity throughout the Diaspora which bears a constructive character and has in it the promise of permanence, derives from the inspiration of Palestine." Palestine's present influence upon the diaspora was "but a dim forecast of the incalculable spiritual impetus that Jewish life will acquire when Palestine civilization shall have grown to its full stature."[43]

Although Kaplan assigned a less transcendent, more temporal role to

Palestine than Finkelstein had, it did not follow that sovereignty was a prerequisite for fulfilling its obligations. Ironically, Kaplan's rejection of the doctrine of the Chosen People, his religious naturalism, and his concept of Judaism as an evolving religious civilization gave Jewish Palestine even greater weight in his scheme for Jewish survival. In a human-centered universe, surely the power of sovereignty offered the potential strength to this end. Moreover, a state promised to alleviate the most pressing problem of all, the saving of the remnant of European Jewry. Nevertheless, in the years the debate raged over statehood, Kaplan's main concern remained the spiritual and cultural condition of the Jews.

Power and politics, however, could not be ignored. As a theologian and an American democrat, Kaplan remained wary of state power. In 1934, he asserted in *Judaism As a Civilization* that nationhood did not confer the right to absolute self-determination. If democratic nationalism was true to itself, "it would have to concede the right of the Jews throughout the world to retain their status as a nation, though the retention of such status involves their becoming a new type of nation—an international nation with a national home to give them cultural and spiritual unity." In conceding this right to the Jews, "democratic nationalism would be living up to its own ethical conception, the conception which sees in internationalism the only hope of civilization."[44]

Twelve years later, as the final stage of the campaign for a Jewish state began, Kaplan addressed the issue once more. What Zionism required, he declared, was not "the sort of irresponsible and obsolete national sovereignty that modern nations claim for themselves. This doctrine of 'absolute national sovereignty' with its assumption that the interests of one's own nation must always override those of other nations, is responsible for the international anarchy of the modern world, and is liable to bring about a catastrophe that will destroy the very foundation of human civilization."[45]

In the *Future of the American Jew*, which he completed in February 1947, he redefined "commonwealth" in typically Kaplanian fashion so that it no longer meant sovereignty but acquired a spiritual and ethical resonance. "A Jewish commonwealth in Eretz Yisrael has become indispensable to us, individually and as an indivisible people," he announced early in the book. But commonwealth status, he explained later, merely implied the occupation of a definite territory and self-government. "The Jewish commonwealth in Eretz Yisrael," he added in italics, "need not and should not be a sovereign nation." Indeed, the term "nation" should be avoided for "it connotes first and foremost an organization of power, in a combative sense.

Religion is altogether precluded, and culture or civilization is decidedly secondary."[46]

Kaplan's understanding of the term "commonwealth" reveals how he was influenced by American political culture. "Four States of the United States are officially designated 'Commonwealth.' They are Massachusetts, Pennsylvania, Virginia and Kentucky." Kaplan then offered this analogy: the Jewish Commonwealth, like Pennsylvania, would command the loyalty and interests of its own citizens; just as Pennsylvania had no political control over citizens of the remaining states of the federal union, neither would the Jewish commonwealth have sovereign power over the diaspora communities. Most striking of all in the analogy are Kaplan's American perceptions of the Jewish diaspora as a federalist polity and the limited sovereignty assigned to a commonwealth.[47]

Despite his notion of limited sovereignty, Kaplan began to edge toward support of a fully sovereign Jewish state in the spring and summer of 1947. Viewing the question of power instrumentally, the means of reaching a larger end that was the survival of the Jewish people, he was able to abandon on pragmatic grounds the ideological stance he had adopted earlier. On the evening of November 29, 1947, following the announcement of the UN General Assembly vote approving the partition plan, Kaplan wrote in his diary, "Considering the dreadful finality that an adverse vote might have had in that it would have put an end to all our hopes of resuming life as a nation in our homeland and would have rendered futile all efforts to keep Judaism alive in the diaspora, we should thank God with the benediction *Gomel.*"[48] (Interestingly, the blessing offered on being delivered from danger—*birkat ha-gomel*—came to Kaplan's mind rather than the *birkat sh'hekhe'yanu*, the blessing of thanks that we were granted to witness this day.)

Nevertheless, the considerations that had led to Kaplan's reservations continued to preoccupy him after the state came into being. Ideologue of American Jewish survival, he called on Israel to reconstruct its inner life to aid diaspora survival more effectively, even if that meant subordinating its sovereignty to a higher one, that of the Jewish people.

In the months following the UN partition decision, the Haganah, the Yishuv's main underground fighting arm, suffered severe defeats. Finkelstein recalls how active Zionists felt that the plan to go ahead with establishing a state could lead to a second Holocaust. In March 1948, Secretary of State George Marshall warned Moshe Sharett, head of the political department of the Jewish Agency, that he saw little chance that the Haganah could stand up to an invasion by the regular Arab armies. For a time in late

March and April, it appeared to some as though America's abandonment of partition in favor of a temporary trusteeship offered a last-minute reprieve from disaster. Postponing the declaration of a Jewish state, scheduled for May 15, would end the fighting and provide a second chance for a political settlement. Eager to win support for trusteeship among American Jews, State Department officials considered inviting Judah Magnes to the United States. Convinced that Magnes's views now accorded with official American policy, the State Department encouraged an ad hoc committee headed by Alan Stroock, who was also the chairman of the board of trustees of the Jewish Theological Seminary, to sponsor Magnes's visit. Finkelstein participated in the early deliberations of the committee.[49]

Suprisingly, when the ad hoc committee met with Magnes on April 26, Finkelstein failed to appear, at the very moment when the attempt to strengthen the hands of the trusteeship forces promised to gather some momentum. The rapidly changing political and military situation may explain Finkelstein's withdrawal from this last-chance peace effort. The UN Security Council had repeatedly shown its inability to mediate a ceasefire, and the trusteeship plan was caught in the mesh of the UN General Assembly. But perhaps most of all, the surge of public support for the embattled Yishuv had reached its peak. Opposing a Jewish state now would have placed him beyond the consensus that had built up so quickly and with such passion. Writing in 1985, in his ninetieth year, Finkelstein recalled his opposition to a Jewish state. He admitted that he had believed the odds were too great. "It did turn out that the people who had faith and were willing to risk everything for the sake of a Jewish state were right."[50]

There were indeed institutional considerations as well. Wealthy and influential supporters, like Alan Stroock and *New York Times* publisher Arthur Hays Sulzberger, adamantly opposed a state. Finkelstein was also well aware that his faculty and even more so, the Conservative rabbinate, were bastions of pro-Zionist and pro-state sentiment. Kaplan caught Finkelstein's dilemma in a diary entry dated February 28, 1948. At the previous meeting of the faculty the granting of an honorary degree was on the agenda. Finkelstein had recommended replacing Moshe Sharett, the leading nominee, with Paul Baerwald, the banker and honorary chairman of the American Jewish Joint Distribution Committee. When partition was carried out, Finkelstein suggested, those responsible would be honored with honorary degrees in a special convocation. Hillel Bavli protested: the Yishuv had to be encouraged now. "At one point Finkelstein screamed at Bavli, and Bavli paled with anger. Bavli charged the Seminary with being among the *sha'a'na'nim* ["the complacent"], and Finkelstein yelled back at him that individually, the men on the faculty, singling out [Simon] Greenberg and me, have worked for Zionism, and that the R.A. [Rabbinical Assembly] both individually and as a group have done more for Zionism than any other group in this country."[51]

There were different faces to spiritual Zionism. Mainstream Conservative rabbis of the stature of Solomon Goldman, Israel Goldstein, and Israel Levinthal were surely spiritual Zionists. They nonetheless held the highest political offices the American Zionist movement offered. To use Finkelstein's words, "they were willing to risk everything for the sake of a Jewish state." Granting this, the fact remains that Kaplan and Finkelstein were important figures in the world of American Judaism and master builders of the Conservative movement who saw themselves as faithful Zionists. However, they perceived their chief mission to be the nurturing and sustaining of a meaningful Jewish life in America. It was an all-consuming task with success uncertain. Eretz Israel was of pivotal importance, a needed cultural and spiritual resource. Until 1945, the issue of Jewish sovereignty appeared to be an academic one, or at most a questionable bargaining point in the political maneuvering of the time. Pursuing it diverted energy from other matters. Defining "commonwealth" and "state" as the supreme and immediate goal of Zionism ran against their spiritual grain. Indeed it diminished the merit of the spiritual center. Finkelstein and Kaplan were in good company. Besides Magnes there was the philosopher Martin Buber who had repeatedly expressed his fear that the single-minded pursuit of political sovereignty would subvert the true goals of Zionism. However, the reality of Jewish need was greater.

The questions the spiritual Zionists posed did not vanish with the creation of the State of Israel. Today, much of American Jewish thought is concerned with reconciling a belief in the centrality of Israel in its transcendent importance for the Jewish people with the reality of the State. Nor is the commitment to a creative Jewish life in America always in harmony with the public and private obligation to the old/new homeland.

# 8    Americanizing Zionist Pioneers

In the course of the 1920s the image of the *halutz* and the concept *halutziut* came to represent the core ideal of Zionism. "Anu banu artza livnot u'li-habonot ba" (a folk song that became popular in Palestine about 1930) captures the essence of that vision: "We have come to the land to build it and to rebuild ourselves in the process." The *halutzim*'s self-image as the vanguard of the Jewish people, totally committed to the redemption of the ancestral land, found widespread acceptance in the Zionist movement and beyond. Addressing an American audience in 1929 on the tenth anniversary of the founding of Hechalutz (the roof organization serving those preparing for *aliyah*), Chaim Arlosoroff, the labor Zionist emissary from Palestine, remarked:

> The name of Hechalutz has witnessed something akin to a triumphal procession around the world. . . . Even those among the Jews who know little about Zionism have—somewhere and at some time—heard its magic ring. When Mr. Winston Churchill, at that time Secretary of State for the Colonies, visited Palestine in 1921, the first question which he is reported to have asked the Governor of the Southern District upon his arrival was, whether there were in the district any of those strange creatures called *halutzim* of whom he had heard talk in Westminster.

Arlosoroff went on to observe that "Hechalutz was the first word of the modern Hebrew vocabulary to gain something like international currency."[1]

In its classic formulation, *halutziut* meant above all else a return to the soil of the Land of Israel. Becoming tillers of the land in the service of the nation also required an inner metamorphosis. "To build and be rebuilt" entailed psychic no less than geographic and occupational redemption. *Hagshama atzmit* (self-realization), the clarion call of the movement, involved the personal fulfillment of the *halutz* ideals through the instrumentality of a disciplined movement and the forging of a collective will. The most effective expression of that will was the collective settlement—the kibbutz and the *kvutza*, and some included the cooperative *moshav*—where means and ends, individualism and communalism, personal conversion and national rebirth merged. For the observer, the apparently un-bounded devotion of the *halutzim* represented the first fruits of Zionist education, the creation of an army of youthful, zealous, fearless, and hard-ened pioneers who were conquering the land with their labor.[2]

This view did not go unchallenged. In the dense political world of Euro-pean Zionism, the *halutz* movement encountered opponents on the right and left. The Zionist right faulted the elitism of *halutziut* and its control-ling collectivist temper. Furthermore, they charged, Hechalutz was a uto-pian movement led by fanatics who were socialist sectarians—and atheists to boot. For some Zionist idealogues on the left, class—creating a Jewish proletariat—was the imperative. Both camps argued that a select *halutz* movement offered no solution for the mass settlement of ordinary Jews which was the overriding need of the hour. In addition, the *halutz* move-ment itself was riven by factional splits fed by clashes over methods, so-cialist theory and ultimate goals.[3]

For the most part, America was spared the acrimony of these debates and the political jockeying they engendered. To some degree, distance and language account for this. The party debates, conducted in Yiddish and Hebrew in Poland and Palestine, were beyond the ken or care of most American Zionists, except for some intellectuals and the socialist Poale Zion, who were more European than American.[4] For the overwhelming majority of American Zionists, their nonideological, philanthropic Zion-ism had little room for such issues as the type of settlers needed in Pales-tine, how they should be trained, what their ultimate purpose should be, and whether a national kibbutz or a federation of independent kibbutzim was preferable. Rather, American Zionist publicists and Jewish educators, with some exceptions, embraced the idyllic image of the *halutzim*. The communal settlements they were building were Zionism's most exalted achievement. Not only were they in the forefront of the renewal of national life; they also offered the world a singular example of a democratic, egali-tarian and just society-in-the-making. Here indeed was evidence for American Zionism's claim that the return to Zion, inspired by the univer-sal prophetic ethic, transcended narrow nationalism.

In its pristine form, this image of the *halutz* crystallized by the early 1920s and continued to represent for American Jewry the essence of the Zionist ideal until the establishment of the Jewish state transformed Zion-ism and its myths. Nevertheless, during the pre-state years, with which we are mostly concerned, some Americans questioned the exalted place as-signed to the *halutzim*. By the late 1920s, critics were commenting upon the ideological rigidity of the kibbutz and the deleterious effect of collectivism on the individual. These critics questioned as well the economic viability of the kibbutz. In 1928, a commission of experts recommended withdrawing financial support from the kibbutzim who were wasting, they declared, the limited resources of the Zionist organization in dubious social experimentation. Only through industrialization and urbanization, they argued, could the country absorb the rising tide of migration. There were others who while admiring the idealism of the kibbutzim were uneasy over the *halutzim's* hostility to religion. However, only during the years prior to and immediately following the establishment of the State of Israel did the *aliyah* of several thousand American *halutzim* and the call from Israel for thousands more to join them provoke any compelling reappraisal of the primacy of the classical *halutz* way. This chapter surveys the rise and decline of the *halutz* image, the uses American Zionists made of it, and finally its redefinition—some would say diminution—after 1948.

The figure of the *halutz,* the invention of the newly formed Zionist youth movements, made its appearance only at the end of the First World War. However, prior to embracing the *halutz* ideal, Zionists in America were stirred by its precursor, the figure of the *shomer,* the guard and lookout. In 1915, Louis Brandeis wrote of the "intrepid *shomrim*" who for him embodied the consummate change Zionism had wrought. A brief consideration of the *shomer* offers some insight into the changing of the legendary guard.[5]

In an address delivered shortly after his return from a visit to Palestine in 1912, the popular Zionist orator, Judah Magnes, captured the image of the *shomer* for his audience. In his report, Magnes ranged widely as he compared the changes that had taken place since his previous visit in 1907. What stood out was the new spirit of the people. The colonists had acquired a new confidence; no longer did they live in "fear and trembling" of their Arab neighbors. The *shomrim* had made the difference. Here were "the beginnings of a Jewish militia, the beginnings of a new type of Jew, [who] were not defending their lives alone, . . . they were defending their country."[6]

The *Young Judaean,* the magazine of the recently established Zionist youth organization, embellished the image. It described the *shomrim* as "stalwart, fearless men whose ability to shoot straight and ride like the wind has put the fear of the Lord upon would-be pilferers."[7] So exhilarating was the *shomer* figure for Henrietta Szold, Zionist leader and founder of Hadassah, that in her 1915 report of the Yishuv's progress, she used these words, in an otherwise dry account, when she discussed the *shomrim*:

> Hashomer has raised the dignity of the Jew in the eyes of his Arab neighbors. A Jew who is a good shot, and rides a horse, bareback if you will, with the same grace as the Arab, and cuts a good figure at that as he gallops 'cross country, exacts respect.[8]

For the American reader, the *shomrim* were the "minute-men," as one account in the *Young Judaean* put it. Jesse Sampter, the poet and Zionist publicist, used another analogy: "They [the *shomrim*] can ride and shoot as well as the Arabs or as our Western cowboys."[9] The *shomer* figure stirred up associations with the frontiersman of the American West, the solitary cowboy of the plains, who imposed order on lawless country when necessary.[10]

Noteworthy for understanding the changes that would take place in the 1920s, when the *shomer* image was replaced by the figure of the *halutz*, was the trait implicitly shared by the Palestinian Jewish hero and his American counterpart. From the American perspective, both were individualists, plucky and unyielding; but whereas the *shomrim* "prepared outlying regions for permanent settlement to be cultivated by others" the *halutz* stood for permanency and collectivism.[11]

In his 1912 report, Magnes touched on other themes later incorporated in the *halutz* legend. One was the sheer joy of the new life that he had not heard before, the *shomer* serenading his girl: " 'Yalda, yalda, yaldati, girl, girl, girl of mine; yonah, yonah, yonati, dove, dove dove of mine'—the song of the *shomer*, of the watchman, to his love—the song of the Jewish guard to the girl whom he would take with him to Jerusalem." Hard-riding *shomrim* fell in love, courted their "girls" on horseback—and all in Hebrew.

A second theme Magnes developed that would be central to the *halutz* ideal was work and self-reliance. "Everyone is working, is trying to find work, is happy in his work, and I suppose what will appeal to an American audience, many are prosperous by reason of their work." Magnes gave particular attention to the first communal and cooperative workers' settlements that were barely two years old. Um Juni (Degania) and Fuleh (Merhavia) were worked by the "Communist men and women." At Kinneret, the young workers governed themselves through their own administrative and agricultural committees, and their own guards stood watch.[12]

From 1918 to 1921, new political and social developments produced the organized *halutz* movement as we know it and bred the legend of the *halutz*. The British occupation, the San Remo peace treaty giving international ratification to the national home, and the beginning of Jewish immigration on an unprecedented scale, rendered the *shomer* myth nearly obsolete. It lingered on for a time intertwined with the new myth. Jesse Sampter, who settled in Palestine in 1919, rhapsodized in a sketch published in the *Young Judeaen* (1920): "I saw spring up, with marvelous quickness, new villages, filled with Jewish men and women, from whose lips came songs of joy and thanksgiving. I saw the *shomer*, astride his spirited steed, a mounted sentinel, guarding the frontier." Sampter then went on to describe *halutzim* draining the swamps of Emek Yizre'el, the Valley of Jezreel.[13]

How quickly the *halutzim* became a staple of Zionist propaganda can be deduced from the remarks Reuben Brainin, the American Hebrew writer, when reporting on his 1926 visit to Palestine in the pages of the *New Palestine*: "The glorification of the *halutz* by our campaign speakers had only served to harden me, to prepare me for disillusionment." Brainin now thought differently. "Whatever you have been reading is pale, colorless, phlegmatic as compared to the spirit as expressed by the *halutzim*." The sheer willpower the *halutzim* displayed, their capacity for service and creation, their hardihood in overcoming difficult conditions were, this literary man wrote, "beyond description." Anticipating a question about the religious beliefs of the *halutzim*—a question Americans frequently asked—Brainin responded that theirs was "the religion of labor." He asked his readers to visualize the quarry at Ein Harod in Emek Yizre'el, where the *halutzim* did the hardest of all physical work. Only then could one understand the meaning of the "religion of labor." "Paid labor," Brainin wrote, "cannot break such stones with a smile and song on the lips."[14]

The single-mindedness and towering inner strength of the *halutzim* who worked the quarries and drained the swamps was magnified tenfold in the eyes of American Jews when Zionist publicists presented them as young intellectuals and professionals who had left behind promising careers for the grueling life of redeeming the land. One American Zionist official, on a mission to Palestine, described "the intense spiritual life" of the *halutzim* (a Hashomer Hatzair group in the Emek) in these words: "You can see men crushing the rocks or digging the soil, and talking about Nietzsche or Weininger, Strindberg or Ibsen, Maeterlinck or Anatol France, Wagner or Beethoven."[15] The eminent Zionist writer Maurice Samuel, in one of his dispatches from Palestine during the summer of 1924, dwelt upon the same phenomenon. This was not the "plain pioneering" and "primitive determination" one found in the early history of an undeveloped country," he noted. "These are civilized and sophisticated men and women, not peasants." Here was "a paradox, if you like, the delicacy of high development combined with the ardor and resistance of the brute. They talk of books and philosophies; their shepherds go into the fields with a Bialik or Ibsen in their pockets; they have their meetings and discussions; they *know* why they suffer and endure." On another occasion Samuel explained how the *halutzim* put their intellectuality to work. He described the nearly thousand *halutzim* living near Petach Tikva. They had been "*luftmenschen,* impractical, useless to themselves and to the world." Within a year they had learned to care for the orchards, to plant, sow and reap. When you speak to them, "they startle you with their modernity. They have organized their field work as work is organized in modern factories," measured a field in hours of work, graphed out, mathematically, the amount of energy the enterprise needed. And their enterprise, their productivity and their élan were amazing.[16] Jewish brains and Zionist idealism, Samuel's readers were expected to conclude, more than compensated for the missing brawn.

This image of the *halutz,* who sacrificed a career at home for a life of labor in the homeland, was not the property of Zionist publicists alone. In the spring of 1923, more than a year before Samuel's articles, the correspondent of the influential *New York Evening Post,* George W. Seymour, published three reports describing his impressions of Palestine. He came to Palestine, he wrote, expecting to find the Zionist dream of creating a Jewish Homeland "doomed to failure." Instead, he found it "destined to be fully realized." Most impressive of all were the accomplishments of "the company of 30,000 Jewish pioneers." In a hyperbolic passage that surely stirred the *Evening Post*'s middle-class, progressive readers, Seymour wrote that a "large percentage" of the *halutzim* were "doctors, lawyers, architects, engineers, university professors, and college students, who surrendered their careers to the hardest kind of manual labor that they might dedicate their lives to the job." Learned men and women engaged not only in roadmaking, bridge-building and other public works, "but toiled long hours throughout the day as carpenters, bricklayers, masons . . . and other skilled or unskilled laborers."[17]

Especially stirring was Seymour's treatment of the *halutzot,* the pioneer women, who insisted on sharing equally the strenuous work of the men. On the construction crew building the road to Tiberias, Seymour encountered women "lifting and carrying stones with their bare hands and devoting hours to crushing them." One of the women, who spoke English, "was a Russian Jewess, a university graduate with an M.D. degree, in a khaki skirt and peaked cap." She was the embodiment of athletic vigor and good health, and her "soft, blue eyes laughed with each stroke of her sledge hammer against the rock she was breaking. 'We are equals with the men in Palestine. We are all working for the same object: to build a nation, and we are in full accord as to the rights and privileges of each other.' " In the next instant, "the steel head of the big hammer came down with a crash on the face of the huge stone, which fell apart in many pieces." Here, indeed, Seymour proclaimed, was the "new feminine militancy of a newborn nation which stands unflinchingly the test of the wilderness in the old land of Israel."[18]

As one would expect from Henrietta Szold, her report of the *halutzim* was less dramatic and more incisive, although no less empathetic, than most accounts. Szold's description was inspired by a four-day stay in Kibbutz Tel Yosef. Meticulously she explained the ideology of the "Gdud-ha-avoda" (the Labor Battalion, the collectivist national organization of *halutzim*), the split with Ein Harod, the economic problems faced by the kibbutzim and agriculture in general. (She was invited to study the account books of the kibbutz.) Szold also described the rhythm of kibbutz life, the organization of work, mealtimes in the communal dining hall, the children's homes, health care, and cultural activities. To communicate the essence of *halutziut*, she focused on the kibbutz women. With her middle-class woman's sensibility, she wrote:

> Do you realize what it means in the way of self-abnegation for those handsome, erect, well-proportioned, vivacious young girls to be going, week-day and Sabbath-day, not to their own trunks or closets for finery that would represent their taste and individuality, but to a common storehouse with its motley assortment of odds and ends in the way of garments?

This was not an essential feature of the commune, Szold explained, although "the zealots" desired to retain it. Nevertheless, "it was a significant illustration of the devotion of our young *halutzoth*."[19]

It is interesting to compare Seymour's and Szold's paean to the *halutzot* with the response of a young American who came to Palestine in 1925 to experience the new life. Fannie Soyer, daughter of a Hebrew writer, teacher of Hebrew literature and a Zionist, had herself studied at the Teachers Institute of the Jewish Theological Seminary. Writing to a friend in America, in Hebrew, she remarked,

> When I was in New York, I considered coming as a *halutza*. I am certain now that I would be unable to stand the [physical] work for more than a

day. In a single year, the beautiful young women become old and coarse, and truly sacrifice their youth. As much as I am impressed by them and respect them, I would be unable to sacrifice myself as they do.[20]

The best of the reporting on the *halutzim* sought to balance the legend with the reality. Lotta Levensohn's account, "The Realities of Ein Harod," followed Szold's example. One of the founding group of Hadassah, Levensohn spent a month working in the kibbutz before she undertook to chronicle her impressions. She, too, included the mundane details of kibbutz living, described her daily work assignments in the fields, and the physical discomforts she encountered. Remarkably, nearly a third of the article dealt with relations between the sexes. "The gossip about the sex life in the Kvutzot seems recently to have died down," Levensohn wrote, "but I feel bound to touch on my observations at Ein Harod in order to present publicly (for the first time, I believe) the evidence of a person who did not form a judgment *after an hour's walk about the camp while the auto was waiting*" (emphasis added).[21]

The charges of immorality, Levensohn thought, could be found in the fact that men and women in some kibbutzim shared the same room (almost always, Levensohn explained, when a casual visitor had to be given a bed wherever one happened to be vacant for the night), and that some couples lived together without being formally married. There were couples, she declared, who had not gone through the marriage ceremony because they opposed it in principle. Yet they "regarded themselves as much married as those who wore wedding rings," and the kibbutz made no distinction whatever. A new set of relationships between the sexes existed in the kibbutz which was vastly superior to what one found anywhere else.

> The general attitude of men and women toward each other is dignified, comradely, wholesome. There is no need or occasion for clandestine relationships. There is nothing to prevent the marriage of two young people who choose each other. In the kvutza, social prestige, economic status, or ambitions of whatever kind have no place. Because all are workers, there is but one social class, one economic status, one standard of living [and] marriage is stripped of all irrelevant impediments, and restored to sheer personal attraction.

If a marriage failed, it was dissolved by mutual consent. There was no stigma. In fact, public opinion "regards it as immoral for people to live together when affection has ceased." Nor did the presence of children offer a problem, since they were all maintained and educated at the expense of the commune. The outdoor life, common occupations, common effort and mutual confidence made for clean and normal relations between the sexes, "so that the furtiveness induced by the artificial stimulations of pandering movies and musical comedies has no place here." There were sex problems, Levensohn conceded: "the preponderance in the number of men, the subtropical climate, and the limited amount of recreation." But they were not "obscene problems of promiscuity or questionable paternity." Thus, in the wonderful world of the *halutzim*, marriage and the relations between the sexes had been elevated to a higher, more noble plane.[22]

Nevertheless, Levensohn's vigorous "defense" of kibbutz morality suggests that allegations of sexual promiscuity were still to be heard. Others beside Levensohn felt constrained to probe the issue. The liberal Protestant minister John Haynes Holmes in his book on Palestine inquired into the sexual morality of the kibbutz; and Judah Magnes in the privacy of his journal recorded a searching interview with Manya Shochet, a leader of the Gdud-ha-avoda, over the rumors of sexual promiscuity.[23] The attention the subject evoked is understandable. Similar accusations directed at Soviet society (communism and free love going together) were commonplace in the United States. The "scandals" connected with Emma Goldman—the immigrant Jewish anarchist who was deported to Russia in 1921—were still fresh in the public's mind. Moreover, America of the 1920s debated with unprecedented candor a set of issues connected with the New Morality and the New Woman—most of it about sex—to the dismay and chagrin of conventional, middle-class America. It is not surprising, then, that some Jewish circles were troubled by this facet of the *halutz* legend, as were others by the open irreligiosity and militant secularism of the kibbutz.[24]

Three influential figures—the writer Ludwig Lewisohn, the philosopher and Zionist thinker, Horace Kallen, and Holmes—visited Palestine during the 1920s and wrote books which reached a readership well beyond the Zionist public. All three praised the *halutzim* but expressed serious reservations regarding the kibbutz enterprise. In a characteristic passage, Lewisohn (whose book, *Israel,* appeared in 1925), juxtaposed the lethargic, backward *fellah,* riding listlessly on a tired donkey, his wife trudging behind, with the sudden appearance of a wagon filled with grain and fruit, "drawn by two vigorous mules." The youthful driver had "a face full of intelligence and energy. In the back of the wagon two others: bare arms and throats, taut muscles, sunbrowned by labor in the open fields despite near-sighted eyes and the foreheads of thinkers. *Halutzim.* These are our people."[25] (The stark contrast between the "primitive" peasant Arabs and the energetic, progressive *halutzim* was a recurring theme in Zionist propaganda films.)

Kallen chose to compare the *halutzim* with the earlier Biluim, the handful of pioneers who came in the 1880s. The *halutzim* possessed a "grand vision." They sought "no simple personal salvation." Their aspiration was "the prophetic one." Like the "sect" of Reform Judaism, "they believed in the mission of Israel and in Jewry's duty and destiny to be a light unto the nations." The kibbutzim and *moshavim* were "endeavors to kindle that light," and the *halutzim* were "the pathfinders and the renewers."[26]

For Holmes, "the shining spectacle of these heroic men and women coming to the worst land with empty hands, not merely to make a living but to restore a commonwealth," were like "the early New England pioneers." But the Puritans had the easier lot, he added. They took over virgin soil of abundant richness, while the *halutzim* were "cultivating a wasted land which will yield its fruits only when watered with men's sweat and tears."[27]

Along with the glorification of the *halutz* legend came unflattering descriptions of their life that called into question not the intentions of the *halutzim* but their fundamental philosophy. Lewisohn described the dinner hour at Ein Harod. "In the huge eating shed several hundred people were eating at the crude tables. The benches had no backs. The dishes and utensils were of the coarsest. There was clatter and noise. There were flies. There was a sense of haste, of improvisation." And yet, to Lewisohn's distress, the young men and women were "quite satisfied with this hubbub, this . . . messiness." In the children's home, parents "snatched what seemed to us a pitiful and again crowded glimpse of both the children and each other before, the dinner hour being over, each had to return to his or her appointed task." For Lewisohn, the liberal American intellectual, the spirit of their "communist austerity" violated the "aim, fruit, goal, meaning of human life—the creative individual." The "large kvutzah" was "a contamination of our life by the supineness, the mass-life, the morbid and dangerous submersion of personality that seems to mark the Russian character whether under Czar or Soviet." True, Lewisohn hastened to add, he found "magnificent self-sacrifice, magnificent fortitude, magnificent singleness of purpose." The kibbutzim were agricultural and industrial triumphs; but as social experiments "they fill my Western mind with misgiving and dismay."[28] Not so the *moshavim*! Each family with its home, gardens, fields, had its privacy and flexibility yet benefited from the cooperative endeavor. Wandering through the gardens and farmyards of Nahalal was "an unforgettable experience." Flowers were all about. The admirable union of harmony and convenience found its expression in the physical layout of the village which "seemed to coincide with the temper of the men and women who live and labor here." No land was held as private property, no hired labor was employed. "Here, too, the social ideals of the Prophets shall prevail."[29]

Holmes came away with impressions similar to Lewisohn's. He noted "the barrenness, grimness, even ugliness of the life which these communal workers are living." In other colonies, he had seen pretty gardens and lawns, but in the communal settlements, he found only the rudiments of existence. At Beth Alfa, where he joined the members for dinner, all ate from a single bowl with a single spoon (an astonishing observation). The houses were "lost in an indescribable mire of mud and slime. No one seemed to have anticipated the winter season, considered providing a row of stepping-stones between the buildings." (Holmes arrived at Beth Alfa on horseback after riding hours in a torrential rain.) On marriage in the kibbutz, he found that "the rigor of the life, if not an established code of law, tends to create a standard of morals more stern than anything the Puritans in their day ever knew." The children's houses moved Holmes, and particularly the enormous sacrifice the kibbutz members made to assure the best conditions and education for the young. Nevertheless, kibbutz education troubled him. "Do children in a communal colony know their parents?" Holmes was reassured by the touching scenes of parental love that he had witnessed in the children's homes. Like Lewisohn, Holmes was enamored with the *moshav*, and for the same reasons: no private ownership of land ("a blow at the first pillar of the capitalistic system"), and no hired labor allowed ("a blow at the second pillar of the capitalistic system—wage labor").[30]

And yet, when Holmes came to list the achievements of Zionism, he returned to the "communal colonies." There he felt "the spirit of dedication not merely to the homeland, but to the world; . . . an enthusiasm not merely to reclaim the land of Palestine, but to fulfill therein those ideals of justice, righteousness and peace which through her prophets are Israel's greatest gift to humankind." Their intention was to build a new kind of nation. "This, to these Communist Jews, has from the beginning of her history been the unique mission of Israel."[31]

Of the three authors, Kallen's observations were based on a well-formulated economic policy for the development of the national home. A co-author of the "Pittsburgh Plan" adopted by the Zionist Organization of America in 1918, he insisted that ideology and politics had no place in building the Zionist homeland. Building the homeland required "business acumen and technical skill," not party functionaries who wrote for journals and swayed audiences. For Kallen, the increase in Jewish population from 10 percent in 1920 to 18 percent in 1926 was "testimony to the place of the Holy Land in the deep heart of Jewry rather than to the abilities of the Zionist administration." The concentration upon agricultural colonization in "a country beautiful but barren" was foolish, more a matter of ideology than nation-building. The large-scale settlement European Jewry required could be achieved only by industrializing the country.[32] Nevertheless, Kallen took the grand tour of Emek Yizre'el with its kibbutzim and moshavim. He, too, found the *halutzim* heroes and the kibbutzim insufferable. This was Ein Harod: "A straggling village; military housing without military tidiness; machinery rusting on the ground; sanitary arrangements a stench and a menace; omnipresent flies over everything; a thick, black, buzzing, beating layer of life on freshly baked bread set out to cool." Here is the Friday night meal at Ein Harod: "The food is being brought in pails and bowls from the kitchen and passed from hand to hand, badly cooked, without nourishment to the eye, unalluring to the palate. But how quickly consumed! While the everlasting doctrinal argument flows high, and the flies buzz."[33] (Interestingly, the three American-born women of genteel German pedigree—Henrietta Szold, Lotta Levensohn and Jesse Sampter—showed forbearance and humility in their visits to Ein Harod, while three renowned gentlemen scholars and moralists—Lewisohn, Holmes and Kallen—failed to see much beyond the flies.)

Legends and myths are for the believers. By the beginning of the 1930s, American Zionists and their sympathizers had embraced the *halutz* legend and Americanized it to fit their needs. *Halutzim* were educated young idealists, who reclaimed deserts and swamps. No less important, they dedicated themselves to creating a moral society where equality, fellowship and the common good would reign. (The critics' words, since they praised as much as they damned, could be filtered to support the legend.) If the *halutzim* were the ultimate Zionists, they were the ultimate Jew, and the prophetic ethic that inspired them made them Americans in spirit. One could now literally sing the praises of the *halutzim* by learning their songs and dances and, in this way, participate vicariously in building the land and being rebuilt. At Zionist gatherings, in the concert hall, among youth groups, even at a conference of Jewish social workers, the folk songs and the hora of the pioneers, reputedly sung and danced into the night after a hard day's work draining swamps, uplifted the participants. As early as 1919, Joseph Reider, a musicologist, writing on the "Revival of Jewish Music," noted the influence of the "folksong of the New Palestine." One example that had reached America was the popular "Po ba'eretz" ("Here in the Land"). "In Zionist circles," Reider declared, "it vies with Hatikvah in popularity." The song was "firm and manly, joyous and hopeful, brimful of verve and resilience, elasticity and sinuosity, and buoyancy and warmth."[34]

For some time the *Young Judeaen* had been offering a song a month from Palestine. Local and national Zionist organizations published song booklets which were used at meetings and by the Zionist choirs that were established. In 1926 a handsomely published collection of Palestinian folk songs appeared that was intended for a wide audience. Selected, arranged and annotated by the composer and musicologist, Abraham W. Binder, after a visit to Palestine, the book went through a second edition in 1929, and in 1933 "Book II" appeared. The song book was used extensively in religious schools. One Jewish educator recalls that "many youngsters made their first contact with Zionist ideas through the new Palestinian music."[35]

In 1926, the *halutz* theme reached the realm of serious music. Jacob Weinberger's full-length folk opera, "The Pioneers (Hechalutz)," won first prize at the international music competition held at the Sesquicentennial Exposition in Philadelphia. Drawing on Yemenite folk themes, Weinberger's *halutzim* abandoned the backwardness and antisemitism of their Polish town for the freedom and rapture of their kibbutz in the Galilee. Eight years later the opera had its world premiere in New York City, with choreography by Dvora Lapson, who began popularizing Palestinian folk dances in Hebrew schools and Jewish centers. In the triumphant final scene of Weinberger's opera, when love conquers all (mostly the objection of the bride's wealthy parents who follow their errant daughter to the wilds of Palestine with a proper groom in tow), Leah and Zev are about to be married (under a *huppah*!) in their kibbutz. A "l'chayim" is raised to the young couple, but Leah is not to be found. Then a comrade finds her in the cowshed:

LEAH:    Why are you celebrating already?
NAHUM:   Leah, enough. It is late enough. Time you stopped working.
LEAH:    And what about the cattle! They must water as well. Soon all my work will be finished.

The assembled wait for Leah to finish caring for the cattle.[36]

During the 1920s, and more so during the 1930s, pageants, exhibitions and especially films became the main vehicles for carrying the *halutz* legend to mass audiences. Zionist films, usually commissioned and financed by the Keren Hayesod (the Palestine Foundation Fund) or the Jewish National Fund, were distributed throughout the Jewish world.

The film that received extraordinary notice, the feature-length *Land of Promise*, opened at New York's Astor Theater on November 20, 1935, to the acclaim of New York's leading critics. The *Times* critic was especially captivated by the powerful contrast. First, one saw Arabs in their "medieval market places" and "sadfaced" *fellahin* in the fields flailing wheat. ("This *was* Palestine, says the camera, before the Jews flocked back to the homeland.")

> Then, suddenly, the lens is opened wide upon a dancing, singing group of young men and women [*halutzim*] on the foredeck of a liner, coming to give new life to the century old city, coming to water its fields, run its factories, build its homes. The effect upon the audience is electric.[37]

Although scenes of Tel Aviv, Jerusalem and Haifa presented bustling urban life in a positive light—construction work, industry, relaxing at the beach, a concert in the Hebrew University's amphitheater on Mt. Scopus, the Technion of Haifa—the heroic figures of the film are the *halutzim*, the tillers of the soil. Water is the leitmotif: *halutzim* drilling for it, directing its flow to the fields, spraying groves; then reaping the harvest and celebrating in a harvest festival and grand parade. Women work alongside men in construction, in field work, in feeding and milking the cows. And there is singing in the dining hall of the kibbutz and more singing on the way to the fields. The success of *Land of Promise* represented the accumulated experience of fifteen years of Zionist filmmaking in Palestine, a spirited producer, gifted director, and a superb cameraman on loan from Fox-Movietone Films.[38]

The Zionists took full advantage of the public relations possibilities of the New York premiere. A distinguished list of guests, headed by Albert Einstein, attended, and the opening ceremonies were broadcast by radio. The *New Palestine* described the "thrilling scene" when a group of "American *halutzim*" arrived from their training farms for the premiere. Dressed in white shirts with pitchforks and rakes on their shoulders, they entered the lobby as "hundreds of people cheered and cameramen eagerly sought to photograph them." The blue-and-white banner strung across Broadway advertising the film gave "poignant evidence to all who pass that Palestine has become a vital reality in Jewish life."[39]

The opening of the Palestine Pavilion at New York's World's Fair (1939) was another landmark mass event. The pavilion ran for nearly two years, and over 2 million saw it. Visitors entered a "Hall of Transformation," ascending stairs that symbolized the rising Jewish immigration to Palestine. Dominating the staircase was "a heroic statue of a *halutz*" and behind the statue a sweeping photomural depicting "the march of the *halutzim*." On the right was a mural showing a huge map of Palestine; opposite were wall photos that "depicted the transformation of swamps into healthful settlements, of rocky hills into a thriving colony, and sand dunes into the modern metropolis of Tel Aviv."[40]

Viewed from afar—through the lenses of the movie camera, the visit to the exhibit hall, the Zionist rally—the "heroic *halutz*," as we have seen, became a stirring myth and slogan for American Zionists. What then happened when young men and women considered becoming *halutzim* themselves? Ironically, when a native American *halutz* movement appeared in the 1930s, it made little impression on the American Zionist public, although it won the approbation of no less a personage than Louis Brandeis. Nevertheless, the endeavors "to make *halutzim* in America," meager as the results were, shed much light on the Americanization of the *halutz* ideal.

As early as 1926, Jesse Sampter articulated the reasoning and motivation behind the call for an American *halutz* movement. Writing in the *New Palestine*, she criticized the existing Zionist youth organizations, with their thousands of members, for "calmly preaching and teaching and collecting and selling, oblivious of those who rebel against the agony of being Zionists—at long distance." Some Americans had settled in Palestine, but they had done so as individuals and had encountered difficulties in adjusting. Needed were groups—"nuclei"—of "several hundred pioneers," who after preparations would join an existing farm commune in Palestine. Sampter was proposing the European *halutz* model: group agricultural training (*hakhshara*) directed to collective settlement in Palestine.[41]

The Zionist youth organizations of the 1930s were either transplants from Europe or American inventions. In the first case, *shelihim*, emissaries from Eretz Israel, almost always sent by a particular kibbutz movement, collaborated with handfuls of immigrants who brought their *halutz* movement affiliations with them from Europe and established Hashomer Hatzair, Gordonia, the Orthodox Hashomer Hadati, Hechalutz, and several training farms. These *halutz* movements were "exclusivist" in the sense that educating their members for kibbutz living was their sole purpose. Their Zionism was embedded in the notion of *shlilat ha-galut* (negation of the Galut): only in Zion could Jews build a creative Jewish life, and for the socialist-Zionists, also a workers' commonwealth. Hashomer

Hatzair (the Young Guard), for example, dropped those members who did not begin their *hakhshara* training at the designated age (usually eighteen) in preparation for *aliyah* to the kibbutz.[42]

Young Judaea represented the American prototype. The oldest and largest of the Zionist youth organizations, it maintained a nonpartisan Zionist posture that enabled it to reach out to a broad stratum of Jewish youth. This was in keeping with the outlook of its sponsors, the Zionist Organization of America (ZOA) and Hadassah. In many places, Young Judaea clubs provided the sole locale for Jewish teenagers to meet in an informal social setting.[43]

In the typology of Zionist youth organizations, the Young Poale Zion Alliance (YPZA), the youth arm of the Labor Zionists, occupied an intermediate position. Immigrant in its origins, the movement's increasingly American-born or American-educated leadership searched for ways to attract native-born Jewish youth to its program. To that end it established a satellite organization, Habonim (the builders), which by 1940 supplanted the YPZA. Through recreational club work, a children's magazine, young adult activities, a network of summer camps modeled after the kibbutz, and leaders drawn from its own ranks who served as role models, Habonim endeavored to impart an interest in Jewish culture, contemporary affairs, socialist-Zionism, and the *halutz* ideal. *Aliyah* and *halutziut* were the most important educational goals of the movement, but not the exclusive ones. Unlike the European *halutz* movements and their American affiliates, Habonim defined itself as "halutz centered and halutziut inspired." It offered, in a somewhat ambiguous formulation, "a synthesis (not a compromise) between *halutziut* and a program for America," in a word, a program that appealed broadly to Jewish youth and simultaneously educated its members to the demanding "*halutz* way of life."

How did Young Judaea, the most American of the Zionist youth organizations, and Habonim, with its Eretz Israel socialist ties and American orientation, respond to the *halutz* ideal?

*Halutziut* first appeared on the agenda of Young Judaea when the 1933 annual convention resolved that "the spirit of *halutz* youth be incorporated in the ideology of Young Judaea and that Young Judaeans be urged to join Hechalutz with a view to ultimately settling in Palestine."[44] In 1935, one of the organization's national leaders returned from a visit to Palestine convinced that Young Judaea's task was "transmitting the current of Jewish life in Palestine to the future *halutzim* of America." At the convention that year, Maurice Samuel, one of American Zionism's foremost intellectuals, spoke ominously about "reorienting" the Young Judaean program "to prepare Jewish youth for such a time *as they may have to emigrate to Palestine*" (emphasis added).[45] The growing virulence of antisemitism as it expressed itself in the public place most likely evoked Samuel's warning.

However, these sentiments led to little else. When Young Judaea published an ambitious educational program, "The Chalutzim Series," its content reflected the organization's equivocations. The introduction to the program declared: "We are taking our clubs through a movement from beginning to end, inviting our members actually to live through, rather than to talk about it, or to play at it." The program was to be as realistic an act of simulation as possible. The authors continued:

> We have chosen the livest, most vital phase of Zionism, and of all modern Jewish life, for that matter, as we say to our Young Judaeans, "This year BE CHALUTZIM! Go to Eretz Israel, found your colony." . . . We hope that many of them will be challenged and inspired with the dynamic urge to go to Palestine and to become builders. But we need Chalutzim here, too.[46]

The *halutz* enthusiasts among the Young Judaean leadership were sufficiently aggressive to elicit an editorial in the *Young Judaean* rejecting the narrow, militant appeal to the "chosen few" that a *halutz*-oriented program implied. The editorial reaffirmed Young Judaea's "all-Jewish programme" which was addressed to "the tens of thousands of America's Jewish youth." Besides, the editorial felt compelled to add, there *were* Young Judaeans in Palestine who were playing important roles in education, industry and culture, and in "commanding posts" in the Zionist executive. Young Judaeans were also to be found serving the cause of Zionism in America, in Zionist districts and Hadassah chapters, in fund-raising campaigns, and in the fields of education and religion. Thus the *halutz* ideal could be stretched to become the "spirit of *halutziut*," defined as devotion to the cause of Jewish survival anywhere. One could be a *halutz* in America! For Young Judaeans, the Americanization of the *halutz* ideal provided uplift and inspiration for the here and now of Jewish living in America.[47]

On first sight, Habonim's "halutz-centered" approach resembles Young Judaea's "spirit of halutziut." However, for Habonim, *halutziut* carried far greater ideological weight. It equated *halutziut* with building a socialist society in Eretz Israel, and it allied itself with the worldwide Hechalutz organization and the kibbutz movements in Palestine. Yet, in important ways, Habonim spoke with a distinctly American voice. It respected individual choice: the decision to become a *halutz* was a private one, to be made without coercion and for "positive" reasons. Eager to reach a wide circle of Jewish youth, Habonim stressed its openness. There was place within its ranks not only for the would-be *halutz*, but for those who chose to remain in America. Striving to maintain Jewish life in America was not to be disdained. In fact, educating for *halutziut*, Habonim argued, made those who remained in America better Jews and Labor Zionists, and activists in the communal life of American Jews.[48]

The "reach out" program never attracted the large numbers the founders hoped for. The movement's dualism did produce some results. On the American side, its graduates entered Jewish communal service—education, the rabbinate, and social work—in significant numbers, and others became the mainstays of Zionist political work and fund-raising. During the 1930s, together with the other youth organizations affiliated with Hechalutz some two hundred completed their training and settled in Palestine. They generally joined kibbutzim associated with their American movement. The attrition rate was high. As many as half were unable to make the adjustment to physical labor and communal living and returned to America. The outbreak of war ended even this modest trickle.[49]

Some changes in attitude toward an American *halutz* movement occurred beginning in 1946. With attention riveted on the embattled Yishuv and its efforts to smuggle survivors of the Nazi horror through the British blockade into Palestine, Zionist organizations mobilized to the hilt for political and fund-raising campaigns and passed tepid resolutions approving of American *halutziut*. Tenuous as these resolutions were, they legitimized the notion that some form of voluntary service in Palestine was praiseworthy.[50]

The period 1946–1952 was the American *halutz* movement's finest hour. The backlog of those who had been unable to go on *aliyah* during the war years (many because of service in the armed forces), the fruits of persevering educational work, and the dramatic events connected with the struggle for Jewish statehood produced a fivefold increase in *halutz aliyah*. For the first time, Young Judaea and Junior Hadassah alumni and members of the Intercollegiate Zionist Federation of America formed *halutz* groups, often to the discomfort, if not outright opposition, of their ZOA and Hadassah sponsors. The number of *hakhshara* farms rose from two to eight. Five kibbutzim with substantial numbers of Americans were founded during these years. Moreover, members of the American *halutz* movement played key roles in the covert operations conducted by the Haganah (the underground military arm of the Jewish Agency) in the United States. They organized and manned the ships purchased in the United States for transporting the "displaced persons" from Europe to Palestine, aided in procuring arms for the Haganah, and helped recruit volunteers to serve in the fledgling Israel Defense Force.[51]

For the leaders of the State of Israel, all this was not enough. To their mind, the thousand or so *halutzim* and volunteers who had settled in Palestine between 1945 and 1948, or had participated in Israel's war of independence, were harbingers of the many times that number who would join in the enormous task of absorbing the tens of thousands of refugees pouring into the country.

The times demanded extraordinary measures. Israel's prime minister, David Ben-Gurion, who had led the Yishuv to statehood, called on American Jewry to provide not only political and financial aid but *aliyah* as well. One of the founders and mentors of the *halutz* movements in Poland and then Eretz Israel, he now argued that the traditional approach of the *halutz* purists was too narrow and restrictive. Raising an elite vanguard through youth movement education was too slow a process. Moreover, the kibbutz, although still important, was no longer the premier instrument of nation-building that it had been for a generation. Consequently, the doctrine of *halutziut* had to be reinvented. The old way should not be abandoned, but the emphasis should be on summoning American Jewish youth in their thousands to provide desperately needed American know-how.[52] The call had to go out that the young state required engineers, scientists, teachers, and administrators—in fact, trained personnel of all kinds. This, too, was *halutziut*. At a closed meeting that Ben-Gurion called in July 1950 to discuss "Our Approach to American Jewry," Abba Eban, at the time Israel's ambassador to the United Nations, put the matter this way:

> One should not identify the concept *halutziut* with "agricultural settlement." One must free this concept *halutz* from its confining framework. ... The physician who immigrates to the country is a *halutz*; also the pilot who joins the air force is a *halutz*; and also a nurse who comes to the country to work in a hospital is a *halutza*; and yes, also one who comes to teach at the university.[53]

Ben-Gurion's reinterpretation of *halutziut* stirred bitter controversy in Israel. It antagonized American Zionist leaders when Ben-Gurion or his ministers appealed to American Jewish youth—whom he assumed were not organizational Zionists but "just good Jews"—to emigrate to Israel.

Crucial for our discussion is the fact that these debates over principle and definition, both in Israel and America, drained the *halutz* ideal of its ideological and organizational specificity. Israel's need for Western *aliyah* and American Zionism's defensiveness—fear of accusations of dual loyalties—spawned a host of programs under the rubric, "service for Israel." Typical was Arthur Hertzberg's suggestion of "limited *halutziut.*" Summer camps should be established in Israel, study programs for college students organized, and a central bureau opened to match professionals with job openings in Israel. Young American Jews should also be asked to volunteer for a year or two of service in kibbutzim and immigrant reception centers.[54] Eban's vision of the *halutz*—physician, pilot, nurse and professor—and Hertzberg's "limited *halutziut*" were a far cry from the heroic model of unconditional *halutziut* and far less threatening for American Jews.

The notion that American Jews *qua* Americans had a unique contribution to make became a way for justifying working and living in Israel. *The Reconstructionist* gave this reinterpretation of the classic version of *halutz-iut* its most striking formulation. Early in the debate, an editorial in *The Reconstructionist* (January 11, 1946) declared: "Trained and healthy young people who can introduce American techniques and 'know-how' and assume leadership among the thousands of refugees who will bring to Palestine only their own broken and starved bodies" was a noble undertaking. "The emphasis will be placed on *experts*, available nowhere in the world at present except in our country." Sensitive to the dual loyalties issue, the editorial continued: "American *halutzim* will not be unique in this role. American Christians have traveled and settled in all parts of the world, as missionaries either of Christian religion or American medicine." Many Americans "spend their years among the 'natives.' "[55] On another occasion, in January 1948, *The Reconstructionist* discussed the role the American immigrant should play in Israel as an "emissary" from America. The American *halutz* should be trained not only to adjust to conditions in Israel but also "to bring to Eretz Yisrael the values of his American experience of which the Yishuv stands in need." How to apply "American democratic principles to the specific conditions of life in Eretz Yisrael should be studied and discussed."[56]

In America, few challenged these new conceptions of *halutziut.* Occasionally, the question arose at Zionist conferences when Israeli leaders reproached their American colleagues for the meager numbers who were settling in Israel. Why was there no great *halutz* movement from America? On one notable occasion, an ideological conference on Zionism and the State of Israel (1953), Ben Halpern, who possessed impeccable Labor Zionist credentials—a former secretary of American Hechalutz and at the time an editor of the movement's *Jewish Frontier*—challenged Ben-Gurion's statist reinterpretation of *halutziut.* Israeli citizens, Halpern remarked, living under the government austerity program, soldiers ordered to work in a frontier kibbutz, or immigrants assigned to development towns in the Negev might be deemed as fulfilling *halutzic* tasks, but this approach was not applicable to American Jewish youth. Halpern explained that for the American Jew the passage to *halutziut* began when Zionism, taken seriously, instilled a sense of the inadequacy of American Jewish life and bred an unwillingness to accept compromises and paths of least resistance. This was the "push." The "pull" sprang from the expectations of building an ideal Zion. "Only if Israel was accepted as a society . . . with potentialities for building toward the envisioned ideal" could a "*halutz* movement hope to bring American Jews to Israel and help them strike roots there." For Halpern, the heart of the matter was "personal conversion, the sense of calling of the halutz."[57] This classic analysis—a throwback to an earlier time—was now largely ignored in Israel as in America. Indeed, only for a brief time had this notion of *halutziut* as applicable to the American scene stirred attention and controversy.

In America, the legend of the *halutzim* remained just that, a legend. It was adapted and popularized to appeal to American sentiments. But the true Americanizers of the *halutz* ideal were the Israelis. Struggling to win the battle for the state, and then facing the floods of immigrants, Israeli leaders extended the *halutz* ideal to include anyone who would volunteer to come to the aid of the nation, or, living in Israel, labor with devotion in his or her station in life. The title *halutz* was easily awarded. *Halutzim* were no longer the elect, and *halutziut* became a conventional slogan. Speaking on "the true mission of Zionism" in 1949, Ben-Gurion declared that "in the forefront of the Zionist movement [was] the promotion of the independent sovereign and *halutzic* State of Israel."[58] The independent sovereign state—*mamlakhtiyut* [statism]—became the determining force shaping the structure and ethos of the society. It replaced *halutziut* as the source of moral strength and expression of the collective will. American Jews followed this lead and transferred their idealization of the *halutz* to the state.[59]

# 9  The "Golden Decade": 1945–1955

Few would deny the proposition that American Jewish life has undergone a radical transformation in the half century since the end of the Second World War. Lucy Dawidowicz, in a synoptic review of American Jewish history, recently captured this sense of major change in two chapter titles. She designated the years 1920 to 1939, "Decades of Anxiety," and the years 1945 to 1967, "The Golden Age in America." "Recovery and Renewal" is how Dawidowicz conceived of the postwar period as a whole.[1]

Remarkably, the essential features of that transformation—the suburbanization of the Jews, the fashioning of a new communal order and the emergence of a collective self-confidence and sense of well-being—were already in place by the mid-1950s. At that point, American Jewry seemed to pause to take stock. The occasion was the yearlong celebration, beginning in the fall of 1954, of three hundred years since the first group of Jews settled on the shores of North America. The flood of tercentenary events intensified group consciousness and pride. The celebrations also encouraged the search for self-definition and self-understanding. Alongside the official and dominant theme of achievement and thanksgiving, a contrapuntal note of disquiet and discontent with the state of American Jewish life was sounded. In this respect, too, the culminating event of the decade set the terms for the years to come. Important publicists and ideologues recognized and debated what Charles Liebman would later pose as the tensions between "two sets of values." In Liebman's formulation, the "ambivalent American Jew" is torn between "integration and acceptance into American society" and "Jewish group survival."[2] Precisely because Jews were fulfilling, at last, their aspiration to integrate into the society at large, identifying with the group and maintaining it were becoming increasingly matters of personal choice. For the most part, Jews responded to their new condition by instinctively adopting a dual construct of identity that aided them in locating and relocating themselves in the volatile pluralism that characterized the nation as well as the Jewish community. This chapter seeks to place the first decade of our times, with its new conditions and new perceptions, in historical perspective. It also examines the Jewish community's endeavors to fix its place on the map of the new era and set its future course.

Surely, the subject most discussed among observers of the American Jewish scene in the late 1940s and the early 1950s was the exodus of Jews from city to suburb. This was the most concrete expression of the new affluence of the rising Jewish middle class. Entering the professions and the higher levels of entrepreneurship on the wave of postwar prosperity, benefiting from the decline in occupational and social discrimination, integrating culturally both in the workplace and in the classroom, and pursuing leisuretime activities similar to those of their social class, the new Jewish suburbanites embraced the tolerant, cosmopolitan image of the suburbs. For the majority of Jews, the creation of an amiable and lenient communal order, religious by definition, went hand in hand with the suburban ethos.[3]

The suburban setting was a far cry from the compact, big-city, middle- and working-class neighborhoods where they had grown up and where some had started their own families during the interwar decades. The Jewish group life in those urban neighborhoods as recalled by the newly arrived suburbanites had contained a multiplicity of synagogues, Jewish secular societies, informal social street settings and "neutral" public institutions that possessed a Jewish ethnic coloration merely by virtue of the high ratio of Jews attending. Less by design than geography, the Jewish neighborhoods had served the broad spectrum of interests, convictions and degrees of Jewish identification both of second-generation Jews and of acculturated immigrant Jews.[4]

The communal order reconstructed during the 1945–1955 decade reflected the new affluence and the rapid pace of social and cultural integration. The synagogue, now including educational and recreational facilities, became the primary guardian of ethnic identity and continuity. The social and educational services of the suburban synagogue expanded enormously when compared to the synagogues of the urban neighborhoods, at the same time as its ritual functions contracted. The years from 1945 through the 1950s witnessed the construction of some six hundred synagogues and temples. In their imposing size and sumptuous architectural design, they reflected their preeminent place in the suburban landscape as the accepted presence of a Jewish community. At the same time, the secular ideologies and particularistic interests that had existed in the urban neighborhoods faded away or were absorbed by the synagogue-centers or by the broad-based federations of philanthropies.

This blurring of differences during the early postwar years enabled the national coordinating agencies of American Jewry to flourish, particularly those agencies which guided fund-raising campaigns and the policy-making implicit in allocating the funds. The local communities channeled vast sums of money and political influence to these bodies through their federations. They, in turn, dispersed overseas relief, aid to Israel, support for the community relations organizations and help for the national denominational and cultural institutions. There is a striking correlation between the enormous increase in the sums raised to aid Jewish displaced persons in Europe and their resettlement in Israel, which peaked between 1946 and 1948, and the decline in such revenue in the 1950s when the overseas crises seemed to have abated and synagogue-building and domestic concerns were high on the community's agenda. Nevertheless, American Jewry was sufficiently affluent and committed enough to Israel to give more aid to the young state than to any other nonlocal cause.[5]

Two compelling experiences during the first few years following the end of the Second World War gave coherence to these developments and provided the basis for the collective behavior of American Jews that has persisted ever since. The first, the establishment of Israel, defined the one arena of greatest concern to the Jews. The second, the emergence of an aggressive liberalism, directed the political energies of the Jewish community into the general American domain. This parity of interests and commitments, which has been at the heart of the Jewish communal consensus for nearly half a century, was firmly in place by the mid-1950s.

In the first instance, at the war's end, American Jews confronted the enormity of the destruction of European Jewry and the urgent need to resettle and rehabilitate the one-third that had survived. This task merged almost immediately with the struggle for Jewish sovereignty in Palestine. Linking the solution of the problem of the survivors with the attainment of statehood created a unity of purpose on a scale unprecedented in the modern history of the Jews.

The American Jewish community mobilized its communal, financial and political resources in a massive outpouring of support. One gauge of this response was the dramatic rise in the contributions to the central communal campaigns. These soared from $57.3 million in 1945 to $131.7 million in 1946 and to $205 million in 1948, when 80 percent of the monies raised went for settling immigrants in Israel. There were other indications of momentous change. Eminent Jews who had taken little part in Jewish affairs now assumed crucial leadership roles, while others who until then had rejected all affirmations of Jewish nationalism rallied their organizations to the common endeavor. Henry Morgenthau, Jr.'s acceptance of the general chairmanship of the United Jewish Appeal in 1946 is one striking case; the collaboration of Joseph Proskauer, president of the American Jewish Committee (AJC), with the Jewish Agency in the final diplomatic push for statehood is another. Political figures and presidential advisors such as Herbert Lehman, Felix Frankfurter, David Niles, Samuel Rosenman and Bernard Baruch overtly or covertly aided the Zionist cause, which they now considered to be the sole means of saving Jews.[6]

The three years between the surrender of the German armies and the declaration of Israel's independence also saw many rank-and-file American Jews take part in European rescue work at considerable personal risk. Soldiers, chaplains and merchant mariners participated in the clandestine operations directed by the Jewish Agency and the Yishuv to transport refugees from the Allied-occupied zones in Germany to Mediterranean ports and from there in ships (purchased in the United States) to Palestine. Arms, too, were acquired surreptitiously in the United States with funds given by wealthy American Jews and shipped illegally to the Jewish underground in Palestine. At the same time, Jewish war veterans were recruited for the fledgling Israeli army.[7]

Pockets of animosity or indifference remained. The small but vocal American Council for Judaism opposed the widespread support for a Jewish state with singular passion. Denouncing Jewish nationalism as an aberration of Judaism and support of a Jewish state as a violation of American loyalty, the council was soon swept to the fringes of the community. Some left-wing circles remained outside the consensus. Pro-Soviet, Jewish radicals, except for the brief period when the Soviet Union supported the partitioning of Palestine, opposed the Jewish state; and a number of ex-socialist writers, the children of Jewish immigrants who were beginning to make their mark in intellectual circles, simply took no notice. However, mainstream Jewish America from the very beginning accepted the state of Israel as haven and protector of the Jews. Sovereignty was recognized as the guarantee of security for the dispossessed.[8]

The alacrity with which statehood was embraced was in fact quite extraordinary. The specter of charges of divided loyalties, and the fear of providing grist for the mills of antisemites, had long haunted the Zionist movement in America. Even after the Biltmore Conference in May 1942 declared a Jewish commonwealth to be the immediate postwar goal of Zionism, the American Jewish leadership (including some Zionists) viewed the demand for a sovereign state as being at best an opening gambit for later bargaining and compromise, or at worst an unrealistic if not perilous political program. Yet four years later, nearly the entire American Jewish community joined in the political battle for a Jewish state. To take one symbolic act, in May 1947, in the absence of David Ben-Gurion, Rabbi Abba Hillel Silver of Cleveland, representing the Jewish Agency (then the shadow government of the state-to-be), presented the case for a Jewish state before the United Nations General Assembly.[9]

Today it is a truism that the security and welfare of Israel have literally become articles of faith in the belief system of American Jews. Nurtured by the writings of publicists and theologians, encapsulated in the slogans of communal leaders and celebrated in commemorative and fund-raising events, Israel, as nearly every observer of Jewish life has suggested, has become "*the* religion for American Jews." One must stress, however, that *the conjunction of circumstances*—the crying need, on the one hand, to resettle the surviving remnant somewhere, and the growing recognition, on the other hand, that establishment of a Jewish state in Palestine was the only feasible means of saving the remnant—was the nexus at the heart of the overwhelming support for statehood between 1945 and 1948.[10]

This coupling of circumstances molded the sentiments and attitudes of American Jews. At its birth, Israel's survival became inextricably bound to that other primal remembrance of our times, the destruction of European Jewry. Later events, such as the alarm for Israel's survival in the weeks preceding the Six-Day War in 1967, demonstrated the depth of American Jewry's concern. True, in the 1950s and early 1960s, other concerns appeared to diminish the emotional identity with Israel that marked the years 1945 to 1948 and the years following 1967. Nevertheless, the transcendent place of the "destruction and renewal" theme in the group consciousness of American Jews was actually set in the formative decade beginning in 1945.

At the same time, American Jews were deepening and intensifying their identity as Americans. America's role in the defeat of Nazism and its emergence as leader of the free world—the one effective force blocking Soviet expansion—induced American Jews not only to participate in the civic and political life of postwar America, but to do so with unprecedented vigor and effectiveness. The high percentage of Jewish participation in elections compared to the voting public as a whole, the prominence of Jewish contributors as financial backers for political candidates, and the increase in the number of Jewish elected officials are some of the outward indications. No less notable is the ease with which political figures of Jewish background began to move out from Jewish organizational life into the larger political world and then, with their enhanced stature, back again to the Jewish. Philip Klutznick is perhaps the most striking example. His Jewish leadership track took him through the ranks of B'nai B'rith to the presidency of the organization in 1953. In a parallel career in government, Klutznick moved from commissioner of Federal Public Housing under Franklin D. Roosevelt and Truman to U.S. representative to the United Nations at various times during the Eisenhower, Kennedy and Johnson administrations and then to a cabinet post during Jimmy Carter's presidency.[11]

Most significant of all was the new departure of Jewish communal institutions in assuming an active role in American civic affairs. Community relations agencies, formerly almost exclusively concerned with discrimination against Jews, now entered the realm of social action in its broadest sense. They lobbied for legislation directed against racial discrimination, in favor of social welfare programs, against weakening trade unionism and for a foreign policy that stressed internationalism, aid to democratic governments, and a tempering of superpower confrontations. So, too, they joined in litigation against racial discrimination and for the strict interpretation of the constitutional principle of separation of church and state. In 1945, the American Jewish Congress created its Commission on Law and Social Action and committed itself to "working for a better world . . . whether or not the individual issues touch directly upon so-called Jewish interests." Soon after, the AJC in a more circumspect manner moved beyond its original purpose (as expressed in its charter) "to prevent the infringement of the civil and religious rights of Jews and to alleviate the consequences of persecution." It now declared its intention to "join with other groups in the protection of the civil rights of the members of all groups irrespective of race, religion, color or national origin."[12]

The religious wings of Judaism followed suit. By the end of the Second World War, both the Reform and Conservative rabbinical associations had long-standing commitments to pursue the goals of social justice, and the Orthodox Rabbinical Council of America began taking a similar stand. In the 1930s, for example, Reform's Central Conference of American Rabbis had declared that the "individualistic, profit-oriented economy is in direct conflict with the ideals of religion." At the same time, the Conservative Rabbinical Assembly of America announced a program for world peace, declared for a thirty-hour work week and proclaimed a goal of "a social order . . . based on human cooperation rather than competition inspired by greed." These resolutions, which undoubtedly reflected the social sensibilities of the rabbis, did not go beyond the ritual of affirmation by the annual conferences. But beginning in the mid-1940s, the Reform and Conservative movements as a whole, and not merely the rabbinate, placed both specific domestic issues and international policy matters on their lay agenda. They established commissions, organized local action groups, and collaborated with parallel Protestant and Catholic agencies on behalf of social justice issues. (In contrast, although the Orthodox Rabbinical Council began adopting annual resolutions on a number of welfare state issues such as price and rent controls and continuation of federal housing programs, social activism did not become an integral part of the Orthodox lay associations.) Thus, the militancy demonstrated by rabbinical leaders and Jewish organizations during the 1960s over civil rights, school integration and the Vietnam War stemmed from the Jewish community's active stand on political issues that began in the 1940s.[13]

In a broad sense, American Jewry's two public commitments—assuring Israel's security and striving for a liberal America (and by extension, a liberal world order)—have constituted the basis for a "functional consensus" ever since the linkage between the two was forged in the aftermath of the defeat of Nazism and the establishment of the Jewish state. On the whole, the two elements have meshed well, and in fact have reinforced each other. American Jewish leaders have presented Israel as both a haven for the persecuted and a doughty democracy surrounded and threatened with destruction by totalitarian Arab regimes allied, until recently, with an expansive Soviet Union. This has been a theme repeated often when U.S. presidents address American Jews and when party platforms are formulated. As a consequence, the dual identity of American Jews has resulted in less anxiety than some would have anticipated. The fear that vigorous support of Israel would give rise to charges of divided allegiance and fan the fires of antisemitism has not been borne out. The patriotic fulminations of right-wing extremists, bearers of a fundamentalist antisemitism, and the revolutionary rhetoric of the radical left that has equated Zionism with racism have of course been causes for concern, but they have not infected mainstream America. This is not to say that a latent disquiet has never been present, rising on occasion to the surface. For example, Jacob Blaustein, president of the AJC, intervened with the government of Israel on a number of occasions until he obtained formal assurances from Prime Minister David Ben-Gurion in 1950 that the Jewish state held no claim on the political loyalties of American Jews, whose sole allegiance, it was stressed, was to the United States.[14]

Nevertheless, American Jews intuitively sensed that the functional consensus based on supporting Israel and defending a liberal America was not sufficient. Needed was a doctrinal or ideological core which, while identifying the group, would also justify the operative elements of the consensus. During the first postwar decade, American Jews almost unanimously viewed religion as that doctrinal core. It was the way Jews identified themselves. Sociologists studying the new Jewish communities documented its currency. They also noted the paradox of Jews defining themselves overwhelmingly by religion while at the same time showing indifference and apathy for actual religious practice. Contemporary observers explained this incongruity as a form of adjustment to an American society that recognized religious activity alone as justifying self-segregation. These were the years when Jewish communal leaders found so congenial the notion that a trifaith America—Protestant, Catholic, and Jewish, "the religions of democracy"—formed the underpinning of the "American Way of Life." This interpretation of American society placed Judaism and its bearers in the mainstream of the nation's cultural and spiritual tradition.[15]

Since Judaism as interpreted by the American rabbi taught its followers to seek social justice, being Jewish in America meant fighting for open housing and fair employment practices, for social welfare and pro-union legislation—in short, for the New Deal, the Fair Deal and their successors. Judaism also demanded fulfillment of the religious commandment that "all Israel are responsible for one another," hence the duty to rescue Jews and strengthen the Jewish state. As individuals, Jews identified themselves as belonging to a religious community. As a group, they acted like an ethnic minority.

It is important to remember that, for American Jews, Judaism and Jewishness became identical only during the decade beginning in 1945. Although such a religious self-definition long preceded the postwar years (it was the cornerstone of American Reform Judaism), the East European immigrants had earlier created an ethnic and secular reality that overran without obliterating the purely religious formulation of Jewishness of the older, established community. One need merely mention the variegated Jewish associational life the immigrants created and the flowering of Yiddish literature—the most impressive cultural creation in a foreign language by an American immigrant group—to indicate the range and depth of this Jewish ethnic world. In acculturated form, significant elements of this world carried over into the second generation. Obviously, Zionism and an aggressively secular Jewish radical tradition stand out. Yet the considerable numbers who were brought up in this milieu in the urban neighborhoods of the years before 1945 failed to seriously challenge or to qualify the religious identification of American Jewry that so quickly became so universal in the post-1945 decade. Surely, the prevailing drive for conformity, which was in part a by-product of the Cold War and the accompanying fear of

Communist influence at home, saw religion (*any* religion, to paraphrase Eisenhower) as the cornerstone of democratic society and an antitoxin against the Communist heresy. And quite possibly the political and financial aid being so prominently extended to the Jewish state was best explained to the nation as religiously motivated. Separation for religious purposes did conform, after all, with patriotic norms. In part, these factors hastened the trends toward consensus within the Jewish community.

On occasion Jewish secular thinkers gave explicit and anguished expression to this change. In 1951, the Labor Zionist Organization published an essay by C. Bezalel Sherman, "Israel and the American Jewish Community." The Labor Zionist movement, an amalgamation of socialist-Zionist parties transplanted to the United States with the mass migration, was staunchly secularist. It had favored the formation of democratically elected Jewish communal polities and bilingual education in a manner similar to its European sister parties. Sherman himself was an ideologue of the organization's left wing. Nevertheless, in reappraising the future of the American Jewish community in the new era ushered in by the establishment of the Jewish state, he abandoned the position that American Jews should strive for the status of nationality. Now he wrote, "America, insensible to the existence of a Jewish nation, insisted on classing them [American Jews] with the religious communities," the only type of ethnic group recognized by "American constitutional life." Sherman continued:

> Jews thus have no other alternative but to constitute themselves as a
> community operating in a religious framework. . . . The irreligious Jew
> . . . will have to accept a religious designation for the group of which he
> wishes to be a member without sharing the tenets of its faith. This is
> the price a secularist Jew will have to pay for his voluntary sharing in a
> minority status.[16]

Ten years later, in his study *The Jew within American Society,* Sherman used this redefinition of Jewish identity to explain Jewish group survival in America. It was the key to understanding Jewish "ethnic individuality." On a note evoking Mordecai Kaplan's analysis of Jewish identity, Sherman concluded: "American Jews can no more conceive of the Jewish faith severed from the framework of Jewish peoplehood than they can conceive of a Jewish community removed from its religious base." Since Jewish peoplehood embraced Jews everywhere, concern for persecuted brethren abroad and the well-being of the state of Israel had increased the sense of "belongingness" among American Jews. "For this reason, they may be expected to continue as a distinct ethnic group—on the level of spiritual uniqueness, religious separateness, ethnic consolidation and communal solidarity, but not in a political sense."[17]

In terms of the Jewish establishment (the synagogue movements, federations, defense agencies and the Zionist organizations), American Jews had created by the early 1950s a consensus and a degree of equanimity they had not known before. They were meeting their dual responsibilities as Americans and Jews admirably. On domestic issues, they aligned with the liberal-centrist position and upheld America's role as defender of the free world. Within the Jewish community, the divisive issues of the interwar years—class differences, the intergenerational tensions between immigrant and native-born, conflicting notions of Jewish identity, the assimilationist-radical deprecation of Jewish life and the strident polemics over Zionism—were vanishing or were gone altogether. Not surprising, then, the tercentenary planners proposed stressing not only communal harmony and achievement but also the beliefs and values Jews held in common with all Americans.

In December 1951, Ralph E. Samuel, the vice president of the AJC, announced the formation of a committee to plan the three hundredth anniversary of the establishment of the first permanent Jewish community in North America. Samuel emphasized the opportunity that the celebrations would provide to pay homage to the "American heritage of religious and civil liberty." American Jews had built a "flourishing American Judaism," he declared, and at the same time they had taken part "in building the American democratic civilization that we have today." In the single reference to contemporary affairs, Samuel concluded his remarks with the note that the tercentenary celebration would demonstrate to the world "the strength of the American people's commitment to the principles of democracy in our struggle against communism and other totalitarianism of our day."[18]

This collective undertaking to popularize an American Jewish ideology proved to be an extraordinary enterprise in itself. It also raised a number of questions. Who indeed did the tercentenary organizers represent? How meaningful and tenable could a least-common-denominator ideology be? What were the constraints the planners faced in relating to the American-political and Jewish-political context? Were the provisional tenets Samuel set forth adequate for setting a course for postwar American Jewry?

In January 1952, when the committee on organization met to launch the tercentenary project, Samuel stressed that the AJC saw its role as initiator rather than sponsor of the enterprise. In fact, it had been the American Jewish Historical Society that had first proposed the tercentenary celebration. Eager for the broadest communal participation it had turned to the AJC for organizational assistance; success of the project depended on leaders whose eminence and integrity assured the nonpartisanship of the endeavor.

In addition to Samuel, who was chosen general chairman, two eminent members of the AJC were appointed to key committees. Simon Rifkind, who had distinguished himself as a federal judge and special advisor on Jewish affairs to General Dwight D. Eisenhower in 1945 and 1946, headed the "committee of 300," the policy-making body of the organization. Samuel Rosenman, also a judge, who had served as a principal adviser to Presidents Franklin Roosevelt and Harry Truman, chaired the program committee. Another important committee, research and publication, was headed by Salo W. Baron, professor of Jewish history at Columbia University.

The composition of the committees reflected nearly the entire spectrum of Jewish religious and communal life. Among the members of the steering committee were Samuel Belkin, president of Yeshiva University; Louis Finkelstein, president of the Jewish Theological Seminary; Israel Goldstein, president of the American Jewish Congress; Samuel Niger, the Yiddish journalist and critic; and Jacob S. Potofsky, president of the Amalgamated Clothing Workers Union.

In April 1953, after nearly a year of deliberations, the program committee, which, in addition to Rosenman, included Benjamin V. Cohen, Adolph Held, William S. Paley and David Sarnoff, submitted its report on the "meaning of the anniversary" to a national meeting of the Committee of 300. Obviously the presence of Paley, the head of CBS, and Sarnoff, the head of NBC, indicated the direction and scale of the celebrations. The proposed theme of the celebration—"Man's Opportunities and Responsibilities Under Freedom," was in fact suggested by Sarnoff, and was approved at this meeting.[19]

The major opening event, the National Tercentenary Dinner with President Eisenhower as guest of honor and keynote speaker, took place on October 20, 1954, at the Hotel Astor in New York. It was preceded and followed by forums, exhibitions, pageants, musical festivals and public dinners organized by local committees in at least four hundred cities and towns. New York, for instance, was the venue of a coast-to-coast radio broadcast of the reconsecration of Congregation Shearith Israel (founded by the original settlers of New Amsterdam) in the presence of represPentatives of the Jewish and Christian congregations that had either aided or functioned alongside it in the eighteenth century. A special national committee supervised the preparation of a national historical exhibit on the theme "Under Freedom," which was shown at the Jewish Museum in New York and the Smithsonian Institution in Washington, D.C. The Chicago committee commissioned Ernst Toch to compose a symphonic suite for the occasion, while the national committee commissioned David Diamond to compose the tercentenary symphony *Ahavah*, which was given its premiere by the National Symphony on November 17, 1954, in Washington. (The other works on the program were Ernest Bloch's *Israel Symphony* and Leonard Bernstein's *The Age of Anxiety*, a thematically balanced program by Jewish composers.) In Atlanta, Georgia, the local committee presented the city with a portrait of Judah P. Benjamin, secretary of state of the Confederacy.[20]

Television played a major role. The main events, such as Eisenhower's address, received national coverage. Leading commercial programs offered commemoration salutes. CBS broadcast a four-part teledrama, "A Precious Heritage," while NBC followed suit with a four-part series entitled "Frontiers of Faith." The tercentenary also generated a plethora of educational material—filmstrips, curricula and guidebooks on American Jewish history—for use in schools and adult education circles that were sponsored and published by the national organizations. B'nai B'rith organized a nationwide search for historical source materials and provided programs and speakers for its lodges and Hillel Foundations. The AJC commissioned a series of studies that it published in the *American Jewish Year Book* and an *Inventory of American Jewish History* to further historical research. A volume of studies subsidized by the Workmen's Circle and other Jewish labor organizations gave special attention to the era of the East European Jewish migration.[21]

This history-mindedness anteceded the tercentenary "revival." It was one expression of a self-assertiveness that stemmed from the new position of centrality that had been thrust upon the American Jewish community. And it paralleled the notion of the "American Century," the conviction that became popular during the war years that America had at last taken its "rightful" place as the leader of the free world and the guardian of world order. This national temper stimulated a reexamination of the American past. Historians and political scientists elaborated the idea of an "American exceptionalism." Typical of their writing was Daniel Boorstin's book *The Genius of American Politics*. "I argue, in a word," Boorstin wrote, "that American democracy is unique. It possesses a 'genius' all of its own."[22]

The new era that began in 1945 was, in a sense, also perceived as "the

American Jewish Century." The conviction that American Jews were at last "making history" required recovering a "useable past" showing that Jews had indeed been "making history" for some time. One important expression of this sentiment was the Hebrew Union College's announcement, in the fall of 1947, of the establishment of the American Jewish Archives to document the historical record of American Jewry. The need for such an institution was explained in these words:

> American Jewry has become the "center" of world Jewish spiritual life. When the Jewish historian of the next generation reaches the year 1939, he will begin a new chapter in the history of his people, a chapter which must be called, "The American Jewish Center." This Jewish community has now become the pivotal and controlling factor in that historic development which began in the thirteenth pre-Christian century in Palestine.[23]

There were more manifestations of a search for "American Jewish exceptionalism." In 1953, the Jewish Theological Seminary established the American Jewish History Center. Soon after, the center commissioned a series of communal studies and organized regional conferences to generate interest in the projects. The tercentenary accelerated this newfound interest in an American Jewish past. Jewish communities—Buffalo, Rochester, Milwaukee, Cleveland and Los Angeles—allocated money for writing their communal histories. In September 1954, a revitalized American Jewish Historical Society convened the most impressive conference of historians ever held on the writing of American Jewish history. Thus the new self-consciousness American Jewry displayed after the conclusion of the war swelled under the impetus of the tercentenary. Pride and awareness of its preeminence in the Jewish world reverberated in the public and institutional interest in recording and interpreting the Jewish experience in America.[24]

One interpretive history of Jewish life in America that appeared during the tercentenary year captured the tercentenary ideology faithfully. Oscar Handlin's *Adventure in Freedom* stressed the process of Jewish integration into a society that was distinguished by its "diversity, voluntarism, equality, freedom, and democracy." Handlin, who taught American social history at Harvard and who had won a Pulitzer Prize for his 1951 study on immigration in American life, *The Uprooted,* was perhaps the most influential writer on the American pluralist tradition. Handlin insisted that American Jews be viewed as one ethnic group among many in a pluralist America that neither impeded nor encouraged ethnic group maintenance. This was the open-ended, wholesome "adventure in freedom." Yet Handlin also struck an ominous note. Although the Jews of America were celebrating the year 1654, they could not forget "the stark facts of our present situation." Jews had not recovered "from the shock of the six million victims of the European catastrophe"; at the same time they shared in the "enormous burden upon American society" which was "locked in unremitting struggle" with "the forces of totalitarianism."[25]

It was the tercentenary theme, "Man's Opportunities and Responsibilities Under Freedom," that required explication. When the program committee presented its recommendations after months of deliberations and after soliciting the opinions of scores of leaders from all fields and walks of life, it explained the criteria it had used in these words:

> The theme should express the outstanding fact of the past 300 years of our participation in America; that it should describe the significance of the present day for American Jews, and that it should express the hopes and aspirations and objectives of the future for ourselves and for all Americans—indeed, for all human beings throughout the world.

When the recommendations were published as a brochure—thirty thousand copies were distributed—no explicit reference was made to the Jewish community itself, or to the American Jew's "responsibility under freedom" to help other Jews, although the members of the committees in their other communal capacities were deeply involved in Jewish affairs. In a section entitled "All-Embracing Nature of Celebration," the committee warned that the tercentenary should not be made "a vehicle for propagation of any particular ideology in American Jewish life. . . . It should be neither Zionist, non-Zionist, nor anti-Zionist. It should not try to formulate or advance any particular definition of Jewishness."[26]

The tercentenary committee defined the principal goal of the observance as a celebration of America's democratic ideals. Thus the American Jewish experience was significant in that it bore witness to the success of this free society. No less important was the emphasis placed on the congruence between Judaism and American democratic ideals. Indeed, the authors of the report declared, "the teachings of the Hebrew prophets have vitally affected the growth of freedom and the development of human dignity in America and throughout the world." In a summing-up statement at the conclusion of the year of festivities, David Bernstein, the tercentenary committee's executive director, justified the choice of the theme in these words:

At a time when the Jewish community and its leaders felt that they were on display before the world, they chose to speak, first, in religious terms and, next, in terms of such political ideas as civic responsibility, strengthening democracy, protecting individual liberty, and expanding civil rights.[27]

Was there perhaps, in the midst of the deserved self-congratulations, also a measure of anxiety and insecurity? What seemed implicit in Bernstein's statement and had been alluded to in Samuel's first announcement of a tercentennial committee four years earlier was stated explicitly in Handlin's measured words. Praising democracy and liberty at a time when the nation was locked in what it perceived to be a global struggle with an aggressive and ruthless totalitarianism was understandable enough. The "golden decade" for American Jews was also the decade of the Cold War, McCarthyism, and fear of communist subversion.

Abroad, postwar America confronted an expansive communist power that now possessed nuclear weapons. Not only had an "iron curtain descended across the continent," in Winston Churchill's words in his March 1946 address, but it was followed by the fall of China to the communists and the invasion of South Korea by the North in 1950. At home, an alarmed government responded with drastic measures to curb and root out real and perceived instances of communist infiltration. It began in 1947, when Harry Truman put into effect his loyalty program, and it ended, at least symbolically, in December 1954 when the U.S. Senate censured its member, Joseph McCarthy—a time span nearly identical with the first years in the new American Jewish postwar era. Thus the years of optimism were also the years of the "Attorney General's list" of subversive organizations, the Alger Hiss case, the loyalty oaths and security clearances, the high-handed investigations of Senator Joseph McCarthy and the congressional committees who went hunting for communists and who blacklisted those they termed "Fifth Amendment Communists."

Here was the snake in the garden: the agony and trepidation caused by the conspicuous presence of Jews among those accused of disloyalty and even espionage, and the presence of a marginal but vocal radical left within the organized Jewish community. Thus the arrest in 1950 of Julius and Ethel Rosenberg for handing atomic secrets to the Soviet Union, and their trial, conviction and execution in 1953, jarred the self-confidence of American Jews. (The trial judge, prosecuting attorney, defense attorneys, and the principal witnesses who turned state's evidence were all Jewish.) Arnold Forster, general counsel of the Anti-Defamation League (ADL), recalled the period as a time when American Jewish leaders "came to fear the establishment of a link between being a Jew and being a 'communist traitor' in the popular mind." A bitter fight ensued within the Jewish community over aiding Jewish victims of the anti-communist crusade. The most prominent instance was the campaign for clemency for the Rosenbergs in which communist and left-wing groups were active.

The AJC created a special committee to combat the "Jewish/communist stereotype." It launched an educational program exposing the techniques and strategies used by the communists to infiltrate Jewish organizations and called on the community to expel Jewish "communist-front" organizations. During the height of the hysteria, the AJC was less than forthright in its commitment to civil liberties. On this last score, in contrast, both the ADL and the American Jewish Congress maintained their aggressive stand in defense of civil liberties. In 1952, at the height of McCarthy's influence, the ADL chose to honor Senator Herbert Lehman at its annual convention because of his opposition to McCarthy. The American Jewish Congress, for its own part, waged an incessant battle against congressional and state legislation that required loyalty oaths, providing legal aid in appealing cases where there appeared to have been infringements of constitutional rights. To a considerable degree, the Red Scare hastened the political integration of American Jews. It greatly weakened Jewish radicalism, fortified the liberalism of "the vital center" and drew American Jews, as never before, into a whirl of "American" issues. In dealing with these issues, both civil libertarians and anti-communist activists operated through Jewish agencies.[28]

The official tercentenary ideology, orchestrated by a group of conservative and cautious leaders, aroused a spirited debate over the direction of American Jewish life. Jewish journals of opinion provided the platforms for a more reflective consideration of the issues. Robert Gordis, editor of *Judaism*, devoted an entire issue to the tercentenary in which contributors evaluated Jewish philosophy, culture and communal life in America. Eugene Kohn gathered a dozen articles from *The Reconstructionist* on the communal and cultural life of American Jews and published them in a volume commemorating the tercentennial. The score of mass-circulation house organs published by B'nai B'rith, Hadassah, the American Jewish Congress and others devoted whole issues to critical essays that examined American Jewish life. For the most part, the conclusions were laudatory and the prognosis for the future optimistic. Typical was Gordis's introduction to the tercentenary issue of *Judaism*. American Jewry, Gordis wrote, had not been "altogether without influence or creativity within the confines of Judaism." It had been innovative in the fields of religion, philan-thropy, education and group-defense. Indeed, "the instruments for a ren-aissance of Judaism, in the days to come, are at hand."[29]

There were also dissenting voices. Horace Kallen, the philosopher and ideologue of cultural pluralism, published a blistering piece in the *Con-gress Weekly* entitled "The Tercentenary, Yomtov or Yahrzeit" ("Holiday or Anniversary of a Death"). He accused the organizers of violating the es-sence of the "American Idea," that is, of his well-known notion of cultural pluralism. Kallen had interpreted American freedom as granting the right to any ethnic, religious or racial group to preserve and diversify its com-munal culture. Nothing in the rhetoric of the tercentenary encouraged American Jews to do this, he argued; even the tercentenary emblem was assimilationist. Not a Hebrew word was on it, and above the menorah that dominated the face of the emblem was a star—but it was a five-pointed, American star rather than the six-pointed Magen David. For Kallen, the challenge of American freedom for the American Jewish community meant creating, first of all, a democratic communal polity. A community so organized would then be able to nurture—and here Kallen employed his famous metaphor of the orchestra—the specifically Jewish part in the total orchestrated production that was the pluralistic culture of the Ameri-can people.[30]

Mordecai Kaplan, the philosopher of Reconstructionism, criticized the planners for failing to confront one of the crucial questions in American Jewish life. "Why is no reference made in all the literature, speeches and lectures concerning the tercentenary to what it means from the standpoint of our survival as a people in dispersion? . . . This is the first time in the history of the Jewish people that it is jubilant over its sojourn in any land outside of Eretz Yisrael." What was the Jewish context of the celebration? What signposts for the future course of American Jewry had the tercente-nary offered? The establishment of the state of Israel had raised the ques-tion of "the ultimate destiny of the Jewish People." Was Eretz Israel to be the ingathering of the exiles or merely the creative nucleus of the Jewish people? Building on his formulation of living in two civilizations (Ameri-can and Jewish), Kaplan emphasized the permanence of diaspora and re-jected the Israel-Zionist claim that American Jews were in *galut* (exile). For Kaplan, the influence of the American democratic tradition on the Jews *and* "the inexhaustible reservoir of Jewish creativity in Israel" promised a creative future for "the American sector of the Jewish people [that had] at last found a resting place for its feet." But these matters had to be debated, clarified and decided upon.[31]

Ben Halpern, the secularist Zionist thinker, began his study of the American Jewish community, *The American Jew: A Zionist Analysis*, by considering the conviction underlying the tercentenary that "America is different." Indeed, it was different, Halpern agreed. In the shadow of Hitler's destruction of Europe's Jews and in the presence of Soviet totalitarianism and Stalin's antisemitism, Jews had special reasons for celebrating America's democratic tradition. However, American Jews had missed one crucial way in which America was different *for them*. As a historic entity, American Jews constituted one of the youngest Jewish centers of the diaspora. In terms of "real history"—of grappling with the specific problems of their existence as a group—American Jewish history began at most with the rise of the first, authentic American Jewish creation, Reform Judaism, and the formation of native American Jewish institutions. Unlike European Jewry, Halpern argued, American Jews had never had to wrestle with the question of emancipation and self-emancipation; American Jewish history began long after the question of equality and political rights was resolved. His analysis led him to conclude that the indigenous ideologies of American Jews, as programs intended to foster a creative Jewish group life, were failing. Neither the secular ideologies such as cultural pluralism and neo-Zionism, nor an innovative religious movement such as Reconstructionism could prevent the erosion of Jewish life. Assimilation? Survival? Was America different than Europe? His answer was: "In Europe, the stick; in America, the carrot." Indeed, Halpern, the fundamentalist Zionist, was utterly pessimistic about American Jewish group survival.[32]

Surely by the final years of the 1950s one could confidently point to a baseline that demarcated American Jewry from what had existed prior to 1945 and that would hold, for the most part, during the decades ahead. The searing recollections of the poverty of immigrant parents or the crushing collapse into destitution of the Depression years had been replaced with an affluence that opened new social opportunities. This affluence enabled the postwar generation to devote some of its time and wealth to societal needs. Establishing entirely new communities in the suburbs demanded an enormous collaborative effort. In addition, the national agencies serving American Jewry as a whole and the needs of world Jewry required politically sophisticated leaders, trained professionals and efficient organization. An organizational ideology developed "of acts and tasks, of belonging and conforming," of *na'aseh venishma*. "To be a Jew," one perceptive observer wrote, "is to belong to an organization. To manifest Jewish culture is to carry out . . . the program of an organization."[33] Support for Israel as refuge and home—which more than sweeping aside its opponents, co-opted them—became the overarching endeavor, the one that transcended the local and the particular. Hence it came to define the active community.

Purely *Jewish* concerns could also be linked to liberal politics through the argument that to support American liberal causes was in the "Jewish interest," or else group interests could be denied in favor of appealing to the universal teachings of Judaism. Whatever the justification, Jewish *communal* participation in American politics in the decade beginning in 1945 became widespread and was found acceptable. For postwar America commended communal ties that encouraged spiritual self-preservation and self-fulfillment. In the state of fluid pluralism then prevailing—of changing self-images and expectations of religious, ethnic and racial groupings—any number of ways were possible for identifying oneself. Understandably, the Jews, eager to take their place in the more tolerant postwar society, defined their group identity to fit the reigning mood. Judaism as ethnic religion and Judaism as "peoplehood," as "religious civilization" and as one of the three "religions of democracy" were some of the terms that came into use. In the case of the tercentenary platform, Judaism became American democracy, reflecting a strand of insecurity that was present during the golden decade.

A number of ideologues were distressed by the assimilationist thrust of this formulation. They called on American Jews to instead confront the complexity of their dual identity, indeed, to view it as the source of an American Jewish distinctiveness. Rabbis and theologians challenged the cult of organization and the emptiness of "religion as the American way." Yet, ideologues and rabbis were also committed to a pluralist America. They collaborated in ways that were inconceivable during the prewar years, not only accepting but applauding the internal pluralism of Jewish group life. Precisely the give and take of contending movements and ideas within a communal consensus indicated a commitment to group survival. One could understand, for example, the much-criticized slogan, "Man's Opportunities and Responsibilities Under Freedom," as a shrewd strategy to maintain the community. (Rabbis used the phrase as the text for their sermons on the need for better Jewish education, support for Israel and a richer synagogal life.)[34] Unmistakably, whatever ideological issues were placed on the Jewish public agenda during the decade beginning in 1945, which have remained there to this day, no longer called into question the worth or desirability of Jewish survival. The issue now would be the quality and character of Jewish group survival.

# 10  Inventing the "New Pluralism"

> The History of ethnicity and ethnic self-consciousness in this country has moved in waves; we are now, in 1965, in a trough between two crests, and the challenge is to describe the shape and form of the next crest. . . . But each time [ethnic self-consciousness] has returned in so different a form that one could well argue it was not the same thing returning at all, that what we saw was not the breakthrough of the consciousness of common origin and community among the groups that made America, but rather that ethnicity was being used as a cover for some other more significant force, which was borrowing another identity.
>
> —Nathan Glazer[1]

This chapter addresses one aspect of Nathan Glazer's 1965 prediction of a "resurgent [ethnic] self-consciousness" and his belief that factors other than group sentiments and loyalties would shape such a resurgence. In fact, within three years of his pronouncement, a well-articulated movement appeared led by a number of social activists, intellectuals, and social scientists to bear out Glazer's prognosis. The movement immediately gained important institutional support, won considerable public notice, and revealed a political potential of some significance. Variously dubbed the "new pluralism" or the "new ethnicity"—the terms were used interchangeably—the movement offered a revised view of American pluralism. It insisted that ethnic group life and ethnic group interests were permanent and central features of American society that necessitated public recognition. Only if public policy responded to the legitimate grievances and needs of the ethnic group, hitherto ignored if not scorned, would it be possible to stop the "polarization" of American society into black and white, haves and have nots.

A number of catchwords used by the movement's leaders sum up the social and political thrust of the new pluralism. The movement was speaking for "Middle Americans" who were variously designated as "working-class ethnics," "blue-collar Americans," or "white ethnics." Accused by elitist liberals of being "bigots," they nevertheless voted with the northern, liberal wing of the Democratic Party; branded "hard-hats" and racists, they were also strong trade unionists, home-owners and proud family men; considered provincial, they viewed themselves as patriotic Americans entitled to protect their hard-won gains. Overwhelmingly the children and grandchildren of Italian, Polish, Slovak, Ukrainian and other Eastern and Southern European immigrants, they were largely Roman Catholics. Because of religion and class, some included the Irish, an older ethnic group, in the white ethnic camp. How remarkable therefore that officials of the American Jewish Committee (AJC) took the lead in formulating the new pluralism that presumed to speak for the needs and aspirations of these working-class, Catholic ethnics.

Beginning in 1968, the AJC became the most influential communal agency to define and propagate the theories, programs and social policies of the new pluralism. That year it organized the first National Consultation on Ethnic America which was held at Fordham University. The Committee then established the National Project on Ethnic America which in 1974 evolved into the Institute on Pluralism and Group Identity and in 1983 into the Institute for American Pluralism. It is this apparent anomaly—the oldest and most prestigious Jewish defense agency popularizing a controversial notion of American group life—that raises questions that go beyond narrow, institutional issues.[2]

Indeed, the full import of the AJC's promotion of the new pluralism becomes apparent when one considers the vastly different perception of American society that guided the Committee during the 1950s and early 1960s. For the Jewish community as a whole those years were marked by a newly found self-confidence and self-definition which also fit the mood of national consensus and purpose. Several events neatly capture the prevailing sense of harmony, rapport and optimism.

In 1954 the AJC played an influential role in planning the yearlong tercentenary celebration of the first settlement of Jews on the North American continent. The occasion provided the opportunity for American Jewry to review its growth from the arrival in New Amsterdam of twenty-three refugee settlers, who were received by an unhospitable governor, to the affluent and influential community of five million three hundred years later. The celebrations became a paean to the American democratic tradition and emphasized the congruity between Judaism and America's ideals.[3]

Soon after the celebrations ended the AJC went a step further to consider group life in America in general and sponsored a conference on the subject. Meeting at Arden House, New York, in November 1956, thirty-three distinguished scholars and men of affairs gathered "to join theory and practice in a consideration of the new patterns of ethnic and religious group life emerging in America."[4]

The conclusions were bland enough to sit well with the consensual, optimistic mood of the late 1950s. For example: "The ethnic group, with increasing emphasis upon religious identification, may be expected to play a continuing but ever-changing role in American life, benefiting both the individual and society." Or: "Within the past two decades these groups have changed markedly in character and concomitant changes in the function of their institutions may also be anticipated. As integration proceeds, their 'defensive' or 'protest' function will become less important. Positive education for their own members as well as service to the community and promotion of the general welfare may be expected to assume greater importance." Under "Problems Ahead" the conference barely hinted at racial tensions. "There is some evidence to suggest that in spite of the rather widespread vertical mobility of Americans today, possibly even because of it, we may anticipate some sharpening of intergroup conflict."[5]

Nor had matters changed much when five years later Oscar Handlin, the Harvard historian and the study director of the Arden House conference, published a number of the papers. In his introductory essay on ethnic groups in American life, Handlin took note of the increasing number of marriages across group lines despite the hostility to them by the ethnic group and used it as paradigm for the openness of American life:

> Marriage in America was not a means of securing the continuity of the group but of satisfying the desire of the individual for fulfillment as a personality, apart from any social considerations. The theme of romantic love grew steadily in importance, and it emphasized the capacity of the individual to surmount the barriers of ethnic differences, as also those of class. It was symptomatic of the conviction that the values associated with the individual invariably took precedence over those of the group. It existed to serve him, not he, it.[6]

In the preface to the volume, Handlin offered his view of America's pluralistic tradition:

> [For some] the retention of group identification is seen as both necessary and desirable for spiritual self-preservation and self-fulfillment, as well as a source of national enrichment. The perpetuation of group loyalties is, from this point of view, consonant with the American pattern, neither impeding integration nor endangering national unity.[7]

Here, indeed, was the essence of the old, or "soft" pluralism in which religious and ethnic groups functioned neither abetted nor impeded by public law, and where group identification was a matter of choice.

During these years perhaps the most popular and influential interpretation of the United States among Jewish religious and communal leaders was Will Herberg's *Protestant, Catholic, Jew.* Herberg, a theologian and sociologist, offered an overarching view of the manner by which America had integrated its immigrant population. Neither a single melting pot model nor the cultural pluralistic model explained the most recent phase of the process. He proposed instead a triple melting pot scheme to explain how the third-generation offspring of the mass migration adopted the American ethos. They had sorted themselves out into the three religious pools, Protestant, Catholic, and Jewish. There they exchanged their fading recollections of their grandparents' immigrant culture for a broader religious identity joining earlier ethnic groups who had preceded them in the process. Of equal worth, "the three great religious communities" constituted "the three basic subdivisions of the American people that is emerging today." They were the "religions of democracy" which formed the underpinning of the "American Way of Life."[8]

For America's Jews, Herberg's analysis placed Judaism, centerpiece of the Judeo-Christian tradition, in the mainstream of the nation's cultural and spiritual tradition. Especially comforting was the conviction that Herberg had correctly gauged the new culture of conformity and consensus that the nation had now achieved. In President Eisenhower's oft-quoted words: "Our government makes no sense unless it is founded in a deeply felt religious faith—and I don't care what it is." Even Glazer and Daniel Moynihan, who in their 1963 study of New York's minorities, *Beyond the Melting Pot*, emphasized the collective interest of the group rather than its customs and culture as the primary factor in its survival, essentially amended Herberg's analysis rather than refuting it. "Religion and race," they wrote in their conclusion, "seem to define the major groups into which American society is evolving as the specifically national aspect of ethnicity declines."[9]

Five years later all had changed. The riots in the black ghettos, the increasingly impassioned opposition to the Vietnam War, the campus uprisings, the radicalization of the civil rights movement, the black power movement, and white opposition to federal programs favoring blacks were tearing the social fabric apart. The 1968 annual statement issued by the National Community Relations Advisory Council—the closest we have to a Jewish state-of-the-nation address—captures the mood of despair.

The Nation is in crisis. . . . When polarizations develop that defy reconciliation, when differences are no longer tolerated, but instead produce violent confrontations, and above all, when substantial segments of the people withdraw and no longer have concern for the preservation of the society itself, we are in grave danger. The nation hangs precariously between anarchy and violence on the one hand and massive repression on the other.[10]

What was a Jewish communal agency like the AJC to do? Pull in its defense perimeter and limit itself to protecting Jewish interests—jobs, neighborhoods, schools—and to repelling the strident antisemitism adopted by black nationalists? During the previous twenty years, as Naomi Cohen in her history of the AJC informs us, the Committee had moved cautiously into the realm of social action, particularly when strong presidential leadership pointed the way. Early in Truman's presidency the Committee joined other civic bodies in supporting legislation and litigation directed against racial discrimination in employment, housing and education. In selected states and cities, Cohen writes, the Committee "assigned special field workers who, alongside the local chapters, helped in the campaigns for local Fair Employment Practices Commissions." Significantly, when it took this first major step to expand the scope of its public concerns, the AJC executive committee found it necessary to declare that such actions were within the powers of its charter: to "join with other groups in the protection of the civil rights of the members of all groups irrespective of race, religion, color or national origin." One could indeed link the broadened involvement of the Committee in American domestic affairs in the 1950s to the founders' justification for establishing the organization a half century before. Not only as Jews, but as Americans committed to the ideals of freedom and equality, they had undertaken "to prevent the infringement of the civil and religious rights of Jews and to alleviate the consequences of persecution."[11] In the name of these ideals and the humanitarian impulses of the American people, they had turned more than once to the national government for its support. Now their civic duty required that they direct their agency to collaborate in redressing the most flagrant of iniquities, racism.

During the Kennedy and Johnson administrations, as the civil rights movement gathered momentum and received presidential support, the Committee played an increasingly active role in the coalition fighting segregation and discrimination. It sponsored social research on race relations as part of a broad program of enlightening the public and influencing social policy. It also initiated training programs to assist blacks in improving their occupational positions, and it aided blacks in establishing their own businesses.[12]

By 1967 the liberal-black coalition was in disarray. Presidential leadership was being wasted on waging a hopeless war. The radicalization of the black protest movement ended white participation in a common undertaking and dealt a near-fatal blow to moderating forces. Perhaps most distressing of all were the portents of a major realignment of political forces: the signs that ultraconservative and jingoist forces were reaching out to tap the fears and prejudices of Northern working-class whites.

For some time now the Committee had been monitoring the rising resentment, anxiety, and anger in the Northern white urban neighborhoods which sat astride the expanding black ghettos. (In New York City a number of sizeable Jewish neighborhoods found themselves in a similar geographic position.) An early expression of the Committee's concern came in a 1964 article in *Commentary* by David Danzig, at the time the AJC's director of programming. Entitled "Rightists, Racists, and Separatists: A White Bloc in the Making?" the article analyzed Governor George Wallace's surprising successes in the presidential primaries in Wisconsin, Indiana, and Maryland. Wallace's most solid constituencies—Southern segregationists and the fundamentalist and nativist ultraright—needed no explanation. However, the alarming fact was that in the spring of 1964 Wallace had done suprisingly well in the heavily Democratic wards of Milwaukee which were predominantly Polish, Italian and Serbian and bordered on the black area of settlement; in industrial Gary, with its large East European and black population; and in Baltimore's Italian and Irish neighborhoods. This working- and middle-class urban population had been one of the mainstays of the old New Deal coalition. It had provided the margin of victory for Harry Truman and John F. Kennedy, and its continued support for liberal candidates seemed essential if the nation's political leaders were to assert themselves once more and deal decisively with the social and racial malaise. Yet the crucial element, Danzig pointed out, had become "militantly 'separatist.'"

In principle, Danzig explained, the working, lower-middle-class ethnic whites had supported civil rights and integration as national goals. However, as court-ordered integration came to the Northern cities, the white ethnics were gripped with "fear that the cherished neighborhood culture" would be destroyed by the expanding black population. Danzig and other social theorists, who would later support the new pluralism movement, justified maintaining the integrity of the ethnic neighborhood with its religious-ethnic communal network of schools, churches, social and recreational clubs, and its similar employment patterns, and its genial family and friendship ties.[13]

During the following years the "white backlash" found its expression in demonstrations against busing and open housing, in violent confrontations between blacks and whites during the ghetto riots, and in municipal politics such as the 1966 New York City referendum on the civilian review board proposal, in which Irish, Italians and the less affluent Jews lined up against imposing outside controls over the police.[14] It was against this background that in the fall of 1967, some members of the AJC's staff, led by Irving Levine, the Committee's director of education and urban planning, began pressing for a major conference on the topic of ethnic America. "I see the meeting," Levine wrote, "as a scholarly one, oriented towards developing a strategy to deal with Ethnic America." The conference would represent a crucial departure in the Committee's traditional approach, replacing a soft pluralism with a hard-nosed, if not a hard "new pluralism."[15]

Levine, who had only recently joined the national staff of the Committee, brought to the task a wealth of experience in the civil rights movement, intergroup relations, and urban affairs. Trained as a social worker, he had served as a community relations field consultant for New York City's Commission on Human Relations in the late 1950s. From 1961 to 1965, he was director of the AJC in Ohio, where he headed the Ohio civil rights legislative campaign and was a leading figure in the United Freedom movement in Cleveland. In recalling those years, Levine described his role in these words: "I became the Jewish professional with ties to the more radical element while the Jewish federation played the role of center moderate on civil rights."[16]

For Levine the increasing tensions within the civil rights movement between white liberals and black power advocates, together with the resentment and anger of Northern, lower-middle-class whites, reached an alarming point when 42 percent of Milwaukee's white ethnics voted for Wallace in the 1964 primary. "White backlash could become white Fascism. I wrote a strategy paper on how Jews might deal with white ethnics. . . . It was an unknown area—[unlike] working with blacks or interreligious relations." Nor had the Wallace threat abated in the spring of 1968 as preparations for the conference on ethnic America moved into high gear. Indeed in the Midwest the Gallop poll gave Wallace 16 percent of the vote.[17] Thus the initial impetus which moved the creators of the new pluralism stemmed to a considerable degree from the urgent need to defuse the white backlash and to save the liberal-progressive coalition from dissolution.

This was to be done, Levine stated in his conference proposal, by identifying "the real problems of lower middle class ethnic groups and speak[ing] creatively to their deepest needs."[18]

Other Committee specialists in urban and intergroup affairs supported this approach. In addition to Danzig, Murray Friedman, who directed the Philadelphia office of the AJC, wrote extensively on the need to recognize the ethnic factor in improving neighborhood life. He advised Levine in preparing the national conference and organized the first AJC-sponsored regional conference in Philadelphia. Welcome support came from Robert C. Wood, the Undersecretary of Housing and Urban Development. His position and academic reputation as an expert on urban affairs gave authority and weight to Levine's approach. In a lecture delivered in November 1967, Wood focused on "the working American—the average white ethnic male." Twenty million strong, they were "deeply troubled," worried about being laid off, suffering from rising taxes and poor neighborhood services, smarting under their image as bigots and upset by their diminished political clout. They were alienated and angry. In line with Wood's analysis, Levine listed twenty-one problems in his conference proposal which required immediate attention. Among them were crime on the streets, the unfair and burdensome tax structure, high medical costs, inadequate leisure-time facilities, the financial burden of parochial education, lack of help in child rearing, and the threat of automation. Levine suggested that the racism of the white ethnics was in large measure an expression of the alienation and frustration of living under these conditions. The white ethnics found little satisfaction or hope for advancement in the workplace, felt themselves slipping into poverty, and, unable to afford any of the amenities of life, lived a drab and constricted existence exacerbated by the visions of affluent America on their TV screens. Close by, a plethora of government-financed programs were directed at the black ghetto. No longer, Levine stressed, could the nation "define the major problem of America only in terms of Negroes. . . . Ethnic groups must feel the security of having someone watching out for them too." By having their needs recognized, white ethnic groups would be brought back "into the mainstream of a progressive America."[19]

The new pluralist strategy, as it was pieced together by Levine and his advisors, also recognized the need to honor ethnic group consciousness and bolster self-esteem. But in 1967 and 1968 there was much unclarity about the meaning and content of ethnic culture and how it related to class. (Writing in 1971, Levine noted: "Most of the issues we projected at the Project's inception were based on the economic circumstances of the group involved—but in each case it has been our purpose to explore and understand the role played by ethnicity.") The theorists of the new pluralism took note of the expressions of black pride, the demands for black studies, and the conscious transformation of black folkways, popular culture, and life styles into a black ethnic culture, a way of life. But an equivalently aggressive response by Italian, Polish and other white ethnic leaders and ideologists was yet to come. Moreover, the term "white ethnic," itself, glossed over the particularistic cultural component. What was *new* about the new pluralism at this time were demands for governmental intervention to alleviate the social and material plight of the white ethnic groups just as government had aided the blacks. Once the passions and the fury of powerless people were directed into meaningful channels, the argument went, the road would be open to bargaining and to accommodation between previously hostile groups. In a word, "depolarization" would lead to "bridge building" and finally to "coalition building"—the slogans of the movement in its first years.[20]

In June 1968, the two-day National Consultation on Ethnic America, as it was called, convened at Fordham University in New York and ushered in the era of the new pluralism. Nearly 150 attended: social workers, scholars, clergymen, trade union leaders, and representatives of ethnic neighborhoods. Among the cosponsors were the Social Action Department of the National Catholic Conference for Interracial Justice, and the International Union of Electrical Workers. In addition to Danzig, Wood and Milton Gordon, Andrew Greeley, the sociologist and author of the influential *Assimilation in American Life*, presented a major paper. Director of the National Opinion Research Center at the University of Chicago, Greeley, a sociologist of ethnicity, was also a Catholic priest, and Irish. His paper, later expanded into *Why Can't They Be Like Us? Facts and Fallacies about Ethnic Differences and Group Conflicts in America*, was published by the AJC and widely distributed. (Wood, by then director of the Joint Center for Urban Studies of MIT and Harvard University, wrote the foreword.) The author, his message, the venue of the conference and the identity of the prime sponsor deftly underscored the ethnic and religious collaboration Levine was seeking.[21]

A year after the New York consultation, the Committee established the "National Project on Ethnic America, A Depolarization Program of the American Jewish Committee" with support from the Stern Family Fund and other foundations. The advisory committee consisted of leading scholars in the field, representatives of a number of ethnic groups, and officials of intergroup relations agencies. However, the Project, directed by

Levine, was staffed solely by AJC professionals who were answerable to the Committee's heads. Since the funding of the Project came primarily from outside sources, Levine and his associates exercised an uncommon degree of organizational autonomy. In fact, as we shall see, a number of the Committee's officials harbored serious misgivings about the entire enterprise yet found it difficult to call Levine to account.

Other "consultations" followed the Fordham conference. The ones in Philadelphia, Chicago, and San Francisco received national attention. The Project staff succeeded in co-opting local church leaders, ethnic organizations, academic institutions, professional communal workers and public agencies. The Chicago consultation led to the establishment of a permanent interethnic agency, which was coordinated by David Roth, the AJC's regional director. Levine and his associate, Judith Herman, traveled widely nurturing interethnic ties, overseeing the conferences, and advising on "action projects" geared to the needs of the local community. In specific places—in poor white neighborhoods in Baltimore, Philadelphia, Newark, and New York—Levine provided staff assistance and subsidized local field workers in establishing community programs. In 1970 and 1971, with additional funds available, the Project expanded its scope, organizing conferences directly or providing guidance for local initiatives in Buffalo, Detroit, Hartford, Pittsburgh, Milwaukee, and Newark. In Boston, the staff undertook the preliminary planning for a conference on ethnic studies and then arranged to have the operating responsibility given to the state's teachers association. In Cleveland, the Project's directors collaborated with Cleveland State University in organizing a "research-action" conference on ethnicity and providing financial support for the resultant training programs in intergroup relations. Hartford and Chicago were chosen as the locales for a study of attitudes of young blue-collar workers. It was conducted under contract for the U.S. Department of Labor. During its first two years the Project generated a remarkable amount of research and publications.[22]

Perhaps its greatest success was the sheer promotion of the notion of the new pluralism. Directly, and by contributing to making the subject of white ethnics newsworthy, Levine was instrumental in gaining the attention of the news media. In its October 9, 1969, issue, *Newsweek* published a series of reports, "The Troubled American: A Special Report on the White Majority." *Time* made the middle American its "Man and Woman of the Year" for 1969. The Project's staff served as a prime resource for WNBC-TV's hour-long program, "The Ethnic Factor," and held meetings with the producer of "All in the Family," the controversial "humorous and ethnic" program. Levine's close working ties with a score of important journalists resulted in feature articles in the major papers throughout the country.[23]

In the fall of 1970, recognition of the AJC's work came in the form of a three-year, Ford Foundation grant. Negotiations began in early 1969. Levine describes the meeting with Mitchell Sviridoff, the Ford Foundation's vice president for national affairs:

> I outlined my idea for the Jewish Urban Action Laboratory. Sviridoff's reaction was that he would have to see a very specific proposal. . . . He also seemed to be telling us that since the Ford Foundation had been making commitments of relatively small amounts to a number of Jewish agencies . . . they were anxious to do somewhat the same for us. . . . It was quite interesting as an aside that with very little time to go into details we also mentioned our concern with white ethnic lower middle class America. Sviridoff's face seemed to light up with considerably more excitement than he showed towards the Jewish project.

Levine suggested that he give Sviridoff the background material the AJC had prepared and meet with his staff.[24]

Whether this meeting influenced the Ford Foundation's reevaluation of its social policies is not clear, although Levine thought so. In the Ford Foundation Report for 1969, Sviridoff proposed new priorities in dealing with America's social problems. "The social programs of the sixties," he wrote, "were targeted in the main at the 'poor' and at 'poverty.' In retrospect, this strategy, while appropriate and necessary in the short run, may have had unfortunate consequences in the longer run. For the polarization that today puts American society under strain stems in large part from the dissatisfactions of whites in the near-poor, lower-middle, and middle classes—those left out of much recent public programming." Levine, in a memorandum to his staff commenting on the Ford Foundation Report, remarked, "I've bracketed a number of paragraphs [in the attached report] that relate to Sviridoff's new emphasis on lower-middle class whites and the problems of racial reconciliation. Sviridoff seems to be adopting AJC's line both generally (in the contents of his writings) and more specifically in our concerns on polarization."[25]

In 1974, a major Rockefeller Foundation award assured the continued operation of the Project. Renamed the Institute on Pluralism and Group Identity, the agency broadened its range of interests to include ethnic studies, the needs of working-class women and their relations to the feminist movement, the family, and the links between ethnicity and mental health. In each of these instances the Institute combined research aimed at shaping social policy, advising and initiating joint programs with public and government agencies, and popularizing the issues. Indeed, there was much truth in the self-congratulatory mood that the AJC's Institute on Pluralism and Group Identity was, in Levine's words, "*the* think tank" on matters of ethnicity and social policy.[26] In the course of ten years, the AJC established itself as a major center for defining the nature and place of ethnicity in American life. It also became a center of controversy from within and from without. Three groups of its critics deserve mention.

Levine's conception of the National Project and then the expanded Institute for Pluralism as "explorer, initiator, communicator, and catalyst" certainly worked in the case of the Catholic social agencies. In 1969 the Catholic Bishops' conference appointed a task force on urban problems headed by Monsignor Geno Baroni and in 1971, with a Ford Foundation grant, Baroni established the National Center for Urban Ethnic Affairs, the Catholic counterpart to the American Jewish Committee's National Project on Ethnic America. Tensions were endemic to the situation. For Baroni, the Committee was an outsider defining the problems, plotting the strategy, and often speaking for a public that was overwhelmingly Catholic.[27]

In 1974, when the Committee received the Rockefeller award, the simmering antagonisms exploded. Catholic leaders including Baroni, Greeley, the Rev. Paul J. Asciolla, the editor of the Chicago Anglo-Italian paper, *Fra Noi*, the Rev. S. M. Tomasi, director of the Center for Migration Studies, all members of the Institute for Pluralism's advisory committee (but who had not been informed of the negotiations), resigned in protest. What especially antagonized them was the moralistic and condescending tone in which the proposal was couched, and which was extensively quoted in the press. Since the Foundation classified the AJC proposal under "Arts, Humanities, and Contemporary Values—The Public Humanities," the Committee was advised to stress the humanistic and ethical goals in its proposal and the uplift effect they would have on the working-class ethnic communities. Asciolla, in a passage that captured the mood of the other letters of resignation, wrote, "The Rockefeller Foundation . . . must finally come to realize that Catholic ethnics have the capability and track record for defining their own 'values,' 'moral concerns' and 'community issues' and that they have the competency of interpreting these humanistic, moral and family values to the media, academics and other 'first rate' intellectual humanists who have never really understood our communities in the first instance."[28] If the culprit was the Foundation, the Committee was the accomplice. At a national conference of Catholic clergy the rancor against the Committee and the Foundation found no rest. A Ukrainian bishop from Philadelphia asked: "How did this happen? Here we've got an Anglo-Saxon foundation giving money to the Jews to study ethnic Catholics in America." An Italian prelate remarked, "They're saying, in effect, that ethnic Catholics are too dumb to study themselves. It's not that the AJC does not do commendable work, but how can they ignore the work done by our own people?"[29]

The Committee itself was of two minds about the entire enterprise, Bertram Gold, the executive vice president, recalled: "There was much opposition to the idea from the beginning among the staff as well as among the lay leaders. 'What do we have to do with organizing the red-necks, forming alliances with them, what about our liberal image?' "[30] Levine himself remembered the early criticism to the idea of building an ethnic coalition. It would be "putting Jews in the middle, between the blacks and the white ethnics, hence eliciting the enmity of both sides," he was told. Furthermore, "nothing would move them [the white ethnics] towards progressive action." And finally, stressing ethnicity means "downgrading" Jewish status from being one of the three major religions to becoming "one of a hundred ethnic groups."[31] In a confidential memorandum to Gold, a senior member of the staff stressed yet another point:

> Some of us feel that it may not be wise, and in the long run not in the Jewish interest, to actively promote ethnic cultures and consciousness, especially of European nationality groups, and more particularly Slavic groups. The fact that under the impact of the black identity movement other ethnic groups may have become more conscious of their own background and interests, does not in itself justify or legitimatize efforts on the part of the American Jewish Committee to become the leader and the mover of an ethnicity project. I have tried to argue in the past that, all other considerations aside and there are many, the revival of the history, culture and ethnic identification of Slavic groups could potentially revive and reinforce anti-Semitism. I have made this point because of my knowledge of some of these Slavic cultures and my personal experience. . . . Frankly, from a Jewish interest point of view, we should welcome the acculturation of these groups into the Anglo-Saxon culture which, with all its limitations, obviously represents a more tolerant, libertarian and democratic tradition. Such acculturation is "good for the Jews."[32]

Supporters of the white ethnic strategy countered with their Jewish reasons. Levine concluded one memorandum to Bertram Gold in October 1974 with the cryptic remark, "This is the time to assert the fact that Jews cannot expect strong support for their major positions unless they have an attitude of reciprocity and compassion for others."[33] More explicitly, the Committee's Midwest director, who had established excellent rapport with Chicago's Italian, Polish and Ukrainian leaders, worked intensively to win their support for Israel and with considerable success. When the Ford Foundation's officer wrote his assessment of the Committee's National Project in 1973, he took note of the "internal debate." The "liberal civil rights coalition was concerned that the project reflected a 'copout' on AJC's commitment to civil rights. A second group expressed concern over the 'anti-Semitism often found among white ethnic groups.' A third group, essentially assimilationist . . . challenged the whole focus on ethnic pluralism."[34]

The new pluralism came under attack from another direction, one which was again close to home. The March 1972 issue of *Commentary* included Harold R. Isaacs's "The New Pluralists," a scathing review of *Overcoming Middle Class Rage*, an anthology of studies on the plight of white ethnic groups. Edited by Murray Friedman, who wrote the main thematic essays, the book also contained key papers given by David Danzig and Irving Levine at the early conferences sponsored by the Committee's National Project on Ethnic America. It thus represented the fullest exposition of the new ethnicity. The June *Commentary* carried Robert Alter's "A Fever of Ethnicity," a slashing criticism of Michael Novak's "intemperate" *The Rise of the Unmeltable Ethnics*, and Norman Podhoretz's editorial, "The Idea of a Common Culture." Taken together, the three pieces represented a rejection of the new pluralism based on the fear that the new pluralists were, wittingly or not, encouraging ethnocentrism, "a certain lunging back into the tribal caves," in Isaacs's words, and "denigrating the ideal of individual autonomy," in Podhoretz's phrase.[35]

Nathan Glazer, perhaps the most astute observer of the ethnic scene, also voiced reservations about the direction the "ethnic resurgence" was taking—if indeed, he speculated, one existed at all. Glazer questioned the viability of the category "white ethnic" itself. But he was most troubled by the implications of the rigorous turn the enforcement of the affirmative action programs had taken, especially the use of minority group quotas in hiring and in professional school admissions. Governmental recognition of group rights was the danger, and the rhetoric of the new pluralism implied just that. Expanding the compensatory measures intended to redress discriminatory practices into corporate privileges for particular racial or ethnic groups, to be enforced by the courts and executed by a heavy-handed bureaucracy, was an aberration of the American democratic tradition. Glazer was troubled by any movement that would further weaken "the primacy of the individual regardless of race, color or creed." In a keynote address to the San Francisco Consultation on Ethnicity in 1971, he sketched a framework within which the discourse on group life in America should take place. The first and most important principle was that

> the *individual* is paramount, not the group. The group has no claim on the individual if he does not want to be a member of the group. It can levy no tax on him, though he may give voluntary contributions. It may levy no loyalty, though he may give voluntary loyalty. Government recognizes the individual, not the group. Only the individual has rights, not the group.[36]

At the Committee's annual meeting in May 1972, the AJC's president, Philip E. Hoffman, devoted much of his keynote address to the issues Glazer and others were raising. The Committee, Hoffman emphasized, remained committed to achieving a truly integrated society. However, he warned, "in our desire to take swift and affirmative action to extend opportunities to disadvantaged minorities we must be careful not to fall into the trap of supporting reverse discrimination." Establishing affirmative action "goals" or "targets" was legitimate, imposing quotas was not. Since its founding, Hoffman reminded his audience, the AJC had fought quotas, "whether they were designed to keep some one out or to bring others in. We will continue to oppose them because they ignore the fundamental principle of democracy: the right to be judged on individual merit, not on such irrelevant considerations as race, religion, ethnic or cultural affiliation." Indeed, in a democracy, Hoffman continued, rights are accorded to the individual, not to the group. And although he granted that special measures were needed "to overcome dramatic and long-standing imbalances in wealth and power, we will insist that these measures be addressed to the individual, not to the group."[37]

Significantly, Hoffman's discussion of minority group quotas led to his remarks about the AJC's National Ethnic Project. A "dramatic emergence of 'group-ism,' " he noted, had produced a vigorous, unself-conscious assertion of group needs, group desires, and group grievances. The purpose of the Ethnic Project was to "defuse these competing groups." Then lapsing into an almost pensive mood Hoffman remarked, "It sometimes seems that our good old American melting pot is feverishly unmelting as, all of a sudden, the many and diverse elements that made up the American stew are popping abruptly out of the broth and back into their separateness. Is this good? Or bad?" His answer was a guarded "good." Group associations should be encouraged. For many they represented "a solid ground on which to stand, a reassuring base from which to go forth, a comforting home to which to return in a despairing and alienating society." At the same time, they must not be allowed to serve as a "battlefield from which to undermine the larger society."[38]

Despite Hoffman's centrist position, differences in nuances remained within the AJC. In a paper delivered before the Committee on Integration of the American Immigration and Citizenship Conference in February 1973, Levine responded to the critics of the new pluralism whom he labeled "reactionaries." What was most discouraging about those who advocated a "return to a laissez-faire economic approach toward the poor . . . was the intellectual cover, intended or not, by the new advocates of 'the limits of social policy.' " These "sophisticated thinkers" had in the past been friendly to ethnic and minority causes. Writing principally in such periodicals as *Commentary* and *Public Interest*, they based their arguments "on the evident failure of government to effectively deliver needed services." Although their criticism was rational enough, what was needed, Levine countered, "is *not* self-imposed limits in social policy programming but the 'fine-tuning' of social policy." He called for "the kind of governmentally supported policies which offer a series of options for people, based on diversity of lifestyles and preferred forms of aid." Instead of more conservative approaches to problems, the nation needed "solutions which seek to carefully preserve and build on those beneficial aspects of 'rootedness,' of neighborhood 'people systems' and communal networks which are still alive."[39]

By the mid-1970s the new pluralism movement was caught between two opposing camps: the liberal, soft pluralists of the pre-1965 era who now feared the "Balkanization" of America and were critical of the social policies of the 1960s (among them social critics like Irving Kristol, Norman Podhoretz and Nathan Glazer); and pre-1965 liberal, civil rights activists, who supported the compensatory programs for blacks and other minorities and wished to apply them, with caution, to other groups. Recalling this period Levine remarked, "I belonged to the liberal wing of the Committee."[40]

The position Levine took as spokesman for the AJC and the Institute for Pluralism on the Ethnic Heritage Studies Program Act offers a further insight into some of the shadings of the new pluralism. The bill was first introduced in November 1969 by Congressman Roman Pucinski, who represented a largely Polish-American district in Chicago. Its purpose was to give every American child an opportunity to study his own ethnic heritage and to appreciate the heterogeneity of American society. Programs—the original language called for centers—would be designed to prepare material and curricula, train teachers, and thereby introduce the study of the ethnic cultures into the school. Cosponsored by Senator Richard S. Schweiker of Pennsylvannia, it became law as an amendment to the Omnibus Higher Education Act of 1972. Congress authorized an expenditure of 15 million dollars. Not until 1974 were funds appropriated and then in the disappointing amount of $2,375,000. Nevertheless, the act was hailed as a new departure for the United States. In the minds of its sponsors, Congress had at last rejected the pernicious notion of the melting pot and recognized through law "the heterogeneous composition of the nation and the fact that in a multiethnic society a greater understanding of the contributions of one's own heritage and those of one's fellow citizens can contribute to a more harmonious, patriotic, and committed populace."[41]

The AJC was active in the framing of the bill and in a consultative capacity during the various stages of its passage. Levine appeared before the House subcommittee on education. He was also instrumental in making one crucial change in the bill. Instead of "centers" dealing with a single ethnic culture as first proposed, Levine warned against their divisive consequences and proposed multicultural centers. The emphasis would be placed on "cross-cultural cooperation"; each center would expose its student teachers to a variety of ethnic cultures and educate them to an appreciation of the totality of a multiethnic society. In his testimony Levine offered an interesting alternative to the proposed heritage studies centers. He called for the establishment of a National Institute on Group Life. His model was the National Institute of Mental Health, a government-supported agency which initiated and coordinated research. In fact, Levine informed the committee, the AJC had proposed to the platform committees of both political parties in 1968 the creation of such an institute. However, his notion of a permanent, comprehensive educational and research agency dedicated to ethnic life was ignored then as it is now. Nevertheless, he did succeed in having the idea of monolithic ethnic centers dropped. Among the new pluralists, Levine and the Institute he built were pragmatic problem-solvers trying to cope with the social realities of the time. On this matter, the AJC was of a similar bent. Bertram Gold recalled: "In a sense [the Institute] was not completely AJC. Thus Irving could try out different ideas without the AJC being fully responsible."[42]

In 1988, the Institute celebrated the twentieth anniversary of the National Consultation on Ethnic America. Appropriately, the conference was held at Fordham University and duly dubbed "Fordham 2." One of the conference's goals—to promote "good intergroup relations and the common interest"—received particular emphasis. Stressing the "common interest" reflected the mounting fears that ethnic lines were hardening at the expense of a shared civic culture. During the heady days of the late 1960s, the new pluralists praised and encouraged the "new awakening" of ethnic and racial identity and pressed for public recognition of group interests and entitlements for white ethnics as well as black Americans. By the late 1970s, calls for ethnocultural changes in the school curricula had gained currency, and the entitlements issue erupted in court challenges to affirmative action quotas in school admissions. (In the celebrated Allan Bakke case, which reached the Supreme Court in 1978, a white applicant who was rejected by the medical school of the University of California at Davis charged the school with reverse discrimination, claiming that less-qualified applicants were accepted under a minorities quota. In an *amicus* brief on behalf of Bakke, the AJC declared itself for "affirmative action without quotas.")[43]

Given the strident debates over ethnic studies, bilingualism, and affirmative action, the Institute devised less controversial programs that were still predicated on the centrality of ethnicity. It designed scores of workshops and research projects on topics such as "The Media and Ethnicity" and "Establishing a Human Relations Program on Your College Campus." The Institute also created a center for the study of "Group Identity and Mental Health" and one for "Women and American Diversity." The shift in emphasis was indicative of a middle road between the new pluralism and soft pluralism, between sanctioning group privileges and a laissez-faire approach to ethnic group life ("pluralistic integration," to use historian John Higham's term). And it conformed with the AJC's formula of "affirmative action without quotas."[44]

From a historical perspective, the interest of the AJC in the new pluralism—and in its various nuances—is noteworthy. The Committee was founded "to prevent the infraction of the civil and religious rights of Jews in any part of the world." Until the 1940s, the AJC avoided public debates over definitions of Jewish group identity in particular and America's national identity in general, except for reiterating its belief in America's democratic ideals. Then, as we noted above, Jewish self-defense was no longer enough. The AJC broadened its scope and joined the struggle for civil rights and the elimination of discrimination and prejudice *for all*. This changed emphasis required that questions relating to the place of diversity and ethnicity in America be addressed. In response to the malaise of the 1960s, the National Project for Ethnic America (including its precursors and successors) undertook no less a task than to redefine American identity and formulate a new public policy for the nation.

These bold initiatives and projects offer some indication of the degree of AJC involvement in national affairs and a measure of the organization's self-confidence. They are traits shared by other Jewish communal agencies, and by many American Jews whose public activism is prompted by their sensibility for civic inclusiveness and their ethnoreligious attachments. Among thoughtful American Jews, this duality has produced a penchant for self-scrutiny which has dwelt tirelessly not only on the meaning of being Jewish in America but on the meaning of America. One thinks of Israel Friedlaender, Judah Magnes, Louis Brandeis, and Horace Kallen, who nearly a century ago interpreted American nationalism as validating diversity. In our times, a host of social critics who identify themselves as Jews and Jewish leaders and scholars have continued to advocate this line of thought, adjusting it to new contingencies and demands. Their writings, teachings, and communal endeavors reflect their wish to maintain a creative duality as Americans and Jews.

# Notes

### Introduction

1.  "The Problem of Judaism in America," in *Past and Present: A Collection of Jewish Essays* (Cincinnati: Ark Publishing Co., 1919), 277–278.

2.  Friedlaender, *Past and Present*, 252–253. Baila Round Shargel discusses the essay in her fine study, *Practical Dreamer: Israel Friedlaender and the Shaping of American Judaism* (New York: Jewish Theological Seminary, 1985), 84–85. (*Jewish Exponent* [Philadelphia], Dec. 20, 1907, 10). The date in Friedlaender, p. 253, is incorrect.

3.  Shargel, *Practical Dreamer*, 3–7; Friedlaender, *Past and Present*, 273.

4.  Friedlaender, *Past and Present*, 260–263.

5.  Friedlaender, *Past and Present*, 273–277, 255–258, 263–267, 274; Shargel, 150, 196–197.

6.  *The Maccabaean* 33 (June 1920): 193; *New York Times*, May 11, 1920, 25; ibid. May 12, 1920, 16; *Der Tog*, May 12, 1920, 1; Arthur A. Goren, "Celebrating Zion in America," in Jeffrey Shandler and Beth S. Wenger, eds., *Encounters with the "Holy Land": Place, Past and Future in American Jewish Culture* (Hanover, N.H.: University Press of New England, 1997), 45–49.

7.  Meyer Weisgal, *Meyer Weisgal: So Far* (New York: Random House, 1971), 109, 115–116; *Chicago Daily Tribune*, July 4, 1933, 1, 4; Atay Citron, "Pageantry and Theater in the Service of Jewish Nationalism in the United States, 1933–1946" (Ph.D. dissertation, New York University, 1989), 37–49; Stephen J. Whitfield, "The Politics of Pageantry, 1936–1946," *American Jewish History* 84, no. 3 (Sept. 1996): 221–251.

8.  Salo Wittmayer Baron, *The Jewish Community: Its History and Structure to the American Revolution* (Philadelphia: Jewish Publication Society, 1942), I:25.

### 1. Strategies of Survival and the Uses of Pluralism

1.  Charles S. Liebman, *The Ambivalent American Jew* (Philadelphia: Jewish Publication Society, 1973); 7–17, 39–41, 149–159; Abraham J. Karp, "Ideology and Identity in Jewish Group Survival in America," *American Jewish Historical Quarterly* 65, no. 4 (June 1976): 310–334.

2.  Among the "Jews who enriched American life" Oscar Handlin mentions Abraham Jacobi, Joseph Pulitzer and Walter Lippman, *Adventure in Freedom* (New York: McGraw-Hill, 1954), 98. All three either avoided, rejected or were indifferent to Jewish identification. Henry Feingold, in his *Zion in*

America (New York: Twayne, 1974), 55, 78, 79, 85, describes August Belmont a number of times as a "Jewish banker." Belmont married an Episcopalian and attended church regularly although he was never baptized.

3. *Jewish Education* 20 (Summer 1949): 110.

4. Isaac B. Berkson, *Theories of Americanization* (New York: Teachers College, Columbia University, 1920), 160–161; Arthur A. Goren, *New York Jews and the Quest for Community* (New York: Columbia University Press, 1970), 121–125.

5. Nathan Glazer, *American Judaism* (Chicago, 1957), 41–42, 151–152; Leon A. Jick, *The Americanization of the Synagogue* (Hanover, N.H.: University Press of New England, 1976), 190–193.

6. Mordecai M. Kaplan, "Judaism as a Civilization: Religion's Place in It," *Menorah Journal* 15 (Dec. 1928): 505–506; "Toward a Reconstruction of Judaism," ibid. 13 (April 1927): 124–130; idem, *Judaism as a Civilization* (New York: Macmillan, 1934), 489.

7. John Higham, *Send These to Me: Immigrants in Urban America*, rev. ed. (Baltimore: Johns Hopkins University Press, 1984), 205–210.

8. "Democracy Versus the Melting Pot, A Study of American Nationality," Part One, *The Nation*, Feb. 18, 1915, 190–194; Part Two, ibid., Feb. 25, 1915, 217–220. Moses Rischin makes the important point that Kallen, in response to John Dewey's criticism, moderated his formulation of a "federal republic of nationalities" and later used the term "cultural pluralism." See Rischin, "The Jews and Pluralism: Toward an American Freedom Symphony," in *Jewish Life in America*, ed. Gladys Rosen (New York: Institute of Human Relations Press of the American Jewish Committee, KTAV Publishing House, 1978), 75–76.

9. *The Nation*, Feb. 25, 1915, 217.

10. Ibid.

11. Ibid., 218.

12. Horace M. Kallen, "Judaism, Hebraism, Zionism" [1910], reprinted in *Judaism At Bay* (New York: Bloch Publishing Co., 1932), 36–39; Sarah Schmidt, "Messianic Pragmatism: The Zionism of Horace M. Kallen," *Judaism* 25 (Spring 1976): 219–221; and, "The Zionist Conversion of Louis D. Brandeis," *Jewish Social Studies* 37 (Jan. 1975): 26–27; Horace M. Kallen, "The Promise of the Menorah Idea," *The Menorah Journal* 49 (Autumn-Winter 1962): 10–12.

13. Will Herberg, *Protestant, Catholic, Jew*, rev. ed. (Garden City, N.Y.: Anchor Books/Doubleday and Co., 1960), 172, 186–188, 231, 246.

14. Ibid., 258, 270–272; Herberg, "From Marxism to Judaism," 3 *Commentary* (Jan. 1947): 25–32; John P. Diggins, *Up from Communism* (New York: Harper and Row 1975), 119–121, 284–302; Hershell J. Matt, "A Tribute to Will Herberg," *Conservative Judaism* 31 (Winter 1977): 5–14; Ben Halpern, *The American Jew* (New York: Herzl Press, 1956), 37–46.

15. Aaron Rothkoff, "The American Sojourn of Ridbaz: Religious Problems within the Immigrant Community," *American Jewish Historical Quarterly* 57 (June 1968): 560–564; Albert Klapperman, *The Story of Yeshiva University* (London: Macmillan, 1969), 94–119.

16. Nathan Glazer, *American Judaism*, 49, 51; Arthur Mann, "Charles Fleischer's Religion of Democracy," 17 *Commentary* (June 1954): 561, 564.

17. *Tzeitgeist*, Jan. 25, Feb. 22, and April 12, 1907, quoted in Jacob Hertz, *Di yidishe sotzialistishe bavegung* (New York: Der Wecker, 1954), 101–102.

18. Moses Rischin, *The Promised City* (Cambridge, Mass.: Harvard University Press, 1962), 95–111; Goren, *New York Jews*, 21–37, 214–229; Naomi Cohen, *Not Free to Desist* (Philadelphia: Jewish Publication Society, 1972), 37–30.

19. Jacob Schiff to Israel Friedlaender, Feb. 16, 1914, Friedlaender Papers (Jewish Theological Seminary).

20. Cyrus A. Adler, ed., *Jacob H. Schiff: His Life and Letters*, vol. 2 (Garden City, N.Y.: Doubleday, Doran and Co., 1928), 164–166; Solomon Schechter, "Zionism: A Statement" [Dec. 28, 1906] reprinted in *Seminary Addresses and Other Papers* (New York: Burning Bush Press, 1959), 91–104.

21. *New York Times*, July 29, 1907, 9; Sept. 15, 1907, part 2, 11; Sept. 30, 3; Adler, ed., *Schiff*, vol. 2, 164–166.

22. Cyrus Adler, *Lectures, Selected Papers, Addresses* (Philadelphia, 1933), 202–206; *American Hebrew*, Feb. 16, 1906, 400; May 18, 777–778.

23. *American Hebrew*, May 23, 1908, 805–807; Nov. 16, 37.

24. Ibid., Oct. 16, 1908, 584.

25. Ibid. The principle of separation of church and state was applied to argue against a broadly conceived pluralistic community. In 1912 a conference of Reform rabbis declared its opposition to organizing Jewish communities on other than a religious basis since that would violate the principle of separation of church and state and "create the impression that the Jews are an *imperium in imperio*." Central Conference of American Rabbis, *Yearbook* 22 (1912): 108–109.

26. Constitution of the Board of Jewish School Aid, Judah L. Magnes Papers, Central Archives for the History of the Jewish People, Jerusalem; *American Jewish Year Book* 19 (1918–1919): 113–146.

27. *American Hebrew*, March 24, 1916, 558; March 31, 587–588, 593. Louis Lipsky, "A Revolution in American Jewry," *The Maccabaean* 30 (June–July 1917): 276–277, 304. For three accounts of the controversy, each focusing on one of three protagonists, see Melvin I. Urofsky, *American Zionism from Herzl to the Holocaust* (Garden City, N.Y.: Anchor Press/Doubleday, 1975), 202–341; Cohen, *Not Free to Desist*, 90–98; Jonathan Frankel, "The Jewish Socialists and the American Congress Movement," *YIVO Annual of Jewish Social Studies* 16 (1976): 202–341. See also Goren, *New York Jews*, 218–227.

28. Zosa Szajkowski, "Private and Organized American Jewish Overseas Relief (1914–1938)," *American Jewish Historical Quarterly* 57 (Sept. 1967): 52, 98;

"Budgeting American Jewish Overseas Relief (1919–1939)," in ibid. (Sept. 1969): 83–113; " 'Reconstruction' vs. 'Palliative Relief' in American Jewish Overseas Work (1919–1939)," *Jewish Social Studies* 32 (Jan. 1970): 15–30; *American Jewish Year Book* 18 (1917–1918): 201, 208–211, 242; Louis Marshall to Felix Warburg, Oct. 26, 1916, Marshall Papers (American Jewish Archives, Cincinnati); Yonathan Shapiro, *Leadership of the American Zionist Organization, 1897–1930* (Urbana: University of Illinois Press, 1971), 53–61, 70–80, 99–134, 181; Urofsky, *American Zionism*, 109–152, 216–230.

29. See above, n. 1.

30. National Conference of Jewish Charities, *Fourth Biennial Session*, May 6–8, 1906, 25.

31. *American Hebrew*, Nov. 10, 1915, 34.

32. Jacob DeHaas, *Louis D. Brandeis: A Biographical Sketch* (New York: Bloch, 1929), 151–152.

33. *Brandeis on Zionism: A Collection of Addresses and Statements by Louis D. Brandeis* (Washington, D.C.: Zionist Organization of America, 1942), 10–11.

34. *New York Times*, April 19, 1909, 9; *New York Evening Post*, April 26, 1909, 8.

35. Michael Kammen, *People of Paradox* (New York: Alfred A. Knopf, 1973), 89–90, 116.

## 2. Pageants of Sorrow, Celebration and Protest

1. For an exemplary study of the phenomenon discussed here, see Kathleen Conzen, "Ethnicity as Festive Culture: Nineteenth Century German America on Parade," in *The Invention of Ethnicity*, ed. Werner Sollors (New York: Oxford University Press, 1989), 44–76. I also benefited from Mary Ryan, "The American Parade: Representations of the Nineteenth Century Social Order," *The New Cultural History*, ed. Lynn Hunt (Berkeley: University of California Press, 1989). For important conceptual insights, see Susan G. David, *Parades and Power: Street Theater in Nineteenth-Century Philadelphia* (Berkeley: University of California Press, 1986), 1–22, 67–72, 166–173.

2. See chap. 3.

3. *Leksikon fun yidishn tiater*, ed. Zalmen Zylbercweig, vol. 3 (New York: Farlag "Elisheva," 1931), 2078–2104; Rose Shomer-Bachelis, *Unzer Foter Shomer* (first part written by Miriam Shomer-Zunzer) (New York, 1950), 122–186; *Tageblat*, Nov. 27, 1905, 1.

4. *Tageblat*, Nov. 26, 1905, 1; *Forverts*, Nov. 26, 1905, 1. For an account of the "elaborate precautions to prevent trouble" see the *New York Times*, Nov. 26, 1905, 12.

5. See *Forverts* and *Varheyt* for Nov. 24, 25, 26 and 27, 1905; and the *Tageblat* for Nov. 24, 26 and 27, 1905.

6. *Tageblat*, Nov. 27, 1905, 1, 8; *Forverts*, Nov. 27, 1905, 1.

7. *New York Times*, Nov. 27, 1905, 9.

8. *Tageblat*, Nov. 27, 1905, 1, 8; Shomer-Bachelis and Shomer-Zunzer, *Unzer Foter Shomer*, 188; *New York Times*, Nov. 27, 1905, 6.

9. *Tageblat*, Nov. 4, 1905, 4; chap. 3.

10. *The Two Hundred and Fiftieth Anniversary of the Settlement of the Jews in the United States* (published as *Publications of the American Jewish Historical Society* 14 [1906]), v–x.

11. See Nathan M. Kaganoff, "AJHS at 90: Reflections on the History of the Oldest Ethnic Historical Society in America," *American Jewish History* 91, no. 4 (June 1982): 467–472; Jeffrey S. Gurock, "From *Publications* to *American Jewish History*: The Journal of the American Jewish Historical Society and the Writing of American Jewish History," *American Jewish History* 81, no. 2 (Winter 1993–1994), 158–162, 167–171; Naomi Cohen, *Encounter with Emancipation: The German Jews in the United States, 1830–1914* (Philadelphia: Jewish Publication Society, 1984), 249–285.

12. See Michael Kammen, *Mystic Chords of Memory: The Transformation of Tradition in American Culture* (New York: Random House, 1991), 93–162, 194–227; John Bodnar, *Remaking America: Public Memory, Commemoration, and Patriotism in the Twentieth Century* (Princeton: Princeton University Press, 1992), 33–35; David Glassberg, *American Historical Pageantry: The Uses of Tradition in the Early Twentieth Century* (Chapel Hill: University of North Carolina Press, 1990), 9–34; John Higham, *History* (Englewood Cliffs: Prentice-Hall, 1965), 6–25.

13. Oscar S. Straus, "Address of the President," *Publications of the American Jewish Historical Society*, no. 1 (Papers Presented at the First Scientific Meeting, Philadelphia, December 15, 1892), 1–4; idem, *The Origin of Republican Form of Government in the United States of America* (New York: G. P. Putnam's Sons, 1885). On Straus's historical writings, see Naomi Cohen, *A Dual Heritage: The Public Career of Oscar S. Straus* (Philadelphia: Jewish Publication Society, 1969), 15, 71–73. For interpretations of the origins of the Society that emphasize the American historiographical context, see Ira Robinson, "The Invention of American Jewish History," *American Jewish History* 81, nos. 3–4 (Spring–Summer 1994), 309–320; and Robert Liberles, "Postemancipation Historiography and the Jewish Historical Societies of America and England," *Studies in Contemporary Jewry*, vol. 10, *Reshaping the Past: Jewish History and the Historians*, ed. Jonathan Frankel (New York: Oxford University Press, 1994), 45–65.

14. See Kammen, *Mystic Chords of Memory*, 134–145; Hasia R. Diner, *A Time for Gathering: The Second Migration, 1820–1880* (Baltimore: Johns Hopkins University Press, 1992), 201–202; Barbara Kirshenlatt-Gimblett, "From Cult to Culture: Jews on Display at World's Fairs," in *Tradition and Modernization* (NIF Pulications 25 [Turku, 1992]), 80–81; Joseph Guttman, "Jewish Participation in the Visual Arts of Eighteenth and Nineteenth Century America," *American Jewish Archives* 15, no. 1 (April 1963), 44; Richard B.

Nicolai, *Centennial Philadelphia* (Bryn Mawr, Pa.: Bryn Mawr Press, 1976), 69, 81; Jonathan Sarna, "Columbus and the Jews," *Commentary* 94 (Nov. 1992): 38.

15. Conzen, "Ethnicity as Festive Culture," 66–69, wherein she cites the *New York Times*, Oct. 8, 1883, 5, and Oct. 9, 2, for accounts of the parades; Frank Trommler and Joseph McVeigh, eds., *America and the Germans: An Assessment of a Three-Hundred Year History*, vol. 1 (Philadelphia: University of Pennsylvania Press, 1985), xi–xiv; H. Arnold Barton, "Swedish-American Historiography," *Immigration History Newsletter* 15, no. 1 (May 1983): 2; Thomas J. Schlereth, "Columbia, Columbus, and Columbianism," *Journal of American History* 79, no. 3 (Dec. 1992): 995–960; John Appel, "Immigrant Historical Societies in the United States, 1880–1950" (Ph.D. diss., University of Pennsylvannia, 1960), 277–288, 329–334.

16. *The Two Hundred and Fiftieth Anniversary*, v–x, 258–261. Although the first twenty-three Jews arrived in New Amsterdam in September 1654, 1655 was chosen as the anniversary year when the Dutch West India Company overruled Governor Peter Stuyvesant and granted "a leave of settlement" to the Jews. For an example of the broad support for holding an anniversary celebration see *Jewish Exponent*, April 14, 1905, 7, and April 21, 1905, 4. For criticism that no Russian Jews were appointed to the executive committee, see *Jewish Criterion*, May 19, 1905, 12; *Hebrew Standard*, May 5, 1905, 8, and May 12, 9; *The American Israelite*, Nov. 16, 1905, 4; *Jewish Exponent*, Nov. 24, 1905, 3, 4.

17. *American Hebrew*, May 5, 1905, 725–731; *Boston [Jewish] Advocate*, May 19, 1905, 1, June 2, 1, and July 7, 1.

18. *American Hebrew*, May 5, 1905, 725.

19. *American Hebrew*, Oct. 6, 1905, 517; *The Two Hundred and Fiftieth Anniversary*, v–x, 242–258. See ibid., 199–232, where excerpts from eleven newspapers appear, and the listing in *American Jewish Year Book* 8 (1906/1907), 148–166.

20. *American Israelite*, Nov. 16, 1905, 3; Nov. 30, 6; *Reform Advocate*, Dec. 2, 1905, 2; *Jewish Exponent*, Nov. 3, 1905, 3, 4, Nov. 24, 1905, 3, 4, Dec. 1, 4, 8.

21. *Two Hundred and Fiftieth Anniversary*, ix. For general accounts, see *New York Times*, Dec. 1, 1905, 1, 4, *Jewish Exponent*, Dec. 8, 1905, 9.

22. *Two Hundred and Fiftieth Anniversary*, 34–35, 72–73, 96, 122–123, 127; Emil Hirsh, "Concordance of Judaism and Americanism," *Reform Advocate*, Dec. 9, 1905, 471–474. In his study *Roger Williams, The Pioneer of Religious Liberty* (New York: Century Co., 1899), Straus presented the historical case for Williams's support for the readmission of the Jews to England; see 3rd ed. (New York, 1936), 174–178. Letters of congratulations were exchanged between Jacob Schiff and H. Gollancz, president of the Jewish Historical Society of England, on the simultaneous celebrations of 250 years of the Whitehall Conference (where the legal basis for the readmission of Jews to

England was established) and the 250th anniversary of the New Amsterdam settlement. See *American Hebrew*, Dec. 1, 1905, 13.

23.  *New York Times*, Nov. 17, 1905, 6.

24.  *The Two Hundred and Fiftieth Anniversary*, 107–108, 122–127; *New York Times*, Nov. 27, 1905, 6. On Kayserling, see Sarna, "Columbus and the Jews," 38–41.

25.  *Tageblat*, Nov. 19, 1905, 4.

26.  *Tageblat*, "English Department," Dec. 1, 1905, 1.

27.  *Forverts*, Dec. 1, 1905, 1, 4; *Varheyt*, Dec. 1, 1904, 1, 4; *Tageblat*, Nov. 27, 1905, 1, 4; *New York Times*, Nov. 27, 1905, 6.

28.  *Forverts*, Nov. 7, 1905, 1, 4, Nov. 23, 1; *Varheyt*, Nov. 23, 1.

29.  See Jonathan Frankel, *Prophecy and Politics: Socialism, Nationalism, and the Russian Jews, 1862–1917* (Cambridge: Cambridge University Press, 1981), 487–492.

30.  *Forverts*, Dec. 2, 3, 4, 1905. See also *Tageblat*, Nov. 29, 30, 1; *New York Times*, Nov. 29, 6.

31.  *Varheyt*, Dec. 4, 1905, 1; *Forverts*, Dec. 4, 1.

32.  *New York Times*, Dec. 5, 1905, 6; *Forverts*, Dec. 5, 1906, 1.

33.  *New York Times*, Dec. 5, 1905, 6.

34.  Ibid.

35.  *American Hebrew*, Dec. 15, 1905, 136.

36.  See *New York Times*, Dec. 5, 1905, 7, for an account of the Temple Emanu-El meeting, and ibid., 6, for a report of the National Committee for Russian Relief's second million-dollar campaign and the report of Jacob Schiff on his diplomatic efforts.

37.  Aaron Antonovsky and Elias Tcherikower, eds., *The Early Jewish Labor Movement in the United States* (New York: YIVO Institute for Jewish Research, 1961), 322–327; N. Goldberg, "Amerikes beytrog zum ershtn mai," *Zukunft* 49, no. 5 (May 1944): 270–271; *Forverts*, May 2, 1903, 1; Ezra Mendelsohn, *Class Struggle in the Pale: The Formative Years of the Jewish Workers Movement in Tsarist Russia* (Cambridge: Cambridge University Press, 1970), 137–140.

38.  A close examination of the American Jewish public response to the Kishinev pogrom in late April and May of 1903 brings into sharper relief the new phase of collaboration that characterizes the 1905 commemorations. In 1903, the notables of the established community initiated seventy-seven protest meetings in fifty cities aross the nation. They were nominally sponsored by "general" committees and featured non-Jewish public figures. (See Cyrus Adler, *The Voice of America on Kishineff* [Philadelphia: Jewish Publication Society, 1904], xvii.) But the Jewish immigrant public failed to unite in or-

ganizing protest meetings, marches and fund-raising drives. See *Forverts,*
April 28, 1903, 1; April 30, 1; May 9, 4.

39.     *New York Times,* Nov. 27, 1905, 7.


## 3. The Rites of Community

1.      For Revel see, *New York Times,* Dec. 3, 1940, 25, Dec. 4, 1940, 27; Aaron
        Rothkoff, *Bernard Revel, Builder of American Jewish Orthodoxy* (Philadel-
        phia: Jewish Publication Society, 1972), 221–223; for Brandeis see, *New York
        Times,* Oct. 8, 1941, 25; Alpheus Thomas Mason, *Brandeis: A Freeman's Life*
        (New York: Viking Press, 1946), 637–638.

2.      *Yiddishes Tageblat,* July 31, 1902, English Department, 1; Jan. 15, 1905, English
        Department, 1; *New York Times,* April 23, 1949, 14; Melvin I. Urofsky, *A Voice
        That Spoke for Justice: The Life and Times of Stephen S. Wise* (Albany: State
        University of New York Press, 1982), 370–372.

3.      Two studies of public funerals deserve mention: Leonard Dinnerstein, "The
        Funeral of Jacob Joseph," *Anti-Semitism in American History,* ed. David A.
        Gerber (Urbana: University of Illinois Press, 1986), 275–301; and Ellen Kell-
        man, "Sholem Aleichem's Funeral (New York, 1916): The Making of a Na-
        tional Pageant," *YIVO Annual* 20 (1991): 277–304. Dinnerstein focuses on
        the riot that marred the funeral in the context of police brutality, ethnic
        group relations, antisemitism, and municipal reform politics. Kellman's
        study pays meticulous attention to the funeral as cultural and social event
        and places it firmly within the context of communal politics.

4.      Kh. Khayus, "Gleybungen un minhagim in farbindung mitn tyt," *Filologin
        shriftn,* vol. 2 (Vilna: Schiftn fun YIVO, 1928), 281–327; Jacob Shatzky,
        "Merkvirdige historische factn vegen der amoliger hevra kadisha," *39th yohr
        cemetery department yohrbuch und barichet* (New York: Arbeiter Ring, 1946),
        28–36.

5.      In this paragraph, I have drawn on two articles of mine, "Traditional Insti-
        tutions Transplanted: The *Hevra Kadisha* in Europe and the United States,"
        *The Jews of North America: Immigration, Settlement and Ethnic Identity,* ed.
        Moses Rischin (Detroit: Wayne State University Press, 1987), 62–78; and
        *Saints and Sinners: The Underside of American Jewish History* (Cincinnati:
        The American Jewish Archives, 1988). See also, Mareleyn Schneider, *A His-
        tory of a Jewish Burial Society: An Examination of Secularization* (Lewiston,
        N.Y.: Edwin Mellen Press, 1991), 83–105.

6.      *Forverts,* Feb. 28, 1903, 1.

7.      J. S. Hertz, *Hirsh Lekert* (New York: Farlag Unser Tsait, 1952); Morris U.
        Schappes, "Hirsh Lekert, Worker Hero," *Jewish Life: A Progressive Monthly*
        (June 1952): 19–21.

8.      Goren, *Saints and Sinners,* 19–21.

9.      Abraham J. Karp, "New York Chooses a Chief Rabbi," *Publications of the
        American Jewish Historical Society* 44, no. 3 (March 1955): 129–187, especially

181–182; Leonard Dinnerstein, *Anti-Semitism in American History* (New York: Oxford University Press, 1994). 275–278, 280–298; Irving Howe, *World of Our Fathers* (New York: Harcourt Brace Jovanovich, 1976), 123–124, 194–195; Gerald Sorin, *A Time for Building: The Third Migration, 1880–1920* (Baltimore: Johns Hopkins University Press, 1992), 176–177.

10. Ephraim Shimoff, *Rabbi Isaac Elchanan Spektor: Life and Letters* (Jerusalem: Sura Institute for Rabbinical Research and New York: Yeshiva University, 1959), 151–154; *Hamelitz* 48 (24 Adar 5656): 2–3; *Hatzfira* 53 (1 Nissan 5656): 252.

11. *Hatzfira* 53, 252; *Hamelitz* 48, 2.

12. See Hebrew section of Shimoff, *Rabbi Isaac Elchanan Spektor*, for the texts of some of the eulogies, 139–158, and the accounts in *Hamelitz* 48, and *Hatzfira* 53.

13. *Yiddishes Tageblat*, July 29, 1902, 1; *New York Times*, July 31, 1902, 2.

14. *New York Times*, July 29, 1902, 8; July 31, 1–2; *Yiddishes Tageblat*, July 29, 1902, 1; July 31, 1, 2; Dinnerstein, *Anti-Semitism in American History*, 278–287.

15. *Yiddishes Tageblat*, July 31, 1902, 1–2; *New York Times*, July 31, 1902, 2.

16. *Yiddishes Tageblat*, July 29, 1902, 1; July 31, 1; the *New York Times* reported that many prosperous Jews "vied with each other in their efforts to secure in advance the right to be buried near him in the cemetery," one merchant offering $5,000 to the Beth Hamidrash Hagadol which had won the right to bury Rabbi Joseph in its cemetery. The offer was rejected (July 29, 1902, 2). Karp writes that the Beth Hamidrash Hagadol won the rights by promising the widow $1,500 and a $15 monthly stipend. *Publications of the American Jewish Historical Society*, 44, no. 3 (March 1955): 180–181.

17. *New York Times*, July 29, 1902, 2; July 31, 2.

18. *Yiddishes Tageblat*, July 31, 1902, English Department, 1.

19. *Yiddishes Tageblat*, Jan. 15, 1905, 1.

20. Cutouts from *New York Evening Sun*, *New York Evening Post*, *New York Times*, *New York Sun*, Jan. 13, 1905, in Kasriel H. Sarasohn Scrapbook, American Jewish Archives, Hebrew Union College Jewish Institute of Religion, Cincinnati, Ohio. The *Evening Post*, for example, commented that "Inspector Titus and Captain Shaw preserved excellent order, which was in sharp contrast to the riots of two years ago, when a crowd of hoodlums stoned the hearse containing Rabbi Joseph's body and assaulted his mourners." Victor R. Greene, *American Immigrant Leaders, 1800–1910* (Baltimore, Md.: Johns Hopkins University Press, 1987), 93–95, used much of the same materials I have in describing Sarasohn's funeral in the context of his discussion of the Jewish immigrant leader.

21. *Yiddishes Tageblat*, Jan. 15, 1905, 1–2; ibid., English Department, Jan. 15, 1905, 1; *New York Sun*, Jan. 15, 1905, Sarasohn Scrapbook.

22. *New York Evening Post*, Jan. 13, 1905, Sarasohn Scrapbook.

23. *Yiddishes Tageblat*, Jan. 15, 1905, 1–2; ibid., English Department, 1; *New York Sun*, Jan. 14, 1905, Sarasohn Scrapbook.

24. *Yiddishes Tageblat*, English Department, Jan. 15, 1905; cutouts from *Evening Post, New York Times*, Jan. 13, 1905, Sarasohn Scrapbook.

25. *Forverts*, June 14, 1909, 1.

26. *Varheyt*, June 12, 1909, 4. For a contemporary critique of Gordin's work see Louis Lipsky, "The Future of the Yiddish Theater," *The Maccabaean* 16, no. 4 (April 1909): 134–38.

27. *Varheyt*, June 12, 1909, 4.

28. *Varheyt*, June 11, 1909, 1, 4; June 12, 1, 4; June 13, 1, 4; *Forverts*, June 11, 1909, 1, 4; June 12, 1, 4.

29. Gordin was buried in Washington Cemetery, Brooklyn, N.Y., in a grave donated by a friend. See Goren, *Saints and Sinners*, 25, n. 30 for the location of the grave.

30. *Varheyt*, June 14, 1909, 1; *Forverts*, June 14, 1909, 1, 8; *New York Times*, May 9, 1902, 9.

31. *Varheyt*, June 14, 1909, 1; *Forverts*, June 14, 1909, 1, 8.

32. *Forverts*, June 14, 1909, 1; *Varheyt*, June 14, 1909, 1. The *New York Times*, June 14, 1909, 7, reported that Rabbi Judah L. Magnes and the Rev. Zvi Masliansky spoke. Both were also on the list of speakers scheduled to address the memorial meeting (*Varheyt*, June 13, 1909, 1) but are not mentioned in the *Forverts* or *Varheyt* reports of the meeting.

33. *Forverts*, June 14, 1909, 8.

34. See, for example, the warm tribute by Bernard G. Richards, a centrist Zionist active in the cultural life of the Lower East Side (*American Hebrew*, vol. 84, June 18, 1909, 172–173), and the critique of Gordin's dramatic work by Louis Lipsky, the Zionist, publicist and theater critic, ibid., 192–193.

35. *Morgen Zhurnal*, June 14, 1909, 1; June 13, 4. The issues of the *Yiddishes Tageblat* are missing for the dates under consideration in the microfilm runs held by the main Jewish research libraries. There are photographs of exposed bodies of Jewish dead. In nearly all cases, they are of pogrom victims and were taken for use as evidence or for propaganda purposes. See Zvi Gitelman, *A Century of Ambivalence: The Jews of Russia and the Soviet Union, 1881 to the Present* (New York: Schocken, 1988), 22, 30–31, 111. Gitelman does bring a photograph of the dead wife of a wealthy Jewish merchant in Siberia and notes in the caption the "combined Christian customs, such as the flowers and candles shown here, with their Jewish beliefs" (p. 85).

36. Leon Stein, *The Triangle Fire* (Philadelphia: J. B. Lippincott Co., 1962) is a detailed account of the fire and its aftermath. See also Charlotte Baum, Paula Hyman, Sonya Michel, *The Jewish Woman in America* (New York: Dial Press, 1976), 148–153.

37. *Morgen Zhurnal*, March 27, 1911, 1; *New York Times*, March 28, 1911, 2;

*Forverts*, March 28, 1911, 5, 8; March 29, 1; Stein, *Triangle Fire*, 101, 105–106, 108.

38. *Morgen Zhurnal*, March 27, 1911, 1; *Yiddishes Tageblat*, March 17, 1911, 1; *Forverts*, March 27, 1911, 1.

39. Maxine Schwartz Seller, "The Uprising of the Twenty Thousand: Sex, Class, and Ethnicity in the Shirtwaist Makers' Strike of 1909," in *"Struggle a Hard Battle": Essays on Working Class Immigrants*, ed. Dirk Hoerder (DeKalb: Northern Illinois University Press, 1986), 254–279. Seller offers the following ethnic make-up of the shirtwaist makers at the time of the strike: "Of a total of 30,000 strikers, approximately 21,000 were Jewish women, 2,000 Italian women, 1,000 were American women, and 6,000 were men, almost all of them Jewish." Her source is John Andrews and W. D. P. Bliss, *History of Women in Trade Unions: Woman and Child Wage-Earners in the United States*, vol. 10 (Washington, D.C.: Government Printing Office, 1911).

40. *New York Times*, March 27, 1911, 1; March 30, 3; March 31, 2; *Morgen Zhurnal*, March 26, 1911, 1; *Forverts*, March 28, 1911, 1; Stein, *Triangle Fire*, 122–124, 128, 149.

41. *Forverts*, March 30, 1911, 1; April 3, 1; Stein, *Triangle Fire*, 135–145.

42. *Forverts*, April 2, 1911, 1.

43. *New York Times*, March 29, 1911, 3.

44. Ibid.; *Morgen Zhurnal*, March 29, 1911, 1.

45. *New York Times*, March 30, 1911, 3; March 31, 2; *Morgen Zhurnal*, March 29, 1911, 1; March 30, 1; Stein, *Triangle Fire*, 148–149.

46. *Forverts*, April 6, 1911, 1; Stein, *Triangle Fire*, 149–152; *Morgen Zhurnal*, April 5, 1911, 1, 4.

47. *New York Times*, April 6, 1911, 1; *Forverts*, April 6, 1911, 8; Stein, *Triangle Fire*, 149, 153–155. With unintentional irony, a historian of cemeteries comments on the monument marking the burial of the unidentified victims: "Though the memorial to the unidentified victims of the Triangle Factory Shirtwaist fire which stands in an empty field in Evergreen Cemetery, Brooklyn, is not lettered in Hebrew (and does not, for that matter, in any other fashion indicate the ethnicity of those it commemorates), it remains as a monument to the early twentieth century Jewish experience in America" (Roberta Halporn, "American Jewish Cemeteries: A Mirror of History," *Ethnicity and the American Cemetery*, ed. Richard E. Meyer [Bowling Green, Ohio: Bowling Green State University Popular Press, 1993], 143). For a photograph of the memorial see ibid., 146.

48. Kellman, *YIVO Annual* 20 (1991): 282–284, 288–297; *Der Tog*, May 14, 1916, 1, 6; *Forverts*, May 14, 1916, 1.

49. Kellner, *YIVO Annual* 20 (1991): 287–288.

50. Kellman stresses the Zionist politicization of the arrangements committee. The Zionists on the committee were "klal yisrael" Zionists, i.e., they emphasized Jewish "peoplehood," "Jewish unity," Hebrew culture, and group sur-

vival in the diaspora. The impeccable literary credentials of the committee may explain the acquiescence of socialists like Abraham Cahan to playing a minor role in the ceremonies.

51.  Kellman, *YIVO Annual* 20 (1991): 288–289. Kellman points out that "two important segments of the community . . . were underrepresented in the *levaye* [funeral]," the socialists and uptown Jews. She ascribes this to their opposition to the Jewish congress movement which Magnes supported at that time.

52.  *Forverts*, May 16, 1916, 1, 8; *Varheyt*, May 16, 1916, 1; *Der Tog*, May 16, 1916, 1; Kellner, *YIVO Annual* 20 (1991): 290–292; *American Hebrew* 99, no. 2 (May 19, 1916): 40.

53.  *Varheyt*, May 15, 1916, 1.

54.  *Der Tog*, May 16, 1916, 4.

55.  *Der Tog*, May 16, 1916, 1; Kellner, *YIVO Annual* 20 (1991): 292.

56.  Kellner, *YIVO Annual* 20 (1991): 301. The unveiling of Sholom Aleichem's monument took place on June 5, 1921, in the presence of family and several thousand Yiddish writers; *Dos Sholom Aleichem Bukh*, ed. Y. D. Berkowitz (New York: Sholom Aleichem Book Committee, 1926), 369, 376–378.

57.  Nakhman Meizel, *Y. L. Peretz, Zein lebn un shafn* (New York: Idisher Kultur Farband—IKUF, 1945), 350–354; *Forverts*, April 6, 1916, 1; April 7, 1; April 17, 1, 4; *East and West*, June 1915, 90–91.

58.  *New York Times*, Sept. 29, 1920, 17.

59.  Ibid.

60.  *New York Times*, Aug. 27, 1936, 21.

61.  *Morgen Zhurnal*, Aug. 27, 1936, 1.

62.  Jacob Adler's funeral in April 1926 had all of the attributes of a funeral pageant of the tradition of the Jewish labor movement: the lying in state, memorial services in a non-religious hall (Kessler's Second Avenue Theater), and the long procession through the streets of the Lower East Side filled with tens of thousands of mourners. *New York Times*, April 2, 1926, 22; April 3, 17. Noteworthy are Adler's intellectual ties with the Jewish labor community and the organizational input of the Jewish Actors Guild and the Jewish Writers Union.

63.  *Forverts*, June 9, 1926, 8. In its editorial on London's death, the *Forverts* stressed that he had represented the Socialist Party *and* the Jewish quarter in Congress and "made the Jewish workers known" (June 9, 1926, 4).

64.  Ibid., June 9, 1926, 1, 8.

65.  *New York Times*, June 9, 1926, 23; June 10, 25; *Forverts*, June 10, 1926, 1, 2, 12. For the photograph of the coffin, see p. 10.

66.  *Forverts*, 1, 2, 12; *Der Tog*, June 9, 1926, 1; June 10, 10.

67.  *Forverts*, Oct. 9, 1933, 1, 5, 7–8, 10; Oct. 10, 1, 4.

68.  *Morgen Zhurnal-Tageblat*, Oct. 9, 1933, 1–2.

69. *New York Times*, Oct. 11, 1933, 23; Oct. 12, 25; *Forverts*, Oct. 10, 1933, 1; Oct. 11, 1; Oct. 12, 1, 8 (*Der Tog*, Oct. 12, 1933, 1, 9).

70. Melech Epstein, *Profiles of Eleven* (Detroit, Mich.: Wayne State University Press, 1965), 338–342; *New York Times*, Oct. 31, 1938, 1, 15.

71. Epstein, *Profiles*, 329–333, 343–344, 347–351; *Forverts*, November 1, 1938, 4. On the front page of the *Forverts* carrying the news of Vladeck's death, the paper published two poems and a feuilleton of his (Oct. 31, 1938).

72. *Freiheit, revolutsianere lider un shirm* (Geneva, Switzerland: Algemine idisher arbeiterbund in lita, poiln un rusland, 1905), 109; *Forverts*, Nov. 3, 1938, 1, 9; *New York Times*, Nov. 3, 1938, 23.

73. *Forverts*, Nov. 3, 1938, 1, 9.

74. *Forverts*, Nov. 1, 1938, 1, 4; Nov. 2, 1, 8.

75. *Freiheit, revolutsianere lider*, 40; *Forverts*, Nov. 3, 1938, 1, 9.

76. *32nd yehrlicher report fun dem cemetery department*, Arbeiter Ring, 1939, 10–16.

77. *New York Times*, Sept. 6, 1951, 31; *Forverts*, Sept. 4, 1951, 1, 9; Sept. 5, 1, 12; Sept. 5, 1, 10–11.

## 4. Socialist Politics on the Lower East Side

1. Moses Rischin, *The Promised City: New York's Jews, 1870–1914* (Cambridge, Mass.: Harvard University Press, 1962), 228–235. For tables of the composition and characteristics of the assembly districts constituting the Ninth Congressional District and the voting results of the 1908 and 1910 elections see, Arthur Gorenstein [Goren], "A Portrait of Ethnic Politics: The Socialists and the 1908 and 1910 Congressional Elections on the East Side," *Publications of the American Jewish Historical Society* 50, no. 4 (March 1961): 227–238. See also, *The Worker* (New York), Nov. 10, 1906, 1; *Zukunft* 13 (Dec. 1908): 768.

2. Also reported in the *New York Times*, Nov. 1, 1908, 5. This was the only direct appeal made by Debs to a particular district that appeared in the socialist *New York Evening Call* during the entire 1908 campaign.

3. *New York Times*, Oct. 19, 1908, 2; *New York Evening Call*, Oct. 13, 1908, 6. The new law required the signature of the voter on registration and election days. If the voter claimed he could not write he was required to answer identifying questions. *New York Times*, Oct. 4, 1908, 5; Oct. 13, 1–2. Goldfogle also succeeded in running on Hearst's Independence League ticket despite court action to remove his name.

4. Abraham Cahan, the powerful editor of the *Forward*, discusses the role of the paper in the trade union and Socialist movement during this period in *Bleter fun mein leben*, vol. 4 (New York: *Forverts* Association, 1928), 536–538, 542–543, 547, 549. The Workmen's Circle branch figures are based on the

membership totals in the *Sixth Annual Report for the Year 1906* and *Proceedings of the Seventh Annual Convention of the Workmen's Circle*, General Executive Committee (New York, 1907), 43–44, and *Eighth Annual Report of the Workmen's Circle for the Year 1908*, General Executive Committee (New York, 1909), 77–81.

5. *New York Times*, Oct. 19, 1908, 2; *Zukunft* (Nov. 1908): 714. On the organization of the campaign see, *New York Evening Call* (1908), Sept. 18, 1; Oct. 17, 1; Oct. 24, 1; Oct. 28, 1. On outside help, see Morris Hillquit, *Loose Leaves from a Busy Life* (New York: Macmillan, 1934), 115; Harry Rogoff, *An East Side Epic* (New York: Vanguard, 1930), 67.

6. *New York Times* (1908), Oct. 26, 3; Oct. 27, 4; Nov. 1, 3; *New York Evening Call* (1908), Oct. 8, 1; Oct. 13, 1, 6; Oct. 17, 1; Oct. 21, 1; Oct. 22, 2; Oct. 23, 1; Oct. 26, 1; Oct. 30, 1.

7. *Zukunft* (Dec. 1908): 768; The *Forverts*'s headline, Nov. 4, 1908, read: "Tammany Does Business with Republicans and Wins over Hillquit." The report was based on a *New York Times* news story (Nov. 3, 1908, 1) of a reputed deal between the Democrats and Republicans whereby Republican regulars would vote for Goldfogle to ensure Hillquit's defeat. The *Zukunft* (Dec. 1908, 768) explained the Hillquit debacle: "As the ships bring the greenhorns the moving vans move out the radicals." For the psychological explanation see *Forverts*, Nov. 9, 1908, 4.

8. Nachman Syrkin, ideologue of the Socialist-Zionist movement, emphasized Hillquit's indifference to the immigration issue as the cause of Hillquit's defeat; *Zukunft* (Dec. 1908): 748. Among the mainline socialist commentators only M. Baranov raised the possibility that ignoring the immigration issue had cost Hillquit the election (*Forverts*, Nov. 12, 1908, 4).

9. Rischin, *The Promised City*, 76–94, 123–143. The authoritative W. Ayer and Sons' *Annual*, 1909 edition, 1143, offers the following 1908 circulation figures for the Yiddish dailies: *Tageblat* (68,442), *Morgen Zhurnal* (67,664), *Forverts* (53,539), and *Varheyt* (59,522). The *American Jewish Year Book*, 1909–1910 (Philadelphia, 1909), 219, lists the following weeklies or monthlies which were published in New York in December 1908: *Arbeiter, Freie Arbeiter Stimme, Der Kibetzer, Dos Naye Leben, Der Yiddisher Kempfer, Die Zukunft*. On the *landsmanshaft* see Lamed Shapiro, "Immigration and the *Landsmanshaft*," *The Jewish Landsmanshaften in New York* [Yiddish] (prepared by the Federal Writers Project, Works Progress Administration) (New York: L. Peretz Yiddish Writers Union, 1938), 27–30. According to Shapiro, 255 societies were established in New York City on the *landsmanshaft* principle between 1906 and 1910. Between 1906 and 1910, 85 *landsmanshaft* branches of the Arbeiter Ring were founded (Shapiro, *Jewish Landsmanshaften*, 32).

10. On the effect of the Kishinev pogrom in 1903 and the Russian Revolution and pogroms in 1905 on Jewish radical circles, see Jonathan Frankel, *Prophecy and Politics: Socialism, Nationalism, and the Russian Jews, 1862–1917* (Cambridge: Cambridge University Press, 1981), 473–499. See also Daniel

Soyer, *Jewish Immigrant Associations and American Identity in New York, 1880–1939* (Cambridge, Mass.: Cambridge University Press, 1997), 49–112.

11.   John Higham, *Strangers in the Land* (New Brunswick: Rutgers University Press, 1955), 128–129, 162–163. Twenty-five bills to restrict immigration were introduced into the House of Representatives alone from July 1907 to August 1908 (*American Jewish Year Book, 1908–1909* [Philadelphia: 1908], 74–76).

12.   *North American Review* 188 (Sept. 1908): 383–384. A *Tageblat* editorial (Oct. 30, 1908, 41) entitled "The Socialist Bingham's Calumnies against the East Side" portrayed Lincoln Steffens's, Robert Hunter's and Morris Hillquit's "preachings on the immorality of the East Side" as giving credence to Bingham's accusations. On the meetings triggered by the Bingham article, see Arthur A. Goren, *New York Jews and the Quest for Community: The Kehillah Experiment, 1908* (New York: Columbia University Press, 1970), 25–42.

13.   *New York Evening Call*, Sept. 12, 1908, 3.

14.   *Varheyt*, Nov. 3, 1908, 4. The *Varheyt*, founded in 1905 by Louis Miller in opposition to the *Forverts*, tried to capture part of the *Forverts*'s socialist following by adopting Jewish nationalist positions while maintaining a radical posture. In the 1908 elections, the *Varheyt* supported the Socialist Labor Party candidate for Congress, Daniel De Leon. See D. Kaplan, "The Varheyt," in *75 Years of the Yiddish Press in the United States of America, 1870–1945* [Yiddish], ed. Jacob Gladstone, Samuel Niger, Hillel Rogoff (New York: Y. L. Peretz Writers Union, 1945), 62–83.

15.   On the rent strike see *New York Times* (1908), Jan. 1, 3; Jan. 2, 8; Jan. 3, 2; Jan. 5, 9; Jan. 6, 7; Jan. 8, 16; Jan. 9, 16; Jan. 11, 8. On the kosher meat boycott, see *American Hebrew*, Sept. 25, 1908, 493. On Julia Richman's campaign, see ibid., April 3, 1908, 652. A District School Superintendent on the Lower East Side, her demand evoked a furor in the Yiddish press and a petition was circulated for her removal (*Varheyt*, Sept. 12, 1908, 4). On the bankruptcy crisis, see *American Hebrew*, Aug. 28, 1908, 395, and Sept. 25, 493.

16.   *Varheyt*, Nov. 3, 1908, 4.

17.   Supra, ch. 1; Frankel, *Prophecy and Politics*, 488–492. In 1903, following the Kishinev and other pogroms, the Executive Committee of the Socialist Party of New York warned Jewish socialists not to desert socialism and be swept along by the stream of Jewish nationalism (*The Worker*, July 12, 1903, 1).

18.   *Tageblat*, Oct. 26, 1908, 4.

19.   Ibid., Nov. 2, 1908, 4.

20.   Ibid., Oct. 30, 1908, 4; Nov. 1, 4; see also *New York Evening Call*, Oct. 28, 1908, 1.

21.   *Tageblat* (1908), Nov. 1, 4; Oct. 30, 4.

22.   Hillquit's native tongues were Russian and German. He learned Yiddish on the Lower East Side but rarely used it on the speaker's platform (Cahan, *Bleter*, vol. 4, 549; *Tageblat*, Oct. 26, 1908, 4).

23. David Shannon, *The Socialist Party in America* (New York: Macmillan, 1955), 47–48; see also Ira Kipnis, *The American Socialist Movement, 1897–1912* (New York: Columbia University Press, 1952), 276–288.

24. Hillquit, "The Stuttgart Resolution on Labor Immigration," *The Worker*, Nov. 9, 1907, 3; Kipnes, *The American Socialist Movement*, 206, 279.

25. *New York Evening Call*, Sept. 12, 1908, 3.

26. The *Varheyt*, Sept. 10, 1908, 1. On one occasion De Leon declared: "The 'agitation' against immigration is directed mainly against the Jews and this is a crime. It is also a crime against socialism. There are no 'progressive' races and 'backward' races. There is only a capitalist class and a workers class." *Varheyt*, Oct. 22, 1908, 1. The *Varheyt*'s longest and most vitriolic attack against Hillquit appeared on Oct. 24, 1908, 4.

27. *Forverts*, Oct. 23, 1908, 4, and *New York Evening Call*, same date.

28. Rogoff, *An East Side Epic*, 57.

29. *Journal of the House of Representatives*, First Session of the Fifty-Seventh Congress, 541. A pamphlet entitled, "Russian Persecution and American Jews," a translation of Goldfogle's speech into Yiddish, was distributed throughout the East Side. The *American Jewish Year Book*, 1909–1910, summarizes the Congressional activity on the passport issue in which Goldfogle's legislative work stands out (pp. 29–64). On Goldfogle's role in Congress as spokesman of the "Jewish interests," see Jacob Magidoff, *Mirrors of the East Side* [Yiddish] (New York, 1923), 117–131; *New York Times*, Dec. 6, 1905, 6; *American Hebrew*, Sept. 11, 1908, 449; *Varheyt*, Sept. 14, 1908, 1.

30. Charles Edward Russell, *Bare Hands and Stone Walls* (New York: Charles Scribner's Sons, 1933), 206. M. Baranov, *Forward*, Nov. 12, 1908, 4. See also Rogoff, *An East Side Epic*, 16.

31. Goren, *Publications of the American Jewish Historical Society*, 228. Percentages have been computed on the basis of the U.S. Bureau of the Census, *Thirteenth Census of the United States: 1910*, Abstract with Supplement for New York, 635–636. See also Jacob S. Hertz, *The Jewish Socialist Movement in the United States of America* [Yiddish] (New York, 1954), 123–128.

32. Hillquit, *Loose Leaves from a Busy Life*, 116. The voting analysis is based on the tables in Goren, *Publications of the American Jewish Historical Society*, 229–231. For Taft's speech, see *New York Times*, Oct. 29, 1908, 1.

33. Hillquit opposed the national executive committee's decision to hire an organizer for Yiddish speakers (Hertz, *The Jewish Socialist Movement*, 91–107, 112).

34. *Forverts*, Oct. 3, 1910, 1; Melech Epstein, *Jewish Labor*, 397–398; Cahan, *Bleter*, vol. 4, 644.

35. Kipnis, *The American Socialist Movement*, 282–288.

36. Shannon, *The Socialist Party in America*, 49–50. For London's report of the Socialist Party convention, see *Zukunft* 14 (July 1910): 410ff.

37. *Forverts*, Oct. 20, 1910, 1.

38. *New York Evening Call,* Nov. 25, 1910, 6; Nov. 29, 6.

39. Ibid. (1910), Dec. 3, 6; Dec. 6, 6; Dec. 7, 6.

40. *Official Canvass of the Vote Cast, The City Record, City of New York,* Dec. 31, 1910, 41. See also Goren, *Publications of the American Jewish Historical Society,* 229–238.

41. *New York Times,* Nov. 9, 1914, 14. For the Congressional election results for 1912 and 1914, see Goren, *Publications of the American Jewish Historical Society,* 226.

## 5. The Conservative Politics of the Orthodox Press

1. "Jewishness and the Younger Intellectuals: A Symposium," *Commentary* (April 1961): 310.

2. Lawrence H. Fuchs, *The Political Behavior of American Jews* (Glencoe, Ill.: Free Press, 1956), 171–204; Edgar Litt, *Ethnic Politics in America* (Glenview, Ill.: Free Press, 1970), 113–126; Werner Cohn, "The Politics of American Jews," in Marshall Sklare, ed., *The Jews: Social Patterns of an American Group* (Glencoe, Ill.: Free Press, 1958), 614–625; Charles Liebman, *The Ambivalent American Jew* (Philadelphia: Jewish Publication Society, 1973), 135–159; Moses Rischin, *The Promised City* (Cambridge, Mass.: Harvard University Press, 1962), 221–235; Ben Halpern, "The Roots of American Jewish Liberalism," *American Jewish Historical Quarterly* 66 (Dec. 1976): 190–214.

3. Irving Howe, *The World of Our Fathers* (New York: Harcourt Brace Jovanovich, 1976), 360–361.

4. *Morgen Zhurnal,* Jan. 29, 1912, 1, 4.

5. For a detailed account of the passport issue, see Naomi W. Cohen, "The Abrogation of the Russo-American Treaty of 1832," *Jewish Social Studies* 25 (January 1963): 3–41.

6. Judah L. Magnes, "A Yiddish Morning Daily" [c. January 1913], Magnes Papers, File 542, Central Archives for the History of the Jewish People, Jerusalem, Israel.

7. Saphirstein to Taft, Jan. 6, 1911 (editorial on immigration policy attached); Charles Hillis, secretary to the president, Nov. 3, 1911 (article on Sherman anti-trust law attached); Saphirstein to Taft, Dec. 21, 1911 (editorial defending Taft on treaty-abrogation controversy attached); Saphirstein to Taft, July 13, 1912 (proposed statement for inclusion in letter of acceptance); Saphirstein to Taft, July 22, 1912 (editorial on award of B'nai B'rith medal attached); Taft to Saphirstein, June 20, 1911 (acknowledging editorial congratulating Tafts on their wedding anniversary); Taft to Saphirstein, Feb. 26, 1912. William Howard Taft Papers, Library of Congress, Washington, D.C.

8. *Der Amerikaner* [weekly magazine of the *Morgen Zhurnal*], Feb. 2, 1913. Translation sent to the president (William Howard Taft Papers, Library of Congress, Washington, D.C.); *New York Times,* Jan. 28, 1912, 1.

9.  Y. Fishman, "44 yohr *Morgen Zhurnal*," in Ya'acov's Glatstein, et al., *Finf un zibstig yohr yiddisher prese in Amerika* (New York: Y. L. Peretz Writers Union, 1945), 64–65.

10. *Morgen Zhurnal*, Jan. 6, 1911, 4; Feb. 16, 1911, 1; Feb. 17, 1911, 4.

11. Leonard Bloom, "A Successful Jewish Boycott of the New York City Public Schools—Christmas 1906," *American Jewish History* 70, no. 2 (Dec. 1980): 180–188.

12. *New York Times*, December 12, 1906, quoted in Bloom, *American Jewish History*, 184–185.

13. *Morgen Zhurnal*, Dec. 10, 1906, 1, 4; Dec. 23, 1906, 1; Dec. 24, 1911, 1; Dec. 27, 1907, 4; *New York Times*, Dec. 25, 1906, 8.

14. *Morgen Zhurnal*, Dec. 17, 1951, 8; Dec. 4, 1906, 1, 4; Dec. 5, 1, 4; Fishman, *Finf und zibstig yohr*, 66. In the interviews with Cannon and Fairbanks, Wiernik recalls acting as interpreter, Levin spoke in German. With the president, the conversation was conducted without an interpreter. Wiernik remarked that Roosevelt's German was better than Levin's.

15. Yacov Shatzky, *Di geshikhte fun yidin in varshe*, vol. 3 (New York: YIVO Institute for Jewish Research, 1953), 27–67, 110–191, 351–405; A. A. Hershberg, ed., *Pinkos Bialystock*, vol. 2 (New York: Bialystok Jewish Historical Association, 1949), 28–53, 74–95; Israel Cohen, *Vilna* (Philadelphia: Jewish Publication Society, 1943), 333–357.

16. *Morgen Zhurnal*, March 2, 1909, 4; March 28, 1909, 4; Feb. 28, 1910, 4; Feb. 24, 1911, 4. On emulating the Reform movement, see Jan. 17, 1911, 4; Arthur A. Goren, *New York Jews and the Quest for Community* (New York: Columbia University Press, 1970), 125–132.

17. *Morgen Zhurnal*, Dec. 2, 1912, 1; Dec. 13, 1912, 4; Goren, *New York Jews*, 81–82, 128; *American Hebrew*, Aug. 11, 1911, 416; Sep. 15, 1911, 591.

18. *American Hebrew*, April 12, 1912, 730; *Morgen Zhurnal*, Aug. 31, 1911, 1; Jan. 23, 1913, 1; Jan. 28, 1913, 4; Jan. 29, 1913, 1; Marshall to Charles M. Stern, March 25, 1912, in *Louis Marshall: Champion of Liberty*, ed. Charles Reznikoff, vol. 1 (Philadelphia: Jewish Publication Society, 1957), 37–38.

19. *Morgen Zhurnal*, April 29, 1912, 4.

## 6. Paths of Leadership

1.  *American Hebrew*, March 3, 1916, 472.

2.  *American Hebrew*, March 31, 1916, 588.

3.  Melvin I. Urofsky, "American Jewish Leadership," *American Jewish History* 70 (June 1981): 401.

4.  *Brandeis on Zionism: A Collection of Addresses and Statements by Louis D. Brandeis* (Washington, D.C.: Zionist Organization of America, 1941), 35, 112; Melvin I. Urofsky, *American Zionism from Herzl to the Holocaust* (Garden

City, N.Y.: Anchor Press/Doubleday, 1975), 155–159; Deborah Dash Moore, *B'nai B'rith and the Challenge of Ethnic Leadership* (Albany: State University of New York Press, 1981), 213–223.

5. I have found the following studies especially helpful: John Higham, ed., *Ethnic Leadership in America* (Baltimore: Johns Hopkins University Press, 1978); Nathan Glazer, "The Jews," in Higham, 19–35; Yonathan Shapiro, *Leadership of the American Zionist Organization* (Urbana: University of Illinois Press, 1971); John Higham, "Leadership," *Harvard Encyclopedia of American Ethnic Groups* (Cambridge, Mass: Harvard University Press, 1980), 642–647; Daniel J. Elazar, *Community and Polity: The Organizational Dynamics of American Jewry* (Philadelphia: Jewish Publication Society, 1976), 257–286; Victor R. Greene, *American Immigrant Leaders: 1800–1910, Marginality and Identity* (Baltimore: Johns Hopkins University Press, 1987), especially 5–16 and the discussion of Jewish ethnic leaders, 85–104.

6. Naomi W. Cohen, *Encounter with Emancipation: The German Jews in the United States, 1830–1914* (Philadelphia: Jewish Publication Society, 1984), 168–172, 188–194; Melvin I. Urofsky, *A Voice That Spoke for Justice: The Life and Times of Stephen S. Wise* (Albany: State University of New York Press, 1982), passim; Arthur A. Goren, ed., *Dissenter in Zion: From the Writings of Judah L. Magnes* (Cambridge, Mass.: Harvard University Press, 1982), 13–28.

7. Cohen, *Encounter*, 39–55, 119–122.

8. Kenneth D. Roseman, "American Jewish Community Institutions in Their Historical Context," *Jewish Journal of Sociology* 16 (June 1974): 31–33; Elazar, *Community and Polity*, 160–163.

9. Moore, *B'nai B'rith*, 74–101; Gary Dean Best, *To Free a People: American Jewish Leaders and the Jewish Problem in Eastern Europe, 1890–1914* (Westport, Conn.: Greenwood, 1982), 65–66, 72–80, 85, 115–117.

10. Naomi W. Cohen, *A Dual Heritage: The Public Career of Oscar Straus* (Philadelphia: Jewish Publication Society, 1969), 55–57; Best, *To Free a People*, passim.

11. M. S. Margolies, "Agudath Horabbonim," in *The Jewish Communal Register* (New York: Kehillah, 1918), 1180–1182; Arthur A. Goren, *New York Jews and the Quest for Community: The Kehillah Experiment, 1908–1922* (New York: Columbia University Press, 1970), 76–85.

12. Judah D. Eisenstein, *Ozar zihronoti* (New York, 1929), 252; Meyer Waxman, "Hayahadut ha'ortedoksit b'amerika," *Luach achiever* (New York: Histadrut Achiever, 1918), 3–13; Herbert S. Goldstein, *Forty Years of Struggle for a Principle, The Biography of Harry Fischel* (New York: Bloch, 1928), 35–36, 42–46, 62–65, 90–95, 124–132; *American Jewish Year Book* (1915), 206–207; Zosa Szajkowski, "Concord and Discord in American Jewish Overseas Relief, 1914–1924," *YIVO Annual of Jewish Social Science* 14 (1969): 100, 103.

13. *American Hebrew*, January 13, 1905; Greene, *American Immigrant Leaders*, 89–95; Szajkowski, *YIVO Annual* 14 (1969): 105; "Gedaliah Bublick," *Universal Jewish Encyclopedia*, vol. 8, 571; Arthur A. Goren, "Orthodox Politics, Repub-

lican and Jewish: Jacob Saphirstein and the *Morgen Zhurnal*," in *Proceedings of the Eighth World Congress of Jewish Studies: Jewish History* (Jerusalem: World Union of Jewish Studies, 1983), 63–71; Arthur A. Goren, "The Jewish Press in America," *The Ethnic Press of the United States*, ed. Sally M. Miller (Westport, Conn.: Greenwood, 1987), 211–212, 216–217.

14.    This paragraph and the following ones draw upon the extensive literature on the Jewish labor movement including: Will Herberg, "The Jewish Labor Movement in the U.S.," *American Jewish Year Book* 53 (1952): 3–74; Jacob Hertz, *Fuftzig yor arbeiter ring* (New York: National Executive Committee of the Arbeiter Ring, 1950); Ben Zion Hoffman, *Fuftzig yor cloak-macher union* (New York: Cloakmakers Local 117, 1936); Irving Howe, *World of Our Fathers* (New York: Harcourt Brace Jovanovich, 1976); Moses Rischin, *The Promised City* (Cambridge, Mass.: Harvard University Press, 1962).

15.    Goren, *New York Jews*, 186–211; Jonathan Frankel, "The Jewish Socialists and the American Jewish Congress Movement," *YIVO Annual of Jewish Social Science* 16 (1976): 202–342.

16.    The tensions between the elitist "leaders from the periphery" and the rank-and-file leadership of East European origins form the central theme of Shapiro, *Leadership*.

17.    On Samuel Dorf see *New York Times*, February 26, 1923, 13, and *American Jewish Year Book* 26 (1924), 616; on Sanders see, *New York Times*, Aug. 19, 1937, 19; Jacob Magidoff, *Der shpiegel fun der east side* (New York, 1923), 131–136; *History of the Independent Order B'rith Abraham* (New York, 1937), 49–51; and Goldstein, *Forty Years*, 78, 230.

18.    Naomi W. Cohen, *Not Free to Desist: The American Jewish Committee, 1906–1966* (Philadelphia: Jewish Publication Society, 1972), 3–18. Between 1911 and 1915, the executive committee of the AJC increased from 14 to 19, the general committee from 75 to 105; *American Jewish Year Book* 14 (1912/1913), 291–293; ibid. 18 (1916/1917), 288–290.

19.    Naomi W. Cohen, "The Abrogation of the Russo-American Treaty of 1832," *Jewish Social Studies* 25 (January 1963): 3–41. On the American Jewish Committee's overcoming Simon Wolf's conciliatory position in negotiating with President Taft, see Louis Marshall to Jacob H. Schiff, February 9, 1911, Marshall to Simon Wolf, June 1, 1911, and August 16, 1911, in *Louis Marshall: Champion of Liberty, Selected Papers and Addresses*, ed. Charles Reznikoff vol. 1 (Philadelphia: Jewish Publication Society, 1957), 77–78, 95–97. For an example of Marshall curbing the initiative of a friendly congressman who was deviating from the committee's strategy, see Marshall to Henry M. Goldfogle, January 27, 1909, March 2, 1911, in ibid., 55–56, 89–90.

20.    Goldstein, *Forty Years*, 86–89.

21.    Mark Wischnitzer, *Visas to Freedom: The History of HIAS* (Cleveland: World Publishing Co., 1956), 61–72, 88–89.

22.    Szajkowski, *YIVO Annual* 14 (1969): 103–109; Jonathan Frankel, *YIVO Annual* 16 (1976): 202–211; *American Jewish Year Book* 17 (1915/1916), 366–369.

23. Melvin I. Urofsky, *American Zionism from Herzl to the Holocaust* (Garden City, N.Y.: Anchor Press/Doubleday, 1975), 120–147; Ben Halpern, *A Clash of Heroes: Brandeis, Weizmann, and American Zionism* (New York: Oxford University Press, 1987), 109–118.

24. *Tageblat*, February 24, 1915, 9.

25. *Forverts*, April 20, 1915, as quoted in Frankel, *YIVO Annual* 16 (1976): 215; idem, *Prophecy and Politics: Socialism, Nationalism and the Russian Jews, 1862–1917* (Cambridge: Cambridge University Press, 1981), 509–547.

26. Schiff to Magnes, May 21, 1915, quoted in Goren, *New York Jews*, 220–221; Marshall to Magnes, May 21, 1915, Magnes Papers, Jerusalem; Reznikoff, ed., *Louis Marshall*, vol. 2, 509–510.

27. Jacob De Haas, *Louis D. Brandeis, A Biographical Sketch with Special Reference to his Contributions to Jewish and Zionist History, with full Text of his Addresses Delivered from 1912 to 1924* (New York: Bloch, 1929), 219–221.

28. Ibid., 228–229.

29. *American Hebrew*, March 31, 1916, 587–588.

30. Frankel, *YIVO Annual* 16 (1976): 300–302, 318–324.

31. *American Jewish Year Book* 23 (1921/22), 269; Joseph C. Hyman, "Twenty-Five Years of American Aid to Jews Overseas: A Record of the Joint Distribution Committee," ibid. 41 (1939/40): 141–147.

32. Szajkowski, *YIVO Annual* 14 (1969): 117–121, 137–140; Baruch Zuckerman, "Dos idish leben in amerika in ershtn fertle fun tzavntzikstn yorhundert," in L. Shpizman, *Geshichte fun der tzionyistesher arbeter bavegung in tzfom amerika*, vol. 1 (New York: Yiddisher Kemfer Publishing, 1955), 33–46.

33. Shapiro, *Leadership*, 78–80; Urofsky, *American Zionism*, 152–155, 169–171, 205. See, for example, Louis Brandeis to Judah Magnes, March 13, 1915, in Melvin I. Urofsky and David W. Levy, eds., *Letters of Louis D. Brandeis* (Albany: State University of New York Press, 1973), vol. 3, 481–484.

34. Brandeis to Felix Warburg, December 31, 1914, in *Letters of Louis D. Brandeis*, vol. 3, 397–398; Brandeis to Judah L. Magnes, July 18, 1915, in ibid., 547–550; Brandeis to Otto Warburg, April 6, 1916, in ibid., vol. 4, 154–160.

35. Louis Marshall to Felix Warburg, October 26, 1916, Louis Marshall Papers, American Jewish Archives. For the background to the dispute see, Szajkowski, *YIVO Annual* 14 (1969): 132–136.

36. *American Jewish Year Book* 18 (1916/17), 90–92; M. E. Ravage, *The Jew Pays, A Narrative of the Consequences of the War to the Jews of Eastern Europe and the Manner in Which Americans Have Attempted to Meet Them* (New York: A. A. Knopf, 1919), 44–61, 80–88; Szajkowski, *YIVO Annual* 14 (1969): 113–114, 131.

37. Judah Magnes to Felix Warburg, March 17, 1920, quoted in Szajkowski, *YIVO Annual* 14 (1969): 142–143. Magnes, Warburg's close advisor, visualized the JDC as the great nonpartisan organ for unifying American Jewry and world Jewry. Its program should be not only the "relief for the individual Jew in distress," but "strengthening the brotherhood and the creative forces

of the Jewish people." Magnes to Warburg, November 30, 1919, P/3 1627, Magnes Papers.

38.  Shapiro, *Leadership*, 181–204; Samuel Halperin, *The Political World of American Zionism* (Detroit: Wayne State University Press, 1961), 191–214; Ben Halpern, *A Clash of Heroes: Brandeis, Weizmann and American Zionism* (New York: Oxford University Press, 1987), 218–232, 244–246.

39.  Ernest Stock, *Partners and Pursestrings: A History of the United Israel Appeal* (Lanham, Md.: University Press of America and Jerusalem Center for Public Affairs, 1987), 130–141; Noach Orian, "The Leadership of Rabbi Abbah Hillel Silver on the American Jewish Scene, 1938–1949" (Ph.D. dissertation, Tel Aviv University, 1982) [in Hebrew], 506–513.

## 7. Spiritual Zionists and Jewish Sovereignty

1.  Ben Halpern, "The Americanization of Zionism, 1880–1930," *American Jewish History* 69 (September 1979): 32–33.

2.  Solomon Schechter, *Seminary Addresses and Other Papers* (New York: The Burning Bush, 1961), 97.

3.  Judah L. Magnes to David Wolffsohn, June 19, 1906, in Arthur A. Goren, *Dissenter in Zion: From the Writings of Judah L. Magnes* (Cambridge, Mass.: Harvard University Press, 1982), 82–83; Evyatar Friesel, "Magnes: Zionism in Judaism," *Like All the Nations? The Life and Legacy of Judah L. Magnes*, ed. William M. Brinner and Moses Rischin (Albany, N.Y.: State University of New York Press, 1987), 72–73; idem, *The Zionist Movement in the United States 1897–1914* [in Hebrew] (Tel Aviv: Hakibutz Hameuchad, 1970), 77–108.

4.  Friesel, *The Zionist Movement*, 109–124, 160–170; Yonathan Shapiro, *Leadership of the American Zionist Organization* (Urbana: University of Illinois Press, 1971), 37–46.

5.  Schechter, *Seminary Addresses*, xxiv; Israel Friedlaender, *Past and Present* (Cincinnati: Ark Publishing Co., 1919), 159–184.

6.  In a letter to Magnes dated March 31, 1908, Schechter wrote: "I had hoped to find peace in Zionism, but my hopes are shattered. When I see men like Ben Jehudah, who forbade his son to read the Bible because he wanted him to be a Jew in the same manner as a Frenchman is a Frenchman (that is, anti-clerical and anti-religious); when I see the prominence given to the productions of the Gordins and other men of the same style; when I see the idol made of the Yiddish language at the expense of the Hebrew, I gain the conviction that Zionism will not fulfill its mission without a thorough cleansing of its anti-religious and anti-Judaism elements. We cannot afford any new destructive forces no matter under what disguises they may appear, be it even under the disguise of Nationalism."
    Elsewhere in the letter Schechter attacked the Socialist-Zionists "who are outspoken enemies of Judaism, if not of the Jews, are traitors of their God

and of their nation." Judah Magnes Papers, Central Archives for the History of the Jewish People, Jerusalem, File 115.

7.  Judah L. Magnes to Mass Meeting of Federation of American Zionists, July 3, 1910, Magnes Papers, File 534.

8.  Baila Round Shargel, *Practical Dreamer: Israel Friedlaender and the Shaping of American Judaism* (New York: The Jewish Theological Seminary, 1985), 8–20, 103–182; Arthur A. Goren, "The Wider Pulpit: Judah L. Magnes and the Politics of Morality," *Studies in American Civilization*, ed. E. Miller Budick et al. (Jerusalem: The Magnes Press, 1987), 106–114.

9.  Melvin Urofsky, *American Zionism from Herzl to the Holocaust* (New York: Doubleday, 1975), 116–163, 427–429; idem, "Zionism, An American Experience," *American Jewish Historical Quarterly* 63 (March 1979): 215–230; Jerold S. Auerbach, *Rabbis and Lawyers: The Journey from Torah to Constitution* (Bloomington: Indiana University Press, 1990), 133–146; *Brandeis on Zionism: A Collection of Addresses and Statements by Louis D. Brandeis* (Washington, D.C.: Zionist Organization of America), 28, quoted in Allon Gal, *Brandeis of Boston* (Cambridge, Mass.: Harvard University Press, 1980), 181–182.

10. Stuart E. Knee, *The Concept of Zionist Dissent in the American Mind, 1917–1941* (New York: Robert Speller and Sons, 1979), passim; Auerbach, *Rabbis and Lawyers*, 141.

11. Quoted in Shargel, *Practical Dreamer*, 171–172, 180.

12. Shargel, *Practical Dreamer*, 15–40; Norman Bentwich, *For Zion's Sake: A Biography of Judah L. Magnes* (Philadelphia: Jewish Publication Society, 1954), 68–75, 97–127.

13. Reprinted in Friedlaender, *Past and Present*, 445–450.

14. Friedlaender, *Past and Present*, 446, 447.

15. *American Hebrew*, June 7, 1918, 114–115. See different version in Friedlaender, *Past and Present*, 488.

16. Friedlaender, *Past and Present*, 488.

17. Israel Friedlaender, "A Few Suggestions Concerning the Relations between the Jews and the Arabs," n.d., Magnes Papers, File 1704.

18. Shargell, *Practical Dreamer*, 180.

19. Herbert Adams Gibbons, "Zionism and the World Peace," *The Century Magazine* (January 1919): 369–372; Israel Friedlaender, "Zionism and the World Peace: A Rejoinder," *Century Magazine* (April 1919): 807–809. For a perceptive discussion of the Gibbons-Friedlaender exchange see, Shargel, *Practical Dreamer*, 171–180. One is left wondering how Friedlaender would have responded to Arab extremism which exploded in the Jaffa riots in May 1921. See ibid., 36–37, for Friedlaender's forebodings.

20. Arthur A. Goren, *New York Jews and the Quest for Community: The Kehillah Experiment, 1908–1922* (New York: Columbia University Press, 1970), 232–234; Goren, *Studies*, 114–115.

21. J. L. Magnes, *War-Time Addresses, 1917–1921* (New York: Thomas Seltzer, 1923), 99–102.

22. Ibid., 96–97.

23. Judah Magnes to Mayer Sulzberger, October 10, 1917, Magnes Papers, File 1348.

24. Magnes, *War-time Addresses*, 105.

25. J. L. Magnes, *Like All the Nations?* (Jerusalem: privately printed, 1930), 5.

26. Ibid., 45–46.

27. Ibid., 53–56.

28. Ibid., 56–57.

29. Ibid., 5; Naomi Cohen, *The Year after the Riots: American Responses to the Palestine Crisis of 1929–30* (Detroit: Wayne State University Press, 1988), 72–74.

30. Harry S. Truman, *Memoirs*, vol. 1 (New York: The New American Library, 1965), 326.

31. *Peace Movements in America*, ed. Charles Chatfield (New York: Schocken Books, 1973), 171–191; idem, *For Peace and Justice: Pacifism in America, 1914–1941* (Knoxville: University of Tennessee Press, 1971), 91–328; Robert A. Divine, *Second Chance: The Triumph of Internationalism in America During World War II* (New York: Atheneum, 1971), 7–28.

32. Roland B. Gittelsohn, "The Conference Stance on Social Justice and Civil Rights," *Retrospect and Prospect: Essays in Commemoration of the Seventy-Fifth Anniversary of the Founding of the Central Conference of American Rabbis, 1889–1964*, ed. Bertram Wallace Korn (New York: Central Conference of American Rabbis, 1965), 89–94, 103–105; *Proceedings of the Thirty-second Convention of the Rabbinical Assembly of America* (New York, N.Y.: 1932), 358–364; *Proceedings of the Thirty-fourth Annual Convention of the Rabbinical Assembly of America* (Tannersville, N.Y.: 1934), 156–164; *Proceedings of the Forty-first Convention of the Rabbinical Assembly of America* (Philadelphia, 1941), 39–50.

33. Divine, *Second Chance*, 36–39, 57–58; Morris R. Cohen, "Jewish Studies of Peace and Post-War Problems," *Contemporary Jewish Record* 4 (1941): 123–125; Salo W. Baron, "What War Has Meant to Community Life," *Contemporary Jewish Record* 5 (1942): 504–505; *Unity in Dispersion: A History of the World Jewish Congress* (New York: World Jewish Congress, 1948), 134–147.

34. Quoted in Divine, *Second Chance*, 37.

35. Goren, *Dissenter in Zion*, 378.

36. Mark Silk, "Notes on the Judeo-Christian Tradition in America," *American Quarterly* 36 (Spring 1984): 65–72.

37. Louis Finkelstein, "Reflections on Judaism, Zionism and an Enduring Peace," *New Palestine* 33, no. 14 (1943): 2–3; Naomi W. Cohen, " 'Diaspora Plus Palestine, Religion Plus Nationalism': The Seminary and Zionism, 1902–

1948," in Jack Wertheimer, ed., *A History of the Jewish Theological Seminary*, vol. 2: *Beyond the Academy* (New York: Jewish Theological Seminary, 1997), 148–150, 155–157.

38. Ibid., 4–5.

39. Ibid., 5–6; Louis Finkelstein, "Zionism and World Culture," *New Palestine*, September 15, 1944, 505.

40. Finkelstein, "Reflections on Judaism," 8.

41. Morris Waldman, *Nor by Power* (New York: International Press, 1953), 258–261. It is interesting to compare Finkelstein's thoughts about a Jewish commonwealth soon after the establishment of the State with his perception of his own views in the 1930s. Writing in 1950, Finkelstein declared: "At the Zionist Convention in 1935, I recall suggesting that to one accustomed to read Scripture, and to read the newspaper headlines in the light of Scripture and the writings of the Talmudic sages, it seemed probably that just as Sennacherib is remembered today primarily as the emperor whose activities were the subject of the prophecies of Isaiah . . . so the future historian of civilization will think of Nazism primarily as the evil which made the third Jewish commonwealth indispensable and inevitable." *Conservative Judaism* 4 (May 1950): 2.

42. Mordecai M. Kaplan, *Judaism as a Civilization* (New York: Macmillan, 1934), 273.

43. Ibid., 251, 278–279.

44. Ibid., 232–233.

45. Mordecai M. Kaplan, *The Future of the American Jew* (New York: Macmillan, 1948), 125.

46. Ibid., 37, 66–67.

47. Bernard A. Rosenblatt formulated this interpretation of "commonwealth" as a limited sovereign state. In his *Federated Palestine and the Jewish Commonwealth* (New York: Scopus Publishing Co., 1941), 39–40, he wrote: "It is necessary to offer *full opportunity for the Jewish National Home to develop as 'The Jewish Commonwealth'*—as free as Pennsylvania or Massachusetts now operate, with full control over their domestic affairs." Such a commonwealth would be joined to a Middle Eastern federation. *Federated Palestine* was reviewed favorably in *The Reconstructionist* of November 28, 1941. "State" and "commonwealth" were often used interchangeably by Zionist leaders. But note David Ben-Gurion's studious evasion of "state" and his use of "commonwealth" in the early 1940s as discussed by Allon Gal, *David Ben-Gurion: Towards a Jewish State* [in Hebrew] (Beersheva, Israel: Ben-Gurion University Press, 1985), 116–117.

48. *The Reconstructionist*, March 21, 1947, 3–4; April 18, 1947, 3–4; April 29, 1948, 3–4. Mordecai M. Kaplan Journals, Jewish Theological Seminary, New York.

49. Goren, *Dissenter*, 53–56, 462–463, 482–488; Menahem Kaufman, *An Ambiguous Partnership: Non-Zionists and Zionists in America, 1939–1948* (Jerusalem:

The Magnes Press, The Hebrew University; Detroit: Wayne State University Press, 1991), 332–333; Zvi Ganin, *Truman, American Jewry, and Israel, 1945–1948* (New York: Holmes and Meier, 1979), 175–176.

50. Louis Finkelstein to Abraham J. Peck, February 25, 1985, American Jewish Archives, Cincinnati.

51. Louis Finkelstein to Abraham J. Peck, February 25, 1985: Goren, *Dissenter*, 462–463, 482–488. Mordecai M. Kaplan Journals, February 28, 1948, Jewish Theological Seminary, New York. Cohen, *Beyond the Academy*, 159–165. In an interview with Simon Greenberg (April 18, 1991), he stressed Finkelstein's perpetual anxiety over the financial condition of the Seminary. While the Seminary's alumni were immersed in Zionist political activity and fund-raising, he felt that they neglected the institution that had nurtured them. The observation reminds one of Schechter's similar concerns over Seminary finances and his resentment when faculty members were active in the Zionist movement, New York Kehillah, or Jewish education.

## 8. Americanizing Zionist Pioneers

1. *Hechalutz*, ed. Chaim Arlosoroff, Shlomo Grodzensky, Rebecca Schmukler (New York: Zionist Labor Party Hitachduth of America and Avukah, American Student Zionist Federation, 1929), 7.

2. Arlosoroff remarked that "Hechalutz became the slogan of every platform-speaker, from the President of the Executive [of the World Zionist Organization] down to the last propagandist somewhere in the darkest province." For a perceptive semantic study of the *halutz* idea see, Henry Neer, "Mihu halutz? gilgulim semantiim shel ha'minuah hahalutzi b'tnuat ha'avoda ha'aretzyisralit" ("Who Is a Halutz? Semantic Changes in the Usage of Halutz in the Labor Movement in Erets Israel"), *Tura Bet* (Hamerkaz l'limudey yahadut, Oranim, Israel), 228–248.

3. Y. Oppenheim, *The Hechalutz Movement in Poland, 1917–1929* [in Hebrew] (Jerusalem, 1982), 150–206, 325–345; Henry Near, *The Kibbutz Movement, A History*, vol. 1: *Origins and Growth, 1909–1939* (Oxford: Oxford University Press, 1992), 97–128.

4. Both the original Hechalutz (founded in 1905) and the one established by David Ben-Gurion and Yitzhak Ben-Zvi during their stay in the United States between 1915 and 1918 were short-lived and limited largely to the Yiddish-speaking members of the Poalei Zion. I have therefore not considered them as germane to a discussion of the Americanization of the *halutz* idea. Cf. Mark A. Raider, *The Emergence of American Zionism* (New York: New York University Press, 1998), 74–98.

5. *Brandeis on Zionism: A Collection of Addresses and Statements by Louis D. Brandeis* (Washington, D.C.: Zionist Organization of America, 1942), 31. For the invention of a *shomer* mythology, see Jonathan Frankel, "The 'Yizkor' Book of 1911—a Note on National Myths of the Second Aliya," in *Religion,*

*Ideology and Nationalism in Europe and America: Essays Presented in Honor of Yehoshua Arieli*, ed. H. Ben Israel et al. (Jerusalem: Historical Society of Israel and Zalman Shazar Center for Jewish History, 1986), 355–384.

6. Judah L. Magnes, "A Message from Palestine: Address Delivered at Cooper Union, on Saturday Evening, May 18, 1912," Magnes Papers (Central Archives for the History of the Jewish People, Jerusalem), P3/1065, 3–4.

7. *Young Judaean*, 4, no. 5 (February 1914): 11. A description of the *shomrim* in the *Young Judeaen* ("Jewish Minute Men," ibid., 3, no. 1 [October 1912]: 20) is apparently based on Magnes's 1912 address.

8. Henrietta Szold, "Recent Progress in Palestine," *American Jewish Year Book* 17 (Philadelphia, 1915), 95.

9. The quotation is from the second edition where the title was changed. *A Guide to Zionism* (New York: Zionist Organization of America, 1920), 170.

10. Jonathan Frankel draws a similar profile from a European perspective. He quotes the Hebrew writer, David Frishman, following a visit to Palestine in 1911: "These youngsters, forever on horseback, forever full of fire, are always, like the Beduin in the desert, out to demonstrate every variety of show and acrobatics on their horses. . . . The main thing is that everybody else should see the [Jewish] people here are harsh and of quick temper and so, out of fear, refrain from theft." Frankel, "National Myths," 371.

11. Szold, "Recent Jewish Progress in Palestine," 95. Henry Near offers a detailed analysis of the differences between the *halutz* and frontiersman images. I have described the *shomer* as I believe he was perceived through *American* eyes. Cf. Near's "Pioneers and Halutzim: Communal Values and Pioneering Images in America and Pre-State Jewish Palestine" (lecture delivered at the Conference of the International Communal Studies Association, Elizabethtown College, July 1991).

12. Magnes, "Message," 5–13.

13. Jessie E. Sampter, "A Vision of Redemption," *Young Judeaen* 11, no. 4 (January 1921): 99. An interesting example of the mythologizing of the *shomer* is the following excerpt from a news story reporting the purported plans of the British army to recruit a rural Jewish constabulary from among the *shomrim*. "Another colony fighter and night-rider of the Ha-Shomerim, called 'the Lion-Hearted' even by his adversaries, is Michael Halperin. Once he entered the lion's cage of a circus-tent packed to the ceiling with Arabs, and there surrounded by five huge, growling lions, sang the Hebrew national hymn, 'Hatikvah,' from beginning to end, just to show his contempt of danger to a handclapping, impressionable crowd of Moslems." *New Palestine* 1, no. 22 (April 2, 1920): 3.

14. Reuben Brainin, "In the Land of Immortals," *New Palestine* 10, no. 3 (January 15, 1926): 54–55.

15. Eva Leon, "With the Chalutzim," *New Palestine* 6, no. 16 (April 18, 1924): 324.

16. Maurice Samuel, "Outposts of the North," *New Palestine* 7, no. 7 (August 22, 1924): 125; ibid. 7, no. 12 (September 26, 1924): 205–207.

17.   The articles sent from Palestine on March 5, 8 and 12, 1923, were published in the *New York Evening Post* and reprinted in the *New Palestine*. George W. Seymour, "Triumphant Advance of Zionism: Described by a Christian Observer," *New Palestine* 5, no. 7 (August 10, 1923): 134–135.

18.   Ibid.: 134, 136.

19.   Henrietta Szold, "Jewish Palestine at Work," *New Palestine* 6, no. 22 (June 6, 1924): 461–462.

20.   Ezra Mendelsohn, "Mo're americanit b'erez yisrael: shlosha mikhtavim m'fani soyer l'rivka letz (1925)" ("An American Teacher in Erez Israel: Three Letters from Fani Soyer to Rivka Letz [1925]"), *Katedra* 72 (June 1994): 96.

21.   In another context in the same article, Levensohn accused Ludwig Lewisohn of making snap judgments and misrepresenting the character of the kibbutz on the basis of a visit to Ein Harod lasting only several hours.

22.   Lotta Levensohn, "Palestine in the Making: The Realities of Ain Charod," *New Palestine* 11, no. 6 (August 20, 1926): 114–115.

23.   Judah L. Magnes [Diaries], March 12, 1925; Judah L. Magnes Papers, File 964, Central Archives for the History of the Jewish People, Jerusalem.

24.   Frederick Lewis Allen, *Only Yesterday: An Informal History of the Nineteen Twenties* (New York: Harper and Row, 1959, first published, 1931), 73–101; William H. Chafe, *The American Woman: Her Changing Social, Economic, and Political Role, 1920–1970* (New York: Oxford University Press, 1972), 94–99; Linda Gordon, *Woman's Body, Woman's Right: A Social History of Birth Control in America* (New York: Grossman Publishers, 1976), 186–202. For a defense of sexual morals in the Soviet Union in response to accusations of promiscuity and the breakdown in family values, see Paul Blanshard, "Sex Standards in Moscow," *The Nation*, May 12, 1926, 521–524; and Waldo Frank, *Dawn in Russia* (New York: Charles Scribner's Sons, 1932), 50–53.

25.   Ludwig Lewisohn, *Israel* (New York: Boni and Liveright, 1925), 150. For the important visit to Palestine of Abraham Cahan, editor of the *Forverts*, see Moses Rischin, "The Promised Land in 1925: America, Palestine, and Abraham Cahan," *YIVO Annual* 22 (1995): 96–100. Cahan extolled the Histadrut, *halutzim*, and kibbutzim in his daily dispatches to the paper.

26.   Horace M. Kallen, *Frontiers of Hope* (New York: Horace Liveright, 1929), 91–92.

27.   John Haynes Holmes, *Palestine To-day and To-morrow: A Gentile's Survey of Zionism* (New York: Macmillan, 1929), 194.

28.   Lewisohn, *Israel*, 178–181.

29.   Ibid., 181–185.

30.   Holmes, *Palestine*, 185, 189–199.

31.   Holmes, ibid., 204–205.

32.   Kallen, *Frontiers of Hope*, 108–114, 117–118. Emanuel Neuman on a visit to Pal-

estine in the summer of 1925 describes being "torn between admiration for the *halutzim* in the Jezreel Valley, and the impressive reality of the rapidly growing town of Tel Aviv" and finally opting for the advantages of urban, industrial development. See, *In the Arena: An Autobiographical Memoir* (New York: Herzl Press, 1976), 82.

33. Kallen, *Frontiers of Hope*, 85–86.

34. Joseph Reider, "A Revival of Jewish Music," *Menorah Journal* 5, no. 4 (August 1919): 225. The song, entitled "Nitzanim," was composed in 1910, the music by Herman Ehrlich and the lyrics by Yisrael Dushman. The opening lines are: "Po be'eretz hemdat avot/tit-gashemna kol ha-tikvot." I am grateful to Dr. Natan Shachar for this information.

35. Abraham Wolf Binder, *New Palestinian Folk Songs* (New York: Bloch, 1926, 1929); idem, *New Palestian Folk Songs, Book II* (New York: Bloch, 1933); Irene Heskes, "A Biographical Sketch of Abraham Wolf Binder," in *A.W. Binder: His Life and Work* (New York: National Jewish Music Council, 1965), 4. Worthy of note was the ambitious plan of the Hechalutz organization to publish an edition of thirty songs in twelve separate folders, "Songs the Chalutzim Sing," to be arranged by a group of "eminent Jewish composers." Four appeared, "Dances of Palestine," arranged by Erich Walter Sternberg and Aaron Copland, "Shepherd Songs," arranged by Paul Dessau, and "Builders' Songs," arranged by Kurt Weill and Darius Milhaud. See advertisements in *Jewish Frontier* 5, no. 6 (June 1938): 24.

36. *New York Times*, November 3, 1956; November 26, 1934. The opera was given in a concert version in Carnegie Hall in 1946. See A. W. Binder, "Jacob Weinberg: 1875–1956, A Tribute," *Jewish Music Notes* (Spring, 1957): 3. The published libretto and music can be found at the Jewish Theological Seminary. Ayalah Goren's research on Binder and Weinberg was most helpful as was her interview with Dvora Lapson in March 1993. John Martin of the *New York Times* wrote: "Her [Lapson's] ballet, based on the Palestinian Hora, spirited and well composed, was quite the brightest spot of the entire production." *Jewish Frontier* 2, no. 6 (April 1935): 29.

37. *New York Times*, Nov. 21, 1935, 2; see also reviews in the New York *Evening Journal*, *World Telegram*, and *American* for the same date. For an account of the making of *Land of Promise* see Hillel Tryster, " 'The Land of Promise': A Case Study in Zionist Film Propaganda," *Historical Journal of Film Radio and Television* 15, no. 2 (1995): 187–217. See also, Ayelet Cohen, "Reyshit ha'kolnoa ha'aretz'yisrali k'mshakef riyonot ha'tkufa," *Katedra* 61 (September 1991): 141–155.

38. Hillel Tryster, "Anatomy of an Epic Film," *Jerusalem Post Magazine* (October 30, 1992): 16–18.

39. *New Palestine* 25, no. 36 (Nov. 22, 1935): 1, 6; ibid. (Nov. 29, 1935): 8.

40. *New Palestine* 29, no. 18 (May 12, 1939): 8; ibid. 29, no. 19 (May 19, 1939): 8–10. Meyer Weisgal, *So Far: An Autobiography* (New York: Random House, 1971), 110–121, 130–139, 149–151, 161–163.

41. Jessie E. Sampter, "Youth and Palestine," *New Palestine* 10, no. 23 (June 18, 1926): 564–565. As early as 1921, "A Message from Our Palestinian Young Judeans," signed by a distinguished list of sixteen, called on America to send "more ideas and men." Eleven of the sixteen were women. *Young Judaean* 9, no. 8 (May-June, 1921): 220–221.

42. Samuel Grand, "A History of Zionist Youth Organizations in the United States from Their Inception to 1940" (Ph.D. dissertation, Columbia University, 1958), 240–241, 248–292, 310–331.

43. Ibid., 43–67.

44. *Young Judaean* 21, no. 8 (Sept. 1933): 10.

45. Ibid. 23, no. 7 (May 1935): 6–7; ibid. 23, no. 10 (October 1935): 12.

46. *The Chalutzim Series*, n.d. [1935?], Central Zionist Archives, E25/330. Among the members of the committee which prepared the series were Ben M. Ediden and Joshua Trachtenberg.

47. *The Young Judaean* (May 1936): 2. I recall one of my Habonim leaders, a former Jewish educator, saying that he thought standing up in front of a Hebrew school class was true *halutziut*. It was surely more difficult than draining swamps.

48. Arthur A. Goren, "Ben Halpern: 'At Home in Exile,' " in *The Other New York Jewish Intellectuals*, ed. Carole Kessner (New York: New York University Press, 1994), 82–85. Mark Raider, *The Emergence of American Zionism*, 125–147; *Youth and Nation*, February 1947, as quoted in *Furrows* 5, no. 3 (March 1947).

49. "Proceedings of Eleventh Annual Conference of the National Council for Jewish Education," May 29–June 2, 1936, *Jewish Education* 8 (1936): 146–147; *The Reconstructionist* 2, no. 10 (June 26, 1936): 5; *Labor Zionist Handbook* (New York: Poale Zion Ziere Zion of America, 1939), 131–133.

50. Murray Weingarten, "Great Expectations, Meager Results," *Furrows* 5, no. 10 (November 1947): 12–15; "Declaration of the National Assembly for Labor Palestine," *Jewish Frontier* 16, no. 7 (July 1949): 21–22; Daniel Frisch, *On the Road to Zion* (New York: Zionist Organization of America, 1950), 46, 76; cf. *The State of the Organization, Report Rendered by Daniel Frisch, President of the Zionist Organization of America*, New York, N.Y., November 13, 1949, 9–10. In its summary of American Jewish communal life, the *American Jewish Year Book* remarked: "The growth of the halutz (pioneer) movement in the United States during 1949–1950 was not commensurate with the number of resolutions passed by leading Zionist organizations in its favor and certainly did not presage a mass exodus of American Jewish youth to Israel"; vol. 52 (1951), 112.

51. Leonard Slater, *The Pledge* (New York: Random House, 1970); Shmuel Ben-Zevi, "The Halutz Movement Develops: 1934–1948," Moshe, "The Zionist T. N. T. Ring," Akiva Skidell, "Aliya Bet Ships," Avraham Schenker, "Retrospect and Outlook," *Pioneers from America: 75 Years of Hehalutz, 1905–1980* (Tel Aviv: Bogrei Hehalutz America, 1981), 83–88, 103–104.

52. Shortly before the creation of the state, Pinkhas Lubianker (later Lavon), one of the prominent figures in the Histadrut, toured the United States to evaluate the work of American Hechalutz. Meeting with the leaders of one of the *halutz* youth movements to hear their problems, he interrupted their report with the remark, "But you are talking of thirty people on hachshara and a movement of a couple of thousand. We are interested in the half-million of eligible youth whom you haven't touched. We are interested in some such project as a 'Congress of Jewish Youth for Erets Israel.' At such a conference we would say what we have to say to thousands at one stroke. We would accomplish in three days what your methods take three years to accomplish." Artie Gorenstein, "Balance-Sheet of American Chalutziut," *Furrows* 8, no. 2 (October 1950): 8; see also Lubianker's "Call to Jewish Youth," *Furrows* 7, no. 1 (Feb. 1949).

53. Zvi Ganin, "New York v'yerushaliim b'sperktiva historit," [with appended document]: "Al haperek: gishatenu l'yahdut amerika, protocol p'gisha b'misrad rosh ha'memshala David Ben-Gurion, July 25, 1950," *Kivunim* (April 1993): 59. Ben-Gurion interrupted Eban at this point and remarked: "Why is it necessary to give the title 'halutz' to all these people?" The remark reflected an inconsistency in Ben-Gurion's use of "halutziut" at this time. In the above discussion he delineated between "olim" (immigrants) and "halutzim"; the latter would settle in agricultural settlements especially in the Negev. He also envisioned the required military training giving recruits "military capacity and the capacity to pioneer" ("kosher tzvai v'kosher halutzi"), i.e., agricultural training in addition to their military training.

54. For the debate over "halutziut," see Henry Near's illuminating "Halutzim v'halutziut b'mdinat yisrael: hebetim semantiim v'historiim, 1948–1956," *Iyunim b'tkumat yisrael* 2 (1992), 116–140. The most important text for Ben-Gurion's thinking is his introduction to *Government Yearbook*, 5712 (1951/52), which is entitled in the English version, "The Call of Spirit in Israel." In the Hebrew edition, the introduction is entitled, "Y'udey ha'ruah v'ha'halutziut b'yisrael" ("The Call of the Spirit and Halutziut in Israel"). On the criticism of American Zionism and the movement's reaction see Urofsky, *We Are One*, 193–195, 258–277, 287–297; Arthur Hertzberg, "New Horizons for the ZOA," *New Palestine* 39, no. 18 (May 27, 1949): 12.

55. *The Reconstructionist* 11, no. 17 (Jan. 11, 1946): 6–7.

56. Ibid. 13, no. 19 (January 23, 1948): 4–6. For an essay which attempts to reconcile *halutziut* with Reconstructionism see, Jack Cohen, "*Halutziut* for American Jews," *The Reconstructionist* 12, no. 17 (December 27, 1946): 10–16, where Cohen expands *halutziut* to include Jewish communal work in America.

57. Ben Halpern, "The Problem of the American Chalutz," *Forum for the Problems of Zionism, World Jewry and the State of Israel* 1 (Dec. 1953): 50–51.

58. *Jewish Frontier* 17, no. 1 (January 1950): 22.

59. It would be interesting to examine the image of the *halutz* as portrayed in commercial and documentary films since 1946. Hollywood produced three films between 1946 and 1960 in which the kibbutz played a role to one de-

gree or another: *Sword in the Desert* (1949), set in 1947; *The Juggler* (1953), set in 1947/1948; and *Exodus* (1960), set in 1947/1948. The great majority of films commissioned by the United Jewish Appeal dealt with refugees and their absorption in Israel. Several films produced by Israeli institutions (Keren Hayesod and Keren Hakayemet) focused on *halutzim* and the kibbutz: *House in the Desert* (1947), the story of kibbutz Beth Ha'arava on the Dead Sea; *Challenge of the Negev* (1951), showing Kibbutz Shuval among other scenes; *The Edge of Danger* (1955), settlers in the border kibbutzim; *The Defenders* (1956), kibbutz Kissufim suffering from terrorist attacks. This suggests that the kibbutz/*halutz* image retained some of its appeal as a representation of heroic Israel but nowhere near the extent that it had prior to the establishment of Israel.

### 9. The "Golden Decade": 1945–1955

1.  Lucy Dawidowicz, *On Equal Terms: Jews in America, 1881–1981* (New York: Holt, Rinehart and Winston, 1982). Murray Friedman in his *The Utopian Dilemma: New Political Directions for American Jews* (Washington, D.C.: Ethics and Public Policy Center, 1985) entitles one of his chapters, "The Golden Age of American Jewry (1945–1965)."

2.  *The Ambivalent American Jew* (Philadelphia: Jewish Publication Society, 1973), vii.

3.  In order of their appearance, some of the key studies of the suburbanization of American Jews are: Herbert J. Gans, "Park Forest: Birth of a Jewish Community," *Commentary* 11, no. 4 (April 1951): 330–339; idem, "Progress of a Suburban Jewish Community, Park Forest Revisited," *Commentary* 23, no. 2 (Feb. 2, 1957): 113–122; Marshall Sklare and Marc Vosk, *The Riverton Study: How Jews Look at Themselves and Their Neighbors* (New York: American Jewish Committee, 1957); Judith Kramer and Seymour Leventman, *Children of the Gilded Ghetto* (New Haven: Yale University Press, 1961); Marshall Sklare and Joseph Greenbaum, *Jewish Identity on the Suburban Frontier: A Study of Group Survival in an Open Society* (New York: Basic Books, 1967).

4.  Deborah Dash Moore, *At Home in America: Second Generation New York Jews* (New York: Columbia University Press, 1981), 19–149, 201–242.

5.  Marc Lee Raphael, *Profile in Judaism: The Reform, Conservative, Orthodox Traditions in Historical Perspective* (San Francisco: Harper and Row, 1984), 119; idem, *A History of the United Jewish Appeal, 1939–1982* (Chico, Calif.: Scholars Press, 1982), 136–137.

6.  Daniel Elazar, *Polity and Community: The Organizational Dynamics of American Jewry* (Philadelphia: Jewish Publication Society, 1976), 297; Melvin I. Urofsky, *We Are One: American Jewry and Israel* (Garden City, N.Y.: Anchor Press/Doubleday, 1978), 144–145; Peter Grosse, *Israel in the Mind of America* (New York: Alfred A. Knopf, 1982), 265–268.

7.  Yehuda Bauer, *Flight and Rescue: Brichah* (New York: Random House, 1970),

241–255; Leonard Slater, *The Pledge* (New York: Simon and Schuster, 1970), 92–97, 120–124, 209–218; Doron Almog, *Harekhesh bartzot-habrit* (Tel Aviv, 1987), 31–34, 43–52.

8. Elmer Berger, *Judaism or Jewish Nationalism: The Alternative to Zionism* (New York: Bookman Associates, 1957), 15–44, 92–107; Thomas Kolsky, *Jews against Zionism: The American Council for Judaism, 1942–1948* (Philadelphia: Temple University Press, 1990), 129–188; Arthur Liebman, *Jews on the Left* (New York: John Wiley and Sons, 1979), 511–515; Sidney Hook, *Out of Step* (New York: Harper and Row, 1987), 5, 33; Nathan Glazer, "Jewish Intellectuals," *Partisan Review* 51 (1984): 674–679.

9. Emanuel Neuman, *In the Arena: An Autobiographical Memoir* (New York: Herzl Press, 1976), 243–245, 349–355; see also Aaron Berman, *Nazism, the Jews and American Zionism* (Detroit: Wayne State University Press, 1990), 178–179.

10. Marshall Sklare, *America's Jews* (New York: Random House, 1971), 211–222; Nathan Glazer, "*American Judaism* Thirty Years Later," *American Jewish History* 77 (1987): 284; Jacob Neusner, *Stranger at Home: The "Holocaust," Zionism, and American Judaism* (Chicago: University of Chicago Press, 1981), 66–67; Chaim Waxman, *America's Jews in Transition* (Philadelphia: Temple University Press, 1983), 114–115, 119–123.

11. Lawrence H. Fuchs, *The Political Behavior of American Jews* (Glencoe, Ill.: Free Press, 1956), 79–120; Charles S. Liebman, *The Ambivalent American Jew*, 136–139, 148–159; Deborah Dash Moore, *B'nai B'rith and the Challenge of Ethnic Leadership* (Albany: State University of New York Press, 1981), 213–221; Waxman, *America's Jews*, 98–103.

12. For this and the following paragraph see Murray Friedman, *The Utopian Dilemma: New Political Directions for American Jews* (Washington, D.C.: Ethics and Public Policy Center, 1985), 1–35; Naomi W. Cohen, *Not Free to Desist* (Philadelphia: Jewish Publication Society, 1972), 384–404; Peter Y. Medding, "Segmented Ethnicity and the New Jewish Politics," *Studies in Contemporary Jewry*, vol. 3, ed. Ezra Mendelsohn (New York, 1987), 26–48.

13. Albert Vorspan and Eugene J. Lipman, *Justice and Judaism: The Work of Social Action* (New York: Union of American Hebrew Congregations, 1956), passim.

14. For the exchange of statements between Jacob Blaustein and David Ben-Gurion, see *American Jewish Year Book* 53 (New York, 1952), 564–565. See also Charles S. Liebman's discussion in *Pressure without Sanctions: The Influence of World Jewry on Israeli Policy* (Teaneck, N.J.: Fairleigh Dickenson, 1977), 118–131. For a recent indication of a continued sensitivity to the question of dual loyalties see, Arthur J. Goldberg, "The Canard of Dual Loyalty," *Hadassah Magazine* (March 1983): 16–17.

15. Will Herberg, *Protestant, Catholic, Jew* (Garden City, N.Y.: Anchor/Doubleday, 1960); for a review of the literature on religious identification, see Waxman, *America's Jews*, 81–95.

16.     C. Bezalel Sherman, *Israel and the American Jewish Community* (New York: Labor Zionist Organization of America, 1951), 12. This caveat appeared on the inside of the title page of the pamphlet: "The particular views expressed by the author do not necessarily constitute the official policy of the Labor Zionist Organization of America."

17.     C. Bezalel Sherman, *The Jew within American Society: A Study in Ethnic Individuality* (Detroit: Wayne State University Press, 1961), 223, 226. For an early statement of this thesis, see idem, "Secularism in a Religious Framework," *Judaism* 1, no. 1 (January 1952): 36–43.

18.     Quoted by Nina Warnke, "The American Jewish Tercentenary" (unpublished mss. presented at the 60th Annual YIVO Conference, October 1988), 1. I am grateful to the author for allowing me to read this illuminating paper on the ideological meaning of the tercentenary.

19.     *American Jewish Tercentenary: 1654–1954, Scope and Theme* (report of steering committee to Tercentenary Committee of 300, National Planning Conference, April 12, 1953); Minutes, Committee on Organization, Tercentenary Celebration of Jewish Settlement in the United States, January 15, 1952, March 24, 1952; Minutes, Steering Committee, American Jewish Tercentenary Committee, June 3, 1952, November 18, 1952; Minutes, National Planning Conference, American Jewish Committee, April 12, 1953; Ralph E. Samuel, to the Tercentenary Committee of 300, Final Report, July 14, 1955. I want to thank Oscar Handlin who allowed me to use his files of the tercentenary committees. He was most directly involved in the committee on research and publications.

20.     See David Bernstein, "The American Jewish Tercentenary," *American Jewish Year Book* 57 (New York, 1956), 101–118.

21.     *National Jewish Monthly* 69 (Sept. 1954): 8–12. Beginning with the October issue, the *Monthly* ran feature stories depicting episodes in American Jewish history. Nathan Glazer, Oscar and Mary F. Handlin, and Joseph C. Blau in *American Jewish Year Book* 56 (New York, 1955), 3–170; Moses Rischin, *An Inventory of American Jewish History* (Cambridge, Mass.: Harvard University Press, 1954); *The Jewish People: Past and Present, 300 Years of Jewish Life in the United States*, vol. 4 (New York: Jewish Encyclopedic Handbooks, 1955) (no ed. named).

22.     Daniel Bell, "The End of American Exceptionalism," *The Public Interest* 41 (Fall 1975): 203–205; Daniel Boorstin, *The Genius of American Politics* (Chicago: University of Chicago Press, 1953), 1.

23.     *American Jewish Archives* 1, no. 1 (June 1948): 2–3.

24.     Moshe Davis and Isidor S. Meyer, eds., *The Writing of American Jewish History* (New York: American Jewish Historical Society, 1957); American Jewish History Center *Newsletter* 1 (Spring 1961).

25.     Oscar Handlin, *Adventure in Freedom: Three Hundred Years of Jewish Life in America* (New York: McGraw-Hill, 1954), vii–viii, 260.

26.     Memorandum, Judge Samuel I. Rosenman to David Bernstein, October 7, 1952; "American Jewish Tercentenary, Scope and Theme (for Steering Committee Use Only)," n.d.

27.     *American Jewish Yearbook* 56 (1955), 103, 107.

28.     Stuart Svonkin, *Jews against Prejudice: American Jews and the Fight for Civil Liberties* (New York: Columbia University Press, 1997), 150–177. Deborah Dash Moore, "Reconsidering the Rosenbergs: Symbol and Substance in Second Generation American Jewish Consciousness," *Journal of American Ethnic History* 8, no. 1 (Fall 1988): 21–37; Arnold Forster, *Square One: A Memoir* (New York: Donald L. Fire, 1988), 126–129; *Congress Weekly*, March 12, 1951, 1–3; ibid., Nov. 16, 1953, 3–10, and Nov. 23, 1953, 10–12.

29.     Robert Gordis, "American Jewry Faces Its Fourth Century," *Judaism* 3, no. 4 (Fall 1954): 298.

30.     Horace Kallen, "The Tercentenary: Yomtov or Yahrzeit?" *Congress Weekly* 21, no. 31 (Nov. 22, 1954): 8–11; "The Tercentenary Symbol and Slogan: An Exchange of Letters," ibid. (Dec. 20, 1954): 14–15.

31.     Mordecai M. Kaplan, "The Meaning of the Tercentenary for Diaspora Judaism," *The Reconstructionist* 20, no. 12 (Oct. 15, 1954): 10, 16–18.

32.     Ben Halpern, *The American Jew: A Zionist Analysis* (New York: Herzl Press, 1956), 11–14.

33.     Harold Weisberg, "Ideologies of American Jews," in *The American Jew: A Reappraisal*, ed. Oscar I. Janowsky (Philadelphia: Jewish Publication Society, 1964), 347–356.

34.     See for example Israel Goldstein, *American Jewry Comes of Age: Tercentenary Addresses* (New York: Bloch, 1955). In an address entitled "Facing the Fourth Century," he notes that the interpretations of the tercentennial theme "can be as varied as the viewpoints of those who interpret it. The theme itself is more Jewish than would appear" (p. 120).

## 10.  Inventing the "New Pluralism"

Irving Levine, former director of the Domestic Affairs Department of the American Jewish Committee, called my attention to unpublished material in the AJC's records office. Unpublished letters, reports, and proposals unless otherwise noted are in the AJC records office and are quoted with the Committee's permission.

1.      Nathan Glazer, *Ethnic Dilemmas, 1964–1982* (Cambridge, Mass.: Harvard University Press, 1983), 17.

2.      Perry L. Weed, *The White Ethnic Movement and Ethnic Politics* (New York: Praeger, 1973), 14–26, is a brief account of the early years of the AJC's new pluralism program; Arthur Mann, *The One and the Many: Reflections on the American Identity* (Chicago: University of Chicago Press, 1979) places the debate over the "new pluralism" within a broad historical context. For Mann's

discussion of the AJC's role as "prime mover of the new pluralist move-ment," see 25–30. In 1996, the Institute was renamed the Arthur and Rochelle Belfer Center for American Pluralism. See *E Pluribus Unum? A Symposium on Pluralism and Public Policy* (New York: American Jewish Committee, 1997), 5–7.

3. *American Jewish Year Book* 57 (1955), 103, 107.

4. American Jewish Committee, "Report of the Conference on Group Life in America," Arden House, November (pamphlet) 1956, i–ii.

5. Ibid.

6. Oscar Handlin, "Historical Perspectives on the American Ethnic Group," *Daedalus* 90 (Spring 1961): 231.

7. Ibid.

8. Will Herberg, *Protestant, Catholic, Jew* (New York: Anchor Books/Double-day, 1955), 94–102, 253, 258, 262.

9. Nathan Glazer and Daniel Moynihan, *Beyond the Melting Pot: The Negroes, Puerto Ricans, Jews, Italians, and Irish of New York City* (Cambridge, Mass.: MIT Press, 1963), 314.

10. National Community Relations Advisory Council, *Joint Program Plans, A Guide to Proper Planning for Jewish Community Relations, 1868–1968*, 7.

11. Naomi Cohen, *Not Free to Desist: A History of the American Jewish Commit-tee, 1906–1966* (Philadelphia: Jewish Publication Society, 1972), 333–335, 384–404.

12. Ibid., 400–404.

13. *Commentary* 38 (Aug. 1964): 28–31; Murray Friedman, "Introduction: Mid-dle America and the 'New Pluralism,' " in *Overcoming Middle Class Rage*, ed. Murray Friedman (Philadelphia: Westminster Press, 1971), 15–31.

14. Allen J. Matusow, *The Unraveling of America: A History of Liberalism in the 1960's* (New York: Harper and Row, 1984), 198–216; Glazer and Moynihan, *Be-yond the Melting Pot* (2nd ed., 1970), ix, xxvi.

15. Levine to Seymour Brief, "Conference on Ethnic America," Sept. 15, 1967. Levine also expressed the hope that the Ford Foundation would become in-terested.

16. Irving Levine Oral History, Dec. 10, 1980, American Jewish Committee; Kevin Lahart, "What Happens When the Melting-Pot Fire Goes Out," *News-day*, June 5, 1971, reprinted by the AJC; Gerald Sorin, "From the Brownsville Boys Club to the Institute for American Pluralism: Irving M. Levine and the Modern Challenge to Jewish Liberalism," in *An Inventory of Promises: Es-says on American Jewish History in Honor of Moses Rischin*, ed. Jeffrey S. Gurock and Marc Lee Raphael (Brooklyn, N.Y.: Carlson Publishing, 1995), 275–282.

17. Levine Oral History, Dec. 10, 1980; Matusow, *Unraveling of America*, 138–139.

18. Proposal for a National Consultation on Ethnic America, prepared by Irving

M. Levine, director of Education and Urban Planning, AJC, Mar. 1968. Levine delivered a paper at the "Conference on the Problems of White Ethnic America" sponsored by the AJC and held in Philadelphia in June 1968. The paper was essentially the text of his March proposal. It was then published as "A Strategy for White Ethnic America" in *Issues in Race and Ethnic Relations*, ed. Jack Rothman (Ithaca: F.E. Peacock, 1977), 270–278. The editor noted: "The paper, written in June 1968, was one of the first efforts to speak to the problems of this country's white ethnic working class, and it formed the philosophy for the National Project of Ethnic America, the predecessor of the Institute on Pluralism and Group Identity of which Irving M. Levine is presently the director" (p. 270).

19.   Murray Friedman, "Is White Racism the Problem?" *Commentary* 47 (Jan. 1969): 61–65; Levine, *Issues in Race and Ethnic Relations*, 272–274; Richard Krikus, *Pursuing the American Dream: White Ethnics and the New Populism* (New York: Anchor Doubleday, 1976), 272; Mann, *The One and the Many*, 19, 22.

20.   "The Reacting Americans: An Interim Look at the White Ethnic Lower Middle Class," AJC, June 1971. The brochure contains excerpts of papers delivered at the National Consultation on Ethnic America in June 1968; National Project on Ethnic America, Interim Report, Oct. 1970–Dec. 1971, 3.

21.   "National Consultation on Ethnic America," June 19–21, 1968, program brochure.

22.   "Reducing Group Tensions: A Strategy for Ethnic Whites," project proposal submitted to the Stern Family Fund by the American Jewish Committee, May 1969; Outline for an AJC White Ethnic Strategy, by Irving M. Levine and Judith Magidson [Herman], July 1969; Irving Levine, National Project on Ethnic America: Interim Report, Oct. 1970–Dec. 1971; "America's Young Workers," Final Report, Submitted to the U.S. Department of Labor Office of Policy, Evaluation and Research, July 1973.

23.   Friedman, *Overcoming Middle Class Rage*, 33–34; "Now That We Are Beautiful, Where Do We Go?" assessment of grants to the American Jewish Committee for the National Project on Ethnic America, Division of National Affairs, Ford Foundation, Feb. 1974, 11–14; *Newsweek*, Oct. 6, 1969; *Time*, Jan. 3, 1970.

24.   Irving Levine to Nathan Perlmutter, Mar. 7, 1969.

25.   Mitchell Sviridoff, "A Perspective on the Seventies," *The Ford Foundation Annual Report 1969* (Oct. 1, 1968, to Sept. 30, 1969), 17–22; Irving Levine to Attendees of Ethnic Strategy Meeting, [*re*] Mitchell Sviridoff–Ford Foundation Report, March 5, 1970.

26.   National Institute on Group Identity and Pluralism, A Proposal Submitted to the Rockefeller Foundation by the American Jewish Committee National Project on Ethnic America, Sept. 1973; Outline for IPGI [Institute on Pluralism and Group Identity] Program Plan, 1978–79, Sept. 29, 1978; Nancy Seifer, "Where Feminism and Ethnicity Intersect, The Impact of Parallel

Movements," AJC, n.d.; Nancy Seifer, "Project Proposal: Reducing Communications Barriers between Working Class and Middle Class Women in America," AJC, Apr. 1975.

27.    Weed, *White Ethnic Movement*, 14–15, 27–38; Mann, *The One and the Many*, 29–36; Frank J. Cavaioli, "In Memoriam, Geno C. Baroni (1930–1984)," *Italians and Irish in America* (Proceedings of the 16th Annual Conference of the American Italian Association, New York: AIHA, 1985), ed. Francis X. Femminella, 13–18; "An Address by Rt. Rev. Mons. Geno Baroni," ibid. 19–25; Geno Baroni, "Ethnicity and Public Policy," in *Pieces of a Dream*, ed. Michael Wenk, S. M. Tomasi, Geno Baroni (New York: Center for Migration Studies, 1972), 3–11.

28.    [Michael Novak], Proposed Action [Summary prepared for presentation to the Board of Trustees of the Rockefeller Foundation], American Jewish Committee—Institute on Group Identity and Pluralism, Feb. 8, 1974; Paul J. Asciolla to Irving M. Levine, June 3, 1974; Geno Baroni to Irving Levine, June 6, 1974; Andrew M. Greeley to Irving M. Levine, May 24, 1974; Irving M. Levine to Geno Baroni, June 30, 1974.

29.    Weed, *White Ethnic Movement* 27–34; *Washington Post*, June 22, 1974; *New York Magazine*, June 24, 1974, 57.

30.    Interview with Bertram Gold, Aug. 26, 1986.

31.    "The New Ethnicity," unpublished paper, 1989, 11.

32.    Yehuda Rosenman to Bertram Gold, Aug. 3, 1972.

33.    Irving Levine to Bertram Gold, Oct. 3, 1974.

34.    "Now That We Are Beautiful," 2–4.

35.    Harold R. Isaacs, "The New Pluralists," *Commentary* 53 (Mar. 1972): 75–79; Robert Alter, "A Fever of Ethnicity," ibid. (June 1972): 68–73; Norman Podhoretz, ibid. (June 1972): 4–6.

36.    Nathan Glazer, "The Issue of Cultural Pluralism in America Today," *Pluralism beyond the Frontier: Report of the San Francisco Consultation on Ethnicity* (pamphlet, San Francisco, 1972), 7. See Glazer's *Affirmative Discrimination: Ethnic Inequality and Public Policy* (New York: Basic Books, 1975), especially 33–76, 168–221, and *Ethnic Dilemmas*, 126–144, 209–229.

37.    Philip E. Hoffman, "Reflections on the Future: Address by the President of the American Jewish Committee to the Committee's Annual Dinner," May 4, 1972, 8–11. Bertram Gold in his address to the same meeting stated: "In the wake of the disillusionment over the snail's pace of social change among the nation's minorities, comes the demand for, and apparent acceptance of, group rights. . . . While we oppose the concept of group rights, we see no problem with the concept of group interests. Group interests are just as real and just as legitimate as transcendent common interests." "Who Speaks for the Jews," text of address by Bertram H. Gold, Executive Vice President of the American Jewish Committee at the Committee's Annual Meeting, May 4, 1972, pamphlet, New York City.

38. Hoffman, "Reflections," 12–13.

39. Irving M. Levine, "Social Policy and Multi-Ethnicity in the 1970s: An Address to the annual Seminar of the Committee on Integration of the American Immigration and Citizenship Conference," Feb. 1973.

40. Levine interview, Dec. 10, 1980.

41. Mann, *The One and the Many*, 37–38; Glazer, *Ethnic Dilemmas*, 135–138.

42. *Ethnic Heritage Studies Centers*, Hearings before the General Subcommittee on Education of the Committee on Education and Labor, House of Representatives, 91st Congress, Second Session, on H.R. 14910 (Washington, 1970). For Levine's testimony, see "Ethnic Heritage Studies Centers Act, Testimony by Irving M. Levine, Feb. 18, 1970," mimeographed; interview with Bertram Gold, Aug. 26, 1986.

43. Sorin, "From the Brownsville Boys Club to the Institute for American Pluralism," 288–289; Irving Levine to Emily Sunstein, [memo] "Beyond Bakke: Ethnic Implications," Oct. 6, 1978. Glazer, *Ethnic Dilemmas*, 106–125, 145–156, 254–273. In Nathan Glazer's 1987 introduction to his *Affirmative Discrimination: Ethnic Inequality and Public Policy* (Cambridge, Mass.: Harvard University Press, 1975, 1987), he remarked that little had changed since the first edition of his book. This did not reflect "stability produced by consensus and compromise," but rather "the stability of trench warfare, in which neither side seems able to advance" (vii). For a recent, more forbearing review of the issue, see Glazer, "In Defense of Preference," *The New Republic* 218, no. 14 (April 6, 1998): 18–25.

44. Institute for American Pluralism of the American Jewish Committee, "1989—Ethnicity in Practice" (brochure); Nancy Seifer, "Project Proposal for a Center on Women and American Diversity," Dec. 1976; idem, "Where Feminism and Ethnicity Intersect: The Impact of Parallel Movements" [issued by the Center on Women and American Diversity], Feb. 1976; Louis Caplan Center on Group Identity and Mental Health, Joseph Giordono, director, "Annual Report, 1978"; Irving M. Levine, "Bolstering the Family through Informal Support Groups," presented at the Philadelphia Conference on "The American Family 1978: Human Values and Public Policy," Apr. 30, 1978. John Higham, *Send These to Me: Immigrants in Urban America* (Baltimore, Md.: Johns Hopkins University Press, 1975, 1984), 242–245, 248.

# Index

# Index

and, 155; in Western Europe, 100; Zionism and, 149

Democratic Party, 86, 205

Dewey, John, 15, 226n8

diaspora, 2, 162, 203; permanence of, 202; relationship with Israel, 8, 131; spiritual (cultural) Zionism and, 147, 159, 160

Dillingham Commission, 87

discrimination, 6, 23, 191, 209, 219

displaced persons, 182, 188

Drachman, Rabbi Bernard, 23, 57

Dreier, Mary, 67

Dubinsky, David, 76, 77, 81

Dulles, John Foster, 157

Eban, Abba, 81, 183, 184

Edelstadt, David, 79

education, 14, 17, 20, 21, 181, 204

Educational Alliance, 32, 33, 34, 70

Einstein, Albert, 79, 178

Eisenhower, Dwight, *140*, 191, 194, 196, 208

emancipation, 203

England. *See* Britain

English language, 19–20, 37, 42

Eretz Israel, 151, 161, 164, 202; *halutzim* in, 179, 180, 181, 183, 184. *See also* Israel, state of; Palestine; Yishuv

Ethical Culture, 20

ethnicity: American nationalism and, 36–37; class divisions and, 117; democracy and, 15; dissolution of, 19; in election campaigns, 83–99; interethnic relations, 6–7; loss of, 13; religion and, 17, 18; resurgent, 205–23; secular dimension of, 16; self-definition and, 26

ethnocentrism, 218

Europe: Jewish communal life in, 10, 109, 113, 114; Jewish emancipation in, 1, 2, 3, 24, 203; Jewish emigration from, 15; Jewish radical-liberal politics in, 100; Orthodox Judaism in Eastern Europe, 51, 52–53; war in, 4; Zionism in, 147

exile, 1, 159, 202

Ezekiel, Moses, 36

Fair Deal, 193

fascism, 77, 158, 211

Federation of American Zionists, 146

Feigenbaum, Benjamin, 41

feminism, 215

films, 177–78, 255–56n59

Finkelstein, Louis: Conservative Judaism and, 164; Jewish historical research and,

196; Judeo-Christian universalism and, 157–61; Zionism and, 5, 145, 155, 156, 162–63, 249n41

First World War, 4, 111, 120, 159; Jewish leadership and, 123–24; Zionism and, 151, 167

Fischel, Harry, 57, 58, 114, 120

Fleischer, Rabbi Charles, 20

Flexner, Bernard, 129

folk songs, 176–77

folkways, 16

Forster, Arnold, 200–201

*Forverts* (newspaper), 20, 33, 34, 50, 73, 93; coverage of funerals, 58, 68, 74–76, 77, 78–79; coverage of Triangle Fire (1911), 65; Jewish leadership and, 115, 122–23; Lower East Side socialism and, 86; on pogroms of 1905, 42, 43–44; Socialist Party and, 96

France, 103

Frankel, Lee K., 129

Frankfurter, Felix, 48, 121, 157, 189

fraternal orders, 112, 118

free love, 173

*Freie Arbeiter Shtimme* (newspaper), 75

Friedenwald, Herbert, 118

Friedkin, Israel, 106

Friedlaender, Israel, 21, 70, 223; on American Judaism, 1–3, 4, 9; murder of, 2, 150; Zionism and, 145, 146, 147, 148, 149–52

Friedman, Murray, 212, 218

funerals, 7, 31–34, 48–50, 232n3

*Future of the American Jew* (Kaplan), 161

garment unions, 73, 116

*gemeinde,* 108

gender, 67

*Genius of American Politics, The* (Boorstin), 197

German Americans, 36–37, 45, 83

Germany, 26, 123, 127; Allied occupation of, 189; Jewish scholarship in, 2

ghettos: black, 208, 211, 212; Jewish, 20, 21, 83, 87

Gibbons, Herbert Adam, 152

Glazer, Nathan, 205, 208, 218–19, 220

*God, Man and Devil* (Gordin), 60

Gold, Bertram, 217, 221, 262n37

Goldberg, Abraham, 61

Goldfogle, Henry, 86, 93, 98, 105–106, 237n3, 240n29

Goldman, Emma, 173

Goldman, Julius, 25, 129

Goldman, Solomon, 164

justice, 191, 192; conservative politics and, 100–109; erosion of communal traditions, 19–20, 51–52; modernization of, 57; public display in United States, 55; Triangle Fire (1911) and, 65–66. *See also* Conservative Judaism; Judaism; Reform Judaism

pacifism, 156–57
pageants, 30, 31, 37, 46, 49; funerals, 72–73, 81–82
Pale of Settlement (Russia), 45
Palestine, 4, 8, 9, 14; American Jewry and, 24, 147, 169–76, 179; ancient, 198; Arabs in, 151–53, 155, 167, 168, 173–74, 178; British control of, 151, 168; protests against British policy in, *138–39;* Reconstructionism and, 16; refugees in, 183; relief aid for Zionists in, 121, 127; Zionist settlement in, 28, 111, 130, 148. *See also* Balfour Declaration; Israel, state of; Zionism
Paley, William S., 196
Panken, Jacob, 74, 91
parochial schools, 14–15, 16, 17
Peoples Relief Committee, 128
Peretz, Isaac Leib, 71
Peskin, Samuel, 20
philanthropies, 23–24, 26, 56, 111, 112, 128–29
Pilgrims, 38, 39–40
Pine, Max, 91, 116, 121
Pinski, Dovid, 69
Pittsburgh Platform (1885), 15
pluralism, 27, 186, 198, 202, 204; cultural, 3, 6–7, 16, 226n8; inventing new forms of, 205–23; within Jewish community, 21, 24, 106, 186, 204; as multiculturalism, 29
Poale Zion, 166, 250n4
Podhoretz, Norman, 218, 220
pogroms, 87, 93, 113, 234n35; 1905 pogroms, 2, 7, 30, 38, 42–46, 89, 119; Kishinev (1903), 89, 119, 231–32n38, 238n10. *See also* anti-semitism
Poland, 17, 50, 127, 183; Bund in, 79–80; Zionism in, 166
Polish Americans, 206, 210, 213, 218, 220
Polish Socialist Party, 76
politics, 5, 29, 100–101, 109, 149. *See also* conservatism; liberalism; socialism
Portuguese empire, Jews and, 35, 40
Potofsky, Jacob S., 196
prayers, 69, 74
"Problem of Judaism in America, The," 1, 3
Proskauer, Joseph, 189

*Protestant, Catholic, Jew* (Herberg), 18, 19, 208
Protestantism, 173, 193, 208; influence on Jewish establishment, 112; liberal internationalism and, 156, 157, 158; Sunday schools, 15. *See also* Catholicism; Christianity
Provisional Zionist Committee, 127
public culture, 7
*Public Interest* (magazine), 220
public schools, 14, 15
Puritans, 174, 175

Rabbi Isaac Elhanan Theological Seminary, 48
rabbis, 51, 107, 156, 163, 191; funerals of, 49; Pittsburgh Platform (1885), 15; pluralism and, 204; public pageants and, 32, 37, 38, 44; on separation of church and state, 227n25; use of English language, 19–20; Zionism and, 150, 164
race, 7, 26, 27, 208, 219
racism, 205, 209, 212
radicalism, 5, 19, 45, 61, 68, 100; civil rights movement and, 208; Cold War and, 200, 201. *See also* socialism; unions
Raisen, Abraham, 81
Ramaz, 72
Rand School, 75, 76
Reconstructionism, 16, 155–56, 202, 203
*Reconstructionist, The,* 184
Reform Judaism, 4, 16, 107, 108–109, 159, 203; commitment to social justice, 191; denunciation of, 115; education and, 14; ethnicity and, 22; First World War and, 153; humanism and, 20; Jewish identity and, 193; Pittsburgh Platform (1885), 15; Zionism and, 149, 174. *See also* Conservative Judaism; Judaism; Orthodox Judaism
Reider, Joseph, 176–77
relief agencies, 127–30, 188
religion, 7, 147–48, 181; Cold War and, 194; decline of, 18; democracy and, 204, 208; education and, 23–24; ethnicity and, 18, 207; freedom of, 36, 40, 195; individual merit and, 219; Jewish identity and, 193; nationalism/nationality and, 16–17, 156; separation of church and state, 22, 24
Republican Party, 5, 86, 94, 101–102, 105
Richman, Julia, 89
Rifkind, Simon, 196
Rockefeller, John D., Jr., 72
Rogoff, Hillel, 93
Roosevelt, Franklin D., 76, 191, 196

synagogues, 21, 30, 39, 195; education and, 23–24; funerals and, 49, 54–55; pogroms of 1905 and, 42, 43, 44; postwar suburbanization and, 187; Union of American Hebrew Congregations, 113

Syrkin, Nachman, 23, 70, 121

Szold, Henrietta, 111, 167–68, 171, 176

Taft, William Howard, 94, 102, 103, 104, 119

*Tageblat* (newspaper), 87, 93, 122; coverage of funerals, 32, 33, 34, 53, 54, 55–56, 58, 68; Jewish history celebrations and, 41, 42; on Morris Hillquit, 89–90; publisher of, 48, 114–15; school strike of 1906 and, 104

Tammany Hall, 83, 84–85, 93, 118, 908

television, 197

theology/theologians, 3, 16, 190, 204

Thomas, Norman, 74, 75, 78

Thomashevsky, Boris, 61

Tobin, Maurice, 81

*Der Tog* (newspaper), 69, 70

Tomasi, Rev. S. M., 216

trade unions. *See* unions

Triangle Shirtwaist Company fire (1911), 62–67, 81, *134*, 235n47

*troyermarsh:* for Triangle Fire victims, 67; for victims of 1905 pogroms, 42–46

Truman, Harry, 156, 191, 196, 200, 209, 210

Union of American Hebrew Congregations, 113

Union of Orthodox Rabbis, 72

unions, 21, 113; Meyer London and, 74–75, 95, 96; Morris Hillquit and, 76, 85, 96; strikes and, 115–16

United Hebrew Trades, 45, 73, 76, 91, 116

United Jewish Appeal, 131, *140*, 256n59

United Nations, 156, 162, 163, 190

United Palestine Appeal, 130, 131

United States: "American Century," 197; American exceptionalism, 10, 147; "Balkanization" of, 220; as center of diaspora, 2, 3; cultural pluralism in, 16; elections in, 5; federalism and commonwealth in, 162; history of Jewish settlement in America, 7, 30, 34–42; Jewish immigration from Eastern Europe, 2, 20–21, 35, 85–87, 113, 146, 193; Jewish integration into, 13; nationalism in, 35–36; Orthodox Judaism and, 103; relations with Russia, 119–20; resurgent ethnicity in, 205–23; separation of church and state, 22, 227n25; turbulence of 1960s/1970s, 18; Zionism and American patriotism, 21–22, *138*, 192

universalism, 20, 149, 150, 153, 158, 166

*Uprooted, The* (Handlin), 198

Urofsky, Melvin, 111, 149

*Varheyt* (newspaper), 33, 41, 93; coverage of funerals, 58–59, 60, 61, 68; on pogroms, 88–89

Vietnam War, 18, 192, 208

Vladeck, Baruch, 48, 73, 74, 77–80

Wagner, Robert, 78

Wald, Lillian, 74

Waldman, Louis, 76

Waldman, Morris, 160

Wallace, George, 210, 211

Warburg, Edward, 79

Warburg, Felix, 25, 102, 121, 126

Warburg, Otto, 127

Weill, Kurt, 82

Weinberg, Joseph, 76, 78, 79

Weinberger, Jacob, 177

Weizmann, Chaim, 128, 130

white ethnic groups. *See* Catholic ethnics

Wiernik, Peter, 106

Williams, Roger, 40, 230n22

Willowski, Rabbi Jacob David, 19

Wilson, Woodrow, 129, 151

Winchevsky, Morris, 61, 70, 81

Wise, Rabbi Stephen S., 4, 24, 79, 111, 112, 121; anti-Nazi protests and, 117; on democracy, 124–26, 130; funeral of, 48; Jewish leadership and, 110, 130–31; lampoon of, *136;* Zionism and, 123

Wolf, Simon, 113

Wolffsohn, David, 146

women, 170–73

Women's Trade Union League (WTUL), 64, 65, 66, 67

Wood, Robert C., 212, 213

working class, 205, 206, 210

Workmen's Circle, 63, 65, 73, 77, 79, 97, 125; cemeteries of, 80–81; growth of, 85; historical research and, 197; *landsmanshaft* associations and, 86; Meyer London and, 96; strikes and, 116; women in, *134*

World Jewish Congress, 130

*World of Our Fathers, The* (Howe), 101

World War I. *See* First World War

**Arthur A. Goren** is Russell and Bettina Knapp Professor of American Jewish
History at Columbia University. His books include *New York Jews and the
Quest for Community, Dissenter in Zion: From the Writings of Judah L. Magnes,*
and *The American Jews.*